Morphology and
Computation

ACL–MIT Press Series in Natural Language Processing
Aravind K. Joshi, Karen Sparck Jones, and Mark Y. Liberman, editors

Speaking: From Intention to Articulation, by Willem J. M. Levelt

Plan Recognition in Natural Language Dialogue, by Sandra Carberry

Cognitive Models of Speech Processing: Psycholinguistic and Computational Perspectives, edited by Gerry T. M. Altmann

Computational Morphology: Practical Mechanisms for the English Lexicon, by Graeme D. Ritchie, Graham J. Russell, Alan W. Black, and Stephen G. Pulman

Morphology and Computation, by Richard Sproat

Morphology and Computation

Richard Sproat

A Bradford Book
The MIT Press
Cambridge, Massachusetts
London, England

Set in Times Roman by Asco Trade Typesetting Ltd. Printed and bound in the United States of America.

Library of Congress Cataloging-in-Publication Data

Sproat, Richard William.
  Morphology and computation / Richard Sproat.
    p. cm.—(ACL–MIT Press series in natural-language processing)
  Includes bibliographical references and index.
  ISBN 0-262-19314-0
  1. Grammar, Comparative and general—Morphology. 2. Grammar, Comparative and general—Morphology—Data processing. I. Title.
II. Series.
P241.S67   1992
415—dc20   91-32327
                                                CIP

Contents

Preface   ix

Introduction   xi

Chapter 1

Applications of Computational Morphology   1

1.1

Introduction   1

1.2

Natural Language Applications   2

1.3

Speech Applications   7

1.4

Word Processing   9

1.5

Document Retrieval   13

1.6

Conclusions   14

Chapter 2

The Nature of Morphology   15

2.1

Introduction   15

2.2

Functions of Morphology   19

2.3

What Is Combined, and How?   43

2.4

Morphemes, the Structure of Words, and Word-Formation Rules   66

2.2.1. Infl or derivation? 19
2.2.2. Derived nominals C Derivational morph 33
2.2.3 Compounding 47

2.5

Morphotactics: The Order of
Morphemes   83

2.6

Phonology   92

2.7

Psycholinguistic Evidence   109

2.8

Final Note   122

2.9

Further Reading   123

Chapter 3   3.1

Computational Morphology   124   Introduction   124

3.2

Computational Mechanisms   125

3.3

An Overview of URKIMMO   145

3.4

Augments to the KIMMO
Approach   153

3.5

The Computational Complexity of
Two-Level Morphology   171

3.6

Other Ways of Doing Computational
Morphology   184

3.7

A Prospectus: What Is Left to
Do   205

3.8

Further Reading   214

Chapter 4   4.1
Some Peripheral Issues   215   Introduction   215

                                                 4.2
                                                 Morphological Acquisition   215

                                                 4.3
                                                 Compound Nominals and Related
                                                 Constructions   230

Key to Abbreviations   241

Glossary   243

Notes   253

References   269

Index   287

Preface

This book is based on some lecture notes that accompanied a tutorial in morphology and computational morphology which I presented the 27th Annual Meeting of the Association for Computational Linguistics, in June 1989. Like the tutorial, the book is intended to serve both as an overview of the issues in morphology and computational morphology and as a review and critique of the literature in computational morphology. I have tried to make only minimal assumptions about the readership. I assume that the reader knows something about linguistics and is at least somewhat familiar with computational linguistics, but I do not assume much more. In particular, I assume no particular knowledge of morphology; I therefore cover a fair amount of material that may be quite familiar to anyone who has studied morphology.

There are a number of people with whom I have had profitable discussions on the material contained herein, or from whom I have received useful comments. I would particularly like to acknowledge Steve Anderson, Bob Berwick, Ken Church, Janet Pierrehumbert, and Evelyne Tzoukermann. Special thanks to my readers, Julia Hirschberg, Rob French, Kathleen Kane, Fernando Pereira, Evelyne Tzoukermann, and Susanne Wolff, for commenting on earlier drafts and offering valuable suggestions. I further thank Conrad Sabourin of Paralingua (P.O. Box 187, Snowdon, Montreal, Quebec, Canada H3X 3T4) for allowing me access to his extensive bibliography of works in morphology and computational morphology. I would also like to thank my wife, Chilin Shih, for discussions of some of the topics covered in this book as well as for love and support.

Finally I would like to acknowledge one other factor: the research environment at Bell Labs. In my own experience, two qualities which have traditionally been most highly prized at the Labs are breadth of scholarship and critical evaluation of ideas no matter what their provenance. It may well be the case that this book fails to adequately cover some aspects of morphology or computational morphology, or that my critique of one or another approach to a problem is not sufficiently thorough. Be that as it may, I am confident that my failings in these areas would have been much greater if I had not been exposed to the stimulating environment at Bell Labs.

Introduction

Suppose you are building a syntactic parser for English. One of the pieces you will need is a module to tell you what words there are in English and what their properties are (e.g., part of speech, subcategorization and tense information for verbs, semantic properties, etc.). In the simplest model for such a module, one would have a dictionary appropriately arranged for easy access and would just look up words in the dictionary when one needed to. The view that word recognition is merely a matter of dictionary lookup is certainly viable in certain cases. Toy parsing systems or parsing systems with small coverage do not need to assume more than this. And speech recognition systems can usually make the assumption at present, since their vocabulary is severely limited in size by current technology.

Still, one might observe that at least some word forms should not have to be in the dictionary in order to be recognized. In English, for example, plural forms of nouns are mostly formed by a very simple process, and it should therefore not be necessary that the word *aardvarks* be in the dictionary; rather, one would list the singular form, *aardvark*, and compute the plural form when one finds it in a text by means of a rule that removes the *-s.* Since the vast majority of English nouns form their plurals by adding some variant of *-s*, it is wasteful to list both singular and plural forms when one can just list the singular form and derive the plural form by means of a rule. Similarly, we know that English verbs (subject to certain restrictions) can take the suffix *-er* to form agentive or instrumental nouns. Similarly, we know that many adjectives can take the suffix *-ness* to form nouns meaning 'the state of *x*', where *x* is the meaning of the adjective. In view of the productivity of these morphological processes, it is missing the point to simply list all the words containing these morphemes (though some might have to be listed, such as those that have idiosyncratic interpretations).

One might, of course, simply ignore these observations and continue adding words one encounters which are not in the dictionary. Certainly the storage of large numbers of words is less of a problem than it used to be, owing to improvements in hardware. Even with these hardware improvements, however, simply listing all words is not generally feasible. A blatant example of why this is so is Finnish, in which a verb can appear in any of several thousand forms. Listing all these forms is infeasible (even with current storage technology). Since most of the forms are formed according to very general and regular morphological processes, to even think of listing them all would be silly. A more subtle but equally compelling argument against simply listing all words in a dictionary is that—even for English (whose inflectional morphology, at least, is more modest than that of Finnish)—one can have a very large list of words yet still encounter many words that are not to be found in that list. To see this, consider that there are about 300,000 different tokens in Associated Press newswire text dating from the middle of February 1988 through December 1988—a total of about 44 million words of text (including numbers, capitalized versions of previously seen words, and so forth). Suppose that you simply collected all the different words you saw, starting in mid-February and ending on December 30, thus obtaining a list of close to 300,000 words. (The fact that about 8 percent of these 300,000 words—about 25,000—can be expected to be typos [Ken Church, personal communication] doesn't affect the point being made here.) Even with that large a list, one can still find in the text for December 31 many words that had not been previously encountered; indeed, a great many newswire stories for that day contain new productive morphological formations. For example, the following words occurred in stories on December 31, 1988, having not been seen in $10\frac{1}{2}$ months' text.

(1) a. compounds:
   prenatal-care, publicly-funded, channel-switching, owner-president,
   logic-loving, part-Vulcan, signal-emitting, landsite,
   government-aligned, armhole, timber-fishing, last-edition, funfest,
   revolution-minded, lap-top

   b. inflections:
   dumbbells, groveled, fuzzier, oxidized

   c. other:
   ex-presidency, puppetry, boulderlike, over-emphasized, hydrosulfite,
   outclassing, non-passengers, racialist, counterprograms,
   antiprejudice, re-unification, traumatological, refinancings,
   instrumenting, ex-critters, mega-lizard

Thus, we have two reasons for being interested in computational morphology:

(2) a. Simply expanding the dictionary to encompass every word one is ever likely to encounter is wrong: it fails to take advantage of regularities.

   b. No dictionary contains all the words one is likely to find in real input.

These two reasons can really be thought of as aspects of the same point. Reason (2a) is the more aesthetically oriented of the two. Linguists would argue that many morphological processes in language are productive and that one should therefore have computational routines to analyze those processes, just as one has computational routines to analyze phrase structure. Furthermore, psycholinguists have argued that humans not only know about morphological structure but also actively parse morphologically complex words, which further suggests that computational models of language should incorporate morphological processing. Nonetheless, one could argue that this is merely a matter of taste. Reason (2b) shows that reason (2a) is more than a purely aesthetic one: precisely because morphology is a productive part of language, people freely generate new words, making use of their knowledge of the morphology of their language. As a consequence, it is fairly hopeless to expect any dictionary to contain all the words one is likely to encounter.

So computational morphology is important. This fact has been recognized for many years. Nonetheless, it is correct to say that morphology has only recently come more to the forefront of computational linguistics. One reason for the previous lack of interest may be the similar lack of interest in morphology that prevailed in theoretical linguistics until the beginning of the 1980s. Another, of course, is that most work in computational linguistics has been done on English. Although, for reasons already given, one really needs to do computational morphology even in English, one can do reasonably well with a large dictionary and perhaps a few simple **affix-stripping** routines to handle regular inflection. This approach fails a great deal sooner for a language with fairly elaborate morphology, such as Finnish. (Not surprisingly, some of the most influential computational work in morphology has come from Finland.)

Fortunately, there have not been many active attempts to dissuade people from doing computational morphology. (In contrast, there have been numerous attempts to argue that machine translation cannot and should not be done—see, e.g. Kay 1986.) The one attempt that I know of to argue against most approaches to computational morphology is that of Wehrli (1985), who proposes instead a relational word-based lexical database in which all words are listed in the lexicon and morphological relations between words are captured by "cross references" (ibid., p. 149) between the entries for those words. Wehrli's argument for this approach versus the approach of actually doing morphological analysis is based upon the observation that many words have idiosyncratic properties that cannot be derived from the properties of the constituent morphemes. That is, one can (possibly ignoring etymological truth) decompose *strawberry* into *straw + berry*, yet that fact alone does not tell us what the whole word means; similarly, knowing that *understand* is morphologically decomposable into *under + stand* tells us nothing about the meaning of that word. Similar considerations apply to *computer, transmission,* and *hardly* (ibid., p. 148).

But these observations are a poor argument against doing computational morphology, for two reasons. First, although it is true that some (or even many) words are noncompositional in the sense just discussed, it is certainly not the case that *all* words are noncompositional. For instance, the properties of the following words can all be derived from the properties of their component morphemes: *giraffes, compiled, radon detector, oafishness.* And in Finnish, the vast majority of the thousands of forms in which a verb can occur will be compositional in this sense. If one is to allow the properties of a subset to determine the way in which the entire set is to be treated, then one may as well take the observation that there are noncompositional phrases—*shoot the bull, by and large, wreak havoc, tread on thin ice*—as arguing that one should not build syntactic parsers.

A second reason that Wehrli's argument is poor is that it makes invalid tacit assumptions about why one might wish to do morphological decomposition. If one morphologically decomposes such words as *strawberry, computer,* or *transmission* with a view to determining their meaning, then one is bound to fail in many cases, as Wehrli argues. But if one is instead interested in how these words are pronounced, and wishes to determine this from the pronunciation of the component morphemes, then one is perfectly safe in morphologically decomposing these words, since there is nothing irregular about their phonology. So, *strawberry* is pronounced with primary stress on the first element, *straw,* just as one would expect from the preferred procedure for stressing nominal compounds in English. Determining the pronunciation of a word from knowledge about its morphological structure is just as valid a reason for doing morphological decomposition as determining its meaning—indeed, text-to-speech systems often incorporate morphological analyzers for precisely this purpose, because in many cases one *must* know about the morphological structure of a word in order to know how to pronounce it. Yet another reason why one might want to morphologically analyze a word is to determine its part of speech. Here again one is not limited by the inability to determine the meaning of a morphologically complex form, since semantic irregularity does not generally correspond to morphosyntactic irregularity. For example, one can determine that *strawberry, transmission*, and *computer* are likely to be nouns simply on the basis of their final morphemes; similar considerations would allow one to analyze *hardly* as an adverb. So, Wehrli's tacit assumption that in morphologically decomposing a word one must needs be interested in computing its meaning is invalid.

In this introduction I have argued that computational morphology is a valid undertaking, and I have argued against the only countersuggestion of which I am aware. The body of the book is organized as follows. In chapter 1, I motivate further the study of computational morphology by discussing a range of applications for programs with knowledge of morphology. In chapter 2, I give an overview of some basic descriptive facts about morphology and some of the issues in theoretical morphology and (lexical) phonology, as well as some of the psycholinguistic evidence for human processing of morphological structure. In chapter 3, I discuss the basic techniques that have been proposed for doing morphological processing and then discuss at length various systems in which some or all of those techniques are used. Finally, in chapter 4, I discuss some interesting areas on the periphery of computational morphology: the analysis of complex nominals in English and the main contributions of connectionism to the computational analysis of words.

Morphology and
Computation

Chapter 1

Applications of
Computational Morphology

1.1 INTRODUCTION

In the introduction, I motivated computational morphology by arguing that the alternative of simply having a huge lexicon is not going to work in general. I also suggested that the huge-lexicon approach is unappealing from a purely scientific point of view. These considerations argue that some nontrivial analysis of morphology will be necessary if one wants to be able to handle words in any general way computationally. Still, it is legitimate to question the extent to which having computational analyzers or generators of word forms is truly useful: if there aren't really any applications, then computational morphology is probably of less general interest than it otherwise might be. At the very least, there will be some who will doubt that computational morphology is a field worth pursuing.

In this chapter I show that morphology is actually quite practically useful, and I demonstrate this by giving a review of a fairly broad range of technological applications for morphological information. I have little to say here about the mechanisms used in the various systems, since extensive descriptions of various techniques for building morphological processors will be given in chapter 3. My point here is merely to show that researchers working on a number of rather different topics have found morphological information to be useful.

The areas I will discuss in the first chapter can be classified roughly as follows:

- natural language applications
  parsing
  text generation
  machine translation
  dictionary tools and lemmatization

- speech applications
  text-to-speech systems
  speech recognition
- word processing applications
  spelling checkers
  text input
- document retrieval

Some of these applications are perhaps fairly obvious (e.g., dictionary tools and lemmatization, parsing, and text generation), some of them perhaps less so. The material outlined above and discussed below will, I hope, serve the purpose of demonstrating the practical utility of computational morphology.

An additional rationale for discussing such a wide range of applications relates in particular to morphological analyzers (as opposed to morphological generators). I would like, as much as possible, to quell prejudices about what kinds of analyses morphological analyzers should produce. (See the discussion of Wehrli 1985 in the introduction.) In much of the literature I find that authors are usually very clear on what they require of the analysis of a word form; however, if one compares different authors, one finds rather different assumptions concerning this point. Some analyzers, for example, merely return the string of morphemes found in a morphologically complex word; others might go a little further and determine that a given word is such-and-such a form of some root. In fact, each of these two kinds of answers may legitimately count as an analysis of the word, and which kind of analysis one chooses depends to a large extent on the intended application. This point is worth keeping in mind while reading this chapter—indeed, for the remainder of the book.

1.2 NATURAL LANGUAGE APPLICATIONS

1.2.1 Parsing, text generation, machine translation, and other text-analysis applications

Traditional natural language applications The most obvious area in which a morphological processing system could be fruitfully applied is in the context of a more general natural language system, such as a parser, a generator, or—something which combines these two technologies—a machine translation system. In a parsing system one needs to know properties of the words that one encounters in text. Such properties would include part of speech (which can often be predicted from the last suffix or the first prefix of the word) and more complex properties, such as the particular thematic role which the subject of the verb bears (see subsection 2.5.1). Since, as we have already seen, it is not practical to simply list all words (even in English), one is bound in general to do some amount of morphological analysis. Similarly, in a generation system one wants to generate forms of words appropriate to a particular context. As we shall see in chapter 3, somewhat less attention has been paid to word-form generation than to word-form analysis, though some systems deal exclusively with generation and one notable system deals with both analysis and generation.

Machine translation, one of the oldest areas of computational linguistics, provided a context for early work on computational morphology; some examples of this work are Andron 1962, Bernard-Georges et al. 1962, Boussard and Berthaud 1965, Brand et al. 1969, Woyna 1962, Vauquois 1965, Torre 1962, Schveiger and Mathe 1965, and Matthews 1966.

Finding word boundaries   In a full-blown natural language system, the importance of morphological analysis is thus clear enough. Now, in many text-based applications one aspect of the task is for the most part trivial: in a good number of orthographic systems, word boundaries are conventionally marked, usually by whitespace. In such cases there is no problem with the most basic question in text analysis—figuring out where the words are. However, even this basic question becomes a nontrivial problem in an orthography (such as that of Chinese) where word boundaries are conventionally not marked and one must therefore segment the text into words. This problem must be solved before other analysis of the text can proceed: a syntactic parser, for example, would need to know which words are found in a sentence. And for a Chinese text-to-speech system (subsection 1.3.1) one minimally needs to know how the characters are grouped into words, since this grouping affects the stress, the intonation, and even the pronunciation of some characters. One application of morphological analysis, then, is to compute the locations of word boundaries where they are not overtly marked. I will briefly discuss how such analysis would be useful in the case of Chinese.

By and large, Chinese characters represent monosyllabic morphemes (though see DeFrancis 1984). Chinese words, like words in English, may be composed of either one or many morphemes; examples of monomorphemic and polymorphemic words are given in (1).

(1) 花   筆   世界   需要   辦 公 室
     huā   bǐ   shì jiè   xū yào   bàn gōng shì
     'flower' 'pen' 'world'   'need'   'office'

Now, since word boundaries are not marked in Chinese, for a sentence like that in (2a) it is not immediately obvious which characters should be grouped together into polymorphemic words. The correct grouping is shown in (2c).

(2) a. 我弟弟现在要坐火車回家

    b. 'my younger brother wants to ride the train home now'

    c. 我〈弟弟〉〈現在〉要坐〈火車〉〈回家〉

       wǒ dìdi xiànzài yào zuò huǒchē huíjiā

       (I younger-brother now want ride train return-home)

The most obvious method—simply looking up the words in a dictionary, which is the normal technique used in toy parsing systems (Yang 1985)—fails when applied to unrestricted text, for two reasons.

The less interesting reason is that, at the present time, large on-line dictionaries for Chinese are not easily available. Now, various methods can be used to supplement this lacuna. Sproat and Shih (1990) report on a stochastic method for segmenting two-character words in unrestricted Chinese text.[1] The basic idea is to estimate, for a large corpus of text, the strength of association of two characters a and b by taking the ratio of how often a directly precedes b ($f(ab)$) relative to how often each of a and b occurs in total ($f(a)$ and $f(b)$).[2] Roughly speaking, one then groups into words the pairs of characters that have the highest values for $f(ab)/f(a)f(b)$. The algorithm works quite well, segmenting about 93 percent of the bimorphemic words in randomly selected texts and of the ones it identified as bimorphemic words, getting about 95 percent correct. One can think of the above-described method as a substitute for a large-corpus-based on-line dictionary (though it can be argued that the association statistics add information that one would not normally find in a dictionary).

The more interesting reason why a dictionary (or a statistical surrogate) is not sufficient is that productive word-building processes in Chinese would not be readily handled by either dictionaries or statistical methods alone. Among such processes are the use of A-not-A verbs in yes/no questions, as in (3a), and the reduplication of certain forms with intensifying meaning, as in (3b).

(3) a. *yào* 'want' → *yào* + *bú* + *yào* 'want not want'

    b. *gāo* + *xìng* 'happy' → *gāo* + *gāo* + *xíng* + *xíng* 'very happy'

Some more conventional approach to morphological analysis would be required in order to allow segmentation of such words in text. A morphological approach has been taken in some work on toy Chinese parsers (Lin

1985), but to my knowledge no such system for handling productive morphology in unrestricted Chinese text has been reported.

1.2.2 Dictionary tools and lemmatization

Using dictionaries Morphological knowledge is useful in various applications having to do with the construction or use of on-line dictionaries. First of all, if one has an on-line dictionary, one might be interested in having tools that allow one, given a word in the dictionary, to give its morphological decomposition, and to produce all the words in the dictionary that are morphologically related to that word in some fashion. One might also like to be able to look up a word that is not explicitly listed in the dictionary but whose morphological analysis is possible because of the dictionary. For example, one might want to look up the Spanish word *puede* 'he/she/it is able' in a Spanish dictionary. Traditional Spanish dictionaries would not list that form; rather, one would have to look up the infinitive form *poder* 'to be able' and use one's knowledge of Spanish to calculate the meaning of *puede*. However, the latter calculation can easily be done by the dictionary access system if it has a knowledge of Spanish morphology. (One could, in principle, merely increase the size of the dictionary so that it will list such forms. However, the number of inflected words in a language such as Spanish is very large, and since many such words are formed by morphologically productive processes there is really no reason not to compute the morphological properties of such words on the fly.)

One novel piece of work in this vein is Feigenbaum et al. 1990, which describes a method for encrypting a dictionary (or another natural language database); the particular natural language Feigenbaum et al. consider is Spanish. The simplest model of a dictionary database, of course, is that one has a set of keys, K. The keys are simply the words of a language. For each $k_i \in K$, there is a value $v_i \in V$, where v_i is some set of interesting properties of k_i; for such a database one would provide a lookup function P with the property that for all $k_i \in K$

$$P(k_i, D) = v_i$$

and for all other k_i

$$P(k_i, D) = \varnothing.$$

The task of encrypting such a database D is to produce from D an encrypted database D', and a corresponding lookup function P', with the properties that

$$P(k, D) = P'(k, D')$$

(i.e., the result of querying both databases with the key k is the same) and that, given P' and D', it is computationally infeasible to reconstruct D.[3] In the scheme of Feigenbaum et al., P' uses an encryption function Enc to encrypt a key k to k'. One then uses the original lookup function, P, to compute $v' = P(k', D')$. Finally one uses a decryption function Dec to compute $v = Dec(v', k)$.

Feigenbaum et al. show how this encryption method can be extended to a Spanish dictionary that has been encoded as a **finite-state transducer** (FST), which is able to compute the properties of words (e.g., *puede*) that are not explicitly listed. The particular architecture for this morphological analyzer is described in more detail in subsection 3.6.3, but the basic idea is that in looking up a word such as *puede* one starts with the FST in a designated initial state q_1. One then finds an arc of the FST labeled with an initial substring (say *pued-*) of the input string, and moves across that arc to the state q_i, which terminates the arc, stripping off the matching letters (*pued-*) of the input string in the process and outputting some grammatical information about the string—e.g. that *pued-* is a stem of the verb *poder*. One is then in state q_i with the remainder of the string being -*e*, which will allow one to follow another arc of the FST to some state q_j, using up the -*e* and obtaining some grammatical information—e.g., third-person present indicative active. So, the FST would report that *puede* is the third-person present indicative active of *poder*. Each move of the FST thus takes an input (sub)string s and an origin state q_i and produces an output string (consisting of grammatical information in our example) S and a destination state q_j; one can then treat the machine as a table where the keys are the concatenation of s and q_i and the values are the concatenation of S and q_j. Feigenbaum et al. show that the above encryption scheme can be applied to this table, and that one can produce a lookup algorithm that will allow one to analyze a Spanish word using this encrypted database. This is a useful result. Although it is desirable to provide morphological-analysis tools for on-line dictionaries, the production of such tools requires even more work than constructing a traditional list-like dictionary (see note 3). The work of Feigenbaum et al. shows that such analysis routines can be encrypted, and hence can be protected.

Dictionary construction In the related problem of dictionary construction, one is interested—often for some particular topic domain—in producing an on-line dictionary from scratch, or at least in expanding a dictionary for better coverage in that domain. An example of the latter kind of work is Wolff 1984. Wolff's domain was medical terminology, and she started with a fairly large (but far from complete) on-line medical dictionary. Her primary purpose was to produce an expanded dictionary that would mark the semantic properties of words, including those words not found in the original dictionary. The strategy adopted was to use the original dictionary to derive a set of morphemes commonly used in medical terminology (e.g., *mening-o-, electro-, -algia, -itis*), the restrictions on those morphemes (e.g., *electro-* is a prefix, *-itis* is a suffix), and the semantic properties of those morphemes (e.g., *appendic-* designates a body part, and words ending in *-itis* designate diseases). This set of morphemes and their properties could then be used to construct plausible entries for an expanded dictionary of medical terminology.

Lemmatization   Yet another topic in the same general vein is **lemmatization**, the problem of finding the dictionary form of a word given some form that actually occurs in text. For example, *dogs* would be lemmatized to *dog*. Several papers would appear to have been devoted to this topic (e.g. Klein and Rath 1981; Drewek and Erni 1982). Lemmatization is normally not an end in itself, but is useful for other applications, such as document retrieval (which I discuss in section 1.5) or indexing.

1.3   SPEECH APPLICATIONS

1.3.1   Text-to-speech

A text-to-speech system is a set of programs that take text as their input and produce speech corresponding appropriately to the given text. The ultimate goal of this technology is to produce speech output that will sound like a human speaker reading a text in his native language. Most text-to-speech systems incorporate some amount of syntactic analysis. Therefore, as one might imagine, the arguments for the importance of morphological analysis for parsing carry over to such systems—indeed, as Klatt (1987) points out (see also subsection 3.6.1 below), one of the major benefits of the MITalk system's DECOMP morphological-analysis module was its ability to provide part-of-speech information for the syntactic analyzer. An additional benefit to morphological analysis in text-to-speech systems lies in providing a decomposition of a morphologically complex word so that the correct pronunciation can be assigned to that word. Here is a simple example from English: One does not want to pronounce the ⟨th⟩ in the word ⟨boathouse⟩ according to the normal pronunciation rules for English, which would yield a pronunciation of either /θ/ or /ð/ for

that digraph. Rather, one wants to note that there is a morpheme boundary between the ⟨t⟩ and the ⟨h⟩. If this were the only example, one would
just list this word as an exception to the general rule. But such compounding is common and productive in English (see subsection 2.2.3), and one
cannot count on listing all the relevant cases. Many text-to-speech systems for English therefore incorporate some amount of morphological
analysis. In addition to DECOMP from the MITalk system, there are
the morphological-analysis routines used in the Bell Labs text-to-speech
system (Coker 1985; Coker et al. 1990). Many languages besides English
require morphological analysis in text-to-speech applications for similar
reasons. For example, a number of the papers from a recent international
workshop on speech synthesis discuss the importance of morphological
analysis for German (Russi 1990; Schnabel and Roth 1990; Zinglé 1990)
and Italian (Martin 1990).

1.3.2 Speech recognition

Speech recognition is one area where morphological analysis will ultimately prove indispensable. This is because the task of a speech recognizer—to
be able to recognize (and ultimately understand) sentences of spoken language—will eventually require the ability to handle unknown words, just
as in a parsing system. To date, however, speech-recognition work has paid
very little attention to morphological analysis. The reason for this can
be seen when one considers that the term "large vocabulary recognition"
means "a vocabulary of about 1000 words or more" (Lee 1989, p. 8). Current speech-recognition technology is simply not able to deal with much
more than this, yet 1000 words is really a minuscule vocabulary for anyone interested in handling natural text or speech. With only about 1000
words as the upper limit, there is often not much reason to incorporate
morphological-analysis routines, and the simple listing of all words (including morphological variants) is thus the norm. The SPHINX system's
vocabulary for the Resource Management Task (Lee 1989, pp. 149–170)
lists many morphological variants, such as *Downes/Downes's, downgrade/
downgraded,* and *length/lengths.*

Still, it should be noted that in some research systems (see, e.g., Roe et al.
1991) morpheme-based (more correctly, morph-based) recognition rather
than word-based recognition is used; full word forms are modeled as a
concatenation of morpheme models. Currently, the advantage of doing
this is that one can reduce the size of the set of forms required to train

the speech recognizer. To train the vocabulary of a word-based recognizer to recognize the word forms *soup, cup, meat, soups, cups,* and *meats,* one would have to provide a few utterances involving each of these word forms. In a morpheme-based recognizer, one would have to provide a few utterances involving *soup, cup, meat,* and *-s*; since it is not necessary to provide instances of each of the full word forms under this approach, the amount of training material can be reduced.

1.4 WORD PROCESSING

In this section I discuss two applications of morphological knowledge that fall under the general rubric of word processing or text entry.

1.4.1 Spelling checkers

McIlroy (1982, p. 91) sketches the early development of the UNIX spelling checker as follows:

Some years ago, S. C. Johnson introduced the UNIX spelling checker SPELL. His idea was simply to look up every word of a document in a standard desk dictionary and print a list of the words that were not found....
The only problems were slowness (the program had to scan the entire dictionary) and the coverage of the dictionary.
The vocabulary of the standard dictionary fell short of covering the vocabulary of real documents in two ways: regularly inflected forms were omitted according to custom, and large classes of common words—proper nouns, abbreviations, and new technical terms—fell outside of the chosen domain of the dictionary. Johnson found that simple-minded stripping of plausible suffixes worked well to recognize inflected words....
The matter of coverage was more difficult. In hopes of broadening coverage, an unabridged dictionary was tried as a standard instead of the desk dictionary—with unfortunate consequences. While the coverage of words that occurred in everyday documents scarcely improved, obscure entries from the unabridged dictionary, such as *yor* and *curn*, often matched mistyped short words....
I decided to attack [the problems of speed and coverage] both at once by constructing a shorter list specialized to its purpose, with no unnecessary words. In particular, the derivation rules were to be augmented, and derivable forms were to be dropped from the list. (The desk dictionary contained over 5000 trivially derived forms in *ly* alone.)

The current version of SPELL knows approximately 30 suffixes and 40 prefixes. Suffixes and prefixes are successively stripped until an exact match is found in the dictionary for the residue. Prefixes are easier than suffixes, since the latter often involve spelling changes and often have ordering restrictions. Some examples of the prefixes and suffixes handled by SPELL are given in (4).

(4) a. *-s* (No other suffix can follow this), *-er, -ism, -ing, -able*

    b. *anti-, intra-, bio-, magneto-, under-*

The above lists gloss over many details; many affixes are prevented from being stripped under conditions where stripping would likely cause problems. Also, there is naturally a stoplist of words and patterns where affixation should not be allowed:

(5) a. Don't strip *-er* after ⟨ct⟩, to avoid *reacter, acter, ...*

    b. *thy* should not be affixed, so as to block *thier*

It should be pointed out that this system is concerned mainly with coverage and reduction in the size of the word list, rather than with producing linguistically correct analyses: "... we are interested in soundness of results, not of method. Silly derivations like *forest = fore + est* are perfectly acceptable and even welcome. Anything goes, provided it makes the list shorter without impairing its discriminatory power." (McIlroy 1982, p. 94) All the same, there is a nontrivial amount of reasonable morphological knowledge in this system. The experience with SPELL suggests that morphology is useful in the domain of spelling correction.

1.4.2 Inputting Japanese text

We now turn to the related problem of inputting text in Japanese. Japanese is written using a combination of syllabic characters known as *kana* (there are actually two sets of these) and morphemic Chinese characters called *kanji*. As a rule of thumb, closed-class morphemes (affixes and clitics) are written with kana and open-class morphemes (nouns, verbs, adjectives) are written with kanji. The number of kanji is quite large (about 3000 are in common use); kana are much more limited (since kana is a syllabary), consisting of about 50 different symbols. Now, any morpheme written in kanji can be transliterated into kana, so many Japanese text-input systems use kana-kanji conversion: input is done by typing in kana, and relevant parts of the text are subsequently converted to kanji. The most simpleminded way of doing this is to provide the typist with a menu of possible kanji for each sequence of kana; this is laborious, however, and the preferred way is to have an algorithm figure out the correct conversion of the input text. Quite a few systems exist for doing this. I will discuss the work of Abe et al. (1986), which involves a nontrivial amount of morphological analysis; the interested reader can also see Becker 1984 for a description of other approaches involving morphological analysis.

There are actually two problems with automatic kana-kanji conversion: segmenting the kana input into words (Japanese writing customs, like Chinese writing customs, do not sanction spaces between words, so people are not used to putting them in) and disambiguating homonyms among the words. Both problems are severe, as figure 1.1 suggests (see Abe et al. 1986, p. 280).

Orthographic Japanese sentences can be thought of as strings of **bunsetsu** (independent content words and their dependent closed-class morphemes). Within bunsetsu the grammatical restrictions are quite tight between morphemes, so it is relatively straightforward to use a grammatical table in computing the possible morphological structures. Compounds, however, consist of several independent words and have far fewer linguistic constraints; also, compounds are freely produced, so compiling a dictionary of such forms is impractical. Abe et al. propose a heuristic statistical model of compounds, making use of generalizations such as the following.

(6) a. Part of speech: About 90% of morphemes in compound words are nouns or their prefixes or suffixes.

   b. Etymology: About 77% of all morphemes in compounds are words of Chinese origin.

   c. About 93% of compound words are 3 to 5 kana in length.

They use these statistical properties to classify compound types into three levels according to the probability of occurrence. The general morphological-analysis routine then uses this table to figure out a likely set of candidate transliterations. The analysis proceeds as follows: First, dependent-morpheme analysis is performed by matching strings over the entire sentence and extracting grammatically well-formed strings of dependent morphemes. Independent-morpheme analysis then proceeds on the remainder of the sentence not parsed into dependent-morpheme strings by checking the more plausible compound types (level 1) first and then checking the less plausible possibilities. At each stage, grammatical connectability between dependent and independent morphemes is verified. In this way a **chart** of plausible morphemes is produced; it is then passed on to syntactic- and semantic-analysis routines for disambiguation. One such chart is shown in figure 1.2.

The entire system of Abe et al. apparently gets around 90.5 percent of its kana-kanji conversions correct (though how this was measured is not stated).

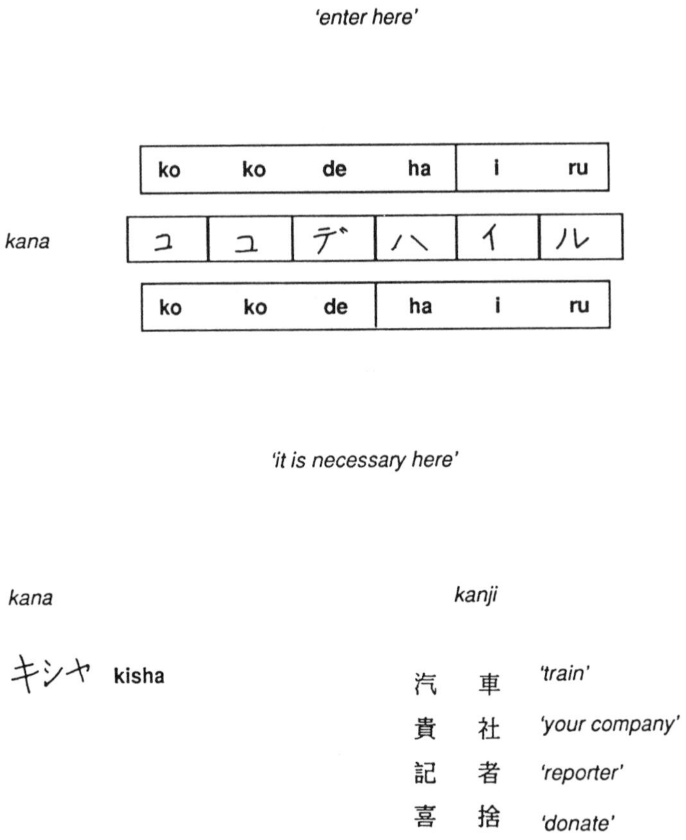

'enter here'

ko	ko	de	ha	i	ru

kana

ユ	ユ	デ	ハ	イ	ル

ko	ko	de	ha	i	ru

'it is necessary here'

kana   *kanji*

キシヤ kisha

汽 車	*'train'*
貴 社	*'your company'*
記 者	*'reporter'*
喜 捨	*'donate'*

Figure 1.1
Some problems with interpreting strings of kana. The top diagram illustrates two possible segmentations of an input sentence corresponding to two different interpretations. The bottom diagram shows how a single kana transliteration can correspond to several different words, written with different kanji characters.

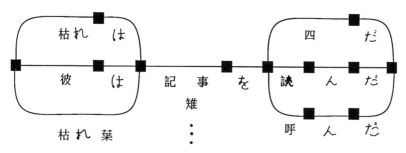

ka	re	wa	ki	ji	wo	yo	n	da
カ	レ	ハ	キ	ジ	ヲ	ヨ	ン	タ

Figure 1.2
A chart of possible transliterations of the sentence *karewakijiwoyonda*, where the correct transliteration means 'he has read the article' (see Abe et al. 1986, p. 282).

1.5 DOCUMENT RETRIEVAL

Yet another application of computational morphology is document retrieval. A number of papers discuss this and related applications (e.g., Dolby et al. 1965; Büttel et al. 1986; Thurmair 1984; Jäppinen et al. 1985; Koskenniemi 1984b; Meya-Lloport 1987). I shall discuss here the early work of Choueka and his colleagues on the RESPONSA project for Hebrew case-law documents, presented in Attar et al. 1978 and elsewhere.

The basic problem of full text retrieval is, given a set of keywords, to find all the texts in a database that contain those words. In English one can for the most part ignore the effects of inflectional morphology in this application, since there is usually little change in the stem; so ⟨church⟩ would serve to specify both ⟨church⟩ and ⟨churches⟩, and those cases where there is an orthographic change (⟨spy⟩ → ⟨spies⟩) can often be handled by fairly trivial routines.

In contrast, in Hebrew and in many other languages the effects of inflectional processes and cliticization can be quite severe. For example, the word *bat* 'daughter, girl' is represented orthographically as ⟨bt⟩ (בת).[4] The plural form of this word is *benot*—written as ⟨bnwt⟩ (בנות)—which itself can be further embedded in a longer orthographic word, ⟨wkšbnwtynw⟩ (וכשבנותינו) 'and when our girls'. Finding the word 'girl' in Hebrew texts thus requires a fair amount of morphological processing. Among other functions, the system reported in Attar et al. 1978 generates, for a given keyword, the set of all possible morphologically related words that one can expect to find in text. More precisely (since, in general, the resulting word set would be too large to be practical), the program actually generates the set of derived and inflected words legally generable from a given root.[5] In the example above, the compound part of ⟨wkšbnwtynw⟩ (וכשבנותינו) would be ⟨bnwtynw⟩—(בנותינו) *benotenu* 'our girls'. This set of words is of manageable size, and from it the cliticized forms which one can expect to find in text can be derived on the fly by simple affix-stripping methods, using a table of possible clitic combinations (which Attar et al. refer to as the 'preposition mask table'). In the example above, ⟨wkš⟩ (וכש) would be known as a possible clitic combination, and this would allow the text form ⟨wkšbnwtynw⟩ (וכשבנותינו) to be split into ⟨wkš + bnwtynw⟩ (בנותינו + וכש), where the second part would be a known derived form.

1.6 CONCLUSIONS

This chapter has presented a number of applications for morphological processing, some of which are probably fairly obvious but others of which one may not have considered. To complete the list of examples, I note that computational morphology has also been used in developing teaching tools for studying morphology itself, both for language learners (Ahmad and Rogers 1979; Holman 1988) and for students of morphological theory (Klavans and Chodorow 1988).

For the remainder of this book I shall be less concerned with the applications of computational morphology and much more concerned with what morphology is like, how one builds morphological processing systems, and what kinds of problems such systems encounter in the world's languages. It should be borne in mind, however, that many of the morphological processing systems I shall discuss in some detail in a later chapter were designed with particular applications in mind—invariably, applications that have been discussed in this chapter.

Chapter 2

The Nature of Morphology

2.1 INTRODUCTION

Suppose one were building a syntactic parsing system for some language, say English. One would normally consider the task of such a system to be to take in sentences and output correct sets of representations of those sentences. If one were more ambitious, one would also be interested in finding the meanings of the sentences. Similarly, a generation system would be concerned with generating sentences appropriate to conveying particular meanings. The task in computational morphology is entirely similar. Morphological analysis (parsing or recognition) is concerned with retrieving the structure, the syntactic and morphological properties, or the meaning of a morphologically complex word. Morphological generation is concerned with producing an appropriate morphologically complex word from some set of semantic or syntactic features.

Now, in the case of sentence parsing one would assume that the system might output a representation of the sentence's phrase structure. Similarly, a generation system would take words or semantic representations of some kind, combine them into phrases, and then ultimately combine those phrases into sentences. In order to be able to accomplish these goals, a syntactic processing system needs to know details of the phrase structure of the language in addition to the syntactic and possibly the semantic properties of individual words. Clearly, then, the designer of such a system would ideally be aware of the kinds of syntactic constructions that would be encountered in the relevant language. And if the system were intended to be readily extensible to other languages, it would be worth considering the syntactic properties of languages in general in order to avoid building a system that would depend too heavily upon the syntactic facts of the language in question.

Returning now to the domain of morphology, we need to understand what kinds of representations a morphological processing system must deal in before we can appreciate the issues involved in designing such a system, or give a fair evaluation of the performance of a particular morphological processing system.

My purpose in this chapter is to present an overview of descriptive and theoretical issues in morphology. The coverage of morphological issues is necessarily somewhat superficial, since this is not a textbook in morphology per se. As a result, it is likely that at least some of the material in this chapter will be familiar to anyone who has taken a course in morphology. On the other hand, since morphology is a rather diverse field that has been studied from many points of view, it is usually true that morphology courses (and morphology overviews) concentrate a few areas while practically ignoring others. So, for example, a lexical phonologist would very likely not have much to say about the interface between morphology and syntax, and someone who was primarily interested in the latter area would very likely have little to say about lexical phonology. In contrast, I have tried to present as broad a range of issues as I feel competent to discuss. I believe that only by considering a broad range of issues—rather than going into great depth in any one area—can one have a good sense of which areas a particular morphological processing system is able to handle and which areas it is lacking in.[1]

One important point to bear in mind is that not all the phenomena I discuss will be evidenced in any one language. So, some phenomena that exhibit themselves in the morphology of Arabic may not be of direct concern to someone whose purpose is to build a morphological processor for French. However, I shall be assuming throughout the broadest possible view of the task of computational morphology, namely that if a language exhibits a particular kind of morphological behavior a model of computational morphology ought to be able to handle it. It will become clear that various computational models of morphology make greater or lesser numbers of simplifying assumptions, and are less or more general as a consequence.

I propose to start the discussion of morphology by looking at a straightforward example from a familiar language and by making some particular observations about the example. The starting point is an instance of verb conjugation in Spanish, namely the form *puede* 'he/she/it can' in a sentence such as (1).

(1) *nadie puede estar contento*
    'nobody can be happy'

There are a number of observations that one can make about this example:

(2) a. *puede* is the third-person singular present indicative of the verb
       poder 'to be able'.

   b. The form *puede* is formed by concatenating the (second
      conjugation) **suffix** -*e* to the **stem** for the verb (*pued*-).

   c. In the form *puede*, the stem vowel has apparently changed from /o/
      to /ue/; note that the stem shows up with /o/ in many other forms of
      the same verb, e.g. *podemos* 'we can'. This change from /o/ to /ue/ is
      obligatory in the sense that *pode is not a well-formed rendition of
      the third-person singular present indicative of *poder*.

The three points in (2), simple though they may be, touch on a broad range
of issues in morphology. Point (2a) brings up the question of the function
of morphology—i.e., what kinds of information morphological forms convey. In this particular example, the form marks the fact that the subject of
the sentence is third-person and singular, the tense marking on the verb
gives information about the 'time' of the action or state, and the use of the
indicative mood (rather than the subjunctive) is consistent with the fact
that the example is a main clause and is interpreted as being a statement of
fact. Point (2b) raises the issue of the forms of morphologically complex
words and out of what kinds of "pieces" they are built. Finally, point (2c)
brings up the question of how rules of phonology (and orthography) interact with morphology. In subsequent sections of this chapter I shall examine the issues that these questions raise. In particular, I shall discuss the
following issues:

(3) a. What sorts of things can morphology mark in different languages?

   b. How are words built up from smaller meaningful units—
      morphemes? What are morphemes, and what can they look like?

   c. What are the constraints on the order of morphemes within words?

   d. Do phonological rules complicate the problem of morphological
      analysis?

I shall also examine briefly the questions of whether and how humans
process morphology in language comprehension and how morphologically complex words are represented in the mental lexicon. To the extent that
one can give useful answers to those questions, one can evaluate the extent
to which computational models of morphological processing are good
models of human processing.

   I hope to dispel in this chapter the idea that morphology and morphological analysis—as opposed to, say, syntax and syntactic analysis—are

⌐trivial.⌐ Although I have never seen it expressed explicitly in published work, I have occasionally encountered that view under other circumstances. The argument for it would appear to be that whereas theoretical morphologists portray word structure as being very intricate and complex, computational morphologists have built working systems that deal with large fragments of the morphology of languages in which the morphology is seemingly quite complex; one is therefore supposed to conclude that theoretical morphology suffers from "ivory-towerism." Well, it is perfectly true that computational systems have been built which have quite impressive coverage. On the other hand, it remains true that morphology is a complex area of inquiry. No existing morphological processing system can handle the entire range of possibilities of morphological expression in natural language; no morphological processing system currently has a good model of the interactions of morphology with syntax of the kind discussed below in subsection 2.5.1; no morphological processing system is really capable of handling the range of complexities evidenced in natural language phonology. Systems with such capabilities are certainly not out of the question, and we may expect the coverage of morphological processing systems to expand in the future. More to the point, systems—such as current ones—that are not fully general can nonetheless be useful in the automatic analysis of the morphology of a language. The point is that the aims of a computational morphologist (at least a relatively pragmatic one) and the aims of a theoretical linguist are overlapping but not identical. A theoretical morphologist is (in principle) interested in why language x has characteristic y, or why all languages have some characteristic y; as a result, the analyses that the theoretical morphologist develops generally attempt to abstract away from the more "surfacey" properties of languages. A computational morphologist, on the other hand, may be interested in more immediate goals, such as providing a working system that will handle 99 percent of the words encountered in newspaper text in some language; as a result, the analyses developed may be much more ad hoc and may not take into account some aspects of morphology that would be important to the theoretical morphologist, simply because those aspects do not occur in language x. These two approaches are not in conflict. Each can learn from the other. The computational morphologist can learn from the theoretical morphologist which issues need to be addressed to make a working system extensible to other languages (or a "toy" system for a language extensible to a "real" system for the same language); the theoretical morphologist can learn something about the complexities involved in building working systems to cover large fragments of a single language (a coverage which theoretical morphologists have not typically aimed for), and in so doing verify the adequacy of particular theoretical models. To a large extent, I believe, this cross-fertilization is taking place; I hope that this will be evident from my discussion of more recent work in computational morphology, in chapter 3.

2.2 FUNCTIONS OF MORPHOLOGY

2.2.1 Inflection versus derivation, plus a look at inflection

Distinctions between inflection and deviation
Morphology conveys information. Exactly how much information and what kind of information is conveyed morphologically varies greatly from language to language. In traditional linguistic description, languages were classified into four broad types which at least partly characterized the ways in which information is morphologically encoded and the amounts and kinds of information so encoded. Bloomfield (1933, pp. 207–208) describes these distinctions roughly as follows:

• *Isolating* languages have no *bound forms*—forms, such as affixes, that must be attached to a word.
• In *Agglutinative* languages, bound forms occur and are arranged in the word like beads on a string.
• *Polysynthetic* languages express morphologically certain elements that often occur as separate words in other languages, such as arguments of the verb.
• *Inflectional* languages show a merging of distinct features into a "single bound form or in closely united bound forms."

An oft-cited example of an isolating language is Mandarin Chinese, which lacks morphological marking for categories such as tense and number:

(4) *gǒu bú ài chī qīngcài*
    (dog not like eat vegetable)

Under appropriate conditions the sentence in (4) can mean any of the following (inter alia):

(5) a. 'the dog (specific) doesn't like to eat vegetables'

    b. 'the dog (specific) didn't like to eat vegetables'

    c. 'the dogs don't like to eat vegetables'

d. 'the dogs didn't like to eat vegetables'

e. 'dogs don't like to eat vegetables'

Thus, *gǒu* 'dog' is not marked for grammatical number or specificity and *ài* 'like, love' is not marked for tense. Indeed, many grammatical distinctions that are marked in other languages morphologically are not overtly marked in Mandarin, or at least are not marked by the attachment of bound morphemes. Still, while it is perfectly true that Mandarin morphology is impoverished in certain ways, it is actually false that bound morphemes do not exist in Mandarin. The nominal suffix *-zi* and the plural suffix *-mén* are bound morphemes. So the classification of Mandarin as an isolating language, if that term is taken to be more than just an approximation, is misleading.[2]

Bloomfield notes that the remaining three classes listed above "were never clearly defined" (p. 208). They also display a hodgepodge of criteria. Agglutinative languages—Turkish is the example usually given—certainly do mark a great number of grammatical categories morphologically. However, the defining characteristic of the agglutinative class, namely the arrangement of morphemes as beads on a string, really has nothing to do with the amounts or kinds of distinctions that are morphologically encoded, but rather has to do with the *way* in which those distinctions are encoded, as we shall see in section 2.3. For now, note the following example from Turkish (Hankamer 1986, p. 43) as an instance of the agglutinative type:

(6) *çöp +lük +ler +imiz +de +ki +ler +den +mi +y +di*
    (garbage + AFF + PL + 1P/PL + LOC + REL + PL + ABL + INT + AUX + PAST)
    'was it from those that were in our garbage cans?'

The term inflectional, at least as defined above, also refers more to the way in which categories are expressed than to what kinds of categories are expressed. The archetypal inflectional language is Latin. Inflectional languages are characterized by heavy use of portmanteau morph(eme)s. In Latin the suffix *-ō* in a word such as *am +ō* 'I love' expresses simultaneously several grammatical categories: first person, singular, present, indicative, active. The Spanish example discussed in (2) also contains a portmanteau morpheme (the suffix *-e*). Again, this is more an issue of the phonological expression of morphological categories than an issue of what kinds of grammatical distinctions are marked morphologically. And it is particularly important not to confuse the terms inflectional language and inflectional morphology; the latter term refers to the *kind* of grammatical distinction encoded, independent of *how* that distinction happens to be overtly encoded in a language. An agglutinative language like Turkish has inflectional morphology even though it does not abound in portmanteau morphemes.

The term *polysynthetic*, in contrast, refers to the amounts and kinds of information encoded morphologically in the language. Typical examples of polysynthetic languages are the Eskimo languages, such as Central Alaskan Yupik:

(7) *qayá:liyú:lú:ní*
   'he was excellent (*-yu-*) at making (*-li-*) kayaks (*qaya:-*)'

In this example (Woodbury 1987, p. 687), a whole sentence consists of one word, including the verb *-li-* 'make' and its object *qayá:* 'kayak', which is **incorporated** into the word (see below on incorporation). Polysynthetic languages, then, would seem to be at the opposite end of the scale of morphological complexity from isolating languages.

So, while the traditional four-way distinction is a somewhat mixed bag of criteria, and was never very clearly defined, there is a core of truth in at least some of the distinctions; it is at least true that some languages encode a great deal more morphologically than others. Indeed, it is often said— somewhat informally—that languages like Central Alaskan Yupik have all their grammar "in the morphology," as opposed to languages like Mandarin, where most relations between grammatical elements are expressed in the syntax. And it is certainly true that building a morphological processor for Central Alaskan Yupik would be a substantially more onerous task than building one for Mandarin.

It is established, then, that languages differ greatly in the amount of information and the kinds of information encoded morphologically; a corollary of this is that the difficulty of constructing a morphological model will also vary widely across languages. More specifically, what kinds of information can be encoded morphologically? As a first cut at an answer to this question let us start with the traditional distinction between *inflectional morphology* and *derivational morphology* (the latter is also traditionally referred to as **word formation**). An intuitive idea of the supposed distinction is that inflectional morphology takes as input a word and outputs a form of the same word appropriate to a particular context; thus, verbal morphology in a language like Spanish (see the example in (2) above) would be considered inflectional, since a word like *puede* 'he/she/it can' is a particular form of the verb *poder* 'to be able', appropriate to the context where the subject is third-person singular, the tense is present, and so forth. Another way to state this is to say that *puede* belongs to the

paradigm of *poder*. A paradigm can basically be thought of as a set of pigeonholes where the set constitutes all the possible inflected forms of the word in question and each of the holes corresponds to a particular function or set of functions. A part of the set of pigeonholes for *poder*—the part with the features 'present' and 'indicative'—would look as follows (as one would find in any standard grammar of Spanish):

(8)   SG   PL
   1   *puedo*   *podemos*
   2   *puedes*   *podéis*
   3   *puede*   *pueden*

(For a relatively recent discussion of theoretical issues involving paradigms, see Carstairs 1984.) Words within the same paradigm, then, are really different forms of the same word; the forms in (8) would often be said to be forms of the **lexeme** *poder* (see Matthews 1974, p. 22).

On the other hand, derivational morphology is (roughly speaking) supposed to take as input a word and output a different word that is *derived from* the input word; this is, of course, why derivational morphology has also been called word formation. So, in English the word *antidisestablishmentarianism* has several layers of derivational morphology[3]:

(9) *establish* → *establish +ment*
          → *establish +ment +ary*
          → *establish +ment +ari +an*
          → *establish +ment +ari +an +ism*
          → *dis +establish +ment +ari +an +ism*
          → *anti +dis +establish +ment +ari +an +ism*

The inflection/derivation distinction seems clear enough in some cases, yet it has always been hard to nail down. For one thing, although one does have an intuition that it is right to say that the forms in (8) are forms of the same word, it is not clear that one can really define the notion of a lexeme in a noncircular way. Therefore, various other criteria have been proposed for distinguishing inflection from derivation. Below I give a sample and some discussion of these criteria, which I have adapted from Wurzel 1989 (pp. 31–42). See Wurzel 1989 for a critique of these criteria. Also see Bybee 1985 for discussions about the problems in distinguishing inflection from derivation.

Inflectional morphology does not change part of speech, whereas derivational morphology may change part of speech.   For example, the plural morpheme -*s* in *boy* +*s* does not change the part of speech of the stem to which it attaches—the word remains a noun. On the other hand, the derivational morpheme -*ness* does change the part of speech of the stem to which it attaches, since it typically attaches to adjectives and makes nouns: *silly/ silli* +*ness*. Problematic from this point of view is inflectional morphology that does change grammatical category. One example is the case of Latin participles, such as *dātus* 'given' (from *dō* 'I give'). On the one hand, participles are certainly part of the verbal paradigm in Latin; on the other hand, they are grammatically adjectives, not verbs.

Inflectional morphology is often required in particular syntactic contexts, whereas derivational morphology is never required by the syntax. A typical example of this distinction would be the fact that nominal case is selected on the basis of the noun's role in the sentence. For example, in the Latin sentence in (10), *puer* 'boy' is in the nominative case because it functions as the subject of the sentence, whereas *Cicerōnem* is in the accusative case since that noun is functioning as the object of the sentence; reversing the case assignment would reverse the grammatical functions interpreted for each of the nouns.

(10) *puer Cicerōnem laudat*
      (boy/NOM Cicero/ACC praise/3/SG/PRES/IND/ACT)
      'the boy praises Cicero'

In contrast, in a sentence such as *everybody desires happiness*, there is no sense that the derivational morpheme -*ness* is required by the syntax, say because *happiness* is functioning as the object of *desire*; any noun can grammatically function as the object of *desire* no matter what the derivational form of the noun. The criterion for distinguishing inflection from derivation presented in this paragraph is closely related to the notion, discussed above, that inflectional morphology produces different forms of the same lexeme; specifically, it produces forms of the lexeme appropriate to a particular context.[4] But the criterion breaks down in other inflectional categories, such as nominal number. In the sentence *everybody desires pumpkins* there is no sense that the plural marking on *pumpkins* is required grammatically.

Since inflection is often required by the syntax, it follows that if a language marks a certain inflectional category then it must mark that category on all appropriate words. So, in a language that marks accusative case on nouns, it ought to be the case that every noun has an accusative case form (though that may in some cases be formally identical to some other case form). In contrast, derivational morphology and the grammatical features it encodes often have no such requirement of generality. For example, although some English occupational terms show gender distinctions—the feminine form often being marked by the suffix *-ess*, as in *waiter/waitress*, *actor/actress*—others do not: *driver/*driv(e)ress, cashier/*cashieress*.

It is important to realize that this is not really a claim about morphology per se, but rather about the lexical or morphological expression of grammatical or semantic features. For example, it is true that all English verbs (with the exception of modals such as *may*) may be marked for past tense, so past-tense formation can be said to be completely productive in precisely the sense that for any English verb there is an associated past-tense form. But it is obviously not the case that past tense is always marked by the same morphological means, since there is a large (though bounded) set of irregular verbs in English—*sing, bring, take, go*—that do not form their past tenses by affixing *-ed*. The affixation of *-ed* is thus not completely productive, but the formation of the past tense *is* completely productive. More formally, one can say that there is a relation P such that $P(v_p, v)$ holds if and only if v_p is the past-tense form of v. P is productive in that for any v_i there is a v_{ip} such that $P(v_{ip}, v_i)$. Note, again, that *this makes no statement about the productivity of morphology that expresses P*. The claim, then, is that "inflectional" relations P are productive whereas "derivational" relations are not.

Even in this relational sense, inflectional morphology is not necessarily always completely productive. Going against the generalization is the observation that in many highly inflected languages inflectional paradigms for various lexemes may be *defective*, or lacking in certain forms. The Latin verb *inquit* 'he says', for example, lacks most of the forms of the Latin verbal paradigm. It is not clear that there is a good semantic reason for this. Rather, it seems to be an arbitrary lexical fact.

And there are certainly non-inflectional relations that appear to be completely productive. Witness the fact that in English virtually any adjective α has a related noun with the meaning 'the degree to which x is α', or 'the state of being α':

(11) *wide*   *width*
     broad   *breadth*
     grammatical   *grammaticality*
     silly   *silliness*
     giraffish   *giraffishness*

repulsive   *repulsiveness*
sarcastic   *sarcasm*

The morphological expression of this relation is by no means regular (though some of the affixes involved are quite productive—see subsection 2.2.2), but the relation itself seems to be as productive as any inflectional relation.

Furthermore, many particular derivational affixes are completely productive. An obvious case involves the prefix *pro-*, which attaches quite freely to nouns as well as to many adjectives:

(12) **pro-**$Nazi$, **pro-**$Stroessner$, **pro-**$Iranian$, **pro-**$nuclear$, **pro-**$civil$-$rights$,
      pro-$Waldheim$, **pro-**$independence$, **pro-**$Western$, **pro-**$Beijing$,
      pro-$development$, **pro-**$environment$, **pro-**$apartheid$, **pro-**$choice$,
      pro-$democracy$

The only restriction on the attachment of *pro-* to a noun would appear to be one of plausibility: *pro-dogfish* seems implausible outside of an appropriate context (e.g., *Charlie the Tuna is pro-dogfish though anti-shark*), but it is not *morphologically* ill formed. Productivity, therefore, bears no special relation to inflectional morphology.[5]

So, the distinction between inflection and derivation—if there is a formal distinction to be made—is at best graded (Bybee 1985, p. 12). Perhaps the most straightforward way to define the inflection/derivation distinction, if one wants to do that, is to define it extensionally, by listing a set of grammatical categories which are inflectional in nature and asserting that morphology which marks those categories is inflectional morphology; everything else is then derivational. If one looks across languages for types of morphology which seem roughly to fit the above criteria for inflectional status (and others), one finds that the same categories show up again and again. A partial inventory of categories which are commonly marked cross-linguistically is given in the following paragraphs. Much of this discussion has been adapted from the treatment of verbal categories in Bybee 1985 (see, e.g., pp. 20–24). For a more complete list of inflectional categories used across languages, see pp. 166–169 of Nida 1949.

Verbal morphology

Grammatical-function-changing morphology Typically, a verb lexically specifies the number of arguments it may take. In many languages, morphological devices modify these lexically specified markings; common examples are causativization, **applicatives**, and passivization,[6] all of which fall under the rubric of what is often called *grammatical-function-changing* morphology (so called because the grammatical functions associated with particular arguments of the verb are changed by the morphology). For example, the most straightforward description of the effects of passive morphology is that the role assigned to the object in an active sentence is assigned to the subject in the related passive sentence. So in the Latin example in (13a), *Cicerōnem* is the object of the active verb *laudat* 'praises'; in (13b), *Cicerō* is the subject of the corresponding passive verb *laudātur*.

(13) a. *puer Cicerōnem laudat*
(boy C. praise/3/SG/PRES/IND/**ACT**)
'the boy praises Cicero'

b. *Cicerō laudātur*
(C. praise/3/SG/PRES/IND/**PASS**)
'Cicero is praised'

Grammatical-function-changing morphology has received by far the most attention over recent years from people interested in the relation between morphology and syntax. The passive is particularly well known from work on syntax because it has been the source of much heated debate. Part of the disagreement between syntactic theories has concerned the mechanism by which the passive exercises its grammatical-function-changing effect. In lexical functional grammar (Bresnan 1982), the passive morpheme—in the Latin example above, the sequence -*ur*—has the morphological effect of changing the verb's argument structure by a rule of the form illustrated in (14), which changes the verb's object into its subject (and concomitantly changes the verb's subject into an optional by-object).

(14) ⟨SUBJ,OBJ⟩ → ⟨BY-OBJ,SUBJ⟩

In government/binding theory (Chomsky 1981), the passive morpheme is supposed to have the effect of simultaneously removing the verb's ability to assign the thematic (θ-) role to the subject and removing the verb's ability to assign Case to the object, thus both allowing and requiring the object to move to the subject position.

The following examples of causative and applicative morphology in the Bantu language Chicheŵa are taken from Baker 1988 (which the reader should see for a recent theory of grammatical-function-changing morphology within the government/binding framework):

(15) a. Causative (Baker 1988, p. 11):
*mtsikana a +na +u +gw +**ets** +a mtsuko*

(girl SubjAgr + PAST + ObjAgr + fall + **CAUS** + ASP waterpot)
'the girl made the waterpot fall'

b. Applicative (Baker 1988, p. 229):
   mbidzi zi +na +perek +er +a nkhandwe msampha
   (zebras SubjAgr + PAST + hand + **APPL** + ASP fox trap)
   'the zebras handed the fox the trap'

In (15a) the noun *mtsuko* 'waterpot', which shows up as the surface object of the sentence, is really notionally a subject; one can understand this by considering that in the English translation of the sentence *waterpot* is the subject of the lower verb *fall*. What the causative morpheme *-ets* does, in effect, is collapse two clauses into one, making the subject of the notional underlying clause the object of the surface clause. Similarly, in (15b), the noun *nkhandwe* 'fox', which shows up as the surface object of the sentence, is really the underlying indirect object (... *handed the trap* **to** *the fox*); the underlying direct object (*msampha* 'trap') surfaces as what is often called the *second object*. The effect of the applicative morpheme *-er* is to promote the indirect object to direct object and to demote the direct object to second object.

Tense and aspect Verbs are commonly marked with indications of the (relative) time at which the situation described by the sentence occurred, or the state of completion of the situation. The former is called tense marking and the latter **aspect** marking. Some languages mark verbs for both tense and aspect; others mark for one or the other. Latin, for example, marks for both. In (16a), the marking *-b-* on the verb marks future tense. In (16b) the marking *-v-* marks perfect aspect:

(16) a. *vir Cicerōnem laudā +***b** *+ō*
     (man C. praise + **FUT** + 3/SG/IND)
     'the man will praise Cicero'

 b. *vir Cicerōnem laudā +***v** *+it*
     (man C. praise + **PERF** + 3/SG/IND)
     'the man has praised Cicero'

Mandarin, in contrast, has no tense markings, but has a rich aspectual marking system (see Li and Thompson 1981, in particular chapter 6), which is marked by various verbal affixes. Some samples are given below of the perfective affix *-le* (17a), indicating that the event described is bounded in time; of the experiential affix *-guo* (17b), indicating that the event in question has been experienced; and of the delimitative aspect, which refers to doing an action 'a little bit' (Li and Thompson 1981, p. 232) and which is morphologically marked by **reduplication** (see subsection 2.3.5) of the verb:

(17) a. *tā shuì +***le** *sānge zhōngtóu*
         (s/he sleep + **PERF** three hour)
         'he slept for three hours' (Li and Thompson 1981, p. 186)

    b. *wǒ chī +***guo** *zhōngguó cài*
         (I eat + **EXP** China food)
         'I have eaten (have had the experience of eating) Chinese food'

    c. *wǒ* **kàn+kan**
         (I **look + look**)
         'I will take a (little) look'

Agreement morphology A final common type of verbal morphology that will be illustrated here is **agreement** between the verb and its arguments for features such as number, person, and gender. (Agreement is also sometimes called concord.) A very common situation, one which is typical for many Indo-European languages, is to require the verb to agree in number and person with the subject of the sentence. Spanish illustrates this nicely (note that the affixes in question are portmanteau morphemes also encoding information about tense and mood):

(18) a. *(yo) pued +***o** *hablar español*
         (I can + 1/SG/PRES/IND speak Spanish)
         'I can speak Spanish'

    b. *los señores americanos no pued +***en** *hablar español*
         (the gentlemen American not can + **3/PL/PRES/IND** speak Spanish)
         'the American gentlemen cannot speak Spanish'

So, in (18a) the suffix *-o* on *puedo* encodes the fact that the subject of the sentence is first-person singular, and in (18b) the suffix *-en* on *pueden* encodes the fact that the subject is third-person plural. Other languages, such as Arabic, also encode gender agreement for certain combinations of person and number; some other languages, such as Georgian and Chicheŵa (on the latter, see Bresnan and Mchombo 1987), encode not only agreement between the verb and the subject but also agreement between the verb and the object.

    Agreement morphology is clearly an important part of the relation between morphology and syntax, since it marks information about the relation between the verb and its arguments. This is particularly the case in so called **pro-drop languages**, such as Spanish and some other Romance languages, where the agreement morphology on the verb is often sufficiently informative to allow the subject to be dropped:

(19) *pued +o hablar Español*
      (can + **1/SG/PRES/IND** speak Spanish)
      'I can speak Spanish'

(But it is not the case that all languages which have rich agreement morphology allow for pro-drop; Russian would be a counterexample to such a claim.) In fact, in some languages, such as Irish (see McCloskey and Hale 1984), agreement morphology on the verb not only allows for pro-drop; it requires it. In such languages, morphological marking for tense and number and overt subjects (or objects) are in complementary distribution. So, in (20a) we have a case of pro-drop in Irish where the subject ('I') is not present as a separate word, although it is morphologically represented by the suffix *-im* on *feicim* 'I see'. In (20b), the presence of the overt first-person subject *mé* renders the example ungrammatical. In (20c) we see that an overt first-person subject is fine as long as the verb (in this case *tá* 'be') does not have any morphological agreement marking itself.

(20) a. *feic +im anois thú*
          (see + 1/SG now you)
          'I see you now'

      b. **feic +im mé anois thú*
          (see + **1/SG** I now you)

      c. *tá mé ag ól fíon*
          (be I Particle drink wine)
          'I am drinking wine'

One can understand this kind of agreement by assuming that the agreement morpheme in question is actually a pronoun which is incorporated into the verb; see Baker and Hale 1990 for a discussion. Thus, the verb *feicim* 'I see' in (20a) provides a subject for the sentence, which cannot then have another subject. Cases like the Irish example are rather like cases of cliticization (to which I return later in the chapter) in that in both situations a single morphological word functions like more than one word syntactically. Such cases are important from the point of view of theoretical and from that of computational morphology, since they suggest that there must be a somewhat more incestuous relationship between morphology and syntax than at first glance there might appear to be.

Greenberg (1966) observed that there are significant cross-linguistic generalizations on what kinds of verbal morphology are expected in a language. In particular, on the basis of a sample of 30 languages from different language families, Greenberg claims (p. 93) that if a language has verbal agreement for person, number, or gender then it must also have mood, or tense, or (presumably) aspectual marking. So, while one finds languages (such as Mandarin) with rich aspectual systems but no person/number agreement, languages which mark verbs for person/number agreement but which lack any verbal markings for tense or aspect are very rare. Greenberg also claims (p. 94) that verbal agreement for gender in a language implies the existence of verbal agreement for number in that language. We will return to the relevance of such implicational universals for the relative order of morphemes within words in subsection 2.5.2. With respect to the issue at hand, the implicational universals suggest that the options that a language has in picking means of morphological expression are by no means completely free.

Nominal and adjectival morphology

We will treat the inflectional morphology of nouns and adjectives together, since there is often much similarity in the morphological behavior of these two categories of words in any given language. The main difference between them, which should be borne in mind, is that typically the inflectional marking on the noun is determined either by the dictates of the desired semantics (in the case of inflection for number), or by the demands of the syntactic context (in the case of inflection for case), or by the inherent lexical properties of the noun itself (as in the case of markings of gender). On the other hand, with one notable exception, all adjectival morphology can be thought of as agreement, much like the verbal agreement discussed above.

Number, case, and gender/noun class   Common inflection categories for nouns and adjectives include the following:

• marking for number (singular, plural, dual, ...)
• marking for case, as governed by verbs, prepositions, or structural position, or to mark various kinds of semantic relations
• marking for gender   (Gender marking is usually lexically specified with a particular noun, but adjectives in many languages must agree with the nouns that they modify or are predicated of.)

For example, in Latin, an adjective of the first and second declension could take any of the following forms, exemplified here by *magnus* 'big' (I am omitting the vocative case, which differs from the nominative only in the masculine singular):

(21)	MASC	FEM	NEUT
SG			
NOM	*magn* +**us**	*magn* +**a**	*magn* +**um**
GEN	*magn* +**ī**	*magn* +**ae**	*magn* +**ī**
DAT	*magn* +**ō**	*magn* +**ae**	*magn* +**ō**
ACC	*magn* +**um**	*magn* +**am**	*magn* +**um**
ABL	*magn* +**ō**	*magn* +**ā**	*magn* +**ō**
PL			
NOM	*magn* +**ī**	*magn* +**ae**	*magn* +**a**
GEN	*magn* +**ōrum**	*magn* +**ārum**	*magn* +**ōrum**
DAT	*magn* +**īs**	*magn* +**īs**	*magn* +**īs**
ACC	*magn* +**ōs**	*magn* +**ās**	*magn* +**a**
ABL	*magn* +**īs**	*magn* +**īs**	*magn* +**īs**

So, Latin distinguishes five cases: nominative, used to mark subjects; genitive, used to mark possessives; dative, used to mark indirect objects; accusative, used to mark direct objects; and ablative, used in a variety of other functions. Latin also has two numbers (singular and plural) and three genders (masculine, feminine, and neuter); again, genders are typically lexically specified for particular nouns, but adjectives like *magnus* must inflect for gender to agree with the nouns they modify or predicate. None of the dimensions of the paradigm in (21) can be considered particularly large. For example, Finnish distinguishes fourteen cases (nominative, genitive, accusative, partitive, inessive, abessive, adessive, ablative, elative, illative, allative, prolative, translative, and instrumental)—fortunately, perhaps, Finnish does not also mark gender.[7]

Familiar languages which have grammatical gender, such as Indo-European or Semitic languages, often distinguish either two (masculine, feminine) or three (masculine, feminine, neuter) grammatical genders. More complex gender-like systems exist, such as the intricate noun-class systems of Bantu languages. The following examples from Swahili are taken from Wald 1987; Bantu class markers are prefixes (shown in boldface in the following):

(22) Class	SG	PL	Gloss
1 (humans)	**m** +*tu*	**wa** +*tu*	'person'
3 (thin objects)	**m** +*ti*	**mi** +*ti*	'tree'
5 (paired things)	**ji** +*cho*	**ma** +*cho*	'eye'
7 (instrument)	**ki** +*tu*	**vi** +*tu*	'thing'
11 (extended body parts)	**u** +*limi*	**n** +*dimi*	'tongue'

Parallel to gender agreement in languages like Latin, Bantu languages exhibit class agreement; for example, modifiers of a noun take agreement prefixes that depend upon the class to which the noun belongs.

Comparison of adjectives   Many languages, including English, express comparison of adjectives morphologically. Commonly expressed morphologically are the comparative and superlative forms. Some languages express more degrees of comparison. For example, Welsh, in addition to comparative and superlative forms, has an equative form:

(23) POS   EQU   COMP   SUP   GLOSS
    gwyn   *gwynn* +**ed**   *gwynn* +**ach**   *gwynn* +**af**   'white'
    teg   *tec* +**ed**   *tec* +**ach**   *tec* +**af**   'fair'

Summary

In these subsections I have sketched some of the more common kinds of inflectional morphology found cross-linguistically. As we have seen, some of the kinds of information marked by morphology in some languages are rather complex; this is particularly true in the case of grammatical-function-changing morphology, since it requires one to look at the morphological structure of the verb in order to figure out how to interpret the relation of the noun phrases in the sentence to the verb.

Inflectional morphology, because of its strong interaction with the syntax and semantics of sentences, seems particularly crucial for computational morphology; indeed, it is probably true that a great deal of the work on computational morphology has concentrated largely on inflectional morphology simply for the reason that in many highly inflected languages this kind of morphology cannot be ignored. Two points should be mentioned in this context. First, precisely because the *inflectional* morphology of English is quite impoverished, there has been an attitude that English *morphology* is trivial; as we shall see in the next subsection, English *derivational* morphology is not trivial. So, while building a morphological analyzer to handle English inflectional morphology may not require much ingenuity, building morphological analyzers to handle the range of derivational possibilities in English has required substantially more ingenuity. Second, while computational models of inflectional morphology may be of primary importance to some computational applications (for example, as a part of a lexical component for a more general natural language analysis system), there are other applications (such as interfaces to dictionaries or morphological front ends to databases or text-to-speech systems—see chapter 1 for a discussion) where the full range of morphological possibilities—inflectional or derivational—are likely to be important. With these points in mind, I turn now to a description of some types of morphological processes that would be called derivational.

2.2.2 Derivational morphology

Derivational morphology involves a much more open-ended set of options than inflectional morphology. The number of different kinds of information that can be marked by morphemes which form new words—i.e., new lexemes—seems to be rather large; a cursory look at what is probably the richest source of information on English word formation (Marchand 1969) reveals that English has a great many derivational affixes, which encode many different kinds of information. There are many quite productive derivational processes in English, and I propose to turn to a description of some of these now. Naturally, within the confines of an overview of this kind the coverage cannot be complete; the interested reader is encouraged to see Marchand 1969 for an extensive discussion.

Deverbal nominal morphology   Two kinds of morphology come under this rubric; one type is the (misnamed) agentive nominal and the other is the **derived nominal**.

Agentive nominals in English are typically formed by the affixation of -*er* to the verb, with the rough meaning of the result being 'one who does *x*' (*x* being the action specified by the verb). Some examples are given in (24).

(24) *adder, baker, catcher, dealer, eater, fighter, grinder, hater, ionizer,*
       jumper, killer, lover, manager, namer, opener, peeler, quitter, roller,
       sitter, timer, user, voter, winner, xeroxer, yodeler, zipper

By and large, the entity denoted by an agentive nominal can be anything that can function as the **external argument** from which the noun is derived; see Levin and Rappaport 1988 for some quite recent discussion of the semantics of -*er* nominals in English. (Such constructions are often called agentive nominals because many of the nouns in question do in fact refer to agents; e.g., a *catcher* is a person who does some act of catching. But, as Levin and Rappaport show, the assumption that -*er* nominals are necessarily semantically agents is incorrect.)

In contrast to agentive nominals, which by and large are quite productive and regular in their semantics and their morphological expression, so-called derived nominals are regular in neither, although there nonetheless exist large pockets of regularity. Semantically, derived nominals are often used to refer to the event corresponding to an instance of the related verb's action (Thomason 1985; Sproat 1985). For example, in (25b) the noun phrase headed by *destruction* refers to an event of the Romans destroying Carthage, as might be felicitously referred to by the sentence in (25a):

(25) a. *the Romans destroyed Carthage*
     b. *the Romans' destruction of Carthage (was fearsome)*

One thing to note with respect to the example in (25b) is that derived nominals are often said to inherit the argument structure of the verbs from which they are derived. So, just as *destroy* takes two arguments, one being the agent of the destruction (*the Romans*) and the other the patient (*Carthage*), so does *destruction*. This is generally true also of agentive nominals (e.g., *Rome was the destroyer of Carthage*), though more restrictions apply on what kinds of arguments can be inherited in such cases. In the case of agentive nominals, the nominal itself is used to refer to the external argument; see Rappaport 1983, Sproat 1985, Safir 1987, and Levin and Rappaport 1988.

However, derived nominals often take on other meanings besides the event reading, although these other meanings do not necessarily preclude the event reading. So, *transmission* has both its automotive reading and the event reading—as in *transmission of information*. (On the other hand, *suction* cannot readily be used to refer to an event of sucking: **John's suction of the milk through a straw.*) Formally too, derived nominals are quite diverse. Many are formed by the suffixation of *-(t)ion*—indeed, verbs ending in *-ate* quite productively form derived nominals in this way, and these nominals tend also to quite freely have the eventive reading. Other forms exist, though: *rely/reliance, engage/engagement, know/knowledge.*[8]

Deverbal adjectival morphology   Foremost among English cases of this kind is the suffix *-able*, which attaches mostly to transitive verbs, with the resultant meaning 'able to be $x$ed', where x is the meaning of the verb:

(26) *parsable, understandable, reachable, likeable, drinkable, eatable*

While there are some restrictions (e.g., *eatable* seems to be rendered bad for some speakers by the existence of *edible*), the affix is, on the whole, productive, in that it attaches quite freely to novel verbs—with predictable semantics.

Deadjectival morphology   English has productive mechanisms for the formation of nouns from adjectives—the suffixes *-ity* and *-ness* in particular. The suffix *-ity* is not completely productive, since it is largely restricted to words of Latinate origin. So we get *rare/rarity, grammatical/grammaticality,* and *grave/gravity*; but not *old/*oldity, red/*reddity,* or *weird/*weirdity.* Even within Latinate adjectives there is not complete productivity, but there are nonetheless areas of complete productivity: so, basically any deverbal adjective ending in *-able* has a related noun in *-ity*: *parsable/ parsability, mashable/mashability, get-at-able/get-at-ability.*[9]

The suffix *-ness* is generally more productive than *-ity,* since it can generally attach to adjectives which *-ity* can also attach to as well as some which *-ity* cannot (see Aronoff 1976, pp. 43–45):

(27)		
rare	*rarity*	*?rareness*
grammatical	*grammaticality*	*grammaticalness*
grave	*gravity*	*graveness*
red	**reddity*	*redness*
weird	**weirdity*	*weirdness*

The meaning of deadjectival nouns in *-ity* and *-ness* is often characterizable as 'the state of being *x*' or the 'extent of *x*', where *x* is the meaning of the adjective:

(28) a. *the grammaticality of this example is not in dispute*
'the state of this example's being grammatical is not in dispute'

b. *the rarity of this coin is truly surprising*
'the extent to which this coin is rare is truly surprising'

As with derived nominals, with which such deadjectival nouns share some properties (Jespersen 1942, p. 85; Sproat 1985, p. 315), many forms have taken on idiosyncratic readings: e.g., *gravity*, which also retains its more compositional meaning, 'state of being grave'.

Denominal morphology   We will take as our example of denominal morphology the suffix *-less*, which attaches to nouns and makes adjectives with the meaning 'lacking *x*', where *x* is the meaning of the noun. It is completely productive, and while there have been cases where a word has taken on idiosyncratic meanings (e.g., *spotless*), there seems to be no problem interpreting any of these forms in a fully compositional way:

(29) *armless statue, beanless chili, catless pet-owner, doorless house, eggless cake, figless newton*

Some productive prefixal morphology   In this subsection we have dealt so far only with suffixing derivational morphology. Here I merely list some examples of productive prefixal morphology in English, all of which are derivational (there are no inflectional prefixes in English):

(30) a. **pseudo-**: **pseudo**-*leftist*, **pseudo**-*military*, **pseudo**-*science*,
            pseudo-*intellectual*, **pseudo**-*pacifist*, **pseudo**-*wood*,
            pseudo-*protection*, **pseudo**-*sympathy*

       b. **semi-**: **semi***arid*, **semi**-*divine*, **semi***formal*, **semi***government*,
            semi*retirement*, **semi**-*subterranean*, **semi**-*natural*, **semi***regular*,
            semi-*coma*, **semi**-*closed*

       c. **un-**: **un***answered*, **un***changed*, **un***able*, **un***known*, **un***substantiated*,
            un*harmed*, **un***committed*, **un***injured*, **un***clear*, **un***founded*, **un***necessary*,
            un*constitutional*, **un***complimentary*, **un***flinching*, **un***lawful*

All of the above prefixes are quite productive, and most of them are regular in their semantics: words formed with *pro-* typically have the meaning 'favoring *x*', and adjectives prefixed with *un-* virtually always have the reading 'the opposite of *x*'.

Summary   The range of functions provided by derivational morphology is less easily laid out than was the case with inflectional morphology, and it seems reasonable to expect that languages differ in what kinds of functions derivational morphology mark more than is the case with inflection. Still, there are functions, such as "agentive" nominal formation, that at least seem to be widespread cross-linguistically.

What is the relevance of derivational morphology to computational morphology? Again, as was noted at the conclusion of subsection 2.2.1, that really depends upon the application for which the system is intended. If one is building a morphological analyzer whose intended function is to provide morphological analyses for a syntactic parser, and if one is working with a highly inflected language such as Finnish, one may be concerned primarily with inflectional morphology and less with more clearly derivational morphology. After all, as long as one's dictionary is sufficiently large, one can cover a great many (though not all) of the lexemes that one is likely to encounter in real text without recourse to analysis, simply because new lexemes are formed at a relatively low rate. On the other hand, lexemes will constantly be showing up in inflectional forms which one has not previously encountered. However, if one is interested in building an interface to a dictionary, or perhaps an interface to a database retrieval system, then one may well be very interested in having a model of derivational morphology in order to be able to capture the often-complex sets of relationships among words in a language. We now turn to a discussion of compounding, which will complete our overview of the functions of morphology.

2.2.3 Compounding (p. 236)

Generally speaking, derivational and inflectional morphology are mediated by the attachment of an affix to the stem form of a lexeme: the genitive singular of the Latin lexeme *magnus* 'big' is formed by attaching *-ī* to the stem of *magnus, magn-*; the English word *nominee* is formed by the attachment of the suffix *-ee* to the stem of *nominate, nomin-*. (In the next subsection I will elaborate on what it means to attach an affix. Note also that a monomorphemic stem form of a lexeme is often called a **root**—a term which I shall use from time to time. See chapter 2 of Bauer 1983 for definitions of *stem* and *root*.)

In contrast, *compounding* consists of the concatenation of two or more lexemes' stems to form another lexeme. The following are some examples of unequivocal compounds from English, where each of these examples is built of the stems of two noun lexemes:

(31) *firefighter, handgun, mountaintop, fairground, firecracker, newspaper, surfboard, roadblock, jailhouse, nighttime, courtroom, policeman, sweatpants, handwriting, songwriter, gunman, sandstone*

Let me start by describing some of the properties of compounds in English, and what makes them both interesting and difficult to analyze in that language. I will then briefly take a look at some of their properties in other languages. I will concentrate on nominal compounds—compounds where the head (see below) is a noun and the resulting compound is also a noun. These constitute the most productive set of compounds in English.

Compounding in English   One of the difficulties with compounds in English is deciding when one has a compound and when one has a phrase. Nominal compounds are instances of modifier-head constructions (Levi 1978). For example, one can think of *handgun* as referring to a particular kind of gun, as determined by the head *gun*, where the modifier *hand* tells you what kind of gun you have. I will have more to say about the semantics of compounds momentarily, but for now note that phrasal—i.e., nonmorphological—constructions, such as *tropical storm*, are also modifier-head constructions. So the functional relationship expressed between the parts of a two-word compound does not readily serve to distinguish compounds from phrases.

Stress is often taken to be the criterion for distinguishing compounds in English from phrases.[10] All the examples in (32a) have stress on the first member (**compound stress**) and are said to be compounds, and all the exam-

ples in (32b) have stress on the second member (phrasal stress) and are said
to be phrases (the primary stressed member is capitalized):

(32) a. *FIREfighter, HANDgun, MOUNTAINtop, FAIRground,*
     FIREcracker, NEWSpaper, SURFboard, ROADblock, JAILhouse,
     NIGHTtime, COURTroom, POLICEman, SWEATpants,
     HANDwriting, SONGwriter, GUNman, SANDstone

   b. *internal EXPECTATIONS, bloody CAMPAIGN, tropical*
      STORM, other SIDE, unilateral ACTION, electronic
      EQUIPMENT, old SKIN, human SUFFERING, congressional
      SOURCE, personal HISTORY

While this is a possible and widely accepted criterion (Bloomfield 1933;
Chomsky and Halle 1968; Liberman and Sproat 1991), it is arbitrary from
many points of view; for more discussion, see Marchand 1969 (pp. 13–15)
and Liberman and Sproat 1991, and see also Ladd 1984 for arguments that
stress should not be taken as criterial. For one thing, it is widely recognized
that there is considerable idiosyncrasy in stress both between speakers and
for individual speakers. Many speakers say *APPLE cake* but *apple PIE*. If
we take stress as a criterion, the former is by definition a compound and
the latter not, but for this example the division seems at best arbitrary from
a semantic point of view: both apple cakes and apple pies are foods made
with apples.

A second way in which the division on the basis of stress is arbitrary is
from the point of view of orthography. In English one may write two-word
compounds as single orthographic words, optionally separating the two
elements with a hyphen: *doghouse* or *dog-house*. It is certainly true that if
one finds a nominal compound so written, stress is virtually guaranteed to
be on the left (in the absence of any discourse context in which some other
stress would be appropriate.) On the other hand, there is little consistency
in orthographic practice (Marchand 1969; Liberman and Sproat 1991);
indeed, one may find ⟨spark plug⟩, ⟨spark-plug⟩, and ⟨sparkplug⟩ within
the same piece of text. And if one finds a premodified nominal written as
two orthographic words, it is still quite possible that the primary stress will
be on the left member. Thus, the number of orthographic words in a premodified nominal will not necessarily distinguish a compound such as
spark plug from a phrasal construction such as *red house*. To add to the
confusion, compounds with more than two members can never be written
together as one word in English; so a cleaner for a pot that holds coffee
could be written ⟨coffee pot cleaner⟩, or ⟨coffeepot cleaner⟩, or ⟨coffee-
pot cleaner⟩, but never *⟨coffeepotcleaner⟩. Notice that this example

would normally be stressed on the leftmost member, as *COFFEE pot cleaner*, thus making it firmly a compound on the above assumption. Thus, while stress may indeed be the correct criterion for distinguishing compounds from phrases, it must be borne in mind that this criterion often seems to make an arbitrary division between cases. Furthermore, from the practical point of view of identifying and analyzing compounds in English text—something desirable in various computational applications— whether or not any given example is a compound on the basis of stress cannot be decided a priori but must be decided on the basis of the analysis of the particular example. (See chapter 4, where I discuss the problem of analyzing compound nominals in unrestricted text for the purpose of calculating their stress pattern for text-to-speech applications.) I shall therefore be somewhat loose in my discussion of compounds in English, including in the discussion cases that are not compounds by the criterion of stress; a more appropriate term might be *complex nominal*, which Levi (1978) used to refer to a subset of premodified nominals including sequences of nouns but also including nouns modified by various denominal adjectives, such as *governmental, environmental,* or *industrial.*[11]

I turn now to two aspects of compounds in English that make their analysis difficult: their interpretation and their structure. The complexity of compound semantics is notorious. At first glance it seems to be the case that almost any semantic relationship can hold between the left member of a compound and the right member (the head). Just consider the following examples, where *coffee* is the left member:

(33) a. *coffee bean*
       'a **bean** of the **coffee** plant'

   b. *coffee house*
      'a **house** where **coffee** is served'

   c. *coffee pot*
      'a **pot** for holding **coffee**'

   d. *coffee filter*
      'a **filter** for brewing **coffee**'

   e. *coffee break*
      'a **break** wherein one drinks **coffee**'

All these definitions are of course simplistic, but taken as a crude approximation they serve to illustrate the point that a wide variety of different relationships are available. Note also that the relationship is not necessarily determined by the head either. Consider other examples with *house* as the head:

(34) a. *dog house*
'**house** where a **dog** lives' (not 'a **house** for serving **dogs**')

b. *tree house*
'**house** in a **tree**' (not 'a **house** for serving **trees**')

c. *fire house*
'**house** where **firefighters** stay' (not 'a **house** for serving **fire**')

Downing (1977) suggested that basically any relation (with a few systematic expectations) can hold under appropriate conditions between the two members of a compound. In contrast, Levi (1978) presented a theory in which the number of relationships was restricted and was expressible by a handful of predicates, such as *make, for,* or *cause.* So, *drug deaths* are deaths *caused* by drugs, whereas a *coffee pot* is a pot *for* coffee. In practice it is not clear that the classification is of much use. For one thing, it is fairly obvious that one can divide up semantic space into a finite number of classes. And the problem with doing so is that many things get thrown into the same bin which one might wish to further subdivide. For example, *coffee pot, coffee filter,* and *coffee house* would all be appropriately classified as involving the *for* predicate despite the fact that they have rather different interpretations. One seems forced to conclude, with Downing (1977), that many of the interpretations come down to issues of pragmatics or real-world knowledge.[12]

There is some correlation between stress behavior and the kind of semantic relationship holding between the two elements of the compound (Fudge 1984). For example, if the left member refers to a time or a location for the head, main stress is often placed on the head—that is, the stress is phrasal:

(35) *Monday MORNING, Washington APARTMENT, winter CHILL*

This is by no means without exception, however—consider *MORNING sickness.*

Turning now to the problem of structure, note that compounds can be quite long in English. For example, some people write things like

(36) *computer communications network performance analysis primer*

The difficulty with such compounds is that the preterminal string of categories often gives no information about the structure, in contrast with the case of normal syntactic parsing, where categorial information can often be helpful; in (36) we have six nouns strung together, and this information does not serve to limit the possible parses. In principle, one could build any

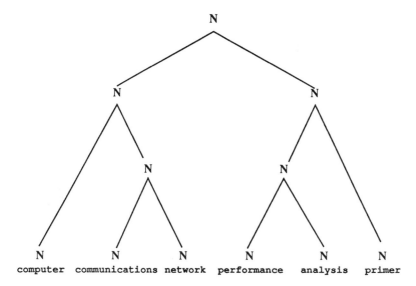

Figure 2.1
A plausible parse tree of the example *computer communications network performance analysis primer.*

parse tree over such examples (and come up with a possible interpretation for the result), yet there is usually one tree that corresponds to the most plausible semantic analysis in any given case; in the case of (36) it would be as in figure 2.1.

Naturally, the appropriate assignment of structure in such cases is intimately tied up with the semantics of the particular case, since it is on the basis of semantics that we must evaluate different structures. So, stress and structure in compounds are both linked to the semantics of these constructions. The difficulty of actually doing a computational analysis of compounds in English is as great as the difficulty of some famous hard problems in syntactic parsing, such as prepositional-phrase attachment.[13]

Compounding in other languages
Not all languages have compounding, but a great many of them do. In at least some other languages, the division between compounding and phrases is somewhat more clear-cut than in English. For example, most Germanic languages have no prohibition on writing multi-stemmed compounds as single orthographic words, as the following example from German shows:

(37) ⟨Lebensversicherungsgesellschaftsangestellter⟩
    Leben +s +versicherung +s +gesellschaft +s +angestellter
    (life + CompAug + insurance + CompAug + company + CompAug +
    employee)
    'life insurance company employee'

Furthermore, morphological markers which are obligatory on phrasal
modifiers are absent when the same modifiers occur within compounds:

(38) a. *rot +* **er** *Wein*
        (red + **NOM/SG/MASC/STRONG** wine)
        'wine which is red in color'

   b. *Rot +wein*
        (red + wine)
        'red wine *qua* category of wine'

In (38a) the adjectival inflectional ending *-er* is obligatorily present, indicating that this is a phrase, whereas in (38b) it is obligatorily absent, indicating that this is a compound.

   Many languages show other overt morphological evidence of compound status for some compounds. Included in such cases are the **augments** found in Germanic languages such as German (see (37) above) and
Dutch. In Dutch, a compound may have no augment at all $(X + Y)$, or
may have the augment *-en-* $(X + en + Y)$, *-e-* $(X + e + Y)$, or *-s-* $(X + s +
Y)$. Which case one gets in a particular compound is largely lexicalized and
learned by native speakers of Dutch, though speakers are often not sure of
which variant to use; Hoeksema (1984, p. 75) notes the case of a butcher
who advertises mutton on different signs in the same shop alternately as
schaap +vlees (sheep meat), *schaap +s +vlees*, and *schap +e +vlees*. Note
that the above-mentioned semantic difficulties for English carry over in
their full glory in other languages that have productive compounding.

Noun incorporation   A rather interesting process related to compounding
found in some languages is *noun incorporation* (Postal 1962; Mithun 1984;
Sadock 1980; Baker 1988). Consider the following example from the Iroquian language Onondaga (see Baker 1988 for a discussion):

(39) a. *Pet waʔ +ha +*HTU *+ʔt +aʔ neʔ o +***hwist** *+aʔ*
        (Pat PAST + 3/MASC,NEUT/SubjAgr + LOST + CAUS + ASP the
        PRE + **money** + SUF)
        'Pat lost the money'

   b. *Pet waʔ +ha +***hwist** *+*AHTU *+ʔt +aʔ*

(Pat PAST + 3/MASC,NEUT/SubjAgr + **money**
+ LOST-CAUS-ASP)
'Pat lost money'

c. *waʔ +ha +*HNI:NU *+ʔ neʔ o +*yvʔkw *+aʔ*
(PAST + 3/MASC,NEUT/SubjAgr + BUY + ASP the
PRE + **tobacco** + SUF)
'he bought the tobacco'

d. *waʔ +ha +*yvʔkw *+*AHNI:NU *+ʔ*
(PAST + 3/MASC,NEUT/SubjAgr + **tobacco** +BUY +ASP)
'he bought tobacco'

In (39a) and (39c) the object noun (given in boldface) is part of its own noun phrase, whereas in (39b) and (39d) it is incorporated into the verb and appears adjacent to the verb stem (given in small capitals). Baker analyzes this phenomenon as involving the movement of a noun into the verb that governs it in the sense of Government and Binding syntax (Chomsky 1981): the structure of (39b) would be roughly as shown in (40).

(40) $[\text{v} \dots \textbf{tobacco}_i + \text{BUY} \dots] \dots e_i$

Other analyses have been suggested; see, for example, Mithun 1984.

Summary The phenomena described in this subsection are but a portion of the kinds of things which morphology can do in a language. From the point of view of someone building a morphological analyzer, it is important to bear in mind the range of information that may be conveyed by morphology, and how that information may be relevant to other components of language, such as the syntax. As we shall see in a subsequent chapter, precious little attention has been paid in the computational literature to really analyzing morphology from the point of view of much of the material discussed in this subsection. Yet, just as arriving at the interpretation of a sentence requires knowledge about the syntactic and semantic functions of the various words in the sentence, so the complete analysis of a word form requires consideration of the functions of the morphology that makes it up.

2.3 WHAT IS COMBINED, AND HOW?

Let us return now to the second of the questions asked above in (3): What are morphemes, and what can they look like? It turns out that it will be rather easier to sensibly consider the answer to the first of these two issues after we have explored the second, and so I will turn first to an overview of the ways in which morphemes are actually 'spelled out'.[14] One thing that should be borne in mind is that in this section we will be discussing the modes of morphological expression that may spell out derivational or inflectional morphology; compounding, as was discussed in the last section, basically involves the concatenation of stems, and therefore does not make use of the range of morphological options that will be outlined here. Let us start with the simplest case.

2.3.1 Purely concatenative morphology: beads on a string

The simplest model of morphology that one can imagine is the situation where a morphologically complex word can be analyzed as a series of morphemes concatenated together. This situation obtains in the case of *puede* in (2); it also obtains in a longer word such as *antidisestablishmentarianism*, which we can analyze as being composed of morphemes strung together like beads on a string, as illustrated in figure 2.2.

Such morphology—the most common kind cross-linguistically—is typically called **concatenative morphology**. As was noted above, agglutinative languages are defined as languages whose (inflectional) morphology is wholly concatenative, and where fairly long words can be formed by the stringing together of morphemes. One such language, is Turkish, in which concatenation is the only morphological device available. Turkish nonetheless gets a great deal of use out of this fairly minimal investment in morphological mechanism, as examples like (6), repeated here as (41), demonstrate.

(41) *çöp + lük + ler + imiz + de + ki + ler + den + mi + y + di*
      (garbage + AFF + PL + 1P/PL + LOC + REL + PL + ABL + INT + AUX + PAST)
      'was it from those that were in our garbage cans?'

Not only is Turkish morphology exclusively concatenative; in addition, all affixes in that language are suffixes too; that is, Turkish complex words (with the exception of compounds) are of the form

(42) *Stem Suffix**.

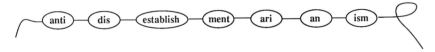

Figure 2.2
An example of purely concatenative morphology: "beads on a string".

Languages can of course have a concatenative morphology which allows prefixes; the English example *antidisestablishmentarianism* has two prefixes, *anti-* and *dis-*. However, there is an asymmetry between prefixation and suffixation cross-linguistically in that suffixing is far more common than prefixing (and other morphological operations). In particular, while many languages exist which only use suffixation, few if any exist which only have prefixes. Also, there are certain kinds of morphological operations which are never marked with prefixes, among them nominal case marking. See Greenberg 1966 for a classic discussion of these asymmetries, and see Cutler et al 1985 for possible psychological bases for the suffixing preference.

Concatenative morphology is a convenient kind of morphology from a computational point of view, since one can often write simple finite-state grammars which can adequately describe such morphology.[15] As we shall see in chapter 3, many computational morphology systems—such as DECOMP and KIMMO (in its original version)—assume a concatenative model of morphology. Although KIMMO is explicitly intended as a general model of morphological processing, it is clear that it was originally designed with Finnish in mind. Hankamer's *keçi* system for Turkish is designed around the fact that Turkish is purely concatenative, and it also takes advantage of the fact that Turkish is purely suffixing: one can often constrain the analysis of a complex word significantly if one knows the stem, and this is much easier to do if the stem is guaranteed to be next to one edge of the word.[16]

2.3.2 Infixation

However, simple linear concatenation is not the only way in which languages can put morphemes together. Apart from attaching to the left or right edge of a word, affixes may also attach as **infixes** inside words. Infixing is not uncommon cross-linguistically, and some language groups, such as the languages spoken in the Philippines, make heavy use of it. Consider the following example from the Philippine language Bontoc (Fromkin and Rodman 1983, p. 115), in which the infix *-um-* turns adjectives and nouns into verbs:

(43) *fikas*   *f-**um**+ikas*
    'strong'   'be strong'
    kilad   *k-**um**+ilad*
    'red'   'be red'

fusul   *f*-**um** + *usul*
'enemy' 'be an enemy'

An infix may not be placed just anywhere in a word; its placement is governed in any particular case by stringent constraints. In Bontoc the infix must be placed after the first consonant of the word to which it attaches. Such cases of infixation are relatively common, and one way to account for them (McCarthy and Prince 1990) is to assume that the infix is really a prefix but that the initial consonant is simply ignored, so that the prefix attaches to the beginning of the word minus the initial consonant. The initial consonant can thus be said to be invisible for the purposes of attachment of the affix.[17] One piece of evidence which suggests that such a view is on the right track is that in many languages, when the stem lacks an initial consonant, the infix actually becomes a prefix.

More generally, the placement of infixes is governed by prosodic principles—that is, principles of phonological constituent structure: words are typically analyzed phonologically as being divided into **syllables**, and syllables are divided into the segments that make them up. Going in the other direction, syllables are combined into prosodic feet. The exact form of a **foot** depends upon the language, and there are theoretical differences depending upon which version of metrical theory one accepts. For our purposes, however, we can define a foot as a sequence of syllables in which either the first or the last syllable bears stress (the choice of first or last usually depending upon the language). From a phonological point of view, then, words have a hierarchical structure as illustrated in figure 2.3. In this figure, following commonly accepted phonological notation, σ represents syllable and F represents foot; the top-level phonological representation of a word is the **phonological word**, represented here as ω.

In the case of (43), the prosodic requirement is expressed as a negative requirement on what prosodic constituent—in this case the consonant beginning the first syllable of the word (its onset)—must be ignored by the infix. In other cases, the infix is marked to attach to a particular kind of prosodic constituent, or between two kinds of prosodic constituents. Consider the following example from Ulwa, a language of the Sumu subfamily of the Misumalpa family spoken in Nicaragua and described in CODIUL 1989.[18] In Ulwa, stress falls on the first syllable in a monosyllabic word or in a polysyllabic word if the first syllable is heavy—i.e., is of the form C(onsonant)V(owel)C or CVV, but not CV. In polysyllabic words where the first syllable is light (CV), stress falls on the second syllable. The following examples, where stress is marked with an accent, serve as illustrations:

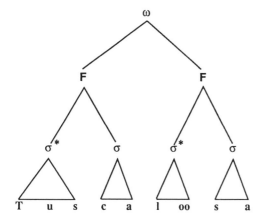

Figure 2.3
Hierarchical prosodic structure. Here σ represents syllable and *F* represents foot.
σ* represents a stressed syllable. Feet are ultimately combined into phonological
words (ω).

(44) Monosyllabic word: *úú* 'house'
      Disyllabic word with heavy first syllable: *súúlu* 'dog'; *yámka* 'good'
      Disyllabic word with light first syllable: *wasála* 'possum'

In metrical terms this stress pattern would be described as follows: build
the largest possible foot dominating at most two syllables at the left edge of
the word subject to the conditions that the rightmost syllable of the foot
bears the stress (the foot is right dominant), and the leftmost syllable may
not dominate a heavy syllable (the foot is quantity sensitive—see Hayes
1980). The metrical structure for the words in (44) is illustrated in figure 2.4.
Now, Ulwa marks possession by attaching one of a series of markers after
the first foot of the noun. If the first foot happens to include the whole
word, then the possessive morpheme is a suffix, but if the word is longer
than the foot, then the possessive morpheme is an infix. Some examples are
given below in (45), and also in figure 2.5.[19] In (45a) are given the forms for
suulu 'dog' (from CODIUL 1989, p. vii); note that the plural forms, with the
exception of the first-person plural inclusive, actually involve two affixes,
one marking the person and the other (-*na*-) marking the number. In (45b)
there are several other examples involving the affixation of -*ka*-. Note that
a number of the examples clearly involve words borrowed from other languages, especially English; the application of a morphological operation to
borrowed vocabulary is generally taken to be an indication that that operation is productive.

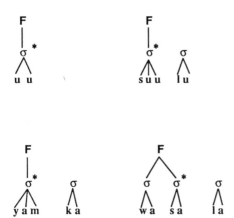

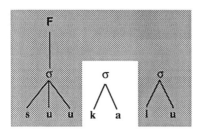

Figure 2.4
Metrical structures for the Ulwa words *uu* 'house', *suulu* 'dog', *yamka* 'good', and *wasala* 'possum'. Asterisk indicates stressed syllable.

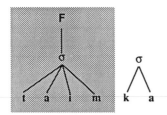

Figure 2.5
The metrical representation of *suukalu* 'his dog' and *taimka* 'his time'. The morpheme (in)to which the affix -*ka*- is attached is in the shaded region.

(45) a. *suu +* **ki**-*lu*
        'my dog'
        suu + **ma**-*lu*
        'your (SG) dog'
        suu + **ka**-*lu*
        'his/her/its dog'
        suu + **ni**-*lu*
        'our (inclusive) dog' (includes both speaker and hearer)
        suu + **ki + na**-*lu*
        'our (exclusive) dog' (excludes hearer)
        suu + **ma + na**-*lu*
        'your (PL) dog'
        suu + **ka + na**-*lu*
        'their dog'

   b. | *baa* | *baa +* **ka** | 'excrement' |
       |-----------|------------------------|------------------|
       | *bilam* | *bilam +* **ka** | 'fish' |
       | *diimuih* | *dii +* **ka**-*muih* | 'snake' |
       | *gaad* | *gaad +* **ka** | 'god' |
       | *iibin* | *ii +* **ka**-*bin* | 'heaven' |
       | *iililih* | *ii +* **ka**-*lilih* | 'shark' |
       | *kahma* | *kah +* **ka**-*ma* | 'iguana' |
       | *kapak* | *kapak +* **ka** | 'manner' |
       | *liima* | *lii +* **ka**-*ma* | 'lemon' |
       | *mistu* | *mis +* **ka**-*tu* | 'cat' |
       | *onyan* | *on +* **ka**-*yan* | 'onion' |
       | *paumak* | *pau +* **ka**-*mak* | 'tomato' |
       | *sikbilh* | *sik +* **ka**-*bilh* | 'horsefly' |
       | *taim* | *taim +* **ka** | 'time' |
       | *taitai* | *tai +* **ka**-*tai* | 'grey squirrel' |
       | *uumak* | *uu +* **ka**-*mak* | 'window' |
       | *waiku* | *wai +* **ka**-*ku* | 'moon, month' |
       | *wasala* | *wasa +* **ka**-*la* | 'possum' |

Thus, Ulwa serves as a nice example of a language in which infixation is clearly sensitive to prosodic structure.[20] While purely concatenative morphology—suffixation and prefixation—is generally straightforward to model computationally, infixation requires more ingenuity. At the very least, a system would have to be able to perform a partial analysis of a word, identify the infix(es), and then resume analysis of the rest of the word. And in order to be able to handle infixing in general, the system would have to model prosodic structure in some sensible way. As we shall see in chapter 3, computational models have been only partly successful at analyzing infixes.

2.3.3 Circumfixation

A somewhat natural antithesis to infixes are **circumfixes**, affixes which attach discontinuously around a stem. Not surprisingly, when one finds such cases, they are usually composed of a suffix and a prefix, each of which may function independently as morphemes. The argument for analyzing the combination as a discontinuous morpheme is that the circumfix has a function that is not derivable from the behavior of the prefix and the suffix of which the circumfix is composed. One example of a circumfix is from Indonesian, in which language the circumfix *kə–an* is composed of the prefix *kə-* (which derives ordinal adjectives from numerals) and the suffix *-an* (which derives nouns from nominal or verbal roots). The circumfixal combination *kə–an* of these two affixes forms abstract nominals from verbs or adjectives; the following examples are from Dolan 1988, p. 78:

(46) *besar*   **kə** +*besar* +**an**
     'big'   'bigness'
     bangun   **kə** +*bangun* +**an**
     'arise'   'awakening'

One can also think of the participle-forming combinations *ge–t* and *ge–en* in German as circumfixes, as illustrated with the following regular verbs:

(47) *säuseln*   **ge** +*säusel* +**t**
     'rustle'   'rustled'
     brüsten   **ge** +*brüst* +**et**
     'brag'   'bragged'
     täuschen   **ge** +*täusch* +**t**
     'deceive'   'deceived'

Although not every verb has the *ge–n* or the *ge–t* combination—verbs derived with a certain class of prefixes regularly do not—the circumfixal combination must be treated as a unit when it is encountered, since the two affixes taken together form the past participle.

2.3.4 Root and pattern (templatic) morphology

Suffixes, prefixes, and infixes all share the property that they consist phonologically of a sequence of segments (or, in the case of circumfixes, two sequences of segments). Now, according to some definitions—e.g., that of Wurzel (1989, p. 28)—the term **morpheme** is limited in its application to entities such as prefixes, suffixes, and roots, which share the property just noted. Therefore, every means of morphological expression which I have discussed thus far in this section is a morpheme, and everything I am about to discuss is not. Certainly this is one possible view, but one of the insights, I believe, of work on generative morphology has been the realization that many morphological mechanisms that seem at first glance to be fundamentally different in kind from the familiar prefixes, suffixes, and infixes are really quite similar to them in one important respect: all of them involve the addition of phonological material. With this in mind, we can redefine the notion **affix**—and more generally **morpheme**—to include any kind of phonological expression of a morphological category μ that involves the addition of phonological material. Many of the means of morphological expression to be discussed below are morphemes under this expanded view. Still, we will see that there are some morphological processes whose characterization as morphemes is potentially problematic. I shall, in any event, discuss the term morpheme further at the end of this section.

Let us start, then, with our first example of nonsegmental morphemes, namely the so-called **root-and-pattern morphology** of Arabic. In Arabic, and in other Semitic languages, verb stems are constructed by combining three elements: a **root**, which usually consists of three consonants; a vowel pattern, which marks information about voice (in Arabic, active or passive) and aspect (in Arabic, perfect or imperfect); and a derivational **template**, which gives the class of the derived verb. The verb classes are called **binyanim** according to traditional Semitic grammar. The following are all forms of the same root, *ktb* 'write' (this is much simplified from McCarthy's [1979, p. 134] table for the perfect aspect):

(48) Binyan	ACT (A)	PASS (UI)	Template	Gloss
I	*k*At*A*b	*k*ut*i*b	**CVCVC**	'write'
II	*k*Att*A*b	*k*utt*i*b	**CVCCVC**	'cause to write'
III	*k*AAt*A*b	*k*uut*i*b	**CVVCVC**	'correspond'
VI	t*A*kAAt*A*b	t*u*kuut*i*b	**tVCVVCVC**	'write to each other'
VII	n*k*AAt*A*b	n*k*uut*i*b	**nCVVCVC**	'subscribe'
VIII	*k*tAt*A*b	*k*tut*i*b	**CtVCVC**	'write'
X	st*A*kt*A*b	st*u*kt*i*b	**stVCCVC**	'dictate'

The consonants provided by the root are given in italics here.

Most current descriptions of this kind of morphology are based on work by McCarthy (1979), who developed an analysis within the framework

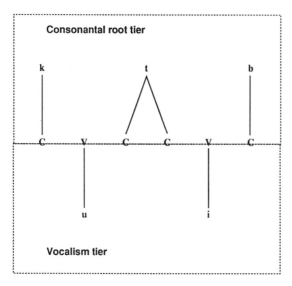

Figure 2.6
The representation of the passive perfect binyan II form for Arabic *kuttib*, from the root *ktb* 'write'. The consonantal root *ktb* and the vocalic morpheme *ui*, which marks voice and aspect, are linked to the consonantal template *CVCCVC*.

of **autosegmental phonology**. The basic idea is that the template can be thought of as contributing the general shape to the word, in terms of an abstract **skeleton** of C and V slots. The root contributes some of the consonantal material, and the vowel material is contributed by the morpheme expressing the voice and aspect. Thus the root and the voice/aspect morpheme contribute the flesh of the word which hangs off the skeleton of the binyan template. In terminology originally borrowed from the autosegmental analysis of tone, the nonskeletal materials are often referred to as *melodies*. Each of the melodies is typically assigned its own plane (or **tier**) in the autosegmental representation, encoding the fact that the consonantal root melody and the vocalic melody behave independently of each other. This will give a structure like that shown in figure 2.6. The consonants of the root are associated with the C slots in the skeleton and the vowels of the root are associated with the V slots. What is important to remember here is that this verb stem has three morphemes in it: the root *ktb* 'write', the passive perfect morpheme *ui*, and the binyan II template morpheme *CVCCVC*. The only thing that is different about Arabic is that the morphemes are put together in a rather different way from the way that morphemes are put together in Turkish or English.

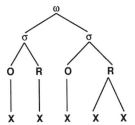

Figure 2.7
A prosodic representation of the Arabic binyan I morpheme *CVCVC*. Following the theory of Levin (1985), the C and V slots are replaced by unlabeled slots X, and syllable structure constraints determine to which positions the consonants and vowels of the root and voice-aspect markers may adjoin.

Levin (1985) and others have reanalyzed these skeletal templates as being prosodic units. For example, the binyan I morpheme *CVCVC* can be reanalyzed as consisting of a pair of syllables (figure 2.7). This alternative view has the theoretical benefit of bringing Arabic verbal morphology under the rubric of the more clearly prosodically defined morphology which we will subsequently examine.

A more recent and more sophisticated approach to Arabic morphology in the same vein is presented by McCarthy and Prince (1990) in their analysis of the Arabic broken plural. In addition to using templatic morphemes in forming different derivational classes of verbs, Arabic forms the plurals of many nouns by similar but more complicated means. A couple of examples of one of the classes—the quadriliteral class—is given in (49).

(49) SG   PL   Gloss
   jundub   *janaadib*   'locust'
   sulṭaan   *salaaṭiin*   'sultan'

McCarthy and Prince argue for a couple of important notions. First of all they propose the notion of a prosodic **minimal word**, which corresponds to a single metrical foot; note that phonological words consist of at least one foot, as figure 2.3 suggests, and that therefore the minimal word must consist of one foot. The minimal word is shown to play a role in defining the way in which affixes attach in many languages. Specifically, it is argued that in many languages the input word is first parsed into a minimal word and its residue. Morphological operations apply to the minimal word, and the output of the operations as applied to the minimal word is then reassembled with the residue. In the notation of McCarthy and Prince (1990), we represent the parsing stage as taking an input *B* and factoring it into the minimal word $B:\Phi$ and its residue B/Φ:

(50) $B = B:\Phi * B/\Phi$.

Here $*$ represents the operation (usually concatenation) whereby the minimal word and the residue combine to form the original. A morphological function F then applies to the minimal word, and the result is combined with the residue:

(51) $F(B) = F(B:\Phi) * B/\Phi$.

Secondly, McCarthy and Prince argue, following Levin (1985), that the CV templates of McCarthy 1979 are properly interpreted as being prosodic constituents.

   McCarthy and Prince analyze forms like those in (49) using these assumptions. The factorization of the input *jundub* is as follows:

(52) *jundub = jun ⌒ dub*.

In (52), *jun* is the minimal word (Arabic closed syllables are metrically heavy and therefore count as feet on their own), *dub* is the residue, and the specific operation used to combine them is concatenation (⌒), with the minimal word on the left and the residue on the right. The morphological function that applies next involves affixing the metrically defined template shown in figure 2.8. The actual affixation to *jun* is shown in figure 2.9, where the linking of the templatic melody /a/ is also shown. The only change in the residue *dub* is to associate the melody vowel /i/, displacing the vowel /u/. The transformed minimal word and residue are then recombined using the same operation as in (52) above, to yield the form *janaa ⌒ dib*. The form *sulṭaan* works the same way, the main difference being that the residue in this case, *ṭaan*, has a long vowel and the plural

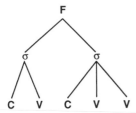

Figure 2.8
The plural template for the quadriliteral class, adapted from McCarthy and Prince 1990. (Note that McCarthy and Prince use a different formalism than the C and V slots used here, for representing the locations to which the melodic segments associate; there is no difference crucial to the present discussion, however.)

therefore inherits the vowel length with /i/ associating to both vowel slots. This inheritance of vowel length is straightforward in the framework of McCarthy and Prince 1990 but was hard to capture in the original framework of McCarthy 1979.

So, as McCarthy and Prince argue, template morphemes and the morphological operations with which they often are associated require a fair degree of reference to prosodic structure. Computational systems for morphological analysis have—with some exceptions—typically been somewhat backward in that they have taken morphological operations to be basically statable on strings of phonemes (or letters). It is of course possible to state prosodic conditions in purely linear (i.e., segmental) terms. However, it is precisely because the purely linear representation of Chomsky and Halle (1968) was cumbersome and theoretically inelegant in handling cases which clearly required some reference to phonological structure that Generative Phonology reintroduced prosodic concepts like syllable and foot quite a number of years ago.

How much of the morphology described in this subsection could one simply ignore in a computational system? It is certainly true that Arabic

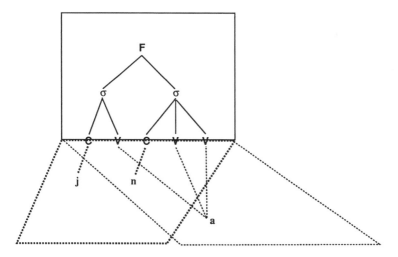

Figure 2.9
The attachment of the plural template for the quadriliteral class to the minimal word *jun*, following McCarthy and Prince 1990. The templatic melody /a/ overrides the /u/ from the stem of *jundub*, which is not represented here. Note that in this autosegmental representation the three components that make up the piece *janaa* are represented as each occupying its own autosegmental plane—these planes intersecting at the skeleton.

dictionaries have to list the binyanim with which a particular verb root occurs, since, if nothing else, the meaning of the resulting derived verb stem is not entirely predictable. In a computational model, then, one might simply enter the various verbal stems in the lexicon, thereby circumventing the necessity for mechanisms to analyze Arabic verbal morphology. However, while this approach might have some appeal in the case of verbs, it is less appealing in the case of broken plurals. While the broken plurals are by no means fully productive, they are nonetheless very widespread. Significantly, certain classes have been applied to loan words, which is usually taken as a good sign that a morphological process is productive, as I suggested in the discussion of Ulwa infixation above. The following examples are from McCarthy and Prince 1990:

(53) Singular   Plural   Gloss (and source)
     baṣṣ   *buṣuuṣ*   'bus'
     bulṭ   *buluuṭ*   'bolt'
     bansil   *banaasil*   'pencil'
     muuṭur   *mawaaṭir*   'motor (vehicle)'

In this respect, Arabic broken plurals are crucially different from English irregular plurals such as *men* and *oxen*, which are a distinct minority in the language and which spread to loans or novel words only under perverse conditions (e.g., *vaxen*). So, although Arabic broken plurals involve rather complicated morphological devices, they are nonetheless much-used constructions. Furthermore, they spell out a rather straightforward and commonplace morphological operation: pluralization. Thus, there is generally no correlation between the complexity of a morphological device and the complexity of what that device is used for, or how much the device is used.

The bias toward concatenative morphology in the design of models of computational morphology is understandable: concatenative morphology is at once easier to process and more common—two characteristics which are surely related. But humans *are* capable of gaining competence in other modes of morphological expression. A general computational model of morphology should therefore be able to handle morphology of the kind discussed in this subsection.

2.3.5   Reduplication

The binyan and broken plural morphemes in Arabic lack their own segmental content. One other kind of morphology that involves such morphemes is **reduplication**. Reduplication comes in two flavors. One, total reduplication, is used, for example, to mark plurals in Indonesian:

(54) *orang*   **orang** +*orang*
    'man'   'men'

In this case, whatever phonological content is in the base word is copied. However, there are cases of total reduplication where things are not so simple. For example, habitual-repetitive reduplication in Javanese (Kiparsky 1987, pp. 115–117) exhibits examples like the following:

(55) Base   Habitual-Repetitive   Gloss
    adʊs   *odas* +*adʊs*   'take a bath'
    bali   *bola* +*bali*   'return'
    bosən   *bosan* +*bosən*   'tired of'
    ɛlɛq   *elaq* +*ɛlɛq*   'bad'
    ibu   *iba* +*ibu*   'mother'
    dolan   *dolan* +*dolɛn*   'engage in recreation'
    udan   *udan* +*udɛn*   'rain'
    djaran   *djoran-djaran*   'horse'
    djaran   *djoran-djɛrɛn*   'horse'
    djaran   *djaran-djɛrɛn*   'horse'

As Kiparsky describes it, if the second vowel of the stem is not /a/—as in the first five examples above—the algorithm is as follows: copy the stem, make the first vowel of the left copy nonlow, with the result that /a/ is changed to /o/ and /ɛ/ is changed to /e/, and change the second vowel to /a/. If the second vowel of the stem is /a/, then the left copy remains unchanged but the /a/ in the right copy changes to /ɛ/. If both vowels are /a/, as in *djaran* 'horse', there are three different possibilities, as shown in (55).

Even more theoretically interesting are cases of partial reduplication, where only part of the stem is copied. Take the case of the Australian language Yidinʸ, described by Nash (1980) and subsequently discussed by McCarthy and Prince (1990). Some examples of Yidinʸ reduplication (from McCarthy Prince 1990) are given in (56):

(56) Singular   Plural   Gloss
    mulari   **mula** +*mulari*   'initiated man'
    gindalba **gindal** +*gindalba* 'lizard'

McCarthy and Prince, following the analysis of Nash (1980), suggest that Yidinʸ reduplication involves copying the minimal word, namely a bisyllabic foot (in this case, the first two syllables). In the case of *mulari* the foot in question is *mula*; in the case of *gindalba* it is *gindal*. So, in a way, the *Yidin*[y] case is much like the Indonesian case, except that a prosodically defined subunit of the word is copied rather than the whole word. The copied material is then prefixed to the stem.

Somewhat more complicated, though more normal for partial reduplication, is the kind of reduplication exemplified in Warlpiri, another Australian language also described by Nash (1980). Some examples of reduplication in Warlpiri are given in (57).

(57) | Base Form | Reduplicated Form | Gloss |
| --- | --- | --- |
| *paṇuṇu* | **paṇu** + *paṇuṇu* | *'dig/PAST'* |
| *tiiḻpaṇkaja* | **tii** + *tiiḻpaṇkaja* | 'split-run/PAST' |
| *wantimi* | **wanti** + *wantimi* | 'fall/NonPast' |

(As Nash describes it, Warlpiri reduplication encodes a variety of semantic properties, including plurality of subject or object.) An examination of (57) shows that the copied material is of the form $CV(C)(C)V$—that is, the initial consonant of the stem and the next two vowels, with possibly one or two intervening consonants. The resulting reduplicative prefix is itself a prosodic foot, but it is important to understand that one cannot analyze this case in the same way as the *Yidin*[y] by simply copying the initial foot of the word: the initial foot of *tiiḻpaṇkaja* is *tiiḻ*, and copying that portion would yield the ill-formed **tiiḻ + tiiḻpaṇkaja*. A now popular analysis for this common kind of phenomenon due to Marantz (1982) has been extended by numerous researchers, including Broselow and McCarthy (1984) and Levin (1985). Basically, such partial reduplication involves the prefixation of a (prosodic) template, much like the prosodic templates of Arabic verbal morphology. In Warlpiri, the prefixed template has the form $CVCCV$. The stem to which the prefix attaches is copied to the left and is associated to the templatic prefix. For Warlpiri, we can assume that the association is "driven" by the segmental melody in that one associates in sequence each of the segments of the copied melody until there are no more available template slots.[21] Thus, for a form like *tiiḻpaṇkaja*, the stem is first copied. Then, the initial /t/ of the stem is associated to the first C of the template, and the /i/ in the second position is associated to the V in the second position of the template. The third segment, /i/, cannot be associated to either the third or the fourth slot in the template, since these are both C; it can, however, be associated to the final slot. Even though the C slots in third and fourth position remain unassociated, no further associations are possible, because it is assumed that autosegmental association lines cannot cross (Goldsmith 1976; Sagey 1988; Coleman and Local 1990):

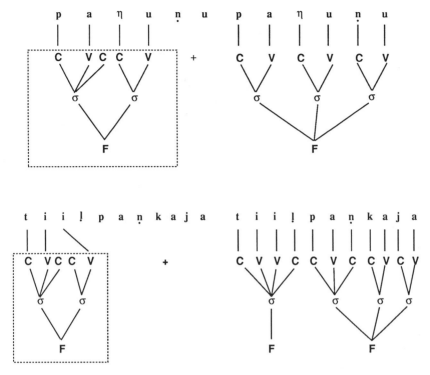

Figure 2.10
Warlpiri reduplication from Nash 1980 following the theory of reduplication
represented in Marantz 1982. Two processes are involved, the first being the
prefixation of the reduplicative prefix (boxed) and the second being the copying of
the segmental material of the word. Only those segments of the copied material
that will fit on the template actually surface.

in order for any subsequent segment to associate with an empty slot in the
prefix, one would have to allow the association line from that segment to
the slot to cross the association line between the /i/ in third position in the
melody and the final V of the prefix. Analyses of two of the examples in (57)
are sketched in figure 2.10. It should be borne in mind that, after reduplication, phonological rules may render the copies nonidentical in the surface
form, though in the above examples of partial reduplication this has not
happened.[22]

Now, following the assumption that Warlpiri-type reduplication involves prefixation of a prosodic template, one would therefore expect to
find suffixing and infixing reduplications. Indeed, one does find such redu-

plications, although prefixing reduplication seems to be the more common —strangely perhaps, since in nonreduplicative affixation suffixation is by far the more common. Infixing reduplication is rare, but it is of theoretical importance since its behavior in the languages in which it does occur provides interesting confirmation of the theory of reduplication proposed originally by Marantz (1982). Given that infixation is, as we saw above, affixation to a (prosodically definable) subunit of a word, and given that in reduplication one copies material from the piece to which one attaches the affix, one would expect that in infixing reduplication one would find that material is copied only from the subunit to which the infix attaches. This seems to be correct. So, in the Australian language Mangaray (Davis 1988; see also Marantz and McIntyre 1986),[23] a template with the shape VCC is infixed after the first consonant of the word; this morpheme marks plurality in Mangarayi. So, for example, *gambura* 'mother's brother' becomes *g-VCC +ambura*. Since this kind of infix is really a prefix on the stem minus the first consonant, we expect copying of material from the subunit to the right, and that is what we find: *g-amb +ambura* 'mother's brothers'.

The insight of this approach to reduplication is that it has made it possible to view partial reduplication as only a *slightly* odd kind of affix. Partial reduplication is an instance of the creative use of pieceparts required for other kinds of morphology: templatic morphology is independently attested in Arabic and other languages where no copying is involved; copying is independently necessary to account for total and "full-minimal-word" reduplication of the kind found in Indonesian. Infixing reduplication adds the independently attested mechanisms needed for ordinary infixation. While previous treatments of reduplication had made use of fairly unconstrained mechanisms in describing reduplication (for example, Aronoff [1976, pp. 64–69] used a transformational grammar rule formalism), the approach suggested by Marantz simplified significantly the description of reduplication by factoring it into simpler and otherwise attested mechanisms.

From a computational point of view, one point cannot be overstressed: the copying required in reduplication places reduplication in a class apart from all other morphology. Most morphological (and phonological) operations can, at least to a first approximation, be described with finite-state machinery (though see below). Reduplication, on the other hand, seems to require mechanisms with memory of the previously seen string, since copying is involved. Indeed, a well-known piece of work on the complexity of natural language, reported by Culy (1985), involves a type of total reduplication found in Bambara, a Northwestern Mande language spoken in Mali. In Bambara, a noun N may be reduplicated as N-o-N, with the meaning 'whatever N' or 'whichever N'. As can be seen from the examples given in (58), the reduplicated nouns may be morphologically very complex.

(58) a. *wulu o wulu*
    (dog o dog)
    'whichever dog'

   b. *wulu + nyini + na o wulu + nyini + na*
    (dog + search + er o dog + search + er)
    'whichever dog searcher'

   c. *malo + nyini + na + filè + la o malo + nyini + na + filè + la*
    (rice + search + er + watch + er o rice + search + er + watch + er)
    'whichever rice searcher watcher' (i.e. 'whoever watches rice searchers')

On the basis of such examples, Culy shows that the set of words produced by reduplication in Bambara is not context-free, and a fortiori that it is not finite state.

2.3.6 'Subsegmental' morphology

So morphemes can consist of some string of segments or they can specify some (prosodic) shape. Morphemes can also consist of less than a segment. An example of this is one kind of plural formation in Irish:

(59) *cat* (/kat/)   *cait* (/kat^j/)
   'cat'   'cats'

In these cases the final consonant of the singular is palatalized to form the plural. One way to represent that is to assume that the plural marker consists of a single feature, [+ high], which becomes associated with what-ever the final consonant of the stem is, as shown in figure 2.11.

Many recent analyses posit the existence of such subsegmental morphemes. Lieber 1987 is an interesting source of such cases. Still, while some cases which seem to involve manipulation of phonological features of the stem can be analyzed in this way, it is not clear that they all can. One particularly tricky case involves ablaut in Germanic languages such as Icelandic. In Icelandic, so-called strong verbs form past tense and past participle stems by changing the stem vowel. There are a number of different classes of verbs, and some of these are exemplified in (60).

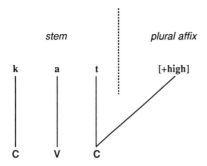

Figure 2.11
Autosegmental representation of the plural of *cat* 'cat' in Irish. The feature
specification [+high], which marks plurality in a subset of Irish nouns, links
autosegmentally to the last consonant slot of the word, rendering the final
consonant palatalized.

(60) a.

Stem	Gloss	PAST/SG Stem	PAST/PL Stem	Past Participle Stem
⟨i⟩		⟨ei⟩	⟨i⟩	⟨i⟩
/iː/		/ei/	/ɪ/	/ɪ/
bít-	'bite'	*beit-*	*bit-*	*bit-*
ríf-	'tear'	*reif-*	*rif-*	*rif-*

b.

Stem	Gloss	PAST/SG Stem	PAST/PL Stem	Past Participle Stem
⟨jó, jú⟩		⟨au⟩	⟨u⟩	⟨o⟩
/joː, juː/		/öi/	/y/	/ɔ/
bjóð-	'offer'	*bauð-*	*buð-*	*boð-*
strjúk-	'stroke'	*strauk-*	*struk-*	*strok-*

c.

Stem	Gloss	PAST/SG Stem	PAST/PL Stem	Past Participle Stem
⟨i, e⟩		⟨a⟩	⟨u⟩	⟨u, o⟩
/ɪ, ɛ/		/a/	/y/	/y, ɔ/
brest-	'burst'	*brast-*	*brust-*	*brost-*
finn-	'find'	*fann-*	*fund-*	*fund-*

Icelandic ablaut is, of course, related to the vowel changes exemplified in
English past tense forms such as *sang* or *ate*; however, ablaut in Icelandic is
more regular and applies to many more verbs than its English counterpart.
While it is relatively straightforward to analyze the vowel changes in Icelandic in terms of feature-changing phonological rules, it is less clear how

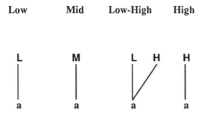

Figure 2.12
The four tonal classes of the Ngbaka verb *a*.

one would provide a simple autosegmental analysis of the kind (appropriate for Irish) given in (59).

One other kind of "subsegmental" morphology that is amenable to an autosegmental analysis is morphology expressed by suprasegmental entities, such as tone. An example of a tonological alternation from Ngbaka, a language of Zaire, is given in (61) (data from Nida 1949). All the examples are verb forms, for which Nida claims four different tonal variants (low, mid, low-high, high) expressing different tense-aspect contrasts (note that low-high gives a contour tone on monosyllables):

(61) Low   Mid   Low-High   High   Gloss
     à   ā   ǎ   á   'put more than one thing'
     kpòlò   kpōlō   kpòló   kpóló   'return'
     b'ìlì   b'īlī   b'ìlí   b'ílí   'cut'

Without knowing more about Ngbaka, one must guess at the most appropriate analysis in this case. However, in accordance with work on the autosegmental phonology of tone initiated by Leben (1973), we can imagine that each of the first four columns in represents a tonal morpheme, namely *L* (for low tone), *M* (for mid), *LH* (for low-high), and *H*. These autosegmental tonal melodies would then be associated with the segmental material of the root as represented for the verb *a* 'put more than one thing' in figure 2.12. So, even with suprasegmentally expressed morphology it seems as if we can preserve the generalization that morphemes add phonological material. We now turn to a couple of types of morphology that seem problematic for that point of view.

2.3.7   Zero morphology

In addition to the various ways in which morphology can add phonological material to a stem, a morphological operation may also have no phonological expression whatsoever. One finds examples of zero morphology in many languages—notably English, in which zero noun-to-verb conversion is quite productive:

(62) a. *I want to* **book** *a flight to Houston*

b. *let's* **table** *the motion*

c. *I need to* **xerox** *this article*

Such examples can be analyzed as involving the addition of a morpheme that has no phonological content—a **zero morpheme**. Thus, *book* in (62a) would be represented as

(63) $book_N + \emptyset_V$

where the zero morpheme $\emptyset$ is marked to attach to verbs and make nouns.

Not all scholars agree on the existence of zero morphology qua morphology. The relationship between *book* as a noun and *book* as a verb could be represented as a purely lexical relation where the two words have two separate dictionary entries but where neither is morphologically derived from the other. From the point of view of computational applications it is probably acceptable to view zero morphology as a lexical relationship. That is, one might have a (lexical) rule which would add V to the list of possible categorial entries for nouns, thus allowing for the possibility that a word which is known to be a noun could be allowed to function as a verb under appropriate circumstances.

2.3.8 Subtractive morphology

Thus, morphological operations can add material in various ways, or they can add nothing. Not surprisingly, perhaps, there are also a limited number of examples of **subtractive morphology**, where material is taken away to mark a morphological operation. One such example is from the Muskogean language Koasati (Martin 1988). In this language the plural form of the verb is (in part) derived from the singular form by deleting the last **rime** of the stem. In (64) the material deleted is indicated in boldface in the singular form:

(64)

SG	PL	Gloss
*pit**af** + fi + n*	*pit + li + n*	to slice up the middle
*las**ap** + li + n*	*las + li + n*	to lick something
*acokcan**a:** + ka + n*	*acokcan + ka + n*	to quarrel with someone
*obakhit**ip** + li + in*	*obakhit + li + n*	to go backwards

Subtractive morphology appears to be genuinely problematic for the view that all morphology consists of the addition of morphemes as suggested in subsection 2.3.4. Although there exist formal phonological mechanisms where, by adding phonological material, one can actually end up removing phonological material, such an approach would, on the face of it, seem to render vacuous any claim that morphological processes must consist of the addition of phonological material. So, it seems as if some morphological processes do not involve morphemes if morphemes, and in particular affixes, are defined as above. Unfortunately, I can do no more than note this as a problem for morphological theory, leaving it unresolved at this point.

2.3.9   What is a morpheme? A more formal definition

In this section I have covered a range of different ways in which morphology is spelled out. The list is not exhaustive, but it should be obvious from even this much that any system which purports to be a general model of a morphological processor will have to contend with a variety of different forms of morphological expression. In particular, one should keep in mind the range of possible means of morphological expression when reading the discussion of computational models in chapter 3; as has been noted above, many such models are designed around concatenative morphology.

But let us return briefly to the question of what a morpheme is. We have looked at a number of kinds of morphological expression which involve the addition of phonological material, although we have seen that the sense in which the phonological material is added is more complicated than simple concatenation. Now, each of the affixes in question that we have discussed "spells out" some morphological category or set of morphological categories. For example, the binyan I morpheme in Arabic spells out the derivational category that takes verbal roots and gives a stem of the verbal class binyan I. Similarly, infixing reduplication in Mangarayi spells out plurality on nouns. We can therefore think of a morpheme more properly as constituting an ordered pair in which the first member of the pair represents the morphological categories which are expressed by the morpheme—i.e., its syntactic and semantic features—and the second member represent its phonological form, along with information on how the form attaches to its stem. Some representative examples are given in (65), where each of the entries in b–d follows the schema in entry a.

(65) a. $\langle \textit{Syntactic}/\textit{semantic features}, \textit{phonological features} \rangle$

    b. $\langle \langle STATE, A \backslash N \rangle, \textit{-ity} \rangle$

c. $\langle\langle BINYAN\text{-}I, ROOT\backslash V\rangle, CVCVC\rangle$

d. $\langle\langle PL, N\backslash N\rangle, \text{-}VCC\text{-}(ignore\ first\ C\ of\ stem)\rangle$

So, the English affix -*ity* in (65b) is represented as having a stative meaning, changes an adjective into a noun,[24] and is phonologically a suffix (see subsection 2.4 for further clarification of this latter point). The binyan I morpheme in Arabic (65c) takes roots and makes a verbal stem of the derivational class binyan I, and it has the templatic form $CVCVC$ phonologically. Finally, the Mangarayi infix -*VCC*- given in (65d) is listed as marking plurals on nouns and infixing after the first consonant of the stem. These representations are not intended to be complete, but one can get the general idea from them. Note that zero morphology could be represented in this scheme by leaving the phonology slot blank. The only morphological operations discussed above that are not obviously representable in this way as morphemes are the cases of subtractive morphology and ablaut.

Still, general though this notion of morpheme is, it does exclude some classes of linguistic entities that have been considered to be morphemes by many authors. Aronoff (1976, pp. 11–14) (see also Wurzel 1989, p. 29) argues that the substring -*mit* in latinate English words such as *permit*, *submit*, *transmit*, and *commit* must be considered a morpheme. The basic argument for this is that the substring has certain predictable properties which cannot be predicted from the phonological form of the string. It is a correct generalization that all verbs which have the relevant substring -*mit* have a related nominal which ends in -*mission*: *permission, submission, transmission, commission*. Since this is not predictable on the basis of the phonological form of -*mit*, it must be the case that -*mit* is lexically marked for this allomorphy. Hence, -*mit* has a life of its own and should be considered to be a morpheme. However, it is rather hard to find a morphological category that -*mit* marks; in particular, there is no predictable semantic content to this morpheme in modern English, though of course it had a definite meaning in Latin. So, the definition that I gave above, which depended upon the notion that a morpheme is a pairing of syntactic or semantic function and phonological form, does not quite capture examples like -*mit*.[25]

2.4 MORPHEMES, THE STRUCTURE OF WORDS, AND WORD-FORMATION RULES

The view that has emerged from the preceding discussion is that a morpheme is a pairing of two linguistic "pieces," one specifying the real morphological content—the syntactic or semantic information—and the other the phonological mode of expression of that content. In the discussion in the previous section, only a few modes of phonological expression— subtractive morphology in particular—might clearly be seen as problematic for such a view.

A natural interpretation of this view of morphemes is that all morphemes, whether roots or affixes, have the same status. The main difference between roots and affixes is that affixes must attach to some stem and usually specify requirements on the properties that must be present on the stem; these properties can be phonological, syntactic, semantic, or any combination of these. We will return later to some examples of the restrictions which affixes specify. Roots (and stems), in contrast, do not specify attachment requirements insofar as they are the things *to which* affixes attach. Thus, while roots (at least in many languages) *may* be free morphemes in that they may be used as words without any further morphological attachment, affixes by definition *must be* attached to something and are therefore always bound morphemes.

Furthermore, it is most often the case that an affix is specified to attach as a sister to exactly one morpheme, with the result that word structure can usually be specified as a binary branching tree; trees are often used to represent the structure of words just as trees are used to represent the structure of sentences. In fact it is often useful to specify two structures for a word, one representing the real morphological structure, encoding the syntactic and semantic information on how the word is built up, and the other specifying the phonological structure of the word; this view of morphology was developed in Sproat 1985 and Sproat 1988 and has been further developed in Inkelas 1989. To take a simple case, the word *unhappiness* would have a phonological and a morphological structure as represented in figure 2.13. One can view linear ordering as being a phonological notion, and so whether an affix is a prefix or a suffix is specified along with the phonological information for that affix. On the other hand, the morphological representation does not have any inherent linear ordering and can be represented as a mobile-like structure.[26] Of course, one still needs to say something about how the order of morphemes is determined. We will return to that topic in the next section.

The two structures are of course related. Roughly speaking (see Sproat 1985, Sproat 1988, and Marantz 1988 for more details), one can represent the relationship as in (66).

(66) If A and B are sisters in morphological structure, and if B is an affix, then the phonological representation of B, denoted as $\Phi(B)$, attaches

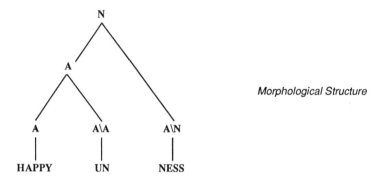

Morphological Structure

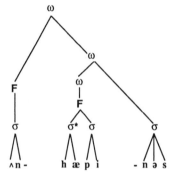

Phonological Structure

Figure 2.13
The phonological and morphological structures of *unhappiness*. Note that one can
view linear ordering as a phonological notion and hence the morphological
structure itself can be represented as a mobile-like structure without any inherent
linear ordering. The morphological level of representation encodes information
such as the category or categorial requirements of the morphemes; for example,
happy is an adjective, and *-ness* attaches to adjectives to make nouns. The
phonological level of representation encodes information on the linear ordering of
morphemes—e.g., whether they are prefixes or suffixes—as well as information on
other phonological properties of the morphemes, such as the phoneme segments
which make them up and their metrical properties. (Note that the prefix *un-* may
bear secondary stress and thus presumably is dominated by its own foot.)

to the phonological representation of A, denoted as $\Phi(A)$. This phonological attachment is denoted by the operator $*$: $\Phi(A) * \Phi(B)$. $*$ is commutative, so that $\Phi(A) * \Phi(B) = \Phi(B) * \Phi(A)$.[27]

This mapping principle will be refined somewhat below. For now, note that this idea helps to clarify the relationship between more commonplace prefixal or suffixal morphologies and more "exotic" morphologies of the type found in Arabic. If one compares the Arabic binyan I form $kVtVb$ 'write' (ignoring the vocalism) with a derived verb in English such as *with + stand*, the main difference between the two cases can be seen to come down to the mode of phonological expression of the morphology, as was noted in subsection 2.3.4. In both cases one is attaching an affix to a verbal root to produce a verb stem. In English this happens to be mediated by prefixation, whereas in Arabic this is mediated by a more complicated autosegmental association between the morpheme ktb 'write' and the binyan I morpheme $CVCVC$. But this is purely a difference in phonological representation; it does not represent a deep difference in morphological structure. Thus, one does not have to conclude, with Selkirk (1982, pp. 2–3), that Arabic differs from English in that (part of) the morphology of the former language cannot be represented as a tree; tree structures are as appropriate for the real morphological structure of Arabic as they are for that of English, the only difference being in the mode of phonological expression.

Now, although in the general case the two structures of a word are isomorphic, a further justification for having two structures is that isomorphism between the phonological and morphological structures does not, in fact, always hold. More generally, it is a fairly traditional observation in morphology that there are really two kinds of words from a structural point of view, namely **phonological words** and **syntactic words**. These two notions specify overlapping but nonidentical sets of entities, in that something which is a phonological word may not count as a single word from the point of view of the syntax (Matthews 1974, p. 32). I turn to these issues in the following subsections. It will turn out that the term *structure of a word* is perhaps misleading.

2.4.1 Bracketing paradoxes: Mismatches between "word-syntactic" and "word-phonological" structure

Let us take as our example of **bracketing paradoxes** the following classic example discussed in Pesetsky 1985. The English adjectival comparative affix *-er* is limited in its distribution: roughly speaking, it can only attach to adjectives which are one or two syllables long (provided they form a single trochaic foot), and it certainly cannot attach to adjectives which are three syllables long:

(67) a. stem with one or two syllables: *sadd* +**er**, *nic* +**er**, *smelli* +**er**, *happi* +**er**

b. stem with three or more syllables: ******curious* +**er**, ******specious* +**er**, ******elegant* +**er**

The possibility of a form like *unrulier* is perhaps not surprising, since one can analyze this form as having a structure where the prefix *un-* is attached to *rulier*:

(68) *[un [ruli er]]*

In fact, given the restriction on *-er* noted above, this is the only possible structure for the adjective. Yet, as Pesetsky notes, this bracketing cannot be right, since it has *-er* attaching to the adjective ******ruly*, but there is no such positive form, only the negative form *unruly*. This suggests that the scope of the comparative *-er* must be outside the scope of the negative prefix *un-*, and that, contrary to what we concluded above, the structure must be as in (69).

(69) *[[un ruli] er]*

So we appear to have arrived at a paradox, in that two different bracketings seem to be required for the same word. Many solutions have been proposed for this and for similar examples (Pesetsky 1979, 1985; Williams 1981; Marantz 1982; Strauss 1982; Sproat 1985; Cohn 1989). I will present the version from Sproat 1985 and Sproat 1988 here, which owes much to the work of Pesetsky. The basic idea is that, whereas we must assume that the true morphological structure of *unrulier* is as in (69), the restriction on the affixation of *-er* noted above is purely a *phonological* restriction; after all, it is based upon the number of syllables in the adjective to which the affix attaches. The suggestion in Sproat 1985 and Sproat 1988 was that *unrulier* has two parallel but nonisomorphic structures: the morphological structure proper and the phonological structure. This is represented in figure 2.14. The implementation of this idea requires only a slight modification of the mapping principle presented in (66) above. The proposal is that the general attachment operator ✳ is translated into the concatenation operator ⌢ whenever one of the attached items is specified as either a prefix or a suffix—i.e., is specified as being linearly ordered with respect to

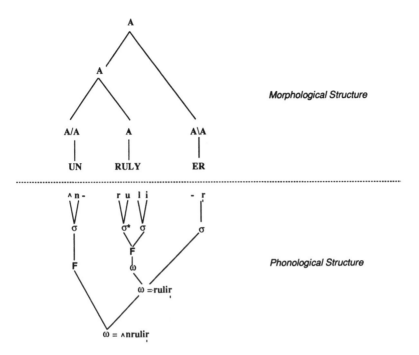

Figure 2.14
The two parallel structures for *unrulier*.

the item to which it is attached. The concatenation operator is not commutative, but it is assumed to be associative. So, the morphological structure for *unrulier* translates phonologically as in (70a); since *un-* is specified as a prefix and *-er* as a suffix, this translates into (70b), but since ⌒ is associative this is equivalent to (70c), which is the structure required by the phonological constraint discussed above.

(70) a. *[[un * ruli] * er]*

   b. *[[un ⌒ruli] ⌒er]*

   c. *[un ⌒[ruli ⌒er]]*

Crucially, although we have described the translation between morphological and phonological structure in terms of a process, the formalism is really intended to describe licit mappings[28] between the two parallel levels of representation. Also, the assumption is that rebracketing of the kind found in *unrulier* is driven by phonological requirements. Later work on bracketing paradoxes (e.g., Cohn 1989) has argued that the phonological requirements which drive reanalysis of structure are generally prosodic in nature.

2.4.2   Cliticization and related phenomena: Further differences between phonological and syntactic words

The bracketing paradoxes just discussed may not be of much direct relevance to the computational analysis of morphology. However, the related phenomenon of cliticization is very common across languages and is of great importance to computational morphology. On the general properties of clitics see Wackernagel 1892, Zwicky 1977, Berendsen 1986, Klavans 1985, Kaisse 1985, Sproat 1988, and Marantz 1988. A **clitic** can be defined as a *syntactically* separate word that functions *phonologically* as an affix and therefore attaches phonologically to a word to its left (encliticization) or to its right (procliticization). Let us take as an example the following words of Warlpiri (see Nash 1980, p. 86):

(71) a. *maliki* + *kiḷi* + *ḷi* + **lki** + **ji** + **li**
         (dog + PROP + ERG + then + me + they)

     b. *kuḍu* + *kuḷu* + *ḷu* + **lku** + **ju** + **lu**
         (child + PROP + ERG + then + me + they)

In (71a), the first two affixes, *-kiḷi* 'PROP' and *-ḷi* 'ERG', are sensibly part of the same word as the noun stem *maliki* 'dog'; the former is a derivational affix meaning 'having' (Nash 1980, p. 23), and the latter is a nominal case marker. On the other hand, there is no sensible interpretation where *-lki* 'then', *-ji* 'me', and *-li* 'they', are part of the same word; they are separate words which have their own function in the syntax. Nonetheless there is strong evidence that the examples in (71) are single phonologically words, since, as those examples show, the vowels on the various suffixes change from /i/ in (71a) to /u/ in (71b). Warlpiri has a phonological process called vowel harmony that forces the vowel of the suffix to agree in certain respects with the vowel of the stem to which the suffix attaches. We will return in section 2.6 to a further description of this phenomenon, as it has received much attention both in the phonological literature and in the computational morphology literature. For now we only need to note that vowel harmony applies only within phonological words in Warlpiri. Therefore both of the examples in (71) are single phonological words, although they are not single words from the point of view of the syntax.

Related examples from more familiar languages include the following:

• The English possessive suffix *'s* syntactically takes a whole noun phrase in its scope, yet both phonologically and orthographically it attaches to the rightmost word in the phrase: *[the queen of England]*'s *hat*

• English auxiliaries have contracted forms which function as phonological (and orthographic) affixes: *he'll come, I'd've done it, who's here*

• French and German prepositions combine with articles in idiosyncratic ways to form phonological words:

French: **de le** *garçon* → **du** *garçon*
　　　　(of the boy)
German: **an dem** *Tisch* → **am** *Tisch*
　　　　(on the table)

Such examples are most clearly important for a morphological analyzer which provides analyses for a syntactic parser. In such cases one needs to provide a morphological analysis which tells the syntactic processor in appropriate circumstances that an input phonological word in fact corresponds to more than one syntactic word. We will return to this point momentarily after reviewing the various notions of word.

2.4.3 What is a word? What information should a morphological analyzer provide?

The conclusion, then, is that what the structure of a word is depends on how you look at it. Furthermore, what a word is depends upon how you look at it. Phonological words and syntactic words, while they may be largely coextensive, are not completely so. Add to this the notion of lexeme or lexicographic word, introduced in subsection 2.2.1, and we have arrived at three different notions of the term word. To complicate matters further, one can note that the **orthographic word** may not correspond to any of the other notions of word; in English the orthographic word does not in general correspond to the phonological word, as we saw in the discussion of compounds above, and in Chinese (as was discussed in chapter 1) there is no such thing as an orthographic word. These points are important to bear in mind when considering computational morphology, since most systems work on orthographic input and assume that the text is neatly segmented into words.

So what kind of information should a morphological analysis system provide, given that the notions of word and word structure seem to be defined in various ways and at various levels? The answer has to be, I believe, that that really depends upon the use to which the system in question is to be put. If one is building a morphological analyzer to interface with a text-retrieval system, then it may be appropriate simply to return the information that a word (say, Spanish *habla* 'speaks') is a form of such and such a lexeme (*hablar* 'to speak'). On the other hand, there are circumstances under which one would prefer to return an analysis that gives the structure of the word, either in a tree-like representation or as a sequence of morphemes. (Most morphological analysis systems, such as DECOMP or KIMMO in its original incarnation, have provided the latter.) So, for a text-to-speech system or a spelling corrector, knowing the sequence of morphemes is important for the application (see subsections 1.3.1 and 1.4.1). And for a natural account of cliticization (and bracketing paradoxes more generally) within a computational framework, one would want to pass off to the syntactic analyzer the sequence of morphemes found and let the latter decide which ones it wants to treat as syntactic words; see the

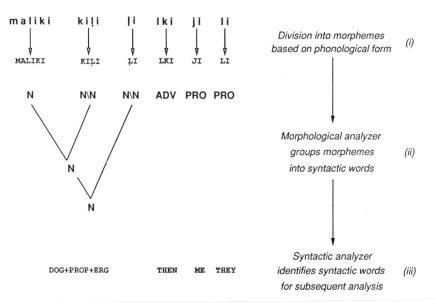

Figure 2.15
Handling cliticization in a computational setting. (i) The morphological analyzer provides an analysis in terms of the sequence of morphemes found. (ii) The morphological analyzer groups together those morphemes that belong as part of the same syntactic word and leaves the remainder unattached. (iii) The syntactic analyzer decides what to do with the unattached morphemes (clitics).

discussion of Sproat and Brunson 1987 in subsection 3.4.4, and see also figure 2.15.

So there is really no hard and fast answer to the question of what kind of analysis a morphological analyzer should provide.

2.4.4 Affixes and word-formation rules

To reiterate, the view of morphology which I have been assuming all along is a view where morphemes—whether they be monomorphemic stems or affixes of one kind or another—are all on a par, and a word is built up by the successive addition of morphemes to stems of increasing complexity. Crucially, *all morphemes are lexical items*, meaning that just as one clearly has to put *dog* in the lexicon of English, so one also has to put (plural) -*s* and -*ity* in the lexicon of English, and the -*VCC*- infix (discussed above) in the lexicon of Mangarayi. A word, then, is much like a sentence in that while the latter is a arboreally arranged sequence of words, the former is an arboreally arranged sequence of morphemes. This view of morphology has been referred to as the *item and arrangement* (IA) model, a term originally due to Hockett (1954) (see also Matthews 1974, pp. 226–227).

Although this is a popular view, it is not the only view of morphology. It is important to discuss the alternative, which is that words are built up via the successive application of **word-formation rules** (WFRs). In this view, which is sometimes referred to as *item and process* (though see Matthews 1974, p. 227, for a discussion on the use of this term), a word-formation rule is a relation *R* which takes as input a stem *S*, and whose output *R(S)* involves changing the phonological form of *S* in some fashion and adding some morphosyntactic features to the features already present in *S*, or possibly changing some features. As an example, consider the affixation of -*ity* in English, which adds the phonological string /-ɪti/ to the stem to which the rule applies and which furthermore changes the input (an adjective) into a noun. Following the notational scheme for word-formation rules developed in Aronoff 1976, we could write this rule as in (72).

(72) $[X]_A \rightarrow [X + \text{ɪti}]_N$

Without going through the various cases again, one may assume that the phonological modes of expression allowed for WFRs are constrained in the ways described in the previous section; for Arabic binyanim, for example, one would have a set of WFRs which take a root as an input and produce an output in which the consonants of the root are appropriately attached to a CV skeleton.

The two views of morphology—the IA model and the WFR view—are not necessarily diametrically opposed (see Matthews 1974, p. 227). Now, in the most extreme view they might indeed be opposed: one interpretation of the rule for *-ity* in (72) is that the sequence of phonemes /-ɪti/ has no status outside the rule that introduces it. That is, /-ɪti/ is not a lexical item, or indeed even the phonological spelling of a lexical item, but just a string of segments introduced by a WFR. The affix *-ity*, on this view, would not belong in the lexicon of English, but would be defined as part of the morphological rule set. A *less* opposed interpretation would be that *-ity* is indeed a lexical item, but that WFRs are responsible for governing how morphemes are combined. In contrast, in a theory of morphology that eschews WFRs, the restrictions on affixation come from lexical specifications on the affixes themselves. So a specification such as the one in (65b) would (at least) be required to restrict the affixation of *-ity* to adjectives in English. This view of morphology, which eschews WFRs altogether, is due in part to Lieber (1980).

As the name suggests, word-formation rules have been used by some authors, most notably Aronoff (1976), to describe word formation proper —i.e., derivational morphology. Still, nothing in Aronoff 1976 would, in principle, rule out the use of WFRs for inflectional morphology also. Indeed, the most recent explicit use of WFRs within the generative morphological tradition for the description of morphological processes in general is found in the *extended word and paradigm* framework (Anderson 1982; Thomas-Flinders 1981) which is itself derived partly from the earlier *word and paradigm* model of Hockett (1954) and Matthews (1972).

A view of morphology that is more in harmony with a WFR-based model than with a WFR-less IA model is the **word-based hypothesis** (Aronoff 1976). In particular, Aronoff claims (p. 21) that "all regular word-formation processes are word-based. A new word is formed by applying a regular rule to a single already existing word." One caveat here: A common view in generative morphology is that all potential words—even words that are extremely arcane, such as *giraffishness*—are taken to be "in the lexicon." The lexicon, on this view, is a *virtual* dictionary in that it contains all morphologically well-formed words; one cannot, in principle, tell when one goes to look up a word in that dictionary whether the word in question had been there before or was created on demand by the productive morphology. So, when Aronoff claims that words are derived from existing words, he includes all potential words as input to word formation; the only things that are excluded as input to *productive* word formation are things that are not words on any definition.

In many cases in English the implementation of Aronoff's word-based hypothesis is straightforward, since many words are derived via affixation from other words. Still, his treatment requires some special assumptions in certain cases. One such case is the suffix -ee, which attaches to verbs and makes nouns with the meaning 'one who has been xed', where x is the meaning of the verb, or 'one who has xed' with certain intransitive verbs:

(73) a. *employ* +ee, *invit* +ee, *stand* +ee, *escap* +ee

   b. *nomin* +ee, *evacu* +ee

The examples in (73b) are of particular interest since they are derived not from *nomin and *evacu, respectively—there are no such words—but from *nomin*ATE and *evacu*ATE. Both of the examples in (73b) can be thought of as derived from other words, then, but only if one has a way of getting rid of the suffix -ate. Aronoff proposes a mechanism, which he calls **truncation**: the WFR for the attachment of -ee includes the specification that the sequence -ate is deleted if present. But, unlike the examples of subtractive morphology which we discussed above and which we saw were *phonologically* defined, Aronoff's truncation is crucially defined to apply to morphemes. In both cases in (73b) the deleted -ate is a morpheme. The sequence *ate* will not delete if it is not a morpheme, so a balloon might be an ?*inflatee* but it could not be an *inflee.

The process of truncation is rather naturally captured by a model that incorporates sufficiently powerful WFRs. In contrast, a model that does not have WFRs but treats morpheme combination as constrained by the lexical specification of the morphemes involved would have to analyze *nominee* as being derived by the affixation of -ee to the stem *nomin*-. (WFRs, at least as described in Aronoff 1976, seem to be a more powerful device than affixation as described in section 2.3. It is hard to tell if this is really true, though, since neither view of morphology has ever been sufficiently well formalized.)

The word-based hypothesis is probably not completely correct; for one thing, there are classic examples in the literature which apparently cannot be derived under the assumption of that hypothesis. The compound *church-goer*, for example cannot be derived either by the affixation of -er to *church-go or by the compounding of *church* with *goer, since neither of those two putative bases exists as an independent word.[29] Nonetheless, as a practical model which is approximately correct, the word-based hypothesis has been argued to be useful in developing computational systems for morphological analysis. For example, the guiding philosophy behind the work presented in Church 1986 is that it is computationally safer to take fewer rather than more steps in the analysis of a word form. Thus, if all words are derived from words which are already to be found in the dictionary—possibly with the application of truncation—the largest number of analysis steps that must be made in handling a novel word form is one. The word-based model is therefore computationally attractive, even if it is not empirically accurate. Of course, Church's computational model differs from Aronoff's theory in that the former assumes that the words of a language are derivable in at most one step from the set of words already listed in a dictionary. As I noted above, Aronoff's theory relates words to entries in a *virtual* dictionary, and the number of derivational steps required between a particular word and an entry in an actual dictionary may be greater than one.

Besides Church's work and that of a few others (e.g., Byrd et al. 1986), most work on computational morphology has assumed some version of the IA view, rejecting a WFR view. This adoption of the IA model does not stem from any deep-seated theoretical motivations. Rather, the reason is more mundane: most morphological analyzers, as has already been noted, and as will be more fully illustrated below, have been designed to handle purely concatenative morphology. There are a few examples of concatenative morphology—such as -*ee* affixation in English—which have been argued to require more mechanisms than a simple-minded IA approach can handle, but the vast majority of such morphology does not have such problems. Thus, the most natural interpretation of a highly agglutinative language such as Turkish is that one constructs words by the successive attachment of morphemes, and one would not feel compelled to treat affixes as *formally* distinct from stems in the description of such a language.

2.4.5   Constraints on affixes (or WFRs)

Having now dealt with one view of what morphemes are, with what word structure is, and with the issue of word formation rules, I will now describe some of the different kinds of restrictions on the attachment of affixes (alternatively, on the application of WFRs) that are observed across languages. This will rather naturally serve as a lead-in to the next section, where we will discuss constraints on morpheme ordering.[30]

Affixes can have a number of different kinds of restrictions on their attachment, which are rather naturally classified according to the particular level of representation at which the restriction applies. Phonological restrictions on affixes specify phonological characteristics which the stem must have in order for the affix in question to be able to attach to that base.

We have already seen some instances of phonological restrictions in the case of infixes. Recall that the attachment site of an infix is often stated prosodically in that the infix is specified to attach to a particular prosodic unit within the word. So, the Ulwa infix -*ka*-, as we saw above, attaches to the right edge of the first foot in the word. In Warlpiri, a number of affixes are sensitive to the prosodic structure of the base word (Nash 1980, pp. 33–34). For example, the ergative affix has one of two allomorphs, depending upon whether the stem consists of one prosodic foot or more than one prosodic foot. In the former case the form of the affix is -ŋ*ku*/-ŋ*ki* (where the vowel depends upon the vowels of the base—see section 2.6) and in the latter it is -*ḷu*/-*ḷi*:

(74) Stem   ERG   Gloss
     kuḍu   *kuḍu* + ŋ**ku**   'child'
     maliki   *maliki* + **ḷi**   'dog'

Another example of a phonological restriction on affixation involves the affixation of the comparative and superlative affixes -*er* and -*est* in English. As we saw above, -*er* is restricted to attach to maximally disyllabic words; see the examples in (67).

Syntactic restrictions on affixes, needless to say, are specifications of the kinds of syntactic features which the stem must have for the affix in question to be able to attach to it. We have seen numerous examples of syntactic restrictions. Case markers on nouns and adjectives, for example, are restricted to attach to nouns and adjectives, as are nominal/adjectival plural markers. The English affix -*able* is (with very few exceptions—e.g., *marriageable*) restricted to attach to verbs. It is probably fair to say that syntactic restrictions on affixes are more common than phonological restrictions: most affixes have some restrictions on the kind of word they may attach to, and at the very least these restrictions usually specify the part of speech to which the word must belong.

Some examples of semantic restrictions are the following, taken from pp. 93–94 of Bauer 1983. Perhaps the most famous example of a semantic restriction on affixation in English is the prohibition on the attachment of the adjectival negative prefix *un-* to an adjective that already has a negative connotation; this observation is attributed to Zimmer (1964). For example (see Bauer 1983, p. 94):

(75) a. **un** +*well*, **un** +*happy*, **un** +*cheerful*, **un** +*optimistic*

     b. *****un** +*ill*, *****un** +*sad*, *****un** +*sorrowful*, *****un** +*pessimistic*

The following example from Italian, attributed to Ettinger (1974), shows a more complex semantic restriction. Italian forms **augmentatives** ('big *x*') from nouns by the addition of the suffix *-one*. For example:

(76) Stem   AUG   Gloss
 canale *canal* +**one** 'canal'
 piazza *piazz* +**one** 'square'
 strada *strad* +**one** 'street'

All the examples in (76) involve man-made objects. With non-man-made objects there appears to be a restriction that prevents the suffix *-one* from being attached to words that denote objects larger than human beings. So, while the examples in (77a) are well formed, the examples in (77b) are ill formed:

(77) a. Stem   AUG   Gloss
  pietrà *pietr* +**one** 'stone'
  fiore *fior* +**one** 'flower'
  ciòttolo *ciòttol* +**one** 'pebble'

  b. Stem   AUG   Gloss
  fiume *fium +**one** 'river'
  lago *lag +**one** 'lake'
  piano *pian +**one** 'plain'

In addition to restrictions that clearly refer to phonological, syntactic, or semantic attributes of the stem, there are also restrictions that seem to be more purely lexical. In English, many latinate affixes are restricted to latinate stems (with a few exceptions—e.g. *oddity*). Consider the distribution of *-ity*:

(78) a. *acid* +**ity**, *precoc* +**ity**, *scarc* +**ity**, *obscur* +**ity**

  b. *good +**ity**, *naked +**ity**, *weird +**ity**, *dark +**ity**

Most analyses assume that there is a lexical feature, [latinate], which is set '+' for those stems that are etymologically derived directly from Latin (i.e., not via French) and '−' for stems not derived from Latin. The affix *-ity* is restricted to attach to [+latinate] stems. Note that which stems are [+latinate] must be learned, though it is probably the case that there are some phonological clues distinguishing latinate from native stems. Note also that a derived word may inherit the feature [+latinate] from the affix by which it was derived. For example, the affix *-able* attaches to verbs in English without regard to their etymology. However, *-able* bears the feature [+latinate], as is evidenced by the completely productive attachment of *-ity* to adjectives formed from verbs with *-able*.

At this point, it is worth describing a couple of the mechanisms that have been proposed in the literature for handling the inheritance of morpho-

logical features. Following Lieber (1980), one can say that the feature
[+latinate] percolates from the affix to the whole word. Lieber's original
model of percolation can be defined roughly as in (79).

(79) In a morphological construction $[_\gamma \alpha\beta]$:

    a. If β is a suffix and if β is specified for a feature F, then γ inherits β's
       specification for F. All features not specified on β are inherited
       from α.

    b. If α is a prefix and if α is specified for a feature F, then γ inherits α's
       specification for F. All features not specified on α are inherited
       from β.

    c. If α and β are both stems and if β is specified for a feature F, then γ
       inherits β's specification for F.

To illustrate (79a) consider the Russian diminutive suffix *-uška*, illustrated
in (80) (examples from Marantz 1984, p. 122):

(80) *baba* (FEM)   'grandmother'
     bab +uška (FEM)   'little grandmother'
     d^{j}ad^{j}a (MASC)   'uncle'
     d^{j}ad^j +uška (MASC) 'little uncle'

In this case β ($= $ *-uška*) is a suffix that is marked with the feature [+diminu-
tive], and this feature is inherited by the whole word. The suffix *-uška*
bears no feature specifications for gender, however, and the gender specifications are therefore inherited from the stem to which the suffix attaches.
This explains why the gender of the diminutive form is identical to the
gender of the noun from which it is derived.

    As an illustration of (79b), consider the English prefix *en-, em-*, which
forms verbs from adjectives or nouns:

(81) *joy*   **en** +*joy*
     noble   **en** +*noble*
     rich   **en** +*rich*
     battle   **em** +*battle*

In Lieber's theory, *en-, em-* is marked categorially as a verb, and this categorial specification is inherited by words derived with this prefix. Clause
(79c) is intended to handle compounds in English. It accounts for the fact
that *hot dog, guard dog,* and *sled dog* are all nouns, even though the left
members are, respectively, an adjective, a verb, and a noun. Since *dog* is
categorially a noun, the entire compound inherits this categorial specification, via (79c).

Another device intended to account for the same range of phenomena is Williams' (1981) notion of head of a word. (See DiSciullo and Williams 1987 for a more recent version of this idea.) In the original formulation, the features of a morphologically complex word are inherited from the head, where the head is the rightmost morphological constituent of the word. This Righthand Head Rule, as Williams called it, was intended to capture the intuition that it is primarily suffixes (and the rightmost members of compounds) which determine the properties (e.g. part of speech) of morphologically complex words. While this generalization is approximately correct for English, note that the prefix *en-*, *em-* appears to falsify it. Moreover, there are a number of languages, including Vietnamese (Lieber 1980, pp. 99–100) and Tagalog, which appear to have many left-headed morphological constructions, thus directly falsifying the Righthand Head Rule, at least as a universal claim. Still, despite the empirical problems with Williams' proposal, the notion head and the associated Righthand Head Rule are frequently cited in the morphological literature, and it is therefore important to be aware of them. In the computational literature, the various mechanisms of featural inheritance have generally been implemented using **unification**-based formalisms (Shieber 1986); see subsection 3.4.3 below.

We have seen that affixes may be restricted in various ways and that therefore a complete description of the behavior of a particular affix may have to take into account its sensitivity to properties of the stem at various levels of grammatical representation. In most computational models of morphology, such constraints have not been particularly well modeled. Most computational models of **morphotactics**—i.e., the ways in which morphemes are put together—have been simple-minded finite-state models. Restrictions on particular combinations of morphemes are largely handled by arbitrary diacritics; morpheme α would be marked in the dictionary with some symbol—say #, which directs the search to another dictionary which lists morphemes capable of following morpheme α. In some cases this is no less enlightening than the linguistic description: the feature [+latinate] is arguably an arbitrary diacritic from the point of view of a synchronic analysis of Modern English. On the other hand, the approach confounds such arbitrary cases with clearly more systematic and nonarbitrary cases, such as the phonological, syntactic, and semantic restrictions discussed above. This criticism does not come down to mere matters of taste, I believe: systematic sensitivity to computable characteristics of stems, such as the phonological sensitivity exhibited by the Warlpiri ergative allomorphs *-ļu/-ļi* versus *-ŋku/-ŋki*, can readily be coded into a system and thus save the trouble of marking each stem as to which affixes it may take. The only presumption is that the system in question have mechanisms available to decide which class a stem falls into. In the case of Warlpiri, one needs to know something about the prosodic structure of the stem; as it turns out, many morphological processing systems cannot trivially compute such properties, although some, such as those discussed in Sproat and Brunson 1987, are designed with precisely this kind of sensitivity in mind.

2.5 MORPHOTACTICS: THE ORDER OF MORPHEMES

Having discussed some of the ways in which individual affixes are constrained, I now turn to a fuller discussion of morphotactics—the ordering restrictions on morphemes. Some of the conditions on morpheme order follow straightforwardly from the kinds of constraints on affixation discussed in the previous section, whereas others will be seen to involve phenomena not previously introduced. Just as a model of syntax for some language must appropriately describe word or phrase order, so a model of morphology must describe the order in which morphemes can appear within the word. For the sake of exposition, I will divide the types of constraints on morpheme ordering into two broad categories: "syntactic" and "other."

2.5.1 Syntactic constraints on ordering

Let us start with a straightforward example involving familiar constraints. What conditions the order of the morphemes in *motorizability*? Why can't the morphemes be placed in any of orders shown in (82)?

(82) a. *itymotorizable, *izemotorability

     b. *motorableizity, *motorabilityize

These examples are morpheme salad composed of the morphemes *motor*, *-ize*, *-able*, and *-ity*. However, the reasons for the saladhood differ in (82a) and (82b). In (82a) the forms violate an obvious constraint: *-ize*, *-able*, and *-ity* are suffixes and therefore cannot appear before the stem. In (82b), the suffixal status of the affixes is not violated, but their syntactic requirements are: *-ize* takes nouns or adjectives and makes verbs, *-able* takes verbs and makes adjectives, and *-ity* takes adjectives and makes nouns. If *motor* is a noun, then the only affix of the set that can attach to it is *-ize*. (Alternatively, on a WFR-based view of morphology, the only WFR of the set that could apply to the input *motor* is the rule introducing *-ize*.) This forms the

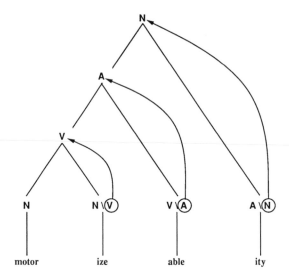

Figure 2.16
The representation of the word *motorizability*. Each affix has as a sister a node of
the appropriate category. Arrows indicate the percolation of categorial features
from the affix to the node dominating it.

verb *motorize*, and the only affix of the set that can attach to that is *-able*,
forming *motorizable*. This leaves *-ity*, which can attach to this adjective to
form *motorizability*. The structure of the word, then, can be given as in the
morphological tree representation in figure 2.16. (Note that the categorial
requirements of the affixes determine only what kind of node they must
attach to in the morphological tree; the linear ordering between sister
nodes is determined by the specification of the affix in question as either a
prefix or a suffix; see the discussion in section 2.4.)

   The ordering constraints just discussed are syntactic in nature, in that
they refer to syntactic features, such as syntactic category, but the constraints pertain to material wholly within the word. More complicated,
and concomitantly harder to model, are syntactic constraints where the
ordering of affixes is sensitive to properties of the sentence in which the
word is contained. I am referring, in particular, to the **mirror principle**
effects discussed by Baker (1985, 1988). In languages that exhibit rich
grammatical-function-changing morphology, it turns out that the order
of the morphemes that mark changes in grammatical function reflects
the order in which the grammatical-function changes in question applied
in the syntactic derivation of the sentence. The claim that this generalization holds universally is the substance of the mirror principle.

Consider the following case from Huichol (an Uto-Aztecan language of Mexico), taken from Baker 1985. Huichol has two syntactic rules that change grammatical functions. One is the applicative rule, which, like the applicative in Chicheŵa (see (15b) above and the surrounding discussion), changes an oblique or indirect object into the direct object. The other is the passive, which, as usual, changes the object into the subject.[31] In Huichol, the application of each of these rules is marked by a distinct morpheme attached to the verb. Now, in English, the rule of dative shift (which changes indirect objects into direct objects) feeds the rule of passive, in that passive can apply to the output of dative shift. So, for example:

(83) a. *John gave the ball to* **Bill**

   b. (via dative shift) *John gave* **Bill** *the ball*

   c. (via passive) **Bill** *was given the ball by John*

Similarly in Huichol, applicative can feed passive. What is interesting about this for our purposes is that, just as the applicative rule applies before the passive rule in the syntactic derivation, so the applicative morpheme on the verb must attach before—i.e., closer to the verb stem than—the passive morpheme in the cases where both rules apply. An example is given in (84) (from Baker 1985, p. 397), where the verb stem is given in plain text, the applicative in boldface, and the passive in small capitals.

(84) *tiiri yi + nauka + ti nawazi me +* puutinanai **+ri** + YERI
   (children four + SUBJ knife 3/SG + buy + **APPL** + PASS)
   'four children were bought a knife'

The way in which this example is derived is sketched in figure 2.17. As is indicated in the example—following the analysis of Baker (1985, 1988)—part of the structure of the verb is built up in tandem with the application of the syntactic rules which the morphology encodes.

A slightly different view of this kind of morphology would be taken within lexical-functional grammar (Bresnan 1982). In that theory, the applicative and passive rules in Huichol (and also the analogous rules in English) are considered to be lexical rules rather than syntactic rules. Thus, the affixation of the applicative and passive markers in (84) would be taken to derive a new verb from the original verb 'buy'. The original verb would be marked to take a subject, an object, and a benefactive, and the verb in (84) would be marked to take (at least) a subject ('four children' in this case) and a so-called second object ('a knife'). As far as the syntax is concerned these are two different verbs lexically marked for different sets of grammatical relations; it is the task of the morphological component of the gram-

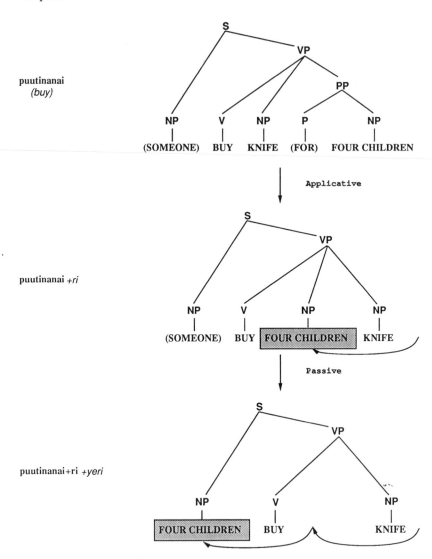

Figure 2.17
The derivation of the Huichol sentence for 'four children were bought a knife'. On
the right is shown the syntactic derivation. On the left is shown the concomitant
building up of the verb's morphological structure.

mar to relate the two verbs, and to note, for example, that the subject in the example in (84) corresponds to the benefactive in the basic form of 'buy'. In any event, such examples are interesting from a computational point of view in that—at least on the view expressed by Baker (1985, 1988)— not only does the verbal morphology give some indication of the rules that have applied in the derivation of the sentence, but it also marks the order in which they have applied. This kind of information would be potentially useful to a morphological processing system designed to interface with a sentence parser for a language, such as Huichol, that has a rich verbal morphology of this kind; see subsection 3.7.3 for more discussion.

2.5.2 Other constraints on ordering

We now turn to nonsyntactic constraints on the order of morphemes. Probably the most popular theory of word structure that purports to account for some aspects of morphotactics is the theory of lexical phonology and morphology (LPM) (Siegel 1974; Allen 1978; Pesetsky 1979; Kiparsky 1982; Mohanan 1986). LPM's basic claim about morphotactics is that the lexicon is organized into ordered strata (Mohanan 1986), each of which is responsible for a certain portion of the morphology. Quite often, the strata are distinguished on the basis of the etymology of the morphemes. For example, in English it has been noticed (Siegel 1974) that latinate affixes such as the negative prefix *in-* and 'native' affixes such as the negative prefix *non-* are ordered: one can place *non-* outside *in-* in words, but not the other way around (note that *in-* assimilates to the following consonant in some cases):

(85) a. **non** +**im** +*partial,* **non** +**il** +*legible,* **non** +**in** +*frequent*

  b. *****in** +**non** +*partial,* *****in** +**non** +*legible,* *****in** +**non** +*frequent*

(Note that *?non* +*partial,* *non* +*legible,* *?non* +*frequent* are marginally acceptable by themselves.) Similarly, the latinate suffix *-ity* cannot occur outside the native suffix *-ish,* although the native suffix *-ness* can:

(86) a. **boor* +**ish** +**ity,** **slav* +**ish** +**ity,** **baboon* +**ish** +**ity,**
        giraff* +ish** +**ity,** **guttersnip* +**ish** +**ity**

  b. *boor* +**ish** +**ness,** *slav* +**ish** +**ness,** *baboon* +**ish** +**ness,**
        giraff +**ish** +**ness,** *guttersnip* +**ish** +**ness**

These facts are handled in LPM by assuming that English contains at least two distinct strata of affixational morphology, one (roughly speaking) for latinate morphology and one for native morphology. Each of these strata is the locus of the morphological rules of its particular type. Furthermore, the strata are ordered so that the latinate stratum feeds into the native stratum, but not the other way around. The two strata are illustrated in figure 2.18.

In addition to these two "etymological" strata, various models of Lexical Phonology—especially that of Mohanan (1986)—posit additional strata for English to handle compounding and inflectional morphology. However, the ordering restrictions accounted for by stratum ordering are crude at best, and can in many cases be explained by other means. For example, as we saw above, latinate suffixes are often constrained to attach to latinate stems, whereas native suffixes are not so constrained. One could capture the ordering restrictions just discussed by simply observing that the relative freedom of native affixes predicts that they can occur outside latinate affixes, but the relative restrictiveness of latinate affixes predicts that they *cannot* occur outside native affixes: once a native affix has been attached to a word the word, is [−latinate] and a latinate affix cannot then generally be attached. In fact, Fabb (1988) argues that a complete account of the ordering restrictions of English suffixes would require quite a large number of rules and principles (including "etymological" principles) and that stratum ordering is effectively doing no work whatsoever in accounting for English morphotactics.

Still, in fairness, it should also be pointed out that one of the claims of the LPM model is that phonological rules which apply to particular classes of affixation—e.g., velar softening in English, whereby the final consonant in *electric* (/k/) is "softened" to /s/ in a derived form such as *electricity*—are indexed so as to apply only at those strata where that morphology takes place, and to be turned off elsewhere. So, velar softening applies at stratum I in English and is turned off at stratum II, thus encoding the fact that this rule can apply with latinate affixes, such as *-ity*, but not with native affixes, such as *-ing* (*hiking* is not pronounced */haʲsɪŋ/*). Rules of stress assignment in English are also marked to apply at stratum I, which accounts for the fact that latinate affixes can shift stress whereas native affixes do not:

(87) latinate   *grammátical*   *grammaticálity*
      native   *grammátical*   *grammáticalness*

The link between types of morphology and types of phonological rules is probably one of the more compelling aspects of LPM.

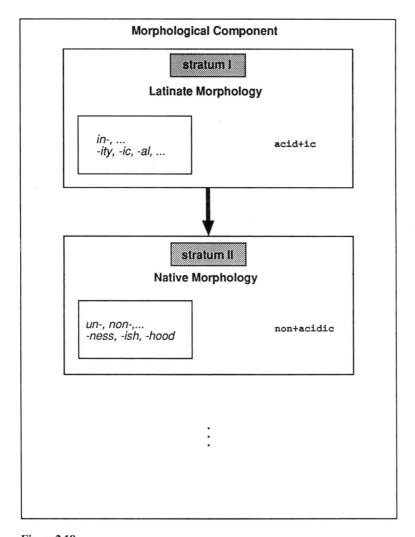

Figure 2.18
Two strata of affixational morphology in English. Stratum I deals mostly with latinate morphology, and stratum II mostly with native morphology. Stratum I feeds stratum II, with the effect that native morphology must be attached outside latinate morphology.

To complete the picture somewhat, I note that various authors have discussed the relation between the functions of particular morphemes and their relative ordering. Such discussions have usually taken the form of implicational universals. For example, Greenberg (1966, p. 95) notes that morphemes marking number on nouns almost always occur closer to the noun than morphemes marking case. Similarly, Bybee (1985, pp. 34–35) notes that markers of tense and aspect almost always occur closer to the verb stem than markers of person agreement. It has been observed that, on the whole, the categories that tend to be marked closer to the stem also tend to be the categories that are more likely to be chosen to be marked at all. Thus, although there are languages that mark tense but not person agreement, there are few languages that mark person agreement but not tense (Greenberg 1966, p. 93). So person agreement is somehow secondary to tense marking, which correlates with the fact that person agreement tends to be peripheral in comparison with tense marking; see also the discussion in subsection 2.2.1. The interested reader is referred in particular to Bybee 1985 for further discussion along these lines.

Needless to say, computational models of morphology must deal with morpheme ordering restrictions of all kinds; it is simply a fact of language that one can usually stack up morphemes in some orders but not in others. It is fair to say that most computational models of morphotactics have not generally been terribly interesting. For the most part they model mor-photactics with purely local finite-state mechanisms. In such systems, for example, one would capture a restriction that morphemes of class β must follow morphemes of class α by setting up a finite-state machine whose only transitions into morphemes of class β come from morphemes of class α. This is arguably adequate for some purposes. Note that the model of morpheme ordering in terms of ordered strata proposed as part of LPM is precisely a finite-state mechanism, and the LPM model can be said to be partially adequate. On the other hand, the syntactic aspects of morphotactics are not modeled particularly well by finite-state mechanisms in the general case, for the same kinds of reasons that finite-state mechanisms have generally been eschewed in syntactic parsing (though see Church 1980): one can find instances of long-distance dependencies in morphology where the existence of one morpheme is allowed by another morpheme which is not adjacent to it. The following example from English will serve as an illustration. Consider the prefix *en-*, noted above in (81). The verbs formed with this prefix behave like normal English verbs in every respect, including the ability to take the suffix *-able* (some of the examples may be implausible on semantic grounds, but all seem morphologically well formed):

(88) *enjoy* +**able**, *ennoble* +**able**, *enrich* +**able**, *embattle* +**able**

Yet *-able* does not attach by itself to the nouns or adjectives to which *en-* attaches:

(89) **joy* +**able**, **noble* +**able**, **rich* +**able**, **battle* +**able**

The problem that the examples in (88) cause for a simple finite-state approach is the following: the suffix *-able* can attach in (88) because the verb-forming prefix *en-* has already attached, yet this prefix is separated from *-able* by the stem to which the prefix attaches. Somehow one needs to be able to encode the relationship between the prefix and the suffix. This is naturally encoded in a tree-like representation, of course, since the node that dominates (say) *enjoy* is labeled as a verb, and *-able* simply attaches to that node. But in a finite-state model one would have to have two different dictionaries, each containing the morphemes *joy, noble, rich, chain,* and *battle* (among others); one dictionary would represent the case where the prefix *en* had not been used, and words in this dictionary would not allow *-able* to follow; the other dictionary would represent the case where the prefix *en-* had been used, and in this case *-able* would be allowed to follow. This setup is illustrated in figure 2.19. (See chapter 3 for a discussion of the notation for finite-state machines used in this book.) Thus, the two dictionaries serve as a kind of memory for morphemes which are not adjacent to, but may be relevant to, the attachment of the morpheme *-able*. The

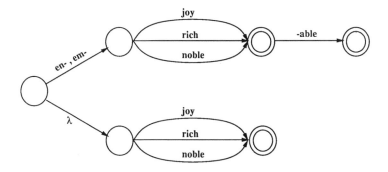

Figure 2.19
Illustration of the problems is encoding morphological long-distance dependencies in a finite-state model of morphotactics. The two separate dictionaries containing identical sets of words serve as a "memory," allowing the suffix *-able* to attach only if the verb-forming prefix *en-, em-* has been attached.

problem discussed here turns out to be an inadequacy of some well-known finite-state models of morphology, in particular the original instantiation of KIMMO (Karttunen 1983, pp. 179–181). In subsection 3.4.3 I shall return to this problem and note that some work has been done on remedying the deficiency.

2.6 PHONOLOGY

Up to this point we have been discussing morphology from the point of view of what kinds of objects morphemes are, what kinds of features they encode, what kinds of shapes they may have, and how and in what orders they may combine. Ideally, then, the task of a morphological analysis system would be to break the word down into its component morphemes and then, for some applications, determine what the resulting decomposition ought to mean. Things are not that simple, however, because of the often quite drastic effects of phonological rules: morphemes often change their shape and are sometimes entirely eradicated by the effects of these rules. Now, it is an explicit assumption of Generative Phonology that if a phonological rule can (reasonably) be written to describe a change in a morpheme, then one should assume that the change is indeed to be captured by a rule, and not by listing two different forms (allomorphs) for the morpheme. By and large this assumption has been carried over into the work on computational morphology, although some work has been proposed (Jäppinen and Ylilammi 1986; Tzoukermann and Liberman 1990) which eschews (on-line) computation of phonological rules, and it is generally true that the extent to which the assumption is carried out in computational work is less than the extent to which it is carried out in theoretical linguistics. Computational morphologists are generally more willing to posit allomorphs and less willing to posit phonological alternations than theoretical linguists. Nonetheless, a fair number of alternations which are described by theoretical linguists in terms of phonological alternations are also so described by computational morphologists.

Not surprisingly, then, a great deal of the effort in constructing computational models of morphology has been spent on developing techniques for dealing with phonological rules. For some computational models, such as KIMMO, the bulk of the machinery is designed to handle phonological rules, and in the original version of that system (Koskenniemi 1983b) the actual *morphology* done is not particularly interesting. Indeed, the term *two-level morphology*, used by Koskenniemi to describe the framework, is really a misnomer: the "two-level" part of the model describes the method for implementing phonological rules and has nothing to do with morphology per se.

This is not a book about phonology, and the discussion will therefore not delve deeply into the massive literature that has accreted on this topic over the past 25 years or so; there are a number of good introductions to phonology, some of which I reference at the end of this chapter. However, I do need to at least discuss the areas that most clearly relate to computational morphology, specifically those areas that either add to the complexity of the problem of morphological analysis in one way or another, or for which interesting solutions have been proposed within the computational literature. I will concentrate on the following areas:

• phonological rules that delete or insert material
• long-distance rules
• notions of structure in phonology
• rule ordering, cyclicity, and the interaction of phonology with morphological structure

I will turn to these issues directly after dealing with one other topic which must be discussed.

2.6.1 ORTHOGRAPHY VERSUS PHONOLOGY

One thing that needs to be borne in mind throughout this discussion is that most computational analyses of morphology assume *written* input. Therefore, properly speaking, the systems do not analyze phonological rules, but orthographic rules. One important difference between the standard orthographies for different languages is the extent to which the orthography is a good phonemic transcription—i.e., a transcription of the pronunciation— for the language in question. In some languages, such as Finnish, the orthography is indeed almost a perfect phonemic transcription, and the results of the phonological rules of that language are reflected in the orthography. So in the KIMMO analyzer for Finnish described by Koskenniemi (1983b) it is fair to say that, although the analyzer works on words represented in standard Finnish orthography, the system is really modeling *phonological* rules of Finnish. At the other extreme (at least for languages which use alphabetic writing systems) is English, where there is a poor correspondence between pronunciation and orthography. As a result, morphological analyzers for English typically deal with orthographic rules which often do not correspond to phonological rules of English:

(90) a. ⟨city⟩ + ⟨s⟩ → ⟨cities⟩ (*⟨citys⟩)

   b. ⟨bake⟩ + ⟨ing⟩ → ⟨baking⟩ (*⟨bakeing⟩)

So (90a) exemplifies the rule that words ending in ⟨y⟩, when adding a morpheme spelled as ⟨s⟩, must change the ⟨y⟩ to an ⟨i⟩, with an ⟨e⟩ being inserted. There is no phonological rule corresponding to this orthographic change. In (90b) the "silent ⟨e⟩" at the end of orthographic words like ⟨bake⟩ is deleted when an orthographically vowel-initial morpheme, such as ⟨-ing⟩, is added. Computational models of this process would have a rule deleting the final ⟨e⟩ under appropriate conditions; there is, however, no phonological deletion rule to which the orthographic deletion corresponds.

So, orthographic conventions of English make some cases more complicated than they are phonologically. There are also cases where the opposite is true:

(91) a. ⟨divine⟩ [dəvaʲn]   ⟨divinity⟩ [dəvɪnɪti]
      ⟨obscene⟩ [ɔbsin]   ⟨obscenity⟩ [ɔbsɛnɪti]

   b. ⟨grammatical⟩ [grəmǽtɪkəl]
      ⟨grammaticality⟩ [grəmætɪkǽlɪti]
      ⟨hospitalize⟩ [hɔ́spɪtələʲz]
      ⟨hospitalization⟩ [hɔspɪtələʲzéʲʃən]

In (91a) the words *divinity* and *obscenity* are analyzable orthographically as the concatenation of the bases, ⟨divine⟩ and ⟨obscene⟩, with the affix string ⟨ity⟩, and with the additional application of the orthographic rule deleting final ⟨e⟩. But the orthography fails to encode the application of some important phonological rules of English, indicated by the phonetic transcriptions of these words, usually termed *vowel shift* and *trisyllabic laxing* in the phonological literature (see, for example, Chomsky and Halle 1968); vowel shift accounts for why the vowels in the second syllables of *divine* and *obscene* are respectively [aʲ] and [i], whereas underlyingly they are argued to be /i/ and /e/; trisyllabic laxing changes underlying *tense* vowels such as /i/ and /e/ into their corresponding lax vowels ([ɪ] and [ɛ]) when they occur in the third syllable from the end; note the vowels in the antepenultimate syllables of [dəvɪnɪti] and [ɔbsɛnɪti]. Neither of these rules' application is represented orthographically. Thus, the orthography in this case gives a more transparent representation of the morphological structure of the word.[32] Similarly, although there is a shift of main word stress in the examples in (91b) when the suffixes *-ity* and *-ation* are added to the stems, English orthography simply does not indicate stress, and one can therefore for the most part ignore the application of stress rules in building a morphological analysis system to parse morphological structure from orthographic input. (Of course, one cannot ignore stress if one wants a text-to-speech system to pronounce the words.)

Even in English, there are some cases where the orthography and the phonology match rather well:

(92) a. ⟨in⟩ + ⟨tangible⟩ → ⟨intangible⟩ (/in-/)
        ⟨in⟩ + ⟨possible⟩ → ⟨impossible⟩ (/im-/)

    b. ⟨dog⟩ + ⟨s⟩ → ⟨dogs⟩
        ⟨mass⟩ + ⟨s⟩ → ⟨masses⟩

In (92a) we see that the latinate negative prefix spelled ⟨in⟩ changes its spelling to ⟨im⟩ when it precedes a labial consonant (such as /p, b, m/); this spelling change corresponds to a phonological change changing the nasal's place of articulation, as indicated by the different pronunciations of the affix under the two conditions. Similarly, with affixes spelled ⟨s⟩ (plural and third-person singular) there is a phonological rule inserting /ə/ between the /s/ and the preceding consonant when that consonant is a coronal strident (/s, z, ʃ, ʒ, tʃ, ʤ/). This is indicated orthographically by the insertion of ⟨e⟩.

I will not have much more to say about orthography, and I will in subsequent discussion characterize the problem faced by morphological analyzers as being one of modeling *phonological* rules, except where it is too blatantly inappropriate. By and large this is justified, since for many languages the orthography mirrors the phonological form much better than is the case in English.[33] With these points in mind, I turn now to a discussion of phonology.

2.6.2   Deletion and insertion rules

Let us start with the assumption that morphemes are represented as strings of phoneme segments. Each segment, in turn, is represented as a vector of phonological features. The morpheme *cat*, for example, is to be represented partially as in (93).

(93)
Feature	k	ae	t
Coronal	−	−	+
Anterior	−	−	+
Voiced	−	+	−
High	+	−	−
Low	−	+	−

This was the view of phonological structure adopted in early work laying the foundations of Generative Phonology (Jakobson et al. 1952; Chomsky and Halle 1968; Johnson 1972). This segmental view of phonological representation is now known to be too simplistic. Nonetheless, it is the view of phonology adopted by most work in computational morphology—largely because such systems deal with orthographic representation, where it makes a great deal of sense to think of morphemes as being represented as strings of letters.

Many phonological rules can be described as changing certain features in one or more phonological segments in a morpheme. For example, consider the nasal assimilation rule in English, exemplified in (92a). Recall that the /n/ in the prefix *in-* (and in other latinate prefixes, such as *con-*) changes into /m/ before labial consonants such as /p,b,m/. One could write the rule segmentally as in (94).

$$(94) \quad n \rightarrow \begin{bmatrix} + & anterior \\ - & coronal \end{bmatrix} / \underline{\hphantom{xx}} \begin{bmatrix} - & continuant \\ + & anterior \\ - & coronal \end{bmatrix}$$

This rule is interpreted as follows: an /n/ gets rewritten as a labial consonant ([+anterior, −coronal]—hence /m/), in the context of another labial consonant.

Now, obviously, if all phonological rules can do is change features on segments, then it will always be true that the surface form of a morpheme will have the same number of segments as its underlying form. However, phonological rules can also delete or insert segments, and this adds to the complexity of the computational problem. For example, as Barton et al. (1987 pp. 150–153), have argued unrestricted deletions can increase the complexity of the recognition problem, owing to the fact that the lexical form of a word may be unboundedly longer than the surface form.[34] Here I will merely note a couple of examples of insertion and deletion rules, and point out that rules which insert or delete segments—or larger units—are fairly common across languages.

As an example of a deletion rule: in Latin, coronal stops /t,d/ are regularly deleted between sonorants and /s/. This explains the alternation exemplified by the nominative forms (suffix *-s*) of the nouns in the third column of (95), where the underlying form of the noun stem is given in the first column and the genitive singular form (suffix *-is*), which retains the underlying stem, is given in the second column (the examples are from Schane and Bendixen 1978, p. 77). The segmental rule formally describing the alternation informally described above is given in (96).

(95) Stem   GEN (-*is*)   NOM (-*s*)   Gloss
     līt-   *lītis*   *līs*   'strife'
     fraud-   *fraudis*   *fraus*   'deceit'
     front-   *frontis*   *frons*   'brow'
     frond-   *frondis*   *frons*   'leaf'
     dent-   *dentis*   *dens*   'tooth'
     sort-   *sortis*   *sors*   'lot'

(96) $\begin{bmatrix} - & continuant \\ + & anterior \\ + & coronal \end{bmatrix} \rightarrow \emptyset / [+ \quad sonorant] \underline{\quad\quad} s$

As an example of an insertion rule, one can take the familiar case of schwa insertion before suffixes of the form -*s* in English, illustrated in (92b).

2.6.3   Long-distance effects: Harmony rules

One area of phonology that has received much attention over the past few years is the analysis of harmony rules, the most famous (and the most common) cases being cases of vowel harmony. We have already considered an example of vowel harmony, in the discussion of Warlpiri in subsection 2.4.2; this example and an example from Finnish will be used in the current discussion. Examples of Warlpiri progressive harmony[35] from (71) above are repeated below in (97a) and (97b), with an additional example in (97c) (also from Nash 1980, p. 86).

(97) a.   *maliki +kiḷi +ḷi +lki +ji +li*
            (dog + PROP + ERG + then + me + they)

     b.   *kuḍu +kuḷu +ḷu +lku +ju +lu*
            (child + PROP + ERG + then + me + they)

     c.   *minija +kuḷu +ḷu +lku +ju +lu*
            (cat + PROP + ERG + then + me + they)

Note that Warlpiri only has three vowels—/i,u,a/—and that two phonological features—[high] and [labial]—are sufficient to distinguish them[36]:

(98) Feature   i   u   a
     High   +   +   −
     Labial   −   +   −

The specification of [labial] is actually redundant for /a/, since, given that in Warlpiri the only [−high] vowel is /a/, [−high] is sufficient to distinguish /a/ from other vowels. Therefore [−labial] is otiose as a *distinctive* feature for /a/.[37] Similar considerations lead to the argument that the specification [+high] is not necessary: given that /a/ is marked for [−high], a lack of marking for height can be taken to mean that the vowel is [+high]. Now, the affixes in (97) all have high vowels that surface as [−labial] just in case the final vowel of the stem is [−labial]; otherwise they surface as [+labial]. Let us assume, then, that the vowels of the suffixes are underlyingly unspecified for the feature [labial]; we notate this underspecified high vowel as /I/. In fact, we can assume that all /u/ in Warlpiri are actually unspecified for [+labial], and that thus all /u/ are underlyingly /I/. These considerations lead us to posit the following revised vowel system for Warlpiri, where a zero in a matrix slot means that the value is unspecified:

(99) Feature   i   I   a
     High   0   0   −
     Labial   −   0   0

Let us furthermore assume that the feature [labial] is assigned its own autosegmental tier in Warlpiri; recall the analysis of Arabic root-and-pattern morphology in subsection 2.3.4. Next we assume that there is a harmony rule that spreads the feature specification [−labial], linked to the vowel slot of syllable n, to the vowel slot of syllable $n + 1$; in this point I follow the analysis of Cole (1987, p. 124). In the case of (97a), we may assume that the [−labial] specification originates in the second syllable of the morpheme *maliki* and spreads to vowels in subsequent syllables, including the last syllable of the stem and all of the affixes. We will assume (following again the analysis of Cole) that there is a prohibition on associating any specification of the feature [labial] to a [−high] vowel in Warlpiri phonology; this is because that feature is never distinctive for [−high] vowels in Warlpiri and, following common assumptions, a *nondistinctive* feature should not be specified until the very end of a (lexical) phonological derivation in a language. Since the harmony rule only spreads [−labial] between vowel slots in *adjacent* syllables, this prohibition on linking [labial] specifications will account for the fact that /a/ blocks harmony; in (97c) the specification [−labial] does not spread across the /a/ in *minija* from the second syllable of that morpheme. The autosegmental representation of the spreading is diagrammed in figure 2.20. Finally, we need to take care of the vowel features that are not underlyingly filled or subsequently filled by harmony—including the /u/ in the suffixes in (97b) and (97c). These specifications can be handled by an ordered set of redundancy rules which apply at the end of the phonological

(a)

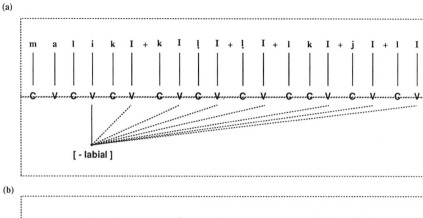

(b)

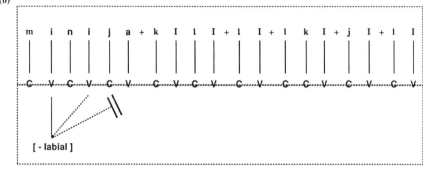

$$I = \begin{bmatrix} + \text{ high} \\ 0 \text{ labial} \end{bmatrix}$$

Figure 2.20
The autosegmental representation of feature spreading in Warlpiri vowel
harmony. The feature specification [−labial] spreads from the first [−labial]
vowel of the stem, filling in that value for subsequent vowels in the word, including
those in suffixes. If an /a/ intervenes, however, the spreading of [−labial] is
blocked for reasons discussed in the text; the blocking is notated with two solid
bars.

derivation:

(100) [0 high] → [+*high*] (/i,u/ are [+high])
 [−*high*] → [−*round*] (/a/ is [−round])
 [+*high*] → [+*round*] (/u/ is [+round])

Long-distance rules of the vowel harmony type are rather common, particularly in certain language families. Altaic languages, for example, are rich in vowel harmony systems, the best-known instance being Turkish. Finno-Ugric languages, including Finnish and Hungarian, also have vowel harmony. In Finnish the harmony system works as follows (I shall merely exemplify the system without giving an analysis). Finnish has seven vowels, represented in (101) by means of the standard Finnish orthography.

(101)
Feature	a	o	u	ä	ö	y	i	e
High	−	−	+	−	−	+	+	−
Low	+	−	−	+	−	−	−	−
Black	+	+	+	−	−	−	−	−
Round	−	+	+	−	+	+	−	−

In all words in Finnish of the form *Stem + Suffix** the vowels must be either all [+back] or all [−back], with the exception of /i,e/ (which are neutral with respect to harmony and can occur with either front or back vowels). The examples of nominative/partitive alternations given in (102) serve to illustrate this; note that the vowels on the partitive suffix -*ta*/-*tä* harmonize with the vowels of the stem.

(102)
NOM	PART	Gloss
taivas	*taivas +ta*	'sky'
puhelin	*puhelin +ta*	'telephone'
lakeus	*lakeut +ta*	'plain'
syy	*syy +tä*	'reason'
lyhyt	*lyhyt +tä*	'short'
ystävällinen	*ystävällis +tä*	'friendly'

Although the long-distance effects of vowel harmony make it appear complicated, it turns out to be rather easy to model in a computational system; indeed, one of the strong points of Koskenniemi's (1983b) treatment of Finnish is its simple model of vowel harmony. This is because vowel harmony can readily be modeled with regular expressions. For example, the well-formedness of sequences of vowels in Finnish words can be partly described using the regular expression (103), which describes harmonizing Finnish vowel sequences as consisting of either (i) a sequence of harmonizing back vowels (/a,o,u/), possibly interspersed with some harmony-neutral vowels (/i,e/), or (ii) a sequence of harmonizing front vowels (/ä,ö,y/), possibly interspersed with some harmony-neutral vowels.[38]

(103) $((a|o|u)^+ \frown (i|e)^*)^+ |((ä|ö|y)^+ \frown (i|e)^*)^+$

A similar description of Warlpiri vowel harmony could be given. We will see how Finnish vowel harmony is actually implemented in the KIMMO system in the next chapter.

Vowel harmony and related autosegmental phenomena (such as tonal phonological rules in many languages—see for example the discussion of the examples of Ngbaka tonal morphology given in (61) and figure 2.12 above) exemplify the inadequacy of the purely segmental representation discussed in subsection 2.6.2. Although it is possible to describe vowel harmony in segmental terms—e.g., by the iterative application of a segmental phonological rule applying to each vowel in turn—and although it is also possible to describe vowel harmony in a basically segmental string representation of the kind used in a computational model such as KIMMO, there is a deeper conceptual issue which such analyses miss and which the autosegmental analysis attempts to capture. What an autosegmental representation like that in figure 2.20 claims is that certain phonological features—such as the feature [−labial] in this particular case—function independently from other features in the language. While there is much debate over which features may function independently and when and how they do so, there is nonetheless a growing understanding that the conception of phonological representation as consisting of a string of segments, each of which is a self-contained bundle of features, is inadequate. It is also clear that the independence of certain features, such as [labial] in Warlpiri, is deeply rooted in speech physiology. For example (simplifying the situation somewhat), the feature [labial] is defined in terms of lip rounding (or protrusion); [+labial] sounds, as for the canonical pronunciation of /o/, tend to have lip rounding whereas [−labial] sounds such as /i/ have no lip rounding. The lips can move independently of the rest of the articulatory apparatus, and so one can easily imagine a historical source for the spread of [−labial] in Warlpiri: in words having stems ending in /i/, speakers came to keep their lips unrounded for the duration of the word, as long as no gesture involving the lips intervened. In this sense, then, the feature [labial], implemented by the lips, could be said to act independently of other features. Speech communication in general, and the representation of speech in phonology in particular, is inherently multi-channel, quite unlike the single-channel model proposed in classical segmental phonology or the string-based implementation of segmental phonology assumed in most work on computational morphology.

2.6.4 Structure in phonology I: The structure of phonological representations

We saw above how prosodic representations were relevant to the description of various types of morphology across languages. Basically, some morphology cannot be concisely described without access to concepts like **syllable, rime** (roughly speaking, the substring of the syllable starting with the **nucleus**—usually the first vowel—and ending at the right edge of the syllable), or **foot**. Of course, these phonological notions have a much more widespread function in languages than merely the description of morphology. In many languages phonology can be shown to make reference to prosodic categories of various kinds, and this is the primary justification for the idea that phonological segments are grouped into onsets and rimes, that onsets and rimes are grouped into syllables, that syllables are grouped into feet, and that feet are grouped into phonological words, as diagrammed (partially) in figure 2.3 above.

Consider for example the criterion for phonological well-formedness of words in Spanish, discussed in Harris 1983. A common question asked by phonologists is whether or not a particular string of phonemes is a **possible word** in some particular language. The textbook example of this point is the *brick/blick/bnick* trichotomy in English. *Brick* is obviously a possible word of English, since it is an actual word of the language. **Bnick*, on the other hand, could not be a word of English, since no English word can begin with the sequence /bn/. Finally, *blick* is not a word of English, but it *could be* a word of English, since many words begin with /bl/ (*blue, blind, blender, blooper,...*) and many words end with /ɪk/ (*thick, Rick, tick, chick, ...*). *Blick* is therefore said to be a possible word of English. The constraints that determine what kinds of strings can be well-formed words (morphemes) are often called **morpheme structure constraints**. English morpheme structure constraints are argued to relate to syllable structure, but the constraints found in Spanish are simpler and thus more straightforwardly demonstrate that phonology needs to make reference to aspects of syllable structure. Harris (1983, p. 9) notes that a Spanish syllable may contain as many as five segments, as in the first syllables (boldface) of the examples in (104).

(104) Example   Gloss
      claustro   'cloister'
      cliente   'client'
      crueldad   'cruelty'
      triunfo   'triumph'

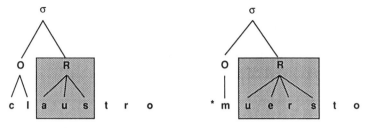

Figure 2.21
The syllable structures for the initial syllables of *claustro* 'cloister' and **muersto* in Spanish, from Harris 1983, p. 9. The impossible word **muersto* violates the constraint that rimes may contain maximally three segments. (Of course, 'O' is 'onset' and 'R' is 'rime'.)

However, not all five-segment syllables are well formed: ***muers**to is not only a nonoccurring word of Spanish, but it is judged by native speakers to be impossible as a word. The reason, Harris argues, is that the correct generalization is not that syllables in Spanish contain maximally five segments, but that rimes contain maximally three segments (and onsets maximally two). A rime in Spanish spans from the first vowel or glide in the syllable up to the end of the syllable. Therefore, while the rime in the first syllable of *claustro* is *(aus)*, in **muersto* it is **(uers)*. The different structures are diagrammed in figure 2.21. Spanish thus provides clear phonological evidence for the existence of subsyllabic constituents such as rime.

Rules of stress are obvious examples of rules that make reference to some aspects of syllable structure. As we saw above in the discussion of infixes in Ulwa, stress assignment can be sensitive to the whether the syllable ends in a vowel (V) or in a more complex sequence (VV, VC). Technically, stress in many (though not all) languages refers to the weight of the rime; often the weight is light if the rime consists of a single vowel slot, and heavy if it is longer. Apart from Ulwa, some other languages with quantity-sensitive stress systems are English, Arabic, and Latin (see Hayes 1980 for a discussion of such issues).

So, phonology—as well as morphology makes crucial reference to prosodic categories, and such categories must therefore be real entities, not merely an epiphenomenal shorthand as they were initially treated in early work on generative phonology. That prosodic categories are demonstrably fundamental to phonology and morphology accords with intuition: notions such as syllable and foot are very old, certainly predating the recent work in generative phonology by a good many centuries. A related point is the observation that whereas many cultures have apparently independently developed syllabaries (writing systems having a different symbol for each syllable), the alphabet, which is basically a segmental representation, was probably invented only once (by Semitic peoples), and all the alphabetic systems in use today are descended from the original system—see p. 77 of Sampson 1985 for a discussion, and see Ladefoged 1982, pp. 219–220, where this claim is explicitly made. So, the notion syllable is even more intuitive than the notion segment.

In contrast, as was noted above, most morphological processing systems have basically assumed a segmental representation; there have been very few active attempts to model prosodic categories. Naturally, just as one can model vowel harmony with regular expressions, and thus handle such rules in the basically segmental representation of KIMMO, one can also model prosodic structure in similar ways. For example, one can define a syllable in a language that has only the syllable types in (105a) by means of the regular expression in (105b).

(105) a. V, CV, VC, CVC

   b. $\sigma = (C)V(C)$

This is what is done in the morphological parsing system reported in Sproat and Brunson 1987, for example. While this approach allows one to refer to syllable-size units—basically by finding all the substrings in an input spanned by σ—it is important to bear in mind that it remains fundamentally lacking in one respect: it would be just as easy to describe a language in which all syllables were of the form $(V)C(V)$, yet no such language exists. Just as the independence of some phonological features (such as [labial] in Warlpiri phonology) is rooted in speech physiology, very likely so are constraints on syllable structure; for a discussion see Ladefoged 1982, chapter 10. So, while one can *describe* syllable structure as in (105b), it is important to bear in mind that this is merely a description, and that notions like syllable are much more fundamental than such an apparently accidental description suggests.

2.6.5   Structure in phonology II: Rule ordering, cyclicity, and related concepts

Let us now turn to issues relating to how generative phonologists conceive of the organization of phonological rules. One device which has been used extensively is *rule ordering*. I will exemplify this with an example from

Finnish. Finnish has a rule that deletes the segment /t/ intervocalically after a weak (unstressed) syllable, which can be written as follows (Keyser and Kiparsky 1984, p. 14):

$$(106) \ /t/\text{-deletion:} \quad \begin{matrix} C \\ | \\ t \end{matrix} \quad \rightarrow \emptyset / \sigma_\omega \underline{\quad} V$$

This applies as in (107).

(107) *naura + ten → nauraen*
      (laugh + 2INF)

Finnish has another rule which turns intervocalic /i/ into the glide /j/:

(108) Glide formation: $i \rightarrow j / V \underline{\quad} V$

In the analysis of Keyser and Kiparsky (1984), glide formation is ordered after /t/-deletion since /t/-deletion can apply so as to enable glide formation to apply (/t/-deletion *feeds* glide formation):

(109) underlying form: *talo + i + ten*
                                     (house + PL + GEN)
       after /t/-deletion: *talo + i + en*
       after glide formation: *talo + j + en*

The ordered rule analysis given above is fairly simple as such analyses go; for an example of a relatively complex analysis where rules stand in fairly intricate ordering relations, see Halle and Mohanan 1985, in particular page 100. Implicit in the analysis above, as in all work in generative phonology, is the idea that rules may look at only one level of phonological representation, namely the form of the input at the time of their application. This is one important way in which the analysis of generative phonology differs from the phonological analyses allowed in two-level morphology.

In addition to arguing that phonological rules may be ordered as described above, phonologists have proposed that some rules are cyclic. The concept of cyclicity in phonology, which dates back to early work in generative grammar—see Chomsky and Halle 1968 in particular—was expressed rather nicely in Pesetsky 1979, which was one of the seminal papers leading up to work in LPM. The idea is simply that as one builds up a word morphologically one submits the output of each instance of affixation to the phonology for the possible application of phonological rules. Thus phonology and morphology are interleaved, as diagrammed in figure 2.22.

MORPHOLOGY   PHONOLOGY

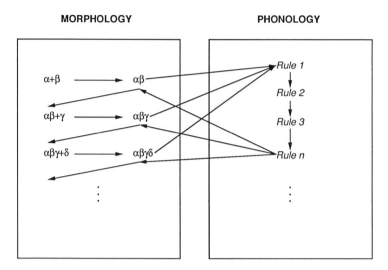

Figure 2.22
The interleaving of morphology and phonology deriving cyclicity, as discussed in Pesetsky 1979.

Consider, as an example, the behavior of third-tone sandhi (3TS) in Mandarin (Shih 1986). Mandarin has four lexical tones, numbered 1 through 4; typical examples are given here in (110).

(110) a. Tone 1 (High Level): *mā* 'mother'

b. Tone 2 (Rising): *má* 'hemp'

c. Tone 3 (Low): *mǎ* 'horse'

d. Tone 4 (Falling): *mà* 'scold'

3TS is a phonological rule in Mandarin that changes a third (low) tone into a second (rising) tone when it precedes another third (low) tone:

(111) Third-Tone Sandhi: 3 → 2/____3

For example, in the morphologically complex word *zǐ* + *cǎo* (purple + grass) 'Lithospermum erythrorrhizon', the underlying third (low) tone of the morpheme *zǐ* changes to the second (rising) tone when it precedes the low-toned morpheme *cǎo*:

(112) *zǐ* + *cǎo* → *zí* + *cǎo*

As Shih shows, 3TS applies cyclically and (word-internally) follows the morphological construction of the word. Examples are diagrammed here in figures 2.23 and 2.24. In figure 23, the morphemes *zǐ* and *cǎo* are com-

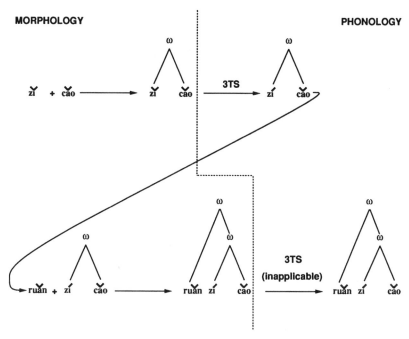

Figure 2.23
The representation of the compound *ruǎn zí + cǎo* (soft purple + grass) 'Arnebia euchroma'. 3TS applies when the inner pair of morphemes—*zí + cǎo*—are combined, and then is blocked from applying when the morpheme *ruǎn* 'soft' is added, since the environment for the rule's application (a sequence of third (low) tones is not present on that cycle.

bined, and the result then undergoes 3TS. That group then is combined with the morpheme *ruǎn* and submitted to 3TS for possible application. In this case the rule cannot apply since, although *ruǎn* has a low tone, *zí*'s underlying low tone has been changed to rising by the application of 3TS on the previous cycle. Turning now to figure 2.24, we again start by combining *mǎ* with *wěi* and applying 3TS. Then we combine it with the morpheme *zǎo*. This time, when the whole sequence is submitted to the phonological rule of 3TS, the rule can apply since there is a sequence of low tones. Mandarin 3TS is a fairly simple and straightforward example of cyclic rule application, but many others can be found in the literature.

On the view of the cycle presented here, then, cyclic rules are intimately intertwined with the process of word building.[39] A consequence of this view, to the extent that it is correct, is that one cannot do morphological

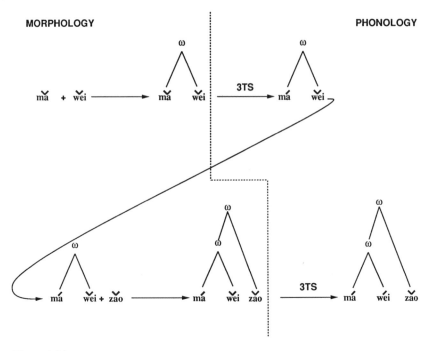

Figure 2.24
The representation of the compound *má* + *wéi záo* (horse + tail alga) 'Sargassum'.
Again, 3TS applies to the inner combination of morphemes, but this time it can still
apply when the morpheme *záo* 'alga' is combined with *má* + *wěi* because there is a
sequence of low tones on *wěi* and *záo*.

analysis by first undoing the phonology and then analyzing the underlying
phonological form into a sequence of morphemes; Anderson (1988) makes
this point. Rather, one apparently must unravel a word by undoing some
phonology, recognizing a morpheme, undoing some more phonology, and
so forth. This makes the general problem of recognizing words look rather
complex from a computational point of view. I shall discuss the computational implications of cyclicity in subsection 3.7.2.

I have already mentioned in section 2.5 one other way in which phonological rules have been claimed to be organized, and that is in the morphological and phonological strata of lexical phonology and morphology. Little work has been done in the computational literature on modeling stratal
domains of rules. However, there has been some such work (e.g. Sproat and
Brunson 1987); see subsections 3.4.4 and 3.7.2 below.

2.7 PSYCHOLINGUISTIC EVIDENCE

In this section I shall examine briefly some of the psycholinguistic evidence for speakers' knowledge about word structure. Specifically, I shall examine the following questions:

• Do humans actually represent morphological structure in their mental lexicons?
• How does lexical retrieval work: how are (monomorphemic) words "looked up" by humans?
• Do humans use their morphological knowledge actively during language use? Or is that knowledge "precompiled" so that the mental lexicon is effectively a list of all words, morphologically simple or complex?

In examining whether humans actively use morphological knowledge during language use, I shall be almost exclusively concerned with the evidence from language comprehension. So the question will revolve around whether hearers *parse* word structure while listening to or reading sentences of their language, as opposed to whether they combine morphemes into words while speaking or writing sentences of their language. (On the latter point I shall only have a few things to say, and I shall address the issue in the first subsection, which is concerned with speakers' knowledge of morphological structure.)

As I have tried to do throughout this chapter, I shall endeavor here to relate the observations concerning human language processing to computational models of morphological processing. A couple of questions can be asked of such models. First, is the model of lexical retrieval used in the system a good model of what humans do? Second, all computational models of any interest involve greater or lesser amounts of morphological decomposition (parsing); are the algorithms and representations employed reasonable models of the way humans do things? Two caveats apply here: First, for many computational systems, the creators of the system never made any claim to psychological reality; rather, they were primarily concerned with building a model capable of handling the facts in as simple and general a manner as possible. It *is* fair to criticize such a system if it fails to capture many linguistically relevant issues, such as some of those discussed in previous sections of this chapter, since such failure means that there are morphological phenomena that cannot be adequately handled by the system. It is *not* fair, however, to argue that the system does not function in the same manner as a human, and this brings up the second caveat: There is absolutely no guarantee that the way in which humans process language is the most *efficient* way to do it, though, to be sure, human language processing is far more *robust* than anything we can currently build. Nonetheless, and with these caveats in mind, there have been a few claims (see, e.g., Koskenniemi 1983b, pp. 141–152, or Karttunen 1983, p. 167) that certain models of morphological processing have some claim to psychological reality; to the extent that those claims have been made, it is fair to compare computational models and human performance.[40]

2.7.1 Knowledge about word structure

Speakers are aware of the morphological structure of their language. There are a number of kinds of evidence for this; two of them will be examined here.

The first kind of evidence comes from the obvious fact that speakers are able to coin, as well as comprehend, new words which are formed in accordance with the morphological rules of the language. Take for an example the word *giraffishness*. The word is perfectly regularly formed according to the rules of English morphology; in particular, the suffix -*ish* makes adjectives out of nouns and -*ness* makes nouns out of adjectives. Yet it is (or at least was) completely novel. This, of course, is somewhat anecdotal, but there have been many scientific studies of speakers' abilities to coin new words; perhaps the most famous of these is the study of Berko (1958), in which preschool and first grade children were presented with pictures of imaginary objects and animals and given nonsense words (which nonetheless obeyed the phonotactic constraints of English), such as *wug*, as names for those objects. They were then presented with pictures showing multiples of the imaginary objects and asked what they saw. When presented with a picture of two wugs, the children responded correctly—in 91% of the cases—with the correct form *wugs*. (The technique developed by Berko has come to be known as a wug test.) By investigations of this kind, Berko showed that even quite young children have some knowledge of the morphological structure of words and can coin new forms on the basis of that knowledge.

A second kind of evidence that speakers are aware of the morphological structure of their language involves evidence from various kinds of aphasia. Aphasias frequently have interesting (though unfortunate) effects on the production and comprehension of various kinds of linguistic structures. I will briefly discuss an example involving a speaker of the Bantu language Ndebele, reported by Traill (1970). Ndebele, like other Bantu languages, has an elaborate system of noun class prefixes; see also (22) in subsection 2.2.1 for an example from Swahili. Traill's subject was described as suffering from "severe expressive aphasia"—in this case (probably simplifying somewhat) a type of agrammatism or Broca's aphasia—caused by a wound to the left side of the head. One morphological deficit which the subject demonstrated was the inability to consistently pick the appropriate prefix for a noun. Occasionally he would even omit the prefix despite the fact that for a noun form to be grammatical in Ndebele it must be marked with a class prefix. For example, Traill (1970, p. 55) notes cases like those in (113), where the subject's utterance (as a single-word response to a question) is given in the first column and the correct form is given in the third column. (In addition to the errors cited here, Traill gave several examples where the utterance was correct; I have omitted these here.)

(113) Utterance   Gloss   Correct Form
     i +*gwatsha*   'rabbit'   **uno** +*gwatsha*
     i +*zulu*   'Zulu'   **isi** +*zulu*
     um +*gwatsha*   'rabbit'   **uno** +*gwatsha*
     ntwana   'child'   **um** +*ntwana*
     komo   'cow'   **in** +*komo*
     gwatsha   'rabbit'   **uno** +*gwatsha*

In the first three forms the stem is combined with a prefix from a different noun class. In the last three forms the stem was produced without a noun class marker at all. Although, as Traill notes, the data are complicated and admit of various interpretations, it seems at least fair to characterize the situation as follows: Before suffering the injury, the subject had represented in his mental lexicon the morphological structure of Ndebele nouns, even for common nouns like *umntwana* 'child'. As a result of the injury, there was an impairment of the mechanism by which the appropriate prefix (or indeed any prefix at all) was combined with the stem, resulting in the errors cited in (113). If this story is correct, we have evidence that speakers are aware of the morphological structure of words, even if the words are very familiar.[41]

2.7.2 Lexical access

Any natural language system, even one that doesn't incorporate a model of morphological analysis, must at least contain a lexicon; there must be some database of the words (or morphemes) of the language, and there must be some means for accessing that database. Similarly, for psycholinguistic models of human language performance, no matter how one interprets the evidence for morphological parsing by humans, one must at least assume that humans have a database of words (or morphemes) and some means to achieve **lexical access** to that database. So, ignoring for now the question of how humans treat morphologically complex words, how are words (or morphemes) looked up in the mental lexicon? Various theories of lexical access have been proposed:

One view is the model of Forster (1976), the basic idea of which is that a stimulus word is accessed by using (some part of) its initial sequence as a key to a bin containing similar words: for written input, for example, the word would be accessed by means of its initial letter sequence. This bin is then searched for an entry similar to the desired word; if a sufficiently similar entry is found, a pointer is followed to a central lexicon, where the entire lexical entry for the word is found. Computationally, this view is most similar to a hash-table representation of the lexical database, with the hash codes generated on the basis of the first few letters; once the relevant bin had been found, that part of the hash table would be searched (linearly?) for the appropriate pointer into the main lexicon. Although hash tables are certainly a computationally efficient way to store lexicons, there is some question as to whether they are the correct model for human word retrieval. At the very least, there are some empirical problems with the particular proposal of Forster (1976), at least on its simplest interpretation. Jarvella et al. (1987) note that Forster's model predicts that the first few letters of the word will cause readers to begin to access the mental lexicon; this prediction appears to be wrong, since it can be shown that presenting the initial portion of a word to subjects slightly ahead of the presentation of the whole word fails to have any effect on their reaction time for the word.[42]

Another well-known model is the cohort model of Marslen-Wilson (1980), which was developed primarily with spoken input in mind. According to the cohort model, at any point during the presentation of a word, the hearer keeps in a "cohort" all words that are consistent with the stimulus heard from the beginning of the word up to the point in question. As the hearer is exposed to more of the word, fewer and fewer words are consistent with the presented stimulus and thus more and more words are dropped from the cohort. Recognition is achieved when there is but one word left in the cohort. The cohort model is similar to the *letter tree* (*discrimination network*, or **trie**) discussed by Knuth (1973) and used quite commonly in morphological analyzers, such KIMMO. I will describe letter trees more fully in the next chapter. For now I merely note that they are another computationally efficient way to store and retrieve words, and that they share with the cohort model the property that as the search algorithm progresses down the word it is simultaneously narrowing the search until eventually a single lexical entry remains. The problem with this type of model is that it would appear—again, on the simplest interpretation—to predict that certain nonwords could be rejected in much less time quickly than it takes to respond affirmatively to real words. With the possible exception of some obscure proper names, no English word starts with the letter sequence ⟨stosh⟩ (or the initial sequence of segments /stɔʃ/). Therefore it ought to be possible, under a letter-tree-type theory, to reject a nonword such as *stoshlobel* on the basis of the initial sequence alone; since that sequence doesn't exist as the initial portion of any word in the lexicon, the search algorithm will not find ⟨stosh⟩ and the search should fail at that point. But, as Forster (1976) suggests (see also Hoeksema 1984, pp. 8–9), nonwords typically take longer to reject than words take to accept, and this suggests that letter-tree-type models cannot, in and of themselves, explain human performance. Also, Katz et al. (1987, p. 246) were unable to confirm the predictions of the cohort model.

The basic mechanisms of the above models do not directly capture what is probably the most unequivocal fact about human lexical retrieval, namely the frequency effect (Bradley 1978); furthermore, *no* computational model of morphology of which I am aware explicitly attempts to model this effect. It is now quite well established that there is a negative correlation between a word's frequency, as measured over a sufficiently large and representative corpus, and the time it takes speakers to react to that word in a lexical decision task. Words that are infrequent take significantly longer to recognize than words that are frequent. This suggests that no matter how the mental lexicon is organized, it must at least have the characteristic that the frequent words are near the "front," where they are easier to get at, and the infrequent words are near the "back."[43] In one sense this is a sensible strategy, and one which is expected: humans organize their mental lexicons in such a way that the words they use or expect to hear the most are easiest to get to and the ones which are used the least are the hardest to get to. Still, it is not clear that this is necessarily the best way to design a computational model, except under the assumption of limited memory resources. If resources are limited, then one might put the most frequent words in a cache and a group of less frequent words in a disk file to be opened when needed; if the local disk becomes full, one could have the least frequent words on a disk file on some other machine. Clearly such a situation would model the frequency effect, at least to some extent. On the other hand, if resources are plentiful, then there is no reason not to put the entire dictionary into a structure, such as a hash table, where they will be equally available; the retrieval of common words would not be impaired, and the retrieval of less frequent words would be improved. Suffice it to say that neural hardware doesn't work this way: people respond more quickly to things that are more frequent (hence more familiar) than they do to things that are less frequent.

2.7.3 Morphologically complex words: Do people parse?

We now turn to the question of most burning relevance to a discussion of morphological processing. Do people parse words? Is there any evidence that, in listening or in reading, speakers actively make use of their morphological knowledge in accessing morphologically complex words?

To be sure, there have been proposals in the literature—(Butterworth 1983, for example)—to the effect that morphologically complex words are not parsed by humans. Under that view, *all* words, morphologically complex or otherwise, are listed in the lexicon, and morphologically complex words are accessed in the same way as monomorphemic words—i.e., by whichever mechanism of lexical access turns out to be correct. To many linguists there is something distinctly unpalatable about that conclusion. Since humans do have knowledge about the morphological structure of their language, it seems odd that they wouldn't make use of that knowledge in parsing words, just as they obviously must make use of their knowledge of sentence structure in parsing sentences. The stock response to that argument, of course, is that the set of words, unlike the set of sentences, is finite. There are two problems with this answer. First of all, even if the set of words is not infinite it is surely very large; this is especially clear in a language such as Central Alaskan Yupik, where entire clauses can be single words. It seems highly improbable that such words are all merely listed in the lexicon; indeed, as I argue in subsection 2.7.4, it seems unlikely that humans can simply store vocabularies with tens or hundreds of thousands of entries. Second, it is not even clear that the set of words *is* finite; in English, for example, compounds are theoretically unbounded in size. Unfortunately, there is no evidence on human processing of languages in which significant parts of the clause may appear within a single word, nor does much evidence exist for languages (such as Turkish) in which a word may merely be very long in terms of the number of affixes concatenated.[44] Fortunately, however, there is sufficient evidence from English and a few other languages to reject the unpalatable assumption. Humans do make use of morphological knowledge in language comprehension and may thus be said to parse words—provided that the notion of parsing words is not interpreted in a simplistic way.

The classic paper which argues that people do morphological decomposition is Taft and Forster 1975. In one of the experiments reported in that paper, subjects were presented with two types of English nonwords. The first type was a real stem produced by stripping off a prefix, an example being *juvenate* from *rejuvenate*. The second was a pseudostem derived by removing a comparable string of letters from the beginning of a word, where that string of letters did not function as a prefix—i.e., it was a pseudoprefix; an example of a pseudostem from Taft and Forster's experiment is ⟨*pertoire⟩, derived by removing the letter sequence ⟨re⟩ from ⟨repertoire⟩. In a reaction-time experiment Taft and Forster found that subjects took significantly longer to classify *juvenate* as a nonword than to do the same with *pertoire*. They explain these results with a model whereby subjects attempt to access a word by first removing an element that looks like a prefix and then looking up the remaining stem; this implies that real stems, such as *juvenate*, will be in the lexicon, but since that stem cannot occur separately as a word it is marked for the affixes with which it combines. Pseudostems, obviously, are not listed at all in the lexicon. The nonword *juvenate* therefore took longer to classify as a nonword, Taft and Forster claim, because subjects found the stem *juvenate* in the lexicon and then searched for a prefix to attach it to. This extra search meant that the rejection of *juvenate* as a nonword took longer than the rejection of *pertoire*, which, being absent from the lexicon, could be rejected fairly quickly. One caveat concerning this work is that, as Emmorey (1988) notes, attempts to replicate Taft and Forster's results have not generally been successful.

Caramazza et al. (1988) report experiments for Italian which further suggest that subjects attempt to morphologically decompose nonwords and, more generally, novel (well-formed) words. In the 1988 paper, Caramazza et al. provide arguments for the *augmented addressed morphology* model (Caramazza et al. 1985), the basic claim of which is that morphologically complex words known to the hearer (or reader), such as *walked* for most English speakers, will activate both the full form of the word (*walked*)[45] and the component morphemes (*walk* and *-ed*). These two sets of morphemes are activated in parallel; however, since *walked* has been previously encountered, lexical access is achieved via that entry rather than via the activation of the component morphemes. On the other hand, if *walked* had not been previously seen or heard by the subject, there would be no activation for the full form, and the form would be accessed via the component morphemes—i.e, via lexical decomposition. This model thus stands in opposition both to models where all forms are listed in the lexicon and to models, such as that of Taft and Forster (1975) which argue that all morphologically complex words must be accessed via lexical decomposition. In one of the experiments testing their model, Caramazza et al. compared reaction times for the rejection of quadruples of Italian nonwords:

(114) a. *cantevi*, where the verb stem *cant-* 'sing' is combined with the legal second-person singular imperfect affix *-evi*. This form is a nonword because *cant-* is a first-conjugation verb, whereas the affix is appropriate for the second conjugation (the correct form is *cantavi*).

   b. *cantovi*, where the verb stem *cant-* is combined with the nonaffix *-ovi*

   c. *canzevi*, where the nonexistent verb stem *canz-* is combined with the real affix *-evi*

   d. *canzovi*, where the word cannot be broken down into any real morphemes

According to the predictions of the augmented addressed morphology model, subjects ought to take the longest to reject **cantevi* in (114a), because both *cant-* and *-evi* are real morphemes and the subject has to ascertain that they are illegally combined. In contrast, the form **canzovi* does not activate any real word (at least not sufficiently), and it certainly does not activate any component morphemes since there are none. Therefore that form can be rejected most rapidly. The cases **cantovi* and **canzevi* are predicted to be intermediate in rapidity of rejection since the component morphemes *cant-* and *-evi*, respectively, are activated, and the subject must therefore ascertain that the complementary piece of the stimulus nonword is in fact not a morpheme. Although Caramazza et al. note that the results are not in perfect agreement with the predictions of the model, it is very clear that subjects do indeed take longer to reject **cantevi*, which strongly supports the theory that they are attempting to access this unknown word via lexical decomposition.

Now, various pieces of psycholinguistic work have suggested that morphologically complex words are listed in the mental lexicon along with the stems from which they are derived (or, if not the stem, some canonical surface form). To put it another way, the mental lexicon is organized into stems (or some canonical form) which have pointers to the various affixes which, when combined with the stems in question, produce related surface forms. Caramazza et al. (1988) make this claim, as do Bradley (1980) and Segui and Zubizarreta (1985). In this context I will discuss a very interesting piece of work done on Serbo-Croatian (Lukatela et al. 1980) which reports on experiments using visually presented materials; a follow-up experiment reported by Katz et al. (1987) replicates the results of the previous experiment using speech stimuli. Serbo-Croatian has a rich nominal inflection system, including six cases and two numbers, making for twelve slots in the paradigm (though, due to syncretism, not all entries are formally distinct). In addition there are three grammatical genders. Serbo-Croatian nominal declensions are exemplified in the following table by the masculine noun *dinar* (115a) 'money' and the feminine noun *žena* 'woman' (115b):[46]

(115) a.

Case	SG	PL
NOM	*dinar*	*dinari*
GEN	*dinara*	*dinara*
DAT	*dinaru*	*dinarima*
ACC	*dinar*	*dinare*
VOC	*dinare*	*dinari*
INST	*dinarom*	*dinarima*

b.

Case	SG	PL
NOM	*žena*	*žene*
GEN	*žene*	*žena*
DAT	*ženi*	*ženama*
ACC	*ženu*	*žene*
VOC	*ženo*	*žene*
INST	*ženom*	*ženama*

Lukatela et al. argue for what they call a *satellite entries* model, whereby nouns are grouped in the mental lexicon around the nominative singular form, which functions as the nucleus of the cluster, and the other cases and numbers are arranged as satellites around the nominative form. This configuration is represented in figure 2.25. In the experiment Lukatela et al. compared subjects' reaction times in a lexical decision task on the nominative singular, genitive singular, and instrumental singular forms of nouns. The results were that subjects recognized the nominative form significantly faster than either the genitive or the instrumental form, but there was no significant difference in the reaction times for the genitive or the instrumental. These results held for nouns of both genders. This, Lukatela et al. argue, supports the satellite-entries hypothesis: nouns are accessed via

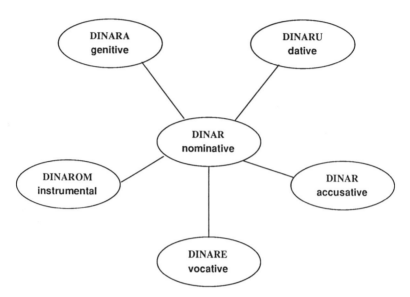

Figure 2.25
The satellite entries model of Lukatela et al. (1980). Represented here are the
singular case forms of the masculine noun *dinar* 'money'. These are clustered
around the nominative-case form.

their nominative singular form, and there is an extra step of computation
to retrieve any of the other case forms in the cluster.

Lukatela et al. contrast the satellite-entries hypothesis with two other
views of the organization of the mental lexicon. One view is that all words,
morphologically complex or otherwise, are simply listed in separate entries, one for each surface form. They argue against that view, based on
observations about the frequency of the various surface forms. On the
separate-entries view, the various forms of the noun ought to be accessed
via their surface form, so that *dinar* (the nominative/accusative suppletive
form) would have a separate entry from *dinara* (the genitive form). Now, for
feminine nouns the genitive *form* (*žene*) is also used in the nominative and
accusative plural; this means that, while the genitive itself is lower in frequency of occurrence than the nominative form, the actual surface form
žene has a higher frequency of occurrence than the surface form *žena*.
So, given the frequency effect, which is shown to be operative in Serbo-
Croatian as in English,[47] one would expect access to the genitive form of
feminine nouns to actually be faster than access to the nominative form.
Yet, as we have seen, this is not the case. Second, Lukatela et al. argue

against various variants of what one might call the naive decompositional view. That view, which is rather of the form of the Taft-Forster model, suggests that, as part of lexical access, one attempts morphological decomposition into stems and affixes. On that view, one would expect the feminine nominative form to take as long to access as the other forms of the feminine. This is because, while on the one hand the nominative form of the masculine appears to be just the stem of the word (e.g. *dinar*), the nominative form of the feminine has an affix (*-a*) just like the other case forms of the feminine. If one were to assume that one affix-stripping operation is as costly as any other, one would then expect no difference with feminine nouns between the access time for the nominative and that for some other case form, such as the genitive. Again, this prediction is not borne out.

But while the work presented in Lukatela et al. 1980 clearly argues against the naive view of morphological decomposition, it does not argue against all conceivable views of how morphological decomposition might operate as part of lexical access. In particular, one should not conclude from this that a satellite-entries view, or some related view, is merely a more sophisticated model where everything is listed in the lexicon—albeit in morphologically related clusters—and that this is therefore entirely inconsistent with a decompositional approach, or any computational model of the same. In fact, one could argue that any sensible computational model of morphology would encode aspects of these psychological models. For example, computational models typically list (explicitly or implicitly), as part of the lexical entry for a stem, the classes of affixes that can occur with that stem; these are referred to as *continuation patterns* in the KIMMO model. Some model of this kind is necessary; one needs to know what sorts of morphemes can be expected to be found after the morpheme which one has already accessed. But this in turn means that one is storing morphologically complex forms with the stems with which they occur, albeit *virtually*. Furthermore, suppose that one is willing to allow that the masculine nominative singular form in Serbo-Croatian is really marked with a null suffix; this is actually one of the possibilities discussed by Lukatela et al. Then one can quite readily model the results of the experiment described above by simply abandoning the assumption of the naive decomposition view that every operation of decomposing is equally expensive: specifically, one can weight the arcs leading from the noun stems to the other case forms so that the traversal between the noun stem and the nominative form is less costly than the traversal between the noun stem and the other case forms. Such a setup is sketched in figure 2.26. This seems ad hoc from a computational point of view, but my point is merely to show that one *can* model the

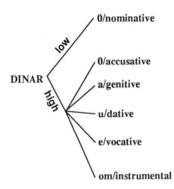

Figure 2.26
How one might implement the results of Lukatela et al. 1980 in a model of
morphological decomposition. The arc to the nominative form is of low traversal
cost, whereas the arc to the other forms is of high traversal cost.

results of Lukatela et al. 1980 within a model of morphological parsing.
Presumably the reason that the nominative form is easier for humans to
access is that it is really considered by speakers of Serbo-Croatian to be the
basic form of the word: in the majority of pedagogical grammars of Indo-
European languages, the nominative is the form under which nouns are
listed. Of course, this observation may help explain the results of Lukatela
et al.: since the nouns were presented in isolation, subjects would be more
prone to recognize nominative forms. Had the nouns been presented in a
sentential context where the genitive case form would be more appropriate, it seems entirely possible that subjects' reaction times would be smaller
for genitive forms than for other case forms. Thus, the results of Luketala et
al. may have been biased by the fact that, in the "null context" in which
they presented the test words, nominative case was somehow more natural;
this in turn suggests that there may be nothing special about the nominative other than being the default case form. In any event, it seems as if the
satellite-entries model and others like it are actually to a large extent in
accord with a more sophisticated notion of how a (psychologically realistic) morphological parsing system might be built, and to some extent in
accord with how such systems already are built.

Thus, there appears to be evidence that people do parse morphological
structure, and there is even some evidence, though this is not generally
agreed upon, that people morphologically decompose words which they
have already heard. It is hard, at this stage, to be more conclusive than I
have been. The psycholinguistics community seems by no means to be

wholly agreed upon the issues discussed here, and I have no doubt that some researchers will disagree strongly with some of the conclusions I have reached. On the other hand, I believe it is fair to say that we will not have arrived at more conclusive evidence on how people parse morphological structure until careful experiments have been performed on language types, such as Eskimo, where significantly more of the grammar is done "in the morphology" than is the case in English, and where, as argued above, it seems implausible to assume that all words are merely listed.

2.7.4 Some final thoughts: Why morphological structure is relevant

But let us temporarily put aside the evidence that we have just considered and ask if there is not a more basic reason why people *must* make active use of morphological structure in language comprehension. For the sake of argument, let us make the assumption that the set of words interpretable to a speaker of English is finite. Since the set is finite, why would one assume that people engage in any decomposition process whatsoever; more generally, why should people make use of morphological structure in any way whatsoever? Isn't human long-term memory effectively infinite? Certainly, storage of a million word forms is not much of a problem for computers these days, and a million word forms will cover a very high percentage of the words one is likely to encounter, whether monomorphemic or otherwise. And while one would still need a morphological decomposition routine for the cases where one encounters an unknown word, a fair amount of text processing *could* be done with table lookup. Since humans have effectively infinite long-term memories, one might assume that they too could store a million separate entries, reserving morphological decomposition and knowledge about morphological structure for those rare cases where a new word is encountered (assuming, of course, that the component morphemes are known).

There are considerations quite apart from morphology which suggest that humans are able to handle the task of handling thousands of items only when there is some inherent structure in those items which they can make use of. As an example consider the case of Chinese characters. An educated reader of Chinese can reasonably be expected to know about 6,000 to 7,000 characters, and this is certainly enough to be able to recognize all the characters in nearly all texts.[48] There are two things to note. First, this number is far smaller than the number of words which people appear to know.[49] Second, there is no question that the set of known Chinese characters is finite. The largest dictionaries of Chinese contain about 40,000 characters, but the majority of these are very rare or obsolete forms. Between 6,000 and 7,000 is as many as a reader of Chinese would ever be likely to need.

Yet despite the fact that the inventory of Chinese characters is relatively small compared with the number of words people know, there is good evidence that Chinese readers do not memorize 6,000 or 7,000 arbitrary shapes. Rather, Chinese readers are aware of the structure of characters— the "grammar" of characters, in fact (Fujimura and Kagaya 1969; Wang 1983)—and are able to put this grammar to use in judging possible (though nonexistent) characters. Thus, any reader of Chinese is capable of judging as a possible character the following example from McCawley's introduction to Quang 1970

because it is made up of a known character,

('turtle', Mandarin *guī*), which is composed according to one of the legal schemes for combining characters into other characters.

It seems (if I am permitted to end on a somewhat philosophical note) that people are bound to try to find structure wherever they are faced with the task of handling thousands of items, even if it is only a few thousand. It should be expected, then, that there would be evidence that morphological structure is both known to and made use of by speakers and hearers.

2.8 FINAL NOTE

In this chapter I have introduced a variety of issues relating to morphology. I have tried, wherever possible, to make appropriate cataphoric references to the material on computational morphology in the next section, so as to make the bond between descriptive, theoretical, and psycholinguistic morphology on the one hand and computational morphology on the other as tight as possible.

One of the points which I hope will have been clear from the discussion in this chapter is that morphology is a complex field, and one cannot

understand it fully without an appreciation of phonology, syntax, semantics, and psycholinguistics. Morphology is truly a crossroads of linguistics
(Bauer 1983, p. 6); it is not really a field unto itself, because to understand
word structure one has to understand many things that touch on areas
outside morphology. This is an important point to bear in mind, because
there is a tendency in some quarters of the computational morphology
world to trivialize the problem, suggesting that the problems of morphology have essentially been solved simply because there are now working
systems that are capable of doing a great deal of morphological analysis.
One should not be misled by such claims. It is perfectly true that there are
now useful working systems that have good coverage of many areas. But
there are still outstanding problems and areas which have not received
much serious attention, as I shall show.

2.9   FURTHER READING

Matthews 1974, Bauer 1983, and Scalise 1986 are basic overviews of morphology; Bauer's book is particularly lucid. Nida 1949 covers a lot of
ground and contains many examples, though the analyses show their age.
Marchand 1969 remains the best description of English morphology. Bybee
1985 contains an interesting discussion of some morphological implicational universals and related issues. Mohanan 1986 is the most comprehensive work outlining the assumptions of the theory of lexical phonology and
morphology. Marantz 1984 and Baker 1988 are good (but highly technical)
discussions of the relationship between syntax and morphology.

Standard textbooks of phonology include Schane 1973, Schane and
Bendixen 1978, and Kenstowicz and Kisseberth 1979, all of which are
out of date with respect to theory. A discussion of relatively recent work
on metrical phonology is to be found in Hogg and McCully 1987. Goldsmith 1989 covers recent developments in metrical and autosegmental
phonology.

Chapter 3
Computational Morphology

3.1 INTRODUCTION

In this chapter I turn to a discussion of computational morphological systems and how they work. I note at the outset that I have not tried to discuss everything that has ever been done on computational morphology. Rather, I have undertaken to describe the basic mechanisms which have generally been used in building computational models of morphology, and I have organized my discussion of various pieces of computational work around those mechanisms. I shall discuss here and there some work which I am familiar with that makes use of mechanisms somewhat different from the norm,[1] but there are many pieces of work which I have not discussed. Pointers to some of the literature which I have not treated can be found in the bibliography.

Since the discussion in this chapter is organized around mechanisms rather than systems, this will not be a historical overview. The first system I shall discuss in any detail, KIMMO, was designed about 20 years after the famous DECOMP system of the MITalk project. However, KIMMO is a good starting point for any discussion of computational morphology for two reasons. First, the computational mechanisms that it uses for handling morphotactics are fairly standard fare in the literature. Second, there is no question that KIMMO has been by far the most successful model of computational morphology, a point to which I will return. But I wish to stress at the outset that I am not presenting a teleological view in which KIMMO is the ultimate culmination of work on computational morphology, nor am I presenting the view that other systems which do not share all the assumptions of that model are inferior clones of KIMMO. Again, for various reasons, the KIMMO model merely serves as a convenient jumping-off point for much other work on computational morphology.

The chapter is therefore organized as follows. In section 3.2 I shall discuss the basic mechanisms for handling morphotactics and phonological rules assumed in what I shall henceforth term URKIMMO—work on so-called two-level morphology by Koskenniemi (1983b) (and its contemporaneous adaptation by Karttunen [1983] and others).[2] In section 3.3 I illustrate how the mechanisms just described were actually put to use in describing some aspects of Finnish phonology and morphology in Koskenniemi's original work, and I outline the linguistic strengths and weaknesses of the approach. In section 3.4 I discuss various adaptations, more or less within the general framework of two-level morphology of the methods used in URKIMMO, especially those adaptations which were specifically designed to overcome linguistic deficits in the original system. In section 3.5 I discuss the computational complexity of the mechanisms used in URKIMMO. In section 3.6 I give an overview of various systems that deviate to greater or lesser extents from the assumptions of two-level morphology, including some historically important work.

Recall from chapter 2 that most work on computational morphology has assumed orthographic input, rather than phonemic input. For the most part this distinction will not be germane to the issues at hand in this chapter. I shall also continue to refer to phonology, unless it is patently clear that the term spelling rules is more appropriate.

3.2 COMPUTATIONAL MECHANISMS

3.2.1 Finite-state morphotactics

Modeling the morphotactics itself   Let us, for the time being, make the false assumption (see section 2.3) that concatenation is the only way in which morphemes may be combined to form words. How would one go about building a model of the morphotactics of a language? That is, how would one build a model that allows all and only the possible morpheme combinations of a language?

Clearly the simplest way to build such a model would be to assume that the allowability of a particular morpheme in a given context depends only upon the morpheme that precedes it. Take a word like *hospitalization*, whose morphological structure is *hospital + ize + ation*. The second morpheme, *-ize*, takes nouns or adjectives and makes verbs. Since we know that *hospital* is a noun, we know that *-ize* can follow it, and therefore that the combination of morphemes *hospital + ize* is acceptable. Looking now to the right, we find the affix -*ation*; this affix forms derived nominals (subsection 2.2.2), taking verbs as input and outputting nouns. Furthermore, it happens to be true that verbs ending in -*ize* invariably take the nominalizing suffix -*ation*:

(1) *nominalization, motorization, skolemization, demilitarization, categorization,* ...

Thus the combination of morphemes *ize* +*ation* is acceptable. So, in order to determine that the placement of -*ize* and -*ation* within *hospitalization* is acceptable, one has only to look at the preceding morpheme.

One can easily model such a system with a **finite-state machine** (**finite-state automaton** or **finite-state transition network**) of the kind familiar from formal language theory (Hopcroft and Ullman 1979; Lewis and Papadimitriou 1981; Harrison 1978). In particular, for some fragment of the morphology of a language L, we can define a machine M as follows (see the definition of a finite-state automaton in Hopcroft and Ullman 1979, p. 17):

(2) $M = (Q, \Sigma, \delta, q_1, F)$, where

- Q is the set of states q of M
- Σ is the finite alphabet of morphemes σ of L
- δ is the transition function from $Q \times \Sigma$ to Q, such that for each $q_i \in Q$ and $\sigma \in \Sigma$ there is a $q_j \in Q$ such that $\delta(q_i, \sigma) = q_j$, where q_j is nonfinal sink state unless morpheme σ is licit at state q_i
- q_1 is the unique initial state of M
- F is the set of final states of M

Figure 3.1 shows a finite-state machine (FSM) that describes a very small fragment of English morphotactics, including the example *hospitalization*. (Note that, as is conventional, transitions to the sink state are not shown.) Imagine, now that we are trying to determine whether *hospitalization* is allowed by the machine in figure 3.1. We will start with the assumption that somehow we know that *hospitalization* is morphologically composed of three morphemes as follows: *hospital* +*ize* +*ation*. (I shall return momentarily to how one would ascertain that, given that the word is written as a string without any information on morpheme boundaries.) So we start with the string of morphemes *hospital* +*ize* +*ation* and with our machine in state 1, the initial state. Because we are in state 1, and our first morpheme is *hospital*, a consultation of our transition function δ gives the value of $\delta(1, hospital)$ as 2. So, we move into that state. Note that we could stop at this point: 2 is a final state, and if *hospital* were the only morpheme of the input we would accept the input as well formed. Next comes the

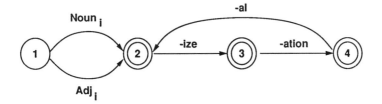

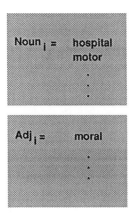

Figure 3.1
An FSM for a fragment of English morphology. Arc labels refer to sets of words
(e.g., *Adj~j~*, consisting of those adjectives that may take the suffix *-ize*) or particular
morphemes (e.g. *-ize*).

The notation for FSMs follows the usage in Hopcroft and Ullman 1979, except
that I shall number the unique initial state of the machine as 1 (Hopcroft and
Ullman use 0). Final states are notated with double circles and nonfinal states with
single circles. Transitions to the sink state are not explicitly shown.

morpheme *-ize*. In this case $\delta(2, \text{-}ize) = 3$ and we therefore proceed to the
latter state. We repeat the procedure in a similar manner for the morpheme
-ation and arrive in state 4, which happily is a final state.

This simple type of model, though demonstrably inadequate to cleanly
handle long-distance dependencies (as we discussed in subsection 2.5.2,
and as we shall discuss further in the context of our discussion of
URKIMMO), is nonetheless sufficiently powerful to handle a fair portion
of concatenative morphology; basically, any morphological system in
which the allowability of a morpheme in position n depends only upon the
morpheme that occurred in position $n - 1$ can easily be so treated.[3]

Modeling lexical retrieval   Let us now return to the issue of how one actually figures out which morphemes make up a string, returning to our example *hospitalization* and continuing to ignore the spelling (or phonological) changes which some of the morphemes—e.g., *-ize*—have undergone. Clearly, if one were informed in the input the morpheme boundaries were, the most straightforward method would be to look up the individual morphemes in some kind of constant-time accessible data structure (such as a hash table) and then check whether the morphemes in question were correctly combined according to the methods described above. However, one is not generally told where the morpheme boundaries lie in the input, and it is therefore much more efficient to use a scheme whereby the morphotactics is folded in with the lexical access. One model of lexical access that is readily adapted to such methods is the letter tree—also called the discrimination network or the **trie**—discussed by Knuth (1973, pp. 481–489).[4] We encountered the letter tree briefly in the discussion of psychological models of lexical retrieval in subsection 2.7.2, where it was noted that such models seem unlikely to be correct as models of human lexical access.

A dictionary is encoded in a letter tree as follows. For each morpheme μ, start by setting the current tree τ to the root node of the letter tree T. Search the daughter nodes of T for the unique node T_{μ_0}, which is labeled with the initial segment of μ, μ_0; if no such node exists, create it. Set τ to T_{μ_0}. Now search the daughter nodes of τ for T_{μ_1}, creating such a node if one does not already exist. Proceed with this algorithm until you have reached the last segment of μ, μ_n. Label the current node as a lexical entry; one would normally mark grammatical information about the morpheme at this point. One looks up a morpheme in the letter tree by an essentially similar method, starting at the top of the tree, and walking down the tree, and searching at each node for a daughter node with the next segment of the input morpheme. Lexical access is successful if and only if one runs out of segments in the morpheme and simultaneously lands on a node that is marked as an entry. Figure 3.2 is a letter tree containing the words *cat*, *catch*, *frito*, *new*, *newt*, *net*, *string*, and *strong*.

In order to make a letter-tree encoding adequate for morphological decomposition, we need to do just one more thing, and that is to encode at the lexical entry of each morpheme μ information about the classes of morphemes that can follow μ. Consider, for example, our minilexicon of English in figure 3.2. Say we want to encode the fact that the plural morpheme -s can attach to any of the nouns *cat*, *frito*, *newt*, *net*, and *string*. What we can do is set up another dictionary—call it *NounSuffixes*—which

Input:
```
  1 2 3 4
  n e w t
```

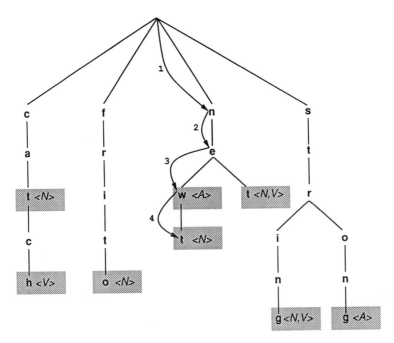

Figure 3.2
A letter tree, following Knuth 1973, containing some words of English and some of
their grammatical features. Also shown is the path one would follow the tree in
looking up the word *newt*.

will contain (among other things) an entry for the morpheme *-s*. Each of
the nouns will contain, as part of its lexical entry, the information that one
can continue the search in the *NounSuffixes* lexicon. Figure 3.3 shows how
one looks up the polymorphemic word *fritos*, using this idea. Koskenniemi
(1983b) referred to the part of a lexical entry that contains information on
where to continue the search as a continuation pattern. In general, the
continuation pattern of a lexical entry will contain names of from zero to
many continuation lexicons—zero if the morpheme with that lexical entry
cannot be followed by any other morpheme. Continuation patterns are, of
course, completely equivalent to the FSM implementation of morphotactics
discussed in the previous subsection, and I leave it as a rather easy exer-

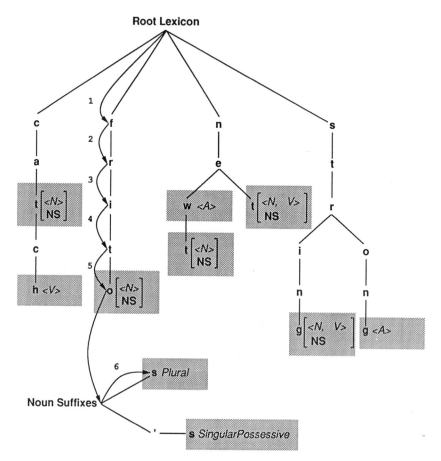

Input:

Figure 3.3
Using continuation lexicons. The lexical entry for *frito* (from the dictionary in figure 3.2) contains information that the plural affix *-s* may follow this noun; **NS** here refers to the noun suffix continuation lexicon.

cise to the reader to come up with an encoding for *hospitalization* in this scheme. It should be borne in mind that this extremely simple mechanism was the *entire* model of morphotactics in URKIMMO (though further restrictions on affixation can be had by the use of selector features; see subsection 3.3.2).

Note also that in the model just represented—indeed in most conceivable computational model of morphotactics—all polymorphemic words that will be accepted by the machinery are *virtually* present in the dictionary. In looking up the word *fritos*, we arrive at the entry for *frito* and find that we can continue the search in the *NounSuffixes* lexicon. Formally, this is equivalent to having the NounSuffixes lexicon attached as a subtree of the node containing the lexical entry for *fritos*. Recall the discussion in section 2.7 of psycholinguistic evidence which suggested that affixed words were represented in the mental lexicon along with their bases; see, for example, the discussion of the satellite-entries model of Lukatela et al. (1980) in subsection 2.7.3. As was noted there, and as is appropriate to raise again in the current context, evidence that affixed forms are "listed" with their bases is actually consistent with any reasonable computational model of morphotactics—finite-state or otherwise. At any point in the analysis of a morphologically complex form, there is generally a strong constraint on the set of possible morphemes which may follow that point, and such constraints are often stated locally—i.e., as part of the lexical information immanent in the last morpheme just examined. So, one would expect that the differences between a theory in which the derived form is quite literally listed with its stem and one in which there is merely a pointer from the base to the lexicon(s) where one may continue the search would be minimal.

In this subsection I have outlined some simple mechanisms for handling lexical retrieval and morphotactics. I want to stress again that these devices are the sum total of the real theory of *morphology* in URKIMMO (and quite a few other morphological analyzers). That is, essentially all of morphotactics, and all of what we have termed the "spelling out" of morphology, is encompassed in what I have just said. Now, I spent a good many pages in chapter 2 describing the various ways in which morphemes can be spelled out and the various kinds of constraints that apply in determining whether a particular morpheme may attach to a particular stem. It is therefore not surprising that there has been work on expanding the set of available options for describing morphology in a computational setting. Particularly dissatisfying is the explicit "beads on a string" assumption built into the morphotactic model used in URKIMMO.

3.2.2   Finite-state phonology

Phonological rules are implemented in various versions of KIMMO as
finite-state transducers (FSTs), a variant of garden-variety FSMs discussed
by (among others) Schützenberger (1961) and Elgot and Mezei (1965). The
difference between an FSM and an FST is that whereas the former accepts
a language stated over a finite alphabet of single symbols, such as the
alphabet in (3a), an FST accepts a language stated over *pairs* of symbols, as
in (3b).

(3) a. $A = \{a, b, c\}$

    b. $A = \{a:a, b:b, c:c, a:b, a:\emptyset, \emptyset:c\}$

One can write regular expressions in terms of an alphabet of paired characters, as in (3b), but instead of the expressions of that language being written
out on single tapes they are written out on pairs of tapes.[5] One tape,
which we can call the *upper tape* or the *lexical tape*, is composed from
characters from the left side of the pairs; the other, which we will call the
lower tape or the *surface tape*, is composed of characters from the right side
of the pairs. So, just as an FSM accepts or rejects a tape written with
symbols from its alphabet, an FST accepts or rejects a pair of tapes where
the upper tape is written with symbols from the left side of the pairs in the
alphabet, and the lower tape is written with symbols from the right side of
the pairs in the alphabet.

Something must now be said about the pairs in the alphabet. In some
of the cases in (3b), *a:a* for example, the meaning of the pair is simply that
an *a* on the upper tape may correspond to an *a* on the lower tape. The pair
a:b means that an *a* on the upper tape may correspond to a *b* on the lower
tape. Finally, *a:∅* and *∅:a* mean, respectively, that an upper tape *a* may
correspond to nothing on the lower tape and that a lower tape *a* may
correspond to nothing on the upper tape.

At the risk of belaboring the obvious, I will give a quick example of how
this all works. Consider the alphabet in (4a) and the regular expression
in (4b):

(4) a. $A = \{a:\emptyset, a:a, b:b\}$

    b. $R = a:a^* \, a:\emptyset \, b:b^*$

The language specified by *R* allows expressions to contain zero or more
cases of upper *a* corresponding to lower *a*, followed by exactly one instance
of upper *a* corresponding to lower ∅, followed by zero or more instances of
upper *b* corresponding to lower *b*. A FST that accepts this language is

Figure 3.4
An FST that accepts $a:a*\ a:\emptyset\ b:b*$. Here, again, the sink state is not explicitly shown.

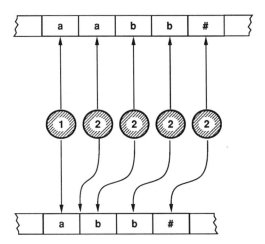

Figure 3.5
The acceptance of the pair $\langle aabb, abb \rangle$ by the FST in figure 3.4. Circles represent the states of the machine after the pairs of symbols indicated by the arrows have been read. I use '#' as the end-of-string symbol.

shown in figure 3.4. This machine accepts all of the pairs strings in (5a) and rejects all the pairs of strings in (5b).

(5) a. $\langle aaabbb, aabbb \rangle$, $\langle a, \emptyset \rangle$, $\langle abb, bb \rangle$

   b. $\langle aaabbb, aaabbb \rangle$, $\langle a, a \rangle$, $\langle bbbb, bbbb \rangle$

Figure 3.5 shows how the pair $\langle aabb, abb \rangle$ is accepted.

Note that an FST (or any FSM) can also be represented as a *state-transition table*. The FST given in figure 3.4 can be represented as in (6), where a final state is indicated by a colon and a nonfinal state by a period.

(6)   a   a   b
   State   a $\emptyset$ b
   1.   1   2   0
   2:       0   0   2

This representation is commonly used in work on finite-state morphology—such state tables are used to represent phonological rules in URKIMMO.

The idea that phonological rules can be implemented as FSTs dates back to Johnson 1972. The formal model of phonology that had been developed at that time (see Chomsky and Halle 1968) was a mathematically powerful theory that, in principle, countenanced arbitrary rewrite rules. As Johnson (1972, p. 43) argued (see also Gazdar 1985): "It is a well-established principle that any mapping whatever that can be computed by a finitely statable, well-defined procedure can be effected by a rewriting system.... Hence any theory which allows phonological rules to simulate arbitrary rewriting systems is seriously defective, for it asserts next to nothing about the sorts of mappings these rules can perform." Johnson went on to show that virtually all phonological rules that had been formulated at the time could be modeled with FSTs. The exceptions to this generalization were rules where features had integral values, including stress and tone rules.[6]

Not only could many rules be implemented as FSTs, but entire modes of rule application could be so implemented; much of the discussion revolves around an example of a consonant harmony process from Sanskrit, where a dental /n/ is changed into a retroflex /ṇ/ when preceded by a continuant retroflex consonant /ṣ, r/ somewhere in the word, provided that there is no intervening palato-alveolar, retroflex, or dental consonant and provided that a sonorant follows the /n/ in question. Like vowel harmony, this consonant harmony process is long-distance in its effects. More relevantly, and also like vowel harmony, it is iterative in its application, applying from left to right in the string wherever it can apply. So, in the example in (7), each /n/ in boldface is changed into an /ṇ/ as triggered by the preceding segments in italics.

(7) uṣnataraanaam → uṣṇataraaṇaam

In traditional generative phonology this iterative application would have been implemented by successive applications of the same rule moving from left to right in the string, but Johnson showed that a single FST applying once to the whole string was sufficient to handle such rules. The FST would be constructed in such a way that the regular expression (8) (here I diverge in detail from Johnson's description, but not in ways that affect the point; see Johnson 1972, p. 33 and elsewhere for discussion of the regular expression implementing this rule) describes the *only* environments in which the pair $n : ṇ$ is allowed by the FST.

(8) $(=:=* R := [-cor] := * - [+son] := =:=*)*$

I need to say a couple of things about the notation of this rule. First of all, I use R to refer to the class of continuant retroflex consonants /ṣ, r/. Of more general interest is the symbol =, which is the 'any' symbol commonly used in work in finite-state phonology.[7] It is due not to Johnson, but rather to Kay and Kaplan (1983) and Koskenniemi (1983b); however, similar variable-type devices are commonly used in linguistic description, including Johnson's work. To understand this symbol, one must first understand that in any two-level phonological description there must be a list of the set of feasible pairs (which Koskenniemi calls concrete pairs) that is the alphabet of all possible correspondence pairs (or correspondences or pairs, as above) of segments given by the rules. This list may be given explicitly in the description, or it may be inferred from the rules of the system; either way, it must be there. Typically, though not always, such a list will include any segment corresponding to itself (e.g., $a:a$, $b:b$,..), but it will also include the list of all correspondences allowed by phonological rules, as in the case of $n:ṇ$ in the Sanskrit rule just described. The list is complete in the sense that only the feasible pairs will be considered when matching two tapes. The interpretation of = is therefore as follows: $=:=$ denotes the entire set of feasible pairs; $=:a$ denotes the set of feasible pairs that have a on the lower tape; similarly, $a:=$ denotes the set of feasible pairs where a is on the upper tape. The only other point that one must understand in order to interpret the use of = in an expression such as that in (8) is that, to match any given correspondence pair $a:b$ in the input tapes to a term in the rule, one always picks the specification that denotes the smallest set of feasible pairs including $a:b$;[8] thus, $=:=$ (or $=:a$, or $a:=$) only matches an input pair if there is no more specific expression matching the pair, hence = implements what phonologists would call the elsewhere case (Kiparsky 1973). It is probably best to see how this all works by considering the workings of an FST that implements the rule above. Actually, since the full implementation of the rule as an FST is somewhat complicated, I will simplify somewhat, partly by considering only the case where [+cor] refers to /t, n/ and [−cor] refers to everything else. The FST is represented as a transition table in (9) and as a diagram in figure 3.6 (see note 8 for the rationale behind having separate columns for $ṣ:=$ and $r:=$).

	ṣ	r	t	n	n	[+son]	=
	=	=	=	ṇ	n	=	=
(9) 1:	2	2	1	0	1	1	1
2:	2	2	1	3	0	2	1
3.	0	1	0	3	0	1	0

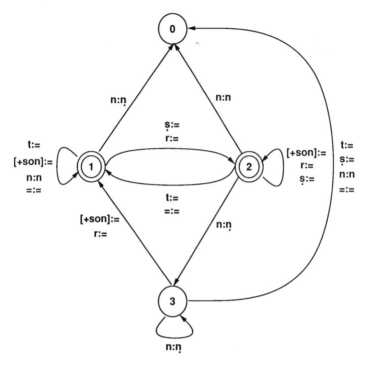

Figure 3.6
A Sanskrit retroflexion engine: an FST implementing part of the Sanskrit
retroflexion rule. To clarify the behavior, the sink state (0) is shown.

An example of the machine specified above accepting the pairing

⟨uṣnataraanaam, uṣṇataraaṇaam⟩,

where the rule has correctly applied, and rejecting the pairing

⟨uṣnataraanaam, uṣnataraaṇaam⟩,

where the rule has incorrectly failed to apply to the first *n*, is shown in
figure 3.7.

   Although the idea that phonological rules could be implemented as
FSTs has its origin in Johnson's work, the first proposal that such machinery actually be used to model phonological rules in a computational system was made in an unpublished (and unfinished) paper by Martin Kay
and Ronald Kaplan (1983) (see also Kay 1985). Note that Kay and Kaplan
were not at the time aware of Johnson's much earlier work on this topic,
and neither was Koskenniemi or Karttunen when they did their first work
in this area (Koskenniemi 1983b; Karttunen 1983). In their proposal, Kay

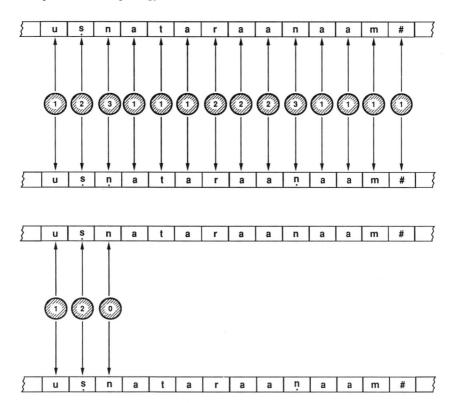

Figure 3.7
How the Sanskrit retroflexion engine works on the pairings ⟨uṣnataraanaam, uṣnataraaṇaam⟩, and ⟨uṣnataraanaam, uṣnataraaṇaam⟩.

and Kaplan outlined two ideas: that phonological rules be implemented as FSTs, as we have seen, and that the individual FSTs be cascaded together in series to mimic the ordered rules of generative phonology. To see how the latter idea works, suppose that Sanskrit has a rule that changes intervocalic /r/ into a nonretroflex /l/ (there is actually no such rule in Sanskrit), and suppose that this rule applies after the retroflexion rule that we have been discussing. Then we would expect the surface form *uṣnatalaaṇaam* from underlying *uṣnataraanam*, because first the retroflexion rule would apply as before, producing *uṣnataraaṇam*, and then the /r/→/l/ rule would apply to yield that surface form. To model this interaction we can simply have the machine that changes /r/ into /l/ take as its upper (or "lexical") tape the lower (or "surface") tape of the retroflexion machine. This machine can be stated as in (10).

(10) $r \rightarrow l$

	r	V	=
State	l	=	=
1:	0	2	1
2:	3	2	1
3.	0	2	0

Figure 3.8 shows how the two machines would be cascaded together.

In general, we can implement n ordered phonological rules by having n FSTs running on $n + 1$ tapes, with $n - 1$ of those being intermediate tapes. Of course, as n becomes large, the system becomes increasingly unwieldly. This is particularly true in the case of recognition, where for any given *surface-side* string to an FST there may be a large number of *lexical-side* strings. In the example shown in figure 3.8, it is possible that the surface /l/ could correspond to a lexical /l/ rather than to an /r/; nothing in the grammar says that it cannot. Thus we very likely will get an increase

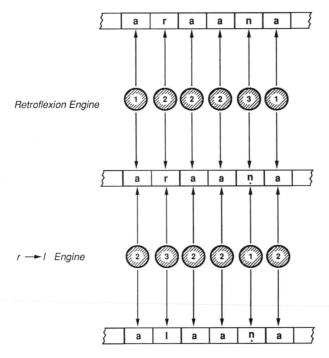

Figure 3.8
Cascading the retroflexion engine and the /r/ → /l/ engine together.

in the number of intermediate tapes, which will get worse (exponentially worse in the worst case) as *n* increases.

There is, at least theoretically, a solution to this problem. It has been known since work of Schützenberger (1961) that any system of cascaded FSTs can be composed into a single FST with the same input/output behavior. But even here, in the worst case, the FST so composed would have as many states as the product of the number of states of the individual machines.[9] In most cases the number of states could actually be reduced by standard minimization techniques (Hopcroft and Ullman 1979, pp. 67–71). Nevertheless, the intermediate machines produced by the composition would still have an unwieldly number of states, and it was in part for this reason that Kay and Kaplan's idea was never successful as a real computational model.[10]

For this reason, among others, Koskenniemi (1983b) proposed that phonological rules be implemented by a set of FSTs operating in parallel rather than in series. In this system, *every* FST sees both the lexical and the surface tapes, and there are only those two tapes—hence the term two-level morphology. The overall look of the system is as sketched in figure 3.9. To illustrate how this design works, let us return to our pseudo-Sanskrit example and consider how one might implement the two

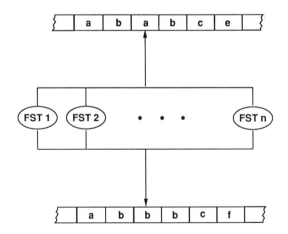

Figure 3.9
The basic architecture of URKIMMO (after Karttunen 1983, p. 176). All the FSTs work in parallel, simultaneously checking the correspondence between the lexical and surface tapes. The machines must be aligned so that when some machine is checking the correspondence between, say, lexical *a* and surface *b*, all other machines are also checking that correspondence.

rules of retroflexion and $r \rightarrow l$ using parallel FSTs. In this particular case, it turns out to be relatively easy to do, since the two FSTs implementing the rules do not have to be changed from the way in which they were previously specified. In general, we cannot expect that a two-level system will so straightforwardly mimic an ordered rule system. Now, one other thing that must be done in order to actually run these two rules correctly is to compute their alignment. Koskenniemi (1983b, pp. 111–112) specifies the aligment algorithm formally; here I will merely describe what the alignment does. The point is that one must know, for every feasible pair, which column in the tabular representation for each FST the pair corresponds to. This is effected by computing, for each pair p and each machine m, the column label that specifies the *smallest* set containing p specified by the column labels of m. For example, the pair $i:i$ would correspond to the column labeled $V := $ in (10) because $i:i$ does not match $r:l$ at all, and while it by definition matches $=:=$, it also matches $V:=$, and the latter specifies the smaller of the two sets, namely just the lexical vowels. In the machine specified in (9), similar considerations lead to the conclusion that $i:i$ matches the column labeled $[+son] := $. These alignments are used to keep the machines "in sync" as the lexical and surface tapes are being compared: as each pair is read off the tapes, the alignments match the pair to the appropriate column of each of the machines, and each machine is then advanced into the next state specified by the column and its current state. Figure 3.10 shows how both machines would proceed in parallel while checking part of the correspondence between underlying *uṣnatalaanaam* and surface *uṣnatalaaṇaam*.

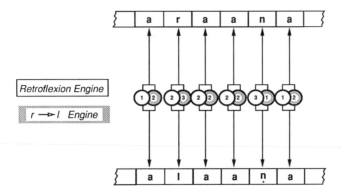

Figure 3.10
Checking the correspondence between *uṣnataraanam* and *uṣnatalaaṇaam*.

One strong advantage of Koskenniemi's proposal is that, unlike cascaded transducers, parallel transducers need not be combined into a single large transducer in order for the system to work. This is due to a difference in computational complexity between the two systems. While uncomposed cascaded FSTs can lead to exponential growth in the number of intermediate tapes, parallel FSTs—*when they are functioning as acceptors of pairs of tapes and when there are no insertions or deletions*—run in linear time. The number of rules—usually termed the **grammar constant**—functions as a constant multiplier; if you double the number of rules, then for every lexical-surface correspondence checked in a pair of input strings the system has to advance the states of twice as many machines, and so the total computation time for accepting a pair of strings is doubled. Nonetheless, the system is still linear. It must be stressed that if there *are* deletions or insertions when the machines are not being run merely as acceptors (as is true in most cases in a morphological processing system), linearity is no longer guaranteed.

Note, however, that although parallel FSTs do not have to be combined into a single machine in order for the system to run efficiently, they *may* be combined; the versions of KIMMO described by Gajek et al. (1983) and by Dalrymple et al. (1987), for example, provide options to perform this combination. That is, the machines may be intersected by means of standard FSM intersection techniques (Hopcroft and Ullman 1979, pp. 59–60). Intersection produces a machine that in the worst case has as many states as the product of the number of states in the individual machines, but again it is usually possible to minimize the result.[11]

The fact that parallel FSTs can be intersected into a single (large) FST brings up a rather important point: Since cascaded FSTs can also generally be composed into single large FSTs, it follows that the the two systems are mathematically equivalent: this is trivial, since if one takes a system of cascaded FSTs and composes it into a single FST then one can interpret the result as a single FST operating "in parallel," and the argument works similarly in the other direction. So, in principle, any system that can be described with cascaded FSTs implementing standard generative phonological ordered rules can also be implemented by a (weakly equivalent) system of parallel FSTs. This is an important point since two-level descriptions are frequently described as being relatively shallow. That is, in generative phonology there is a general tendency to try to reduce the number of lexical forms of a given morpheme to one form in the ideal case, with the burden of describing the alternations in the forms of morphemes being placed on the phonological rule component. On the other hand, in two-level descriptions, one often finds that morphemes are listed in various allomorphs, with a concomitant reduction in the number of rules. This difference is generally attributed to the fact that all two-level rules must compare lexical and surface forms (Anderson 1988, p. 530), and there is some truth in that: rule interactions, which may be easy to state in terms of ordered rules, are often much more difficult to state in a two-level model.

Consider, for example, the following pair of rules—stated in standard generative phonological notation, where the first rule deletes a lexical intervocalic glide and the second is a vowel assimilation rule which turns the sequence $/Vi/$ (where V is a vowel) into $/ii/$ (this is an oversimplified version of a pair of rules that apply in Standard Arabic):

(11) a. $\{w, y\} \rightarrow \emptyset / V - V$

    b. $V \rightarrow i / - i$

With a lexical form like *quwila*, the first rule applies to produce *quila* and the second applies to this form to produce *qiila*. This sequence of rules is easy enough to implement as a pair of cascaded FSTs, but when implementing a two-level version one has to be slightly careful. A two-level machine that implements (11a) is represented by (12) (where W represents the set $\{w, y\}$)

(12)	V	W	=
State	V	0	=
1:	2	0	1
2:	2	3	1
3.	2	0	0

This takes care of deleting the intervocalic glide, but in writing the machine implementing rule (11b) one must take into account the possibility that a deleted segment can intervene. This is because we want the vowel assimilation rule to apply across deleted segments, but at the same time we do not want it to apply across any other segments. Therefore we cannot simply treat the pair $W : \emptyset$ as falling under the class $=:=$, but must explicitly give transitions for the deletion case. The reader should verify that the machine represented by (13) has the desired behavior.

(13)	V	i	=	=
State	i	i	$\emptyset$	=
1:	2	1	1	1
2.	2	1	2	0

The addition of one extra column in the tabular representation of the FST may not seem like a great expense. However, as the interactions expressed by ordered rules become increasingly complicated, more and more care must be taken to ensure that the action of one rule is not nullified by the failure to encode the consequences of that rule in other rules. Because of such difficulties in encoding the complicated interactions found in ordered rule systems, two-level descriptions tend to be fairly shallow. Nonetheless, it is important to bear in mind that this shallowness of description is not a mathematical necessity but rather a matter of ease of description.[12]

3.2.3 Putting it all together

We have now described some basic mechanisms for doing finite-state morphotactics, and one now-popular mechanism for implementing phonological rules as FSTs. In order to understand a KIMMO-style system, it remains only to see how these two ideas are combined.

In our discussion of FSTs, we have been primarily characterizing them as acceptors of pairs of tapes. As far as computational morphology is concerned, however, the real utility of FSTs comes from their ability to function as *transducers* (as their name would suggest). In this usage, an FST takes a lexical-side tape and outputs the set of surface-side tapes that match the lexical-side tape according to the specifications of the machine; alternatively, inputting a surface-side tape will cause a set of lexical-side tapes to be output. This brings up an important property of FSTs that makes them ideal for implementing phonological rules: they are inherently bidirectional and can be run either as an analyzer or as a generator. URKIMMO is thus both a morphological generation system and a morphological analysis system. However, in all versions of KIMMO of which I am aware, generation is very uninteresting, consisting merely of providing a lexical string and having the system produce the set of all possible surface forms corresponding to the lexical string. One might expect that a real word-generation model would accept as input some set of semantic features and provide as output a word or a set of words satisfying the featural requirements. I will have little to say about generation here.

Recognition is more interesting. One takes as input the surface form of a word, and rather than using the FSTs to check the correspondence of the input string to a single lexical string one instead checks the correspondence with the set of strings provided by the dictionary. Lexical access proceeds much as before, but this time, instead of the match between the lexical and surface forms being a literal character match, the FSTs determine whether the given surface character can be paired with the lexical character at the current node in the lexical letter tree. (In the case where the machines allow a deletion to occur, the pointer into the lexical letter tree is advanced to the next node in the letter tree but the pointer to the surface form is not advanced; in the case of an insertion, the converse state of affairs holds.) In a typical situation, it will often be necessary to try multiple branches in the letter tree before the correct match is found, and this is one of the sources of computational complexity in KIMMO systems. Suppose for example that we have an orthography-based morphological analyzer for English and we want to look up the word ⟨Friesian⟩. We know that a surface ⟨i⟩ can correspond to a lexical ⟨y⟩, as in the case of surface ⟨fries⟩ corresponding to lexical ⟨fry+s⟩. The match $y{:}i$ further entails that an ⟨e⟩ be inserted and that either a surface s or a surface d (as in ⟨fried⟩, corresponding to ⟨fry+d⟩) must follow, but this is all fine since the initial surface substring ⟨Fries⟩ meets those requirements; we may therefore postulate that it corresponds to lexical ⟨fry⟩ followed by the affix ⟨s⟩. Only when the second surface ⟨i⟩ is reached do we realize our mistake (since there is no further lexical material that can follow the affix ⟨s⟩ in English), and we are forced to backtrack all the way to the point where we made the incorrect assumption that surface ⟨i⟩ corresponds to lexical ⟨y⟩. At that point, we would try the alternative that surface ⟨i⟩ corresponds to lexical ⟨i⟩, and the lexical retrieval would finally succeed. Therefore a two-level system must incorporate a search strategy. Koskenniemi's system happens to use breadth-first search; see Koskenniemi 1983b p. 135, for some justification of this choice.

Relating directly to the previous issue is the important point that FSTs, in their uses as generators or analyzers, can often not be determinized— even when the machine *is* deterministic when viewed as an acceptor of pairs of strings (Barton et al. 1987, pp. 146–149). As an example of an FST that is nondeterministic as a generator, and furthermore cannot be determinized, consider (14) (adapted from Barton et al. 1987, p. 148):

(14)	x	x	a	b
State	a	b	a	b
1.	2	3	0	0
2.	2	0	4	0
3.	0	3	0	4
4:	0	0	0	0

This machine converts a lexical level *xxxxxb* into a surface *bbbbbb*, and a lexical level *xxxxxa* into a surface *aaaaaa*. However, until it reaches the final character of the lexical string there is no way for the machine to know, given a lexical x, whether it should be outputting a or b. In order to run this machine as a generator, a decision must be made by a controlling mechanism to output one of the two possible surface characters—say a—with the possibility that the decision could prove to be the wrong. If it does prove wrong (because the final lexical character turns out to be a b), then the controlling mechanism must backtrack the machine to the beginning of the lexical string, and start over outputting b for lexical x. This inherent nondeterminism is another source of computational complexity in KIMMO systems (see section 3.5), but not one that generally causes serious problems in practice.

3.3   AN OVERVIEW OF URKIMMO

3.3.1   Koskenniemi's rule formalism

I begin this section by briefly describing the rule formalism used by Koskenniemi (1983b), because it is somewhat different from what one finds in standard Generative Phonology. Two-level rules have the following basic syntax:

(15) CP **op** $LC - RC$

CP stands for *correspondence part*, and is a regular expression over the alphabet of feasible pairs, though it frequently consists of just a single pair. LC and RC stand for *left context* and *right context* respectively, and these are also regular expressions over feasible pairs. The operator **op** is one of four types, and there are correspondingly four types of rules, as listed in (16). (I diverge here from the notation used by Koskenniemi [1983b] and use instead that used by Dalrymple et al. [1987], which is slightly clearer.)

(16) a. Exclusion rule: $a:b/ \Leftarrow LC - C$

     b. Context restriction rule: $a:b \Rightarrow LC - RC$

     c. Surface coercion rule $a:b \Leftarrow LC - RC$

     d. Composite rule: $a:b \Leftrightarrow LC - RC$

The exclusion rule (16a) states that a may not be realized as b in the context $LC - RC$. The context restriction rule (16b) states that a may be realized as b only in the given context, and nowhere else. The surface coercion rule (16c) states that a must be realized as b in the given context. The composite rule (16d) is a combination of a context restriction rule and a surface coercion rule; it states that lexical *a* must correspond to surface *b* in the given context, and that this correspondence is licit only in that context.

Koskenniemi's formalism also provides for some abbreviatory devices. For example, in addition to being able to state rule correspondence parts and contexts in terms of feasible pairs, one can use *abstract pairs* involving pairs of variables over lexical and surface characters. As an example, consider the following rule, which says that a coronal stop may correspond to a coronal continuant if and only if it is preceded by a lexical vowel and followed by a lexical front nonlow vowel:

(17) $T : S \Leftrightarrow V := - \, I :=$

   Conditions:
   $T = \{t, d\}$
   $S = \{s, z\}$
   $V = \{i, e, a, o, u\}$
   $I = \{i, e\}$

Abstract pairs allow for a way to refer to natural classes of segments.

Of course, the above formalism for expressing rules is just that—a formalism: in order to be able to use the rules in a working system, one must compile them into FSTs. The following FST would implement rule (17), for example:

(18)	I	V	T	T	=
State	=	=	S	T	=
1:	2	2	0	1	1
2:	2	2	4	3	1
3:	0	2	0	1	1
4.	2	0	0	0	0

In Koskenniemi's original work this compilation was performed by hand; Antworth (1990, pp. 49–94) gives an extensive description of how to perform hand-compilation of two-level rules. However, it is also possible to compile FSTs automatically, as I shall describe in subsection 3.4.1.

Having four different types of rules may seem rather baroque in view of the fact that in traditional Generative Phonology there is only one kind of rule—the rewrite rule, as in (19).

(19) $a \rightarrow b / LC - RC$

Yet there is much that is implicit in generative phonological descriptions that is simply being made explicit in two-level descriptions (Antworth 1990, p. 32ff.). For example, if (19) is an obligatory rule, and if furthermore there is no other means by which an *a* could change into a *b*, then this rule is equivalent to a composite rule, as in (16d). If the rule is optional, however, it is equivalent to a context-restriction rule, as in (16b). Again, if the rule is obligatory but there are other rules which also allow *a* to change into *b*, then (19) is equivalent to a surface coercion rule. In fact, the only way in which a standard Generative rule is not directly interpretable is as an exclusion rule.[13]

3.3.2   Koskenniemi's description of Finnish

Koskenniemi presents a "comprehensive" description of modern Standard Finnish that "covers the full inflection of nouns, adjectives and verbs, in-cluding affixation of possessive suffixes and clitics, and compounding" (1983b, p. 48).[14] The description is adequate to handle the roughly 18,000 different verbal forms found in Finnish (including various nominal-case forms of the various verbal participles). Before embarking upon his description, Koskenniemi lays out a couple of philosophical points wherein his approach differs from other descriptions of Finnish. These points are described below.

A shallow description   First, Koskenniemi is "cautious" with the rules in that, unless an alternation is very productive, he would rather describe that alternation by listing two allomorphs of the same morpheme in the lexicon than describe it using a rule. In this sense Koskenniemi's description is shallower (in a nonpejorative sense) than more traditional generative descriptions which attempt to push the view "one morpheme, one form" at the cost of increasing the number of rules and the complexity of their interaction. As I argued above, a shallower description is not a mathematically necessary consequence of adopting the two-level model, although there is no question that the two-level model renders unwieldly a description involving many rules with complex interactions. For Koskenniemi, his decision to adopt a shallower description was "partly a consequence of the structure of the two-level model, and partly of personal choice" (1983b, p. 47).[15]

Koskenniemi's rule set (1983b, pp. 79–99) consists of somewhere between 14 and 55 rules, depending upon whether you count as single rules the many minor rules which Koskenniemi groups under one heading. For example, the Vowel Harmony rule (his rule 5) is stated to consist of two subrules (I am adapting Koskenniemi's notation somewhat), and it is a somewhat arbitrary decision whether to count this as one or two rules:

(20) a. Back Vowel Harmony: $\{A:a\,|O:o|\,U:u\} \Rightarrow =: Vb = (-Vf)^* -$

    b. Front Vowel Harmony:

$$\{A:\ddot{a}\,|O:o|\,U:y\} \Rightarrow \{\#\mid =:Vf\} =:(-Vb\}^* -$$

where

$$Vf = \{\ddot{a}, \ddot{o}, y\}$$

$$Vb = \{a, o, u\}$$

Here /A/, /O/, and /U/ represent vowels which are lexically unspecified for backness (see the discussion of vowel harmony in subsection 2.6.3 above), and $-Vf$ and $-Vb$ refer, respectively, to the set of everything that is not a front vowel and the set of everything that is not a back vowel.

It is hard to make a sensible comparison between the number of rules in Koskenniemi's description and a generative treatment such as that of Keyser and Kiparsky (1984; discussed in the previous chapter). The latter uses about 13 ordered rules—not including vowel harmony and "other rules," which they do not discuss—but it is clear that their treatment is far from complete. I shall therefore merely make some spot comparisons between the two analyses, because I believe that at least some comparison is useful.

Let us first consider the interaction between /t/-deletion and glide formation, discussed in subsection 2.6.5 above. The derivation of *talojen* 'house/PL/GEN' is repeated for convenience as (21).

(21) underlying form: *talo +i +ten*

                          (house + PL + GEN)

      after /t/-deletion: *talo +i +en*

      after glide formation: *talo +j +en*

Koskenniemi (1983b, p. 86) also assumes a rule of glide formation, which (with the notation changed somewhat) can be presented as in (22).

(22) $i:j \Leftrightarrow =: V =: \emptyset^* \; "+" - V$

That is, a lexical /i/ corresponds to surface /j/ when preceded by a surface vowel, any number of deleted elements, and a morpheme boundary (implemented as a lexical character $+$), and when followed by a vowel. Koskenniemi does not, however, invoke a rule of /t/-deletion. Rather, he lists in the lexicon a number of variant forms of the genitive plural suffix, one of which (p. 56) has the lexical form $\& +ien$. (Note also that, unlike Keyser and Kiparsky, Koskenniemi assumes that the morpheme spelling out genitive plural is a portmanteau morpheme, rather than a sequence of -*i* 'PL' -*(t)en* 'GEN'.) The character $\&$ is a diacritic—a segment whose purpose in life is to trigger a morphophonological rule; Koskenniemi terms these diacritics *selector features*. The function of this selector feature is to restrict affixation of the & + *ien* genitive plural allomorph to stems ending in single rounded vowels or stems ending in a consonant on the surface. This restriction is mechanically accomplished by a context-restriction rule that limits & to occur in the stated phonological environment. Such selector features serve an important function in URKIMMO descriptions: they are used to impose further restrictions on affixation over and above what is accomplished by continuation pattern. Such restrictions are often stated phonologically, as is the case with & + *ien*, but they may in principle be stated in terms of other selector features. Since selector features depend for their operation on finite-state two-level rules, they do not actually add to the power of the URKIMMO formalism.

Returning to our example, we would have the following lexical and surface strings for *talojen*:

(23) t   a   l   o   &   +   i   e   n
     t   a   l   o   Ø   Ø   j   e   n

As a second comparison, consider the derivation of *purra* 'bite/INF', derived in Keyser and Kiparsky's model (pp. 17–18) from *pur +ta* 'bite + INF'; the /t/ of the infinitive suffix is somehow changed to /r/. To handle this alternation, Keyser and Kiparsky invoke the rule of consonant gradation, a complex rule by which geminate (doubled) stops (/kk/) become degeminated (/k/) and nongeminate stops become weakened (including such weakenings as /t/ becoming /r/ after another /r/). In Keyser and Kiparsky's model (and in other Generative descriptions of Finnish) consonant gradation applies when the consonant in question is the onset of a closed syllable. But the /t/ of the infinitive suffix is the onset of an open syllable, not a closed syllable, so how does consonant gradation apply? Keyser and Kiparsky propose that the underlying form of the infinitive suffix is really *-taC*, where *C* is a consonantal slot linked to no segmental material; this C slot does not surface as a segment (because nothing is ever linked to it), but it serves in their model to close the syllable, thus rendering the initial /t/ eligible for consonant gradation. The derivation thus proceeds as in (24).

(24) underlying form: *pur +taC*
      after consonant gradation: *pur +raC*
      surface form: *purra*

Not surprisingly, Koskenniemi's analysis is different. Although he has a rule of consonant gradation, he does not invoke that rule to handle this example; rather, he assumes that the infinitive suffix contains a /D/, which has a diacritic function and for which there are special rules which mimic consonant gradation somewhat. In particular, /D/ is mapped to /r/ following another /r/. The underlying and surface forms of *purra* are thus (roughly) as in (25).

(25) *p   u   r   D   a*

    p   u   r   r   a

Finally, consider how the allomorphic alternation in the illative ('into *x*') singular ending is handled in the two approaches. The facts are that the illative shows up either as *-seen* or as *-hVn*, where V is a copy of the preceding vowel.[16] The allomorph *-seen* occurs "after double vowels in stems with at least two syllables" (Koskenniemi 1983b, p. 96), and the allomorph *-hVn* occurs after diphthongs and monosyllabic stems ending in vowels:

(26) Base Form   Illative   Gloss

    maa   *maa + han*   'earth'

    vapaa   *vapaa + seen* 'free'

Koskenniemi uses selector features to handle the alternation; for example, he gives the lexical form of *-seen* as *5 + seen*, and he has a rule that restricts '5' to occur in two-syllable words ending in a long vowel. Keyser and Kiparsky take a rather different approach: they argue that words such as *vapaa* are underlyingly *vapaCa*, where again C is an empty C slot with no segmental material. They posit a rule of allomorphy that (roughly) changes *-hVn* into *-seen* when preceded by a single vowel which is itself preceded by an empty C slot.

In giving these comparisons, I hope to have given something of a flavor of the difference between a typical Generative description and a typical URKIMMO description. To some extent, URKIMMO descriptions are more direct, making less use of rules and more use of representational differences; this was the case in the treatment of the example *talojen*. In other cases, the URKIMMO description actually seems to invoke more rules than a Generative description; this was the case in the treatment of the infinitive ending, where Koskenniemi did not attempt to invoke the rule of consonant gradation to account for the alternation. In still other cases, as in the selection of illative allomorphs, the two analyses are arguably quite similar, though they use different devices. All in all, Koskenniemi's description does not seem to fare badly. Certainly it is more surfacey than a Generative description, in that it frequently assumes multiple underlying forms for a morpheme rather than invoke rules to handle the alternations. This seems unpalatable to a Generative phonologist, but one could argue that this is largely a matter of taste. Koskenniemi's description also makes much use of ad hoc selector features. Notice, however, that Keyser and Kiparsky's analysis is by no means without its share of hackery, the empty C slot in the infinitive ending being a rather clear example of this. Also on Koskenniemi's side is the fact that his model can be claimed to be reasonably complete; it is rather hard to know how complicated and ad hoc Keyser and Kiparsky's analysis would become if scaled up to cover most of Finnish morphophonemics.

A "psychologically real" description   Koskenniemi's second point is that, unlike many other descriptions of Finnish, his model is intended to be a "dynamic model which is interpreted also as a model of the morphological performance of a Finnish speaker-listener" (1983b, p. 47). This is, of course, a claim about the psychological reality of the description, and one must therefore be careful in evaluating the extent to which Koskenniemi is successful. Certainly his model analyzes many Finnish word forms (as would any competent speaker of Finnish) and does so reasonably quickly (as would a human speaker-listener).

   Furthermore, Koskenniemi (1983b, pp. 141–152) claims that morphological production errors by Finnish-speaking children and aphasics appear to support the two-level model. Most such errors, apparently, involve lexical errors such as the misselection of affixes (see the discussion of Ndebele aphasic data in chapter 2 above) or allomorphs of stems, and rarely involve misapplication of phonological rules. This at least argues for a model in which allomorphy and affix selection are handled differently from phonological rules. Also, Koskenniemi suggests that the two-level model has an advantage over more traditional Generative Phonology-style descriptions: there is no psycholinguistic evidence for errors involving the intermediate levels of representation that are traditionally posited in such analyses.

   Nonetheless, there are a couple of issues which need deeper consideration. First, linguistic theories (as Alec Marantz once noted) do not wear their psycholinguistic (or computational) interpretation on their sleeves, and it is therefore perfectly conceivable that a psycholinguistic model consistent with the data and with traditional Generative Phonology could be forthcoming. (Still, on Koskenniemi's side is the point that well-developed theories of this kind have not been abundant.[17]) Second, Koskenniemi is correct that the absence of errors involving truly productive phonological rules in Finnish (and elsewhere) suggests that such rules are learned very quickly (because children tend not to make errors involving them) and that, once learned, these rules are not easily broken (because aphasics, who show other kinds of linguistic deficits, apparently rarely show deficits involving these rules). Still, while one may readily understand why productive phonological rules are quickly learned (such rules tend to be very pervasive, and there is therefore much overt evidence in the child's early data), it is less clear why such rules could not be damaged. All phonological descriptions, including Koskenniemi's, present productive phonological alternations as formal machines, and machines can be broken. That is, I could as easily damage the operation of Koskenniemi's rules—e.g., by switching around some of the transitions on his vowel harmony machines—as I could damage the lexicons, and I could thus readily produce an "aphasic" version of URKIMMO that (according to Koskenniemi) would model no human aphasic. So, Koskenniemi may be correct to point out (1983b, p. 151) that "the status of being a 'rule' correlates" with observations about what kinds of mechanisms are likely to show errorful behavior and that "if one strives for realistic descriptions, this criterion can be used for determining which alternations should be described with two-level rules." Still, it is not clear by what means (other than stipulation) one can really explain the correlation between what things are encoded in URKIMMO as FSTs and what things fail to develop bugs in humans.

I have already discussed the issue of whether letter trees constitute a psychologically realistic model of lexical retrieval in subsection 2.7.2, and will therefore say nothing more about that here.

3.3.3 Other issues

Although URKIMMO does indeed work well for Finnish, Finnish morphology is really very simple, at least at the level of description given. This may seem like a heretical statement: Finnish, along with Turkish, is famous for long words built up of many morphemes. On the other hand, Finnish phonological rules are, as we have seen, either quite local in their effects (as is the case with consonant gradation) or are long-distance rules which have a simple and elegant finite-state description (as is the case with vowel harmony). There are no rules comparable in complexity to English stress, where a finite-state analysis, though probably possible, would nonetheless be difficult (Gazdar 1985). There is no evidence for a phonological cycle in Finnish (unlike English), and so a potentially problematic set of phonological rule interactions is removed (see also subsection 3.7.2.).[18] Furthermore, Finnish morphology is purely concatenative, and this is the simplest kind of morphological combination.

The basic difficulty with Finnish words comes down to one thing: they are long. But the length of words should not be taken as a measure of the complexity of the morphology. In syntactic parsing, a longer sentence is not necessarily a more complex sentence, and the really difficult problems in syntactic analysis—such as prepositional phrase attachment— can arise even in quite short sentences. Similarly, a long word is not more complicated merely because it is long and contains many more morphemes. Now, it is certainly true that genuinely hard problems, such as the semantic interpretation of compound words (see section 4.3), arise in Finnish, as they do in English; however, most morphological analyzers— and KIMMO-style analyzers are no exception—do not even deal with these aspects of the problem. One should therefore not conclude that because URKIMMO works on Finnish it will *necessarily* be an appropriate model for handling other languages.

Nonetheless, it is true that the techniques in KIMMO are applicable to a wide range of languages, and it is for that reason that the KIMMO framework has been by far the most successful morphological processing model ever proposed. Indeed, it has had roughly the effect on computational morphology that Chomsky and Halle 1968 had on phonology in the late 1960s and the early 1970s. Because the rules and the lexicons are strictly separate from the controlling mechanisms, it is relatively easy to write descriptions of new languages without much understanding of how the whole system works: one need only rewrite the grammar; the program remains the same. As a result, many descriptions of various languages, including such typologically different languages as Rumanian, Old Church Slavonic, Japanese, and English, have been produced in KIMMO-style frameworks. KIMMO-style models have been put into practical use in a number of applications, including serving as the morphographemic front end to the SRI PATR grammar and as the morphological processing system in at least one machine-translation installation (ALPNET; see Beesley 1989a).

There has also been a fair amount of work devoted to dealing with the inadequacies of the URKIMMO model, within the general spirit of the two-level framework. Let us now turn directly to a discussion of this topic.

3.4 AUGMENTS TO THE KIMMO APPROACH

The well-being of a theoretical framework can be measured not only by the amount of work that strictly adheres to all of its assumptions, but also by the amount of work that proposes improvements to the model while still staying—or at least purporting to stay—largely within the bounds of the model. For that reason it is significant that there has been a fair amount of work which, roughly speaking, can be said to fall within the two-level model, but which at the same time addresses problems that were not neatly solved within Koskenniemi's original framework. The work that I shall describe in this section can be characterized as improvements to Koskenniemi 1983b. Some of these improvements, such as the rule compiler, have been strictly technological, while others have been of a more theoretical nature.

I should point out that the dividing line between the work I describe in this section and the work I shall describe in section 3.6 is arbitrary to some extent, and perhaps the division will not please everyone. Roughly speaking, the work described in this section adopts more assumptions of the two-level model than does that in section 3.6. On the other hand, since some of this latter work certainly postdates Koskenniemi 1983b, and since practically everybody who writes about computational morphology today compares their work with Koskenniemi's, even some of that work is influenced by the ideas of the two-level model.

3.4.1　A rule compiler

As was noted above, Koskenniemi coded his original rules by hand, although he did (very briefly) sketch a rule compiler. Hand-coding rules as FSTs is not very hard once you get used to it; I feel it is a useful exercise for anyone interested in computational phonology and morphology, since it forces one to think very carefully about how such a rule operates. Be that as it may, hand-coding can be quite tedious if one wants to describe a language with a large number of rules. Clearly a compiler that could take two-level rules in the format in (16) and compile them into FSTs would be a useful tool.

A rule compiler was reported in Koskenniemi 1986 and more thoroughly described in Dalrymple et al. 1987 (where it is called TWOL). In order to illustrate how the compiler works, I will describe the basic algorithm for compiling a surface coercion rule ($\Leftarrow$ rule). (This is less complicated than compiling a context-restriction rule ($\Rightarrow$) or a composite rule ($\Leftrightarrow$), but more complicated than compiling an exclusion rule ($/\Leftarrow$).) Here I follow in large part the discussion on pp. 35–38 of Dalrymple et al. 1987. Let us imagine that we wish to compile the surface coercion rule (27).

(27) $b\!:\!v \Leftarrow V\!:\!V - V\!:\!V$

The first step in compiling a rule into an FST (whether compiling it by hand or designing an algorithm to do the compilation) is to consider what situations the rule excludes. Koskenniemi (1983b, p. 40) terms the set of conditions excluded by the rule the *rejection set* for the rule. What the rule in (27) demands is that a lexical /b/ be realized as a surface /v/ between two vowels. In order to figure out the rejection set for the rule, one first needs to know what *other* things a /b/ could correspond to besides /v/. Let us suppose that the set of feasible pairs of which /b/ is the lexical character is as follows: $\{b:b \; b:v \; b:p\}$. Then what rule excludes is any situation in which one has any number of pairs, followed by $V:V$ followed by either $b:b$ or $b:p$, followed by $V:V$, followed by any number of pairs—i.e., any case where an intervocalic lexical /b/ does *not* correspond to surface /v/. We can express this rejection set as the regular expression (28), where (following Dalrymple et al. 1987) pi^* refers to any possible string of feasible pairs.

(29) $pi^* \; V:V \; (b:b \,|\, b:p) \; V:V \; pi^*$

The next stage is to build a machine that accepts only strings of feasible pairs that come from this rejection set. To do this, we build machines that accept pi^*, $V:V$, $(b:b\,|\,b:p)$, and then concatenate them as required by (28). Each of the basic machines is easy to build: pi^* just has a single state, which is both an initial and a final state, and there are arcs for every feasible pair leading from that state back into itself; the $V:V$ machine has arcs for all possible vowel pairs (e.g. $a:a$, $i:i$...) leading from the initial state to the single final state, and all other arcs leading to a sink state; finally, the $(b:b\,|\,b:p)$ machine has arcs labeled $b:b$ and $b:p$ leading from the initial state to the single final state, and all other arcs leading to a sink state. Concatenation of these machines can be accomplished using standard methods (Hopcroft and Ullman 1979, pp. 31–32). To concatenate machines M_1 and M_2, one forms a third machine M_3 whose set of states consists of the union of the states of M_1 and M_2, whose alphabet consists of the union of the alphabets of M_1 and M_2, whose initial state is the state corresponding to the initial state of M_1, and whose final states are those states corresponding to the final states of M_2. The transitions of M_3 consist of the union of the transitions of M_1 and M_2 plus, for each state corresponding to a final state of M_1, an ε-transition (a transition that does not read a symbol on the machine's tape(s)) to the state corresponding to the initial state of M_2.[19]

We now have a machine that will accept all and only the strings of pairs we do not want. We can easily get the desired machine by taking the machine complement of our rejection-set machine, again using standard techniques. To complement a machine M_1, one first produces an equivalent deterministic machine M'_1 (Hopcroft and Ullman 1979, pp. 22–27) and then constructs a third machine, M_2, which is identical to M'_1 except that for any final state in M'_1 the corresponding state in M_2 is marked as non-final and for any nonfinal state in M'_1, the corresponding state in M_2 is marked as final. See p. 59 of Hopcroft and Ullman 1979 for further details.

This, then, is the basic algorithm for generating FSTs corresponding to surface coercion rules. In addition to compiling the various types of rules, the TWOL system checks for possible conflicts between rules and attempts to resolve those conflicts—a useful tool if one is attempting to build a fairly sizeable rule set. For example, it is possible that, in addition to rule (27), we have some other rule which actually allows $b:p$ to occur in some environment which is a subset of the environments specified by $V:V - V:V$. Of course, the FST we have just built would override the specification of this other rule and would render $b:p$ impossible in any intervocalic environment. However, we can resolve the conflict between the two rules by simply removing $b:p$ from the disjunction of pairs which go into the construction of the rejection-set machine. The modified rejection set would then be simply (29).

(29) $pi^* \ V:V \ b:b \ V:V \ pi^*$

3.4.2   Negative rule features

As we saw in subsection 3.3.2, arbitrary diacritics were used in the URKIMMO model to control the application of morphological and two-level rules. In order to account for the fact that one gets epenthesis of $\langle e \rangle$ in the plural form $\langle$potato$es\rangle$ but not in the form $\langle$pianos$\rangle$, one could mark the lexical entry *piano* with a diacritic whose sole function is to prevent the application of the $\langle e \rangle$-epenthesis rule to that form. As Bear (1988) points out, this is a poor way to implement lexical idiosyncrasy, since not only does it require that one mark diacritics in lexical items but it also requires that the two-level rules be written so as to be sensitive to the presence of those diacritics. As an alternative, Bear adopts *negative rule features*, a device familiar from Generative Grammar. Under this scheme, *piano* would be marked as $[-\langle e \rangle$-epenthesis$]$. When a morpheme is accessed during the analysis of a word form, the analyzer looks in the lexical entry of the morpheme to see if there are any negative rule features. If a rule specified by one of those features has applied in the analysis currently under consideration, that analysis is ruled impermissible.[20]

3.4.3   Improvements in morphotactics and word syntax

As we saw in subection 2.5.2, a purely finite-state model of morphotactics leads to a somewhat inelegant model of long-distance dependencies: in order to capture the fact that -able attaches to verbs formed with the prefix en- we had to have two identical dictionaries, whose only difference was that one of the dictionaries functioned as a memory for the fact that the prefix en- had occurred. Now, one could partially solve this problem by using some arbitrary selector feature, say '#', which would be part of the lexical entry of all verb stems, and also the prefix en-. The suffix -able would have its own selector feature, say '&', which would be constrained by a two-level rule to occur only in strings where there was a previous occurrence of '#' (Karttunen [1983, p. 181] also makes this point):

(30) $\& := \Rightarrow \# := =:=^* -$

Of course, we would want to block -able from attaching to a word when a noun-forming deverbal suffix was attached even when en- was present: -able does not attach to ennoblement. This would lead to the introduction of further arbitrary selector features. Clearly what is needed is some real model of word syntax.

One solution, due to Bear (1986), is to implement a **unification** scheme for **directed acyclic graphs** (DAGs) which runs off a grammar written in the PATR formalism (Shieber 1986). Consider the following English rule (Bear 1986, p. 276):

(31) %   verb   →   verb   +   ing
     %   1   2   3

    1. $\langle 2\,cat \rangle = verb$

    2. $\langle 3\,lex \rangle = -ing$

    3. $\langle 2\,form \rangle = inf$

    4. $\langle 1\,cat \rangle = verb$

    5. $\langle 1\,word \rangle = \langle 2\,word \rangle$

    6. $\langle 1\,form \rangle = [tense : pres - part]$

As the analysis progresses, a DAG representing the possible analyses is built by unifying features of the current morpheme into it. So, according to the rule in (31), if the analyzer encounters the lexical entry -ing and has analyzed an infinitive verb already, then a new DAG is constructed representing the -ing form of the verb. Note that the rule above, and other rules like it in Bear's system, implement fairly standard theories of word syntax, such as those of Lieber (1980) and Selkirk (1982). In such a framework one can readily state restrictions necessary to handle long-distance dependencies of the kind involving *en-* and *-able*. All that is necessary is to include a word-syntax rule which states that *en-* attaches to nouns or adjectives and that the result of attaching *en-* is a verb; another rule would allow *-able* to attach to verbs, forming adjectives.

Beesley (1989a) and Trost (1990) have adopted Bear's idea. Beesley, for example, uses a unification scheme to handle Arabic discontinuous verbal morphology, which is reminiscent of the German *ge-t* and *ge-en* circumfixes discussed in chapter 2 above. (This should not be confused with the nonconcatenative morphology found in Arabic.) A paradigm for the active imperfect of the first binyan verbal form of *ktb* 'write' (stem *ktub*) is given in (32).

(32)

	SG	DU	PL
1	a + *ktub* + **u**	na + *ktub* + **u**	na + *ktub* + **u**
2/M	ta + *ktub* + **u**	ta + *ktub* + **aani**	ta + *ktub* + **unna**
2/F	ta + *ktub* + **iina**	ta + *ktub* + **aani**	ta + *ktub* + **na**
3/M	ya + *ktub* + **u**	ya + *ktub* + **anni**	ya + *ktub* + **uuna**
3/F	ta + *ktub* + **u**	ta + *ktub* + **aani**	ya + *ktub* + **na**

Consider the form *ya* + *ktub* + *u* 'he writes'. The prefix *ya-* occurs in a number of positions in the paradigm. An examination of the positions in which it occurs reveals that it encodes the following set of features (this is simplified somewhat from Beesley's treatment):

(33) $ya- = (PERSON = 3 \wedge$
$((GENDER = M \wedge (NUMBER = SG \vee NUMBER = DU)) \vee$
$(GENDER = unspecified \wedge NUMBER = PL))$

Similarly, the suffix *-u* occurs in a number of different paradigm slots:

(34) $-u = ((PERSON = 1 \wedge GENDER = unspecfied \wedge NUMBER = unspecified)$
$\vee (PERSON = 2 \wedge GENDER = M \wedge NUMBER = SG)$
$\vee (PERSON = 3 \wedge GENDER = unspecified \wedge NUMBER = SG))$

Clearly the prefix *ya-* and the suffix *-u* are ambiguous taken by themselves. On the other hand, *ya* + *ktub* + *u* is not ambiguous. One can pick the correct combination of features by unifying the feature structures for the two affixes, which results in the following feature structure for the whole combination:

(35) $ya-u = (PERSON = 3 \wedge GENDER = M \wedge NUMBER = SG)$

Work by Ritchie and his associates (Russel et al. 1986; Ritchie et al. 1987) extends Bear's approach for English. In addition to making use of unification as the method for handling syntactic features, they also adopt general *feature passing conventions* based on the syntactic theory GPSG (Gazdar et al. 1985).[21] One convention is the *word-head convention*, which Ritchie et al. (1987, p. 296) state as follows:

(36)   The WHead feature-values in the mother should be the same as the WHead feature-values of the right daughter.

This basically encodes the Righthand Head Rule (Williams 1981), which, as was noted in chapter 2 above, is incorrect as a generalization about morphology but is approximately correct for English. What (36) says is that for a predetermined set of WHead (word head) features, a complex word inherits the values for those features from the right daughter. For example, Ritchie et al. assume that the set of WHead features includes a plurality feature PLU. So, a word like *dog +s* would inherit the feature specification $(PLU +)$ from the affix -*s*, which is lexically specified with that feature specification.

3.4.4   Nonconcatenative morphology

Probably the most obvious sense in which the URKIMMO framework is inadequate is that it is hard to build analyzers that handle anything but prefixation and suffixation—the most mundane kind of affixation. In this subsection I discuss various proposals on how to improve this state of affairs.

Before I turn to the improvements, however, it is helpful to clarify the extent to which one can handle phenomena like infixation, templatic morphology, and reduplication strictly within the descriptive framework of Koskenniemi 1983b. It will be clear that one can describe this kind of morphology, but only at some cost.

3.4.4.1   Nonconcatenative morphology within URKIMMO

Infixation   Antworth (1990, pp. 156–157) discusses how to handle a simple case of infixation in Tagalog, where, rather as in the case of the related language Bontoc described in chapter 2, an infix (-*in*-) is inserted after the first consonant of the root:

(37)   *pili*   *p-in +ili*   'choose'

       tahi   *t-in +ahi*   'sew'

       kuha   *k-in +uha*   'take'

Antworth suggests representing the infix lexically as $X+$ (the '$+$' character is not necessary and is apparently there for cosmetic reasons) and writing a two-level rule to handle the spelling out of this affix:

(36) $X:\emptyset \Rightarrow -+:\emptyset\, C\emptyset:i\emptyset:n\, V$

This rule merely deletes the X and inserts /in/ after the first consonant of the root; Antworth's rule compiles into a machine with six states.

Things get significantly more complicated when one tries to describe a more intricate system of infixation, such as that found in Ulwa. As we saw in subsection 2.3.2, infixes in Ulwa are placed after the first foot of the word. There is no way in Koskenniemi's framework to refer directly to "the first foot of the word," so one must build into one's FST-based description a part that mimics prosodic structure. An analyzer that handles all the regular cases of Ulwa infixation has over 70 states.

As Antworth (1990, pp. 11–12) notes, tables that implement nonconcatenative morphology "often get very large and run slowly." For example, in my implementation of Ulwa infixation, analysis of the word $on+ka\text{-}yan$ 'his onion' is blocked 50 times by the infixation FST, meaning that 50 possible analyses were proposed only to be rejected later because of the infixing grammar. (Actually, matters can be improved somewhat by factoring the single large machine into several machines which perform different parts of the puzzle. For example, if one factors the problem into (i) locating the infix correctly, (ii) defining the prosodic shape (CV) of the infix, and (iii) correctly choosing the surface segments of the infix, one ends up with three machines with (roughly) 10, 20, and 10 states respectively, or half the number of states in the single big machine; see Barton et al. 1987, pp. 145–146, for some discussion relating to this issue.)

Templatic morphology   A machine that handles the class of Arabic broken plurals discussed in subection 2.3.4 has about 10 states. Such a machine is of reasonable size, but it will handle only one of the several ways in which Arabic nouns may form broken plurals; furthermore, in addition to handling the nominal plurals, one would need a set of machines to handle the verbal paradigm; finally, one would have to make sure that the machines interact appropriately with various phonological rules of Arabic, including some rules that delete or insert material. A fully developed description of Arabic within the URKIMMO framework would be very complicated.

Reduplication   As was noted in subsection 2.3.5, reduplication is a unique kind of affixation in that it evidently goes beyond the realm of the finite state. There is, however, an uninteresting sense in which most (if not all) reduplication _is_ finite-state. With the possible exception of total reduplication, all reduplication involves the copying of a strictly bounded amount of material. In Warlpiri, as we saw, reduplication involves the prefixation of a $CV(C)(C)V$ template, and the association of material from the stem to fit into that template. Note that the template is maximally five segments long, and since Warlpiri, like any other language, has only a finite number of segments, it follows that there are only a finite number of forms which the reduplicative prefix can take. So, one _could_ model Warlpiri reduplication by enumerating all the possible forms of the prefix and then making sure that each form was matched to the following stem.

In this vein, Antworth (1990, pp. 157–158) shows how to handle one type of reduplication in Tagalog, where the first CV of the stem is simply copied:

(39) _pili_   **pi** +_pili_   'choose'

       tahi   **ta** +_tahi_   'sew'

       kuha   **ku** +_kuha_   'take'

He implements this with two machines: one that makes sure that the consonant in the reduplicative prefix is the same as that in the stem, and one that similarly takes care of the vowel (note that this requires a set of states for _each_ consonant and vowel). Antworth's consonant and vowel machines have 10 and 11 states respectively. Note, however, that he does not represent all the consonants that could occur initially in a root in Tagalog—the full machine would be much larger. Needless to say, an approach like this would not work very well for Warlpiri: I estimate that a machine with over 14,000 states would be necessary to encode all the possible forms which the reduplicative prefix could take.[22] (This estimate is based on Nash's [1980, pp. 67–68] description of Warlpiri phonotactics. For a stem beginning with $CVCCV$, which would be copied by reduplication, there are roughly 13 possible initial consonants, 7 possible vowel combinations, and 137 possible medial consonant clusters, for a total of 12,467 possible forms of the reduplication morpheme. For a stem beginning $CVCV$ there are 13 possible initial consonants, 18 possible medial consonants, and 7 possible vowel combinations, for a total of 1638. Finally, for CVV stems, there are 13 possible initial consonants and 3 possible vowel combinations, for a total of 39. The sum of these totals is 14,144. Note that this number encodes only the possible forms of the prefix; to make sure that the reduplicative prefix also matches appropriately with the stem to the right, we need somewhere between 1.5 and 2 times as many states.)

3.4.4.2 Proposed improvements

Infixation   I know of no work within the two-level approach which specifically addresses the problem of how to handle infixation in an interestingly general way. One non-two-level system that *does* allow a reasonable treatment of infixation is AMPLE, which will be discussed in subsection 3.6.5. To extend two-level morphology to handle infixation one would need to develop a mechanism for modeling prosodic constituency, perhaps along the lines of Sproat and Brunson 1987 (see below).

Templatic morphology   There have been a few different proposals for how to handle the templatic morphology found in Arabic. (Note that the only proposals concern how to deal with verbal morphology; I know of no serious attempts to model the more complicated broken plurals discussed in McCarthy and Prince 1990.) Probably the best-known attempt is that of Kay (1987). His suggestion was to replace the single lexical tape of URKIMMO with three tapes, one handling the skeletal affix (the binyanim), one handling the root consonant lexicon, and one handling the vowel morphemes. Consider Kay's example involving the word *aktabib*,[23] where one matches the input to three taps as shown in figure 3.11. The alignment between the tapes is controlled by an FST which reads all four

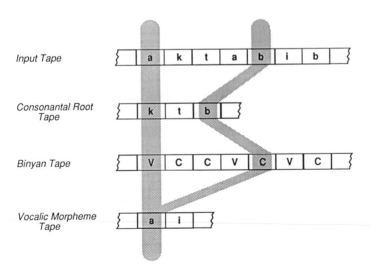

Figure 3.11
The analysis of the Arabic word *aktabib* as proposed by Martin Kay. The FST controlling the analysis reads four tapes instead of two.

tapes, instead of a pair of tapes. Figure 3.11 shows two stages in the matching procedure. The first is the initial state. The second is the first matching of a /b/ on the input tape with a lexical /b/ in the verbal-root tape; at this stage the lexical vowel /a/ has matched two occurrences of /a/ in the input. At all stages in the analysis the skeletal tape and the input tape are kept in lock step; Kay's FST uses the skeletal tape to compute the alignment between the input tape and the root and vowel tapes.[24] (Kataja and Koskenniemi [1988] discuss a system for Akkadian (another Semitic language with template morphology) for which they propose viewing the association of roots to patterns as the (virtual) intersection of the root and pattern lexicons. They do not discuss an actual implementation of this idea, although they claim that the tools exist to do the job; one assumes that the implementation would look rather like Kay's implementation for Arabic.)

Now, to my knowledge, Kay's proposal has never actually been used to develop a large-scale morphological analyzer for Arabic. One KIMMO-style system that apparently does constitute a serious attempt to cover a large portion of Arabic morphology is the system reported in Beesley 1989a. Beesley makes use of a method for traversing multiple lexicons which he calls "detouring." Unfortunately the details of the detouring algorithm are not reported (for intellectual-property reasons), but from having experimented with my own implementation of KIMMO adapted for Arabic I assume that the method works somewhat as follows: Unlike Kay's proposal, which requires a four-tape FST, here we use a conventional two-tape FST. However, in contrast with the situation with URKIMMO, where (with a depth-first search) we have only one dictionary open at any given time, under the detouring proposal we have multiple dictionaries open. In Beesley's published description he uses two dictionaries, one representing the verbal consonantal roots and the other the binyan templates precompiled with the vowels; thus, instead of combining three elements (e.g., *ktb*, *CVCVC*, and *ui*) one combines just two (*ktb* and *CuCiC*).[25] The two types of lexicon are arranged in the standard letter-tree configuration, but in this case one jumps back and forth from tree to tree rather than descending through a single tree at a time. The method would seem to be that one keeps the skeleton-plus-vowel lexicon aligned with the input tape (allowing, of course, for the possibility that some FSTs may admit deletions or insertions) but that when one encounters a variable character such as '−' in the lexicon (standing, roughly, for 'C') one detours into the root lexicon to retrieve the next appropriate consonant. For a form like *aktabib*, the analysis would proceed as is shown schematically in figure 3.12.[26]

Beesley's system is rather ingenious in another way: Arabic, like Hebrew, is typically written unvocalized (without vowel markings), and one must therefore infer the pronunciation of the vowels in a given word from the sentential context and from one's knowledge of the Arabic lexicon and Arabic morphology. As a result, a form written in (transliterated) Arabic as *ktb* could correspond to *kataba* 'he has written' or *kutiba* 'it was written', among other words. Now, for unvocalized text, a morphological analyzer for Arabic should produce analyses consistent with the surface form, and thus (as a side effect) produce all possible vocalizations of an unvocalized text that are consistent with the morphology. Beesley handles this by allowing lexical short vowels to delete in most contexts, by always admitting the pairs $a:\emptyset$, $i:\emptyset$, and $u:\emptyset$ in those contexts. A surface form *ktb* would then match with lexical analyses *kataba* and *kutiba* as desired. However, Beesley's system also admits the pairs $a:a$, $i:i$, and $u:u$ in general, allowing him to also handle cases where full vocalization is given (*kataba*), or even cases of partial vocalization—as very occasionally happens in Arabic text when it is crucial to distinguish two forms, e.g. passive *kutb* from active *katb*.

Other prosodic morphology: reduplication   A two-level model for Warlpiri that handles reduplication in that language is reported in Sproat and Brunson 1987. I will describe this model at some length here, since, in addition to its model of reduplication, a few other augmentations to the standard two-level approach were proposed which deserve some discussion.

Since several parts of Warlpiri morphology require reference to prosodic categories, we incorporated a model of prosody into the system which allows direct reference to constituents such as syllable or foot. The particular prosodic parsing method used was the **matrix chart parsing** algorithm described in Church 1986 and used by Church to describe prosodically based phenomena in English. In addition, the matrix parsing scheme was used to run a finite-state grammar describing the phonological well-formedness of Warlpiri words (more on this below). Finally, since the scheme mimics finite-state machines, we used it to implement two-level phonological rules. The details of the algorithm are not crucial to the present discussion, and I refer the reader to Church 1986. It is worth noting here that in the particular version of the matrix parsing algorithm used, an analysis of an input string is not performed strictly from left to right. Rather, terminal

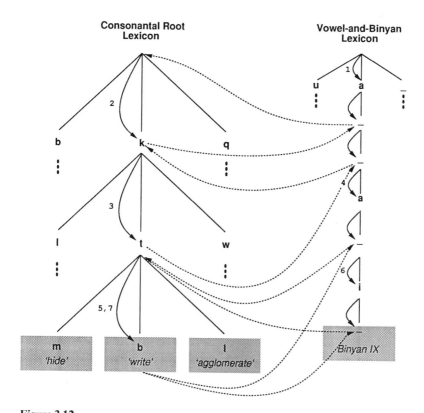

Figure 3.12
The analysis of *aktabib* following a path through multiple lexicons along the lines
of Beesley 1989a. Note that the repetition of the last character of the root *ktb* would
have to be handled in this system by a statement in the grammar that would allow
step 7 to retrace the same branch as step 5. Presumably one would do this by
marking the lowest "empty" branch in the vowel-and-binyan lexicon with a special
symbol whose interpretation is 'repeat the previous root consonant'.

node labels are first assigned to each element of the input, so that the entire input is scanned before any further structure is built.

As an illustration of how the parser makes use of prosodic structure (and other information) in handling reduplication and other aspects of Warlpiri morphology, consider the parsing of the word *paŋu +paŋu +ṇu* (REDUP + dig + Past) 'dug repeatedly'. Here REDUP is the verbal reduplication morpheme described in subsection 2.3.5. Note also that the verb stem—underlyingly *paṇi*—has undergone *regressive* vowel harmony, whereby the final vowel of the stem has been changed to /u/ because of the /u/ in the suffix -*ṇu*. We assume an input that not only has segmental information but also is appropriately marked for stress. In this particular example, the input would look as follows, following Nash's (1980) description of the stress pattern of Warlpiri:

(40) páŋupàŋuṇu

The parser first finds the prosodic constituents. The prosody of Warlpiri is simple in that syllable types are limited and phonological words reliably take a single primary stress on the first syllable. The prosodic constituent grammar contains the following rules, among others:

(41) a. $\sigma \rightarrow CV$

     b. $F \rightarrow \sigma_{stressed}\sigma^*$

     c. $\omega \rightarrow F_{primary\,stress}F^*$

In the particular example, the rules tell us that the syllables are /pa/, /ŋu/, /pa/, /ŋu/, and /ṇu/, that the feet are /paŋu/ and /paŋuṇu/, and that there is a single prosodic word, namely /paŋupaŋuṇu/.[27]

Having computed the prosody, the parser next searches for the morphemes that might plausibly make up the word. Since the entire system reported in Sproat and Brunson 1987 was built around the non-left-to-right matrix chart parsing methodology, we did not implement a letter-tree-based lexicon with continuation dictionaries, but rather stored all morphemes in a hash table. Lexical access was facilitated, however, by the fact that—with a very limited and well-defined class of exceptions—Warlpiri morphemes must be syllabifiable strings. Since we have already computed the syllabic structure of the word (and since a morphological analysis must span the entire input), we can severely limit the number of substrings which have to be checked for possible morphemic status. A further complication in lexical access is the obvious fact that the surface form of a morpheme may, as a result of phonological rules, be different from the underlying form. In Warlpiri the differences are minimal, and in our system they reduce to the effects of regressive vowel harmony and progressive vowel harmony. In the case at hand the sequence *paŋu* may have come from underlying *paŋu* or underlying *paŋi*. The latter is a morpheme of the language, and we therefore pick it; this choice must be later licensed by the operation of the vowel harmony rules, to which I return below.

Of course, another way in which the surface representation of a morpheme may differ from its underlying representation is if it does not contain any segmental information, but merely information about prosodic shape. This is the case with the reduplication morpheme *CV(C)(C)V*, which Sproat and Brunson referred to as a "bimoraic foot" (roughly speaking, a foot with two vowel slots). Whenever we see a bimoraic foot, we posit the existence of verbal reduplication subject to immediate verification if it matches the phonological material to its right. For Warlpiri, "match" means a perfect match with an equal amount of material to the right, but in other languages where other phonological processes may interact with reduplication more sophisticated matching would be necessary; obviously the habitual-repetitive reduplication in Javanese described in the previous chapter would necessarily involve a more complicated procedure. Since we already know the prosodic structure of the string, it is easy to directly refer to "bimoraic feet." In *paŋupaŋunu*, the first sequence *paŋu* is a bimoraic foot. Since it matches appropriately with the sequence to its right, we can posit the existence of a verbal reduplicative affix at this point.

Having proceeded to this point, we have a chart of possible morphemes. In the case at hand the chart has a path consisting of *REDUP*, *paŋi*, and *nu*. We now check that the hypothesized sequences of morphemes are well formed from a morphophonological point of view. Succinctly put, Warlpiri words consist of an optional prefix, followed by a root, followed by some number of suffixes; in addition, the stem plus suffixes form the domain over which the two rules of vowel harmony apply. This can be formalized with the following finite-state rules, where a well-formed *Vowel Harmony Domain* is defined to be the intersection of (correct) applications of vowel harmony and the concatenation of a root with some number of suffixes:

(42) a. *Word → (Prefix) ⌢ Vowel Harmony Domain*

   b. *Vowel Harmony Domain → (Root ⌢ Suffix*) ∩ Vowel Harmony*

Phonological rules in the Sproat-Brunson system are essentially the same as standard two-level rules: the rules check to see that the sequence of surface segments can be paired with the sequence of lexical segments in the underlying morphemes and that the surface string is well formed according

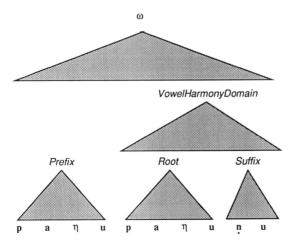

Figure 3.13
The structure of the Warlpiri word *paŋupaŋuṇu* 'dug repeatedly' as analyzed by the system reported in Sproat and Brunson 1987.

to the regular expressions implementing the rules.[28] One difference is that phonological rules in the Sproat-Brunson system were defined—as indicated in (42)—for particular domains of application, rather than continuously applying as in normal KIMMO models. This aspect of the model is interesting from the point of view of Lexical Phonology. Just as in the LPM model, phonological rules are restricted to apply within certain domains (strata), so in this model vowel harmony is restricted by the grammar to apply only in the domain *Root ⌢ Suffix**.[29] The example at hand, *paŋupaŋuṇu*, passes the constraints in (42), since, among other things, the application of regressive vowel harmony is evidently restricted to the root and suffix domain. The structure assigned to this input is given in figure 3.13.

At this point, we know what the chart of morphemes is, and we know what order the morphemes occur in. This information—but not information about phonological rule application or other aspects of phonological structure—is passed off to the (morpho)syntactic analyzer. (The particular analyzer used was due to earlier work by Brunson [1986].) One consequence of passing the information in this way is that the (morpho)syntactic analyzer has no access to any kind of information about the phonological structure of the word, with the result that the structures that the syntactic analyzer builds are likely to show mismatches with the phonological structure of the kind described in section 2.4. Of course, this (desirable) property will characterize any system where the model of (word) syntax is conceptually separate from the more phonological aspects of the analysis. Systems of the kind proposed in Bear 1986 could also have this property.

The implementation of prosody in the Sproat-Brunson system has other applications in Warlpiri. Recall from subsection 2.4.5 that certain Warlpiri affixes take different allomorphs depending upon the prosodic structure of the base word. Since one can refer directly to prosodic constituents in the system, it is quite easy to implement the constraints on those affixes. Now, note that Koskenniemi (1983b, pp. 92–97) uses selector features to handle some similar cases in Finnish, where certain affixes attach only to bases with certain syllabic structures. The implementation of prosodic notions is possible in the URKIMMO framework, but the tools were not really available in that system for manipulating prosodic constituents in a clean and simple way. Nonetheless, it suggests that if the original formalism of URKIMMO were augmented with a sensible implementation of prosodic structure, and with some additional mechanisms such as copying, it would be adequate to model the behavior of the Sproat-Brunson system for Warlpiri. The idea would be to have a left-to-right model where the lexical access, phonological rules, and prosodic parsing were carried on in tandem. This would overcome the only legitimate objection to Sproat and Brunson's proposal, namely that lexical access as implemented was inefficient. This inefficiency was only a consequence of using the non-left-to-right matrix parsing method. If that method were replaced with finite-state machines to handle prosody and with standard FSTs to handle the phonological rules and phonological well-formedness, and if, furthermore, the (morpho)syntactic analysis were carried on in parallel (perhaps by an approach such as that of Bear [1986]), there is no reason why the augmentations proposed in Sproat and Brunson 1987 could not be incorporated into an efficient morphological parsing system adequate to handle languages like Warlpiri. However, not only languages like Warlpiri but also languages like English could benefit from such information: although the computation of stress in English is complicated by the fact that it may have to be assigned cyclically (following analyses dating back to Chomsky and Halle 1968, it is at the very least clear that it depends crucially on information such as syllable structure (in particular syllable weight) and foot structure.

In addition to Sproat and Brunson's work, Dolan (1988) discusses a system for handling Indonesian morphology, which is in many ways quite similar to the proposals just discussed. More recently, Cahill (1990) has reiterated the point that a morphological analyzer needs to use information about prosodic structure.

Other nonconcatenative morphology   I am unaware of any work on languages where tone is morphologically significant, although I have no particular reason to believe that morphological tone changes pose any special problems for two-level finite-state morphology.

Zero morphology, as was suggested in a previous chapter, may well be best handled in a computational system by simply allowing (appropriate) lexical entries which are ambiguous as to category, or whatever other feature the zero morpheme manipulates.[30] As far as I can tell, any computational model of zero morphology would be equivalent to this suggestion.

Subtractive morphology—presumably since it is relatively infrequent—has attracted no attention. One certainly could handle it, to a degree, in a two-level model. For example, Koasati subtractive morphology, discussed in subsection 2.3.8, could be handled by a rule that deletes a sequence /VV/ or /VC/ when it precedes a lexical '$', which is an arbitrary diacritic triggering the deletion. A machine that implements such a rule is given in (43).

(43)   V   C $ =
           ∅   ∅   ∅   =
    1:     2   0   0   1
    2.   3   3   0   0
    3.   0   0   1   0

As for ablaut, one piece of work somewhat in the KIMMO tradition which treats ablaut as a productive process is Cornell's (1988) work on Icelandic.[31] The model differs from the two-level model in that it proposes cascaded transducers. The ablaut machine changes, for example, the preterite stem *gaf* 'gave' into the lexical form of the stem *gef* 'give'; this rule applies close to the lexical level and takes as input the output of other machines which apply closer to the surface level. In addition to allowing transductions on surface to lexical characters, Cornell's machines also introduce morphosyntactic features. For example, the ablaut machine has an arc labeled with the pair *e:a* to handle the transduction from *gaf* to *gef*, and in addition this arc is labeled as $[+Pr] := $, meaning that it introduces the morphosyntactic features [+Preterite] at the same time as it makes the transduction from surface /a/ to lexical /e/. Unfortunately it is hard to evaluate the success of this model, because it was apparently not implemented at the time of publication of Cornell 1988.

3.5 THE COMPUTATIONAL COMPLEXITY OF TWO-LEVEL MORPHOLOGY

Although there has been been little general work on the computational complexity of morphological processing systems, the much-cited work of Barton (1986) and Barton et al. (1987) deals specifically with the computational complexity of KIMMO-type two-level morphological systems. Since we have just reviewed the architecture of URKIMMO and its relatives, it is appropriate to raise the issue of complexity at this point. I shall start by showing why the KIMMO model isn't necessarily efficient; I shall then sketch Barton's ingenious proof that KIMMO-generation is NP-hard. Barton also shows that KIMMO-recognition is NP-hard (Barton et al. 1987, pp. 140–143), and that KIMMO-recognition with unrestricted deletions is PSPACE-hard, but I will largely omit discussion of those proofs here, since the general flavor of the issue can be gleaned from the proof about KIMMO-generation; see subsection 3.5.4, however.[32]

3.5.1 Why KIMMO isn't necessarily efficient

Initial claims about the complexity of two-level morphology were made by Karttunen (1983, p. 167) (see also Koskenniemi 1983b, p. 156):

One important consequence of compiling the grammar in this way [as FST—RWS] is that the complexity of the linguistic description of a language has no significant effect on the speed at which the forms of that language can be recognized or generated. This is due to the fact that finite state machines are very fast to operate because of their simplicity. Thus the number of such machines produced by the conversion and the number of states in each machine has only a minimal effect on processing time. Although Finnish, for example, is morphologically a much more complicated language than English, there is no difference of the same magnitude in the processing times for the two languages....

It also has some psycholinguistic interest because of the common sense observation that we talk about 'simple' and 'complex' languages but not about "fast" and "slow" ones.[33]

Barton et al. (1987, p. 125) refer to the view expressed here that finite-state machinery implies efficient processing as The Lure of the Finite State; contrary to what Karttunen suggests, finite-state machinery does not guarantee efficient processing.

Both the lexicon and two-level rules can lead to complexity and concomitant inefficiency in the KIMMO model. First, the lexicon, as has been noted above, can often be a problem because the KIMMO analyzer, running in recognition mode, often chooses the wrong path. As Barton et al.

note (p. 127), there are really two issues here. One is that it is often the case that a given lexical item will specify several continuation lexicons, whereas in any given case only one of those (typically) has any chance of being the right path to follow. Nonetheless, in the standard KIMMO implementation one must check every one of those continuation lexicons to see if a possible analysis might lie down that path. Even if such tentative paths are killed off quickly, going down them nonetheless takes time, leading to inefficiency. A particularly bad property is that it may well be the case that affixes in different sublexicons share initial segments. This means that the identical surface-lexical correspondence will be checked each time a new lexicon is opened. Barton et al. (1987, pp. 155–159) propose solutions to these problems that involve merging the many lexicons into one, so that only one lexicon must be searched.

Second, the dictionary can also conspire with the two-level rules to yield complexity. As we saw above in subsection 3.2.3, analysis of the word *Friesian* in English requires some backtracking because the analyzer must be initially unsure as to whether a surface $\langle i \rangle$ corresponds to a lexical $\langle i \rangle$ or to a lexical $\langle y \rangle$. This second issue is much more deeply ingrained in the architecture of KIMMO systems, and is directly related to the observation, noted in subsection 3.2.3, that FSTs (whether running in recognition or generation mode) cannot be determinized. That is, as long as there are machines that allow a surface $\langle i \rangle$ to correspond either to a lexical $\langle y \rangle$ or to a lexical $\langle i \rangle$, and as long as the factors that condition the choice between the alternatives are not deterministically predictable from the left-hand context, the system is inherently nondeterministic. Therefore, there is no way that the system can generally know whether to transduce a surface $\langle i \rangle$ into a lexical $\langle i \rangle$ or a lexical $\langle y \rangle$, and therefore there must be some amount of backtracking.

The sense in which the dictionary conspires with the two-level rules in the preceding case is precisely that the dictionary often does not provide enough constraints. Obviously, if one is at a node in the dictionary where the only daughter is labeled $\langle y \rangle$, then the possibility that a surface $\langle i \rangle$ may correspond to a lexical $\langle i \rangle$ can be killed immediately. This did not obtain with *Friesian*, because both *fri* and *fry* are possible lexical initial substrings of English words. This situation, which is bad in the case of analysis, is much worse in the case of KIMMO generation: here there are *no* constraints on the output of the machines other than the constraints provided by the (lexical) input and the machines themselves.[34] Indeed, it is for this reason that it is most straightforward to prove the complexity of KIMMO-generation, and I turn now to this issue.

A standard technique for proving the complexity of problems in general and natural language analysis problems in particular is *reduction*. Simply put, one shows that a problem whose complexity is known can be represented as a particular instance of the problem at hand; the latter problem is thus at least as complex as the former. Barton et al. make much use of this technique, and an example of the genre is provided by Barton's proof (Barton et al. 1987, pp. 135–140) that KIMMO-generation is NP-hard. Barton shows that a known NP-hard problem, namely *Boolean satisfiability* (henceforth SAT) can be encoded as a KIMMO-generation problem, and therefore KIMMO-generation is NP-hard; it is therefore not generally tractable.

The problem in SAT is to decide, for a formula in conjunct normal form (CNF) of n variables, whether there is some assignment of T and F to the variables such that the entire formula is true. In the case of the formula in (44), we ask whether such a consistent assignment of T and F can be made to x, y and z.

(44) $(\neg x \vee y) \wedge (\neg y \vee z) \wedge (x \vee y \vee z)$

This problem is known to be NP-hard; in other words, it is not known to be solvable by a deterministic Turing Machine in polynomial time. Hence, the problem is said to be intractable.

Barton's proof of the NP-hardness of KIMMO-generation consists in showing that one can encode SAT as a KIMMO-generation problem. For any formula, such as the one in (44), the system will ascertain whether or not there are consistent assignments of truth values to variables such that the whole formula is true, and if there are such assignments, what they are. Barton encodes the problem as in (45).

(45) a. lexical characters:
- The set of variables $\{x, y, z \ldots\}$
- '−' encoding negation
- ',' encoding conjunction (no character of disjunction is needed)

b. surface characters:
- truth assignment $\{T, F\}$, ',', and '−'

c. For each variable u, a 'u-consistency' machine for that variable:

	u	u	=
	T	F	=
1:	2	3	1
2:	2	0	2
3:	0	3	3

d. A machine to determine satisfaction:

	=	=	−	,
	T	F	−	,
1.	2	1	3	0
2:	2	2	2	1
3.	1	2	0	0

The variable-consistency FSTs simply enforce the same truth assignment to each variable across the entire formula. It can easily be verified from the state diagram that as soon as a variable is assigned a truth value, it must retain that truth value or the FST will enter the sink state. The satisfaction FST looks at the surface string to ensure that each group of the CNF formula being examined is true; it ends up in state 2 (the only final state) whenever the current group contains at least one T or $-F$. The system is guaranteed to find an answer, but on many formulas this requires significant amounts of backtracking. For example, in handling a case such as the one in (46) (from Barton et al. 1987, p. 170), the system advances and then backtracks seven times before arriving at the conclusion that there is no solution to this particular formula.

(46) $(x \lor y \lor z) \land (\neg x \lor \neg z) \land (\neg x \lor z) \land (\neg y \lor \neg z) \land$
    $(\neg y \lor z) \land (\neg z \lor y)$

The reason for this is that nothing in this formula allows the system to definitely fix the value of the variables early in the input string, and it must therefore try all possible value settings; since only $x = F$, $y = F$, $z = F$ is ruled out by the satisfaction requirement in the first clause of the formula, that leaves seven other possibilities, hence seven advances and backtracks. To underscore how bad this particular problem is, Koskenniemi and Church (1988) point out that the generation time grows exponentially with the number of variables.

One must conclude, therefore, that the KIMMO model does not (contra Karttunen and others) guarantee efficient processing: it is possible to encode very hard problems in the system, and (not surprisingly) the system performs generally poorly on such problems. The question now remains how to interpret this result. Barton et al. (1987, chapter 6) offer one answer: The KIMMO framework as it stands is inadequate as a model of the computational description of natural language morphology because the formalism does not allow one to distinguish genuinely computationally difficult problems such as SAT from the typically easier problems that one finds in natural language. This state of affairs can be improved, however, by imposing further constraints, as I shall briefly describe in the next subsection. A second answer is offered by Koskenniemi and Church (1988) in their reply to Barton's reduction: Barton is correct, but that is of little consequence to the description of natural language, since systems can be and have been built which describe natural languages efficiently. I describe their answer in subsection 3.5.3. Finally, I discuss a further suggestion, namely that at least some of the necessary constraints can be derived from noncomputational linguistic considerations, and that one might furthermore use the poor performance of KIMMO-type systems on SAT problems to explain the nonoccurrence of SAT-like processes in real natural languages.

3.5.2 Barton's constraint propagation

As Barton et al. note (1987, p. 162), there is something rather unnatural about the SAT reduction: surely one does not expect that real natural languages such as Finnish or Warlpiri would show phonological processes of the complexity of SAT problems. Yet the SAT reduction is allowed by the KIMMO formalism, and this leads them to ask whether there might not be a way of constraining the formalism so as to allow "easy" problems of the kind one finds in natural languages, but to reject truly "hard" problems. What characterizes natural, easy problems is *not* the fact that backtracking is unnecessary in the KIMMO formalism for such problems; we have already seen that this is not the case. Rather, what characterizes typical easy problems is that there is normally a piece of the input from which one can deduce the answer to the rest of the input. Now, note that the SAT problem has rather the character of vowel harmony: in both cases, there is a long-distance constraint (in SAT it is the 'u'-consistency machines) that must be satisfied. To use the example of Barton et al. consider the case of regressive vowel harmony in Warlpiri, in particular *pirri + kuju + ŋu* 'scatter + PAST'.[35] The normal surface (and lexical) form of the verb stem would be *kiji*, but it surfaces in this form as *kuju* because of the effects of regressive harmony. Now, in a KIMMO model of Warlpiri generation there is no way to know how one should translate the lexical /i/ until we reach the very end of the word and then realize that the suffix contains a /u/, which triggers regressive harmony. If one has chosen to translate /i/ as /i/ (the default assumption), one will therefore be required to backtrack and instead translate the /i/s as /u/s. This situation differs from the case of hard SAT problems, however: the correct answer to the Warlpiri regressive harmony generation problem can be known just as soon as one has reached the suffix, and one therefore really does not need to guess. As Barton et al. also note, this also characterizes "easy" SAT problems such as (47) (Barton et al. 1987, p. 170).

(47) $(\neg y \lor z) \land (x \lor y) \land \neg x$

In this case, unlike the case in (46), the solution is fairly easy to deduce. One need only look at the final clause, $\neg x$, and realize that x cannot be true. Therefore, by the second clause, y must be true. Finally, by the first clause, z must be true. As in the case of Warlpiri regressive harmony, the problem is easy because one can systematically deduce the values of individual variables without having to try all possible combinations. Unfortunately, however, the KIMMO architecture does not perform well on the formula in (47): it backtracks five times before deciding on the only solution. Since the solution is easily deducible, this brute-force approach fails to take advantage of the structure of the problem.

Barton et al. propose a method of *constraint propagation*, based on the constraint-propagation method that Waltz originally applied to vision (see Winston 1984), that allows one to deal with an easy problem—but not a hard problem—by observing where constraints apply in the particular problem at hand, and propagating those constraints so as to reduce the amount of search. To illustrate this method, in figure 3.14 I give what Barton et al. term a *tableau* for a short (and easy) SAT formula: $(x \lor y)$ $\land \neg y$, which translates as $xy, -y$ in Barton's reduction. The rows represent the individual machines of the system, and the columns represent all of the possible combinations of input state, feasible pair, and output state in which each of the machines could be at each of the successive input characters.[36] For example, in the first column, the x-consistency machine could start in state 1, 'read' pair $x : T$, and go into state 2; or it could read pair $x : F$ and go into state 3. Some constraints of the system are already evident here: for example, I have not included transitions out of state 1 for the x-consistency machine in the second column, since (given that we have already read an x in the first position) there is no way that the x-consistency machine could be in state 1 in that column.

The real work of the constraint-propagation method is shown in figure 3.15, however. The circled numbers by each of the crossed-out items indicate the order in which we deduce that the items should be crossed out. To start with, we observe that for the transduction to be successful no machine can enter a sink state. That rules out (1) in the third column. Furthermore, since any arcs leading out of state 1 for the satisfaction machine in

	x	y	,	-	y
x-consistency	<1, x:T ,2> <1, x:F 3>	<2, y:T ,2> <3, y:T ,3> <2, y:F ,2> <3, y:F ,3>	<2, :,: ,2> <3, :,: ,3>	<2, ÷, ,2> <3, ÷, ,3>	<2, y:T ,②> <3, y:T ,③> <2, y:F ,②> <3, y:F ,③>
y-consistency	<1, x:T ,1> <1, x:F ,1>	<1, y:T ,2> <1, y:F ,3>	<2, :,: ,2> <3, :,: ,3>	<2, ÷, ,2> <3, ÷, ,3>	<2, y:T ,②> <3, y:F ,③>
SAT	<1, x:T ,2> <1, x:F ,1>	<1, y:T ,2> <1, y:F ,1> <2, y:T ,2> <2, y:F ,2>	<1, :,: ,0> <2, :,: ,1>	<1, ÷, ,3>	<3, y:T ,1> <3, y:F ,②>

Figure 3.14
The tableau for xy, $-y$ following Barton et al. 1987. Circled entries in the final columns represent final states for the machines.

x	y	,	-	y
<1, x:T, 2> <1, x:F, 3> ⑯	<2, x:F, 2> ⑪ <3, x:F, 3> ⑩ <2, y:F, 2> <3, y:F, 3>	<2, ;;, 2> <3, ;;, 3>	<2, ÷, 2> <3, ÷, 3>	<2, x:T, 2> ⑥ <3, x:T, 3> ⑤ <2, y:F, 2> <3, y:F, 3>
<1, x:T, 1> <1, x:F, 1> ⑮	<1, x:F, 2> ⑨ <1, y:F, 3>	<2, x:F, 2> ⑧ <3, ;;, 3>	<2, x:F, 2> ⑦ <3, ÷, 3>	<2, x:F, 2> ④ <3, y:F, 3>
<1, x:T, 2> <1, x:F, 1> ⑭	<1, x:F, 2> ⑬ <1, x:F, 1> ② <2, x:F, 2> ⑫ <2, y:F, 2>	<1, x:F, 0> ① <2, ;;, 1>	<1, ÷, 3>	<3, x:T, 3> ③ <3, y:F, 2> ②

Figure 3.15
Constraint propagation at work.

the third column go into the sink state 0, there is no point in even proposing that we start out in 1 in the third column for that machine. Therefore, all arcs leading into state 1 for the satisfaction machine in column 2 can safely be eliminated; hence the deletion labeled (2). Now, all machines must show a transition to final states in the right-hand column for the analysis to be successful. The satisfaction machine would not be in a final state if y were true since it would put that machine into state 1, and we therefore delete that transition in (3). According to what is left in the satisfaction automaton row for the last column, the only successful transition implies that y is false. This means that we can eliminate *all* arcs in the entire tableau that have y corresponding to T (deletions (4), (5), (6), (9), (10), (11), (12), (13)), and at the same time we can eliminate any arcs that lead into states for which the only possible translation is for y to be true ((7), (8)). This massive elimination of possibilities has rendered some transitions pointless, since they lead only to transitions that have been eliminated. Hence, we can eliminate (14), and since we deduce from this that x must be true, we can eliminate (15) and (16). So, by applying constraint propagation in this example, we have deduced the answer. According to Barton et al. (1987, p. 182), the constraint-propagation algorithm runs in time polynomial with the size of the automata and the input. Since for the SAT reduction the number of automata is equal to one plus the number of variables, the constraint-propagation method is an improvement over the KIMMO method, which runs in time exponential in the number of variables.

Although the method works for easy cases of SAT, and for natural cases like Warlpiri vowel harmony, it fails for the hard cases of SAT: constraint propagation for a formula like (46) merely deduces that each variable could be either true or false (Barton et al. 1987, p. 185). We therefore appear to have drawn a line between the hard cases and the easy (natural) cases: only in the latter cases does constraint propagation provide a solution.

3.5.3   Koskenniemi and Church's reply

So there is a problem with KIMMO. Perhaps, as Barton et al. propose, there is a partial solution. On the other hand, is the problem that Barton notes a serious one for evaluating KIMMO models as models of *natural* languages? Koskenniemi and Church (1988) argue that it is not.

As was noted above, the variable consistency machines are reminiscent of vowel harmony or other vowel harmony processes, and SAT problems are generally solved by KIMMO systems in time exponential with the number of variables—i.e., the number of (long-distance) harmony processes. Koskenniemi and Church point out that although a number of languages have one harmony process (including Finnish) and a few have two (Warlpiri might be considered an instance of this), there are no reliable reports of languages with three or more harmony processes. Therefore, the potential for exponentiality is never likely to be realized in any practical application of the model to real data. Of course, Barton et al. make the same point when they concede that the SAT reduction is unnatural.

Koskenniemi and Church also present data demonstrating the performance of Koskenniemi's Finnish analyzer on words derived from a Finnish newspaper corpus of approximately 400,000 tokens; of these, they selected all words with 17 or more letters, plus all words from 700 words of selected running text.[37] They then measured the number of steps it took Koskenniemi's analyzer to recognize the words, and compared this number with the length of the input words. Their results were as follows: the number of analysis steps for all but two of the words were well modeled by linear regression on the length of the input, with a constant of 2.43 steps per letter as the multiplier of the length term in the equation

(48) $steps = c + 2.43 \cdot length.$

Of the two outliers, one was a genuinely ambiguous word with a false (garden) path; they do not report what caused the other outlier. Recall that the KIMMO system is set up to return *all* possible analyses of an input form; a truly ambiguous word would therefore be expected to take longer than predicted by the formula in (48). Koskenniemi and Church's plot for the data minus the two outliers is given in figure 3.16. One point that is obvious from looking at the figure is that the relationship is not entirely linear: clearly some points fall well above the line and some fall well below it. One assumes that this is because KIMMO systems backtrack for reasons having to do with the dictionary itself or with the ambiguity of phonological rules besides harmony; thus, if one were to compare words of length *n*, one would expect some of these words to take somewhat longer to process than others. Nonetheless, the overriding trend in the data appears to be the linear relationship between word length and the number of analysis steps. What this suggests is that, except in cases of genuine ambiguity or garden-pathing (where even a human might be led astray), the KIMMO analyzer for Finnish works fairly efficiently. This we can attribute to the fact that Finnish, like any natural language, has few harmony processes. Barton's reduction, while correct, would appear to have little practical consequence.

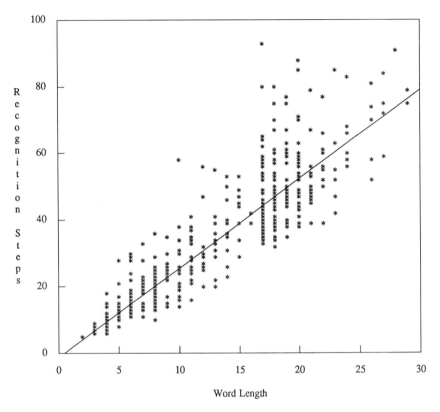

Figure 3.16
Word length as a predictor of the number of analysis steps (for unambiguous
words only), from Koskenniemi and Church 1988.

3.5.4   A consensus?

Koskenniemi and Church point to the small number of harmony processes—i.e., just one— as being a crucial factor in the success of the Finnish model. There are some other factors, however, and to fully understand
how to evaluate this debate it is important to realize what those are.

First, Koskenniemi and Church's argument involves the *recognition* of
Finnish words. Now, as was noted above, Barton actually proved NP-
hardness of both KIMMO generation *and* KIMMO recognition. The
proof for recognition is similar to the proof for generation, except that the
variables now constitute the surface level and the values the lexical level.
Instead of having a satisfaction machine, one uses the lexicon to limit the
variable values to all and only the possible combinations of *T* and *F* that

will yield a "true" morpheme. Each morpheme represents a clause in the SAT formula (actually a variant of SAT called 3SAT [Barton et al. 1987, pp. 52–55]), and a whole formula consists of some number of morphemes concatenated together, where each morpheme must be true for there to be a solution. The lexicon in this reduction is rather unlike natural language lexicons, since the only "morpheme" that is not a lexical item is the one that consists of a string of Fs. Natural language lexicons are typically much more constrained than this, meaning that in many cases one would not need to pursue a path simply because there is no lexical item that would fit the path. So, it is hard to find a natural example that is really similar to Barton's proof of the complexity of KIMMO recognition. Part of KIMMO's success lies in this fact.

Second, Finnish vowel harmony is progressive, with the "trigger" for the harmony always being near the beginning of the word. Thus, Finnish is like the easy SAT case in (47), but with the added advantage that the $\neg x$ clause is at the beginning, thus setting the value for that variable at the outset. This means that, both for analysis and for generation, Finnish will be even easier than some easy SAT problems, since there will never be a case where the decision to spell out a particular vowel in Finnish depends upon a decision that is far removed to the right. It turns out that most harmony systems are like this; Warlpiri regressive harmony and some more exotic bidirectional systems are in the minority. Of course, for Warlpiri, one will get nondeterminism.[38] However, even here the situation is not terrible. Since lexical /i/ can show up only as /i/ or /u/ on the surface, the worst that can generally happen in generating a form like *pirri +kuju +ņu* is that the system would make the wrong choice, and this would require a single backtrack. The system would therefore still be running linearly, but it would take twice as long to run as an equivalent case of progressive harmony.

Finally, a crucial aspect of Barton's reduction is satisfiability itself. Note that without the satisfiability constraint, and with only the consistency constraint, the problem becomes one of simply producing a consistent set of truth assignments for variables—a problem very far from being NP-hard. Yet nothing in natural language phonology corresponds to satisfiability. I am aware of no constraints which specify that a certain feature must be assigned a particular value (e.g., that the feature [back] must be assigned the value '−') in at least one segment of every morpheme of every word of the language, yet something like this would have to exist for satisfiability to have a reasonable chance of being natural. Thus, while there is no doubt that Barton et al.'s easy SAT example is *more* like a natural harmony process, even that easy case is arguably too hard, since some amount of inferencing involving satisfiability is required—e.g., steps (1), (2), and most crucially (3) in figure 3.15, which depend on properties of the satisfiability machine. Natural harmony systems are not logic puzzles; rather, the values of the variables are set—normally near the beginning of the string, less often near the end—and the system works to maintain consistency in the assignments. One wonders, therefore, if the computational solution that Barton et al. propose is really right. Certainly constraint propagation limits the set of possible grammars to a more reasonable set, but even that set may be too large.[39]

While the solution to the problem that Barton et al. raise could lie in limiting the power of the computational mechanism, as they suggest, it is also possible that one might look for constraints in the grammar which might explain the limits; furthermore, one might actually use the complexity of certain encodable systems to explain why such systems are never, in fact, encoded. Barton et al. discuss these two points (pp. 162–167). They note, first, that not all computational difficulties can be removed by constraints on the grammatical formalism; they cite as evidence the case of syntactic center embedding, which most likely has a processing explanation, not a grammatical one. Second, they warn against giving too much credence to a theory of performance that depends upon the properties of brute-force search.

Let me address this second point first. While it is true that brute-force search, and the backtracking that it typically necessitates, may well be incorrect models of human morphological processing, Koskenniemi and Church show that one can have a model that uses this kind of search and have efficiency to boot: the claim that "the adoption of brute-force search leaves unexplained the oft-cited rapidity with which humans process most linguistic inputs" (Barton et al. 1987, p. 165) is therefore simply untrue. It is true that general search procedures "implicitly assume that the natural problem has no *special structure*" (Barton et al. 1987, p. 165, emphasis theirs), and this is a legitimate criticism of the fairly simple-minded searching methodology which KIMMO-type models assume. On the other hand, it does seem as if even this simple-minded model is sufficient to give one possible explanation as to why human languages do not have SAT-like harmony systems: such systems are simply too complex to process efficiently, and it is therefore understandable that they have not evolved, or that they would quickly become simpler if they were somehow introduced. So, while I do not believe for a moment that KIMMO-type systems are particularly psychologically realistic, it does seem as if their architecture can explain the unnaturalness of extremely complex systems of the kind used in Barton's reduction.

As for the first point, it seems at least plausible to believe that part of the unnaturalness of SAT follows from principles which are not computational. Why is it that languages do not have many vowel harmony processes? Koskenniemi and Church (1988) suggest that one reason may be that there simply aren't enough distinctive features to allow for multiple independent and noninteracting vowel harmony processes.[40] In particular, they claim that there are typically not enough vowel features in most languages to make a system with four vowel harmony rules even possible (p. 336). Though it is a research project in itself to work out the details of this claim in an adequate fashion, there is nonetheless a measure of plausibility here. Of course, this limitation on the number of possible distinctive features for vowels (or any segment) is undoubtedly extra-grammatical in origin; presumably its origins lie in the anatomy of the human speech apparatus and the acoustic properties of the vocal tract. Crucially, however, the explanation would not be computational.

3.6 OTHER WAYS OF DOING COMPUTATIONAL MORPHOLOGY

We now turn to a discussion of some approaches to computational morphology that differ from the KIMMO approach to various extents. The decision to discuss some systems here, rather than above in the discussion of augments to the KIMMO approach, is somewhat arbitrary. For example, the Spanish morphological analyzer presented by Tzoukermann and Liberman (1990) and discussed below could be viewed as an "augment" of the KIMMO approach, since it is a *reductio* of some assumptions of that approach. On the other hand, some of the systems—such as DECOMP, which predates Koskenniemi's work by many years—clearly deserve separate discussion.

I want to stress that the work that I discuss here is limited to a few examples from the published literature with which I am familiar. Some pointers to other apposite literature can be found in the discussion of applications of computational morphology in chapter 1.

3.6.1 MITalk's DECOMP module

As I noted in chapter 1, morphological analysis is an important part of text-to-speech conversion for many languages. It is therefore of interest that one of the earliest strands of research on morphological analyzers was connected with the work on the English text-to-speech system MITalk. The work on MITalk's various modules dates back to the early 1960s (Allen et al. 1987, p. 1), and the work on morphological decomposition dates back to the mid 1960s[41]; see also Klatt 1987, pp. 772–773, for a concise discussion of DECOMP.

The main motivations for development of the DECOMP module were among the considerations outlined in the introduction to this book. Storage space was one consideration, since "a comprehensive word lexicon [one that simply listed all the words—RWS] would have to store all regularly inflected forms, which places a large burden on the storage required" (Allen et al. 1987, p. 24). And coverage was the other consideration, since even a very large dictionary would not contain all the words encountered in typical text: as Allen et al. note (p. 24), compounds such as *earthrise* and *cranapple* are freely formed in English. Furthermore, one cannot simply ignore morphological structure in English text-to-speech, since letter-to-sound rules often depend upon it. The ⟨th⟩ in ⟨hothouse⟩ is not pronounced the same as the ⟨th⟩ in ⟨thistle⟩, because in the former case the ⟨th⟩ crosses a morpheme boundary. By analyzing morphological structure, DECOMP served as one source of pronunciations for words in MITalk.

In what follows I will give an overview of the various components of DECOMP, which are listed in (49).

(49) a. a model of English morphotactics

  b. a recursive morph partitioning algorithm

  c. spelling-changing rules for use at morpheme boundaries (i.e., a model of English **morphographemics**)

DECOMP's morphotactic model   The lexicon used by DECOMP consists of about 12,000 morphs (this term is used by Allen et al. to refer to the orthographic representation of the morphemes of English). The morph lexicon was developed from the approximately 50,000 distinct words in the Brown corpus (Kucera and Francis 1967) by starting with a "nascent lexicon containing all bound morphs and function words" (Allen et al. 1987, p. 2) and successively analyzing the Brown-corpus words according to the lexicon; this procedure "led to the interactive addition of new morphs."

DECOMP had a finite-state model of morphotactics, which was stated in terms of linguistically motivated morph types. Some examples of DECOMP's types are given in (50).

(50) a. A morph is a *free root* if can appear either alone or with prefixes and suffixes: *side, cover, spell*.

b. *Absolute* morphs disallow most affixes (except perhaps some inflectional suffixes): *the, into, of*.

c. *Prefix* morphs: *pre-, dis-, mis-*

d. *Left-functional roots* must always be followed by a derivational suffix: *nomin-* (e.g., *nominate, nominee*).

e. *Derivational* suffixes: *-ness, -ment, -y*

Some examples of the rules represented by DECOMP's finite-state model are given in (51).

(51) suffix → (derivational | inflectional)
word → (affixed-word | absolute-word)
affixed-word → {prefix} effective-root {suffix}
effect-root → (root | lf-root deriv | ...)

In addition to the finite-state machinery there is a scoring mechanism for deciding upon the best parse when several parses are available. Costs are associated with each transition in the FSM, and the parse with the least total cost is favored, as will be exemplified more fully below. The following (hand-tuned) costs were used (Allen et al. 1987, p. 33):

- 34 units for each prefix
- 35 units for each deriv
- 64 units for each infl
- 101 units for the first effective root and 133 units for each additional effective root

One consequence of this scoring mechanism is that compounding—the combination of two effective roots—is much more costly than affixation, and we thus avoid the analysis of a word like *hippies* as being a compound of *hip* and *pies*; this point will be relevant in the discussion of the decomposition of *scarcity* given below.

The morph partitioning algorithm The finite-state morphological model described above and the model of spelling changes to be described below constitute DECOMP's grammar of English morphology. As with any computational model of grammar, one needs, in addition to the grammar, a means of searching the space of possible analyses. Allen et al. (1987, pp. 28–29) refer to the search mechanism in DECOMP as the *morph partitioning algorithm*, which is a depth-first recursive procedure defined as in (52).

(52) find the longest morph which matches the *right* end of the current
string
while there is a longest match **do**
   if the matching morph is compatible with the current state
     then remove the matched letters from the right side of the string;

      i. update the current state and score as a function of type of the
matched morph

     ii. find a set of possible spelling changes at the right end of the
remainder

    iii. attempt a recursive decomposition for each spelling variation

    iv. save the results of the best-scoring for each spelling variation

     v. restore the remainder string, state and score to their original
values

   end if
   find the next longest morph which matches the right end of the
string
end while

DECOMP thus differs from KIMMO in that it starts analyzing at the right edge of the word and works backward. This was done, according to Allen et al. (p. 29), because in an earlier version of the system (before the finite-state grammar had been implemented) "it was observed that the best decomposition was found first by stripping off suffixes before searching for roots and prefixes," and this design decision was retained in subsequent versions.

English spelling changes DECOMP has a very simple model of spelling changes: spelling changes may append a letter, delete the last letter, or change the last letter, so only a single letter at the end of a morph may be affected. Various spelling changes are considered. For example, if the stem ends in $\langle ck \rangle$, then a variant ending in $\langle c \rangle$ is tried: this case would come up, for example, in the analysis of $\langle picnicking \rangle$, from $\langle picnic \rangle + \langle ing \rangle$.

Each morph in DECOMP's lexicon has a spelling change code indicating that spelling changes are either forbidden, required, or optional (Allen et al. 1987, p. 34):

(53) a. *forbidden*: $\langle alloy \rangle$ does not double the $\langle y \rangle$ in $\langle alloying \rangle$.

    b. *required*: $\langle scar \rangle$ doubles the $\langle r \rangle$ in $\langle scarred \rangle$.

    c. *optional*: $\langle change \rangle$ may undergo spelling change in $\langle changing \rangle$,
but does not in $\langle changeable \rangle$.

An example of DECOMP's operation and a synopsis   Allen et al. (1987, pp. 36–37) give as an example the decomposition of the word *scarcity*. The interest of this word is that, although there is only one correct analysis— *scarce + ity*–the example is in principle ambiguous since one could analyze it as a compound of *scar* and *city*. Note that correct pronunciation [skɛrsɪti] depends upon getting the analysis correct in this case; from the incorrect analysis one would predict something like [skarsɪti]. (Another possible analysis, *scar + cite + y*, is attempted during the analysis but is almost immediately rejected as too costly.) Since the morph partitioning algorithm works from right to left and attempts the longest match first, the first analysis it tries is the wrong one, since of the two analyses described *scar + city* has the longer orthographic right-hand member. Since this incorrect analysis involves two roots, the cost of the analysis is 234 by the scoring mechanism given above. The correct analysis (*scarce + ity*), which is tried subsequently, has a score of 136 (1 root ($=101$) plus one derivational affix ($= 35$)) and therefore wins. DECOMP returns the following analysis (adapted from Allen et al. 1987, p. 37)[42]:

(54) Spelling: ⟨scarcity⟩
     Syntactic features: singular noun
     Decomposition: ⟨scarce⟩ [skɛ'rs] adjective
                        + ⟨ity⟩ [ɪti] noun suffix

(As this example suggests, it is somewhat questionable whether DECOMP is really better off by decomposing from right to left, as Allen et al. claim. Given that it is preferable to find the best decomposition early in the search, then one might be better off in this case by looking for the maximal match from the *left* edge of the word; this would be ⟨scarc(e)⟩, and this path would immediately lead to a correct analysis. At the very least, it is not obvious that one generally benefits much by proceeding from right to left.)

With its morph lexicon of 12,000 entries, DECOMP is claimed to be able to handle on the order of 120,000 English words: as Klatt (1987, p. 773) points out, this allows for the compact representation of a fairly large vocabulary. According to Church (1986) and also Klatt, DECOMP could handle correctly about 95% of the words found in running text. Klatt suggests that the greatest advantage of DECOMP (over and above its ability to provide pronunciations for morphologically complex words) is the fact that it provides part-of-speech information, which is useful for subsequent syntactic analysis (see Allen et al. 1987, chapter 4).

DECOMP is an important system for a number of reasons. First, although its development dates back about 25 years, making it one of the earliest serious morphological analysis systems, its coverage is quite impressive. Also, it is important from a sociological point of view: the linguistic analysis modules of the MITalk system in general (and DECOMP in particular) owe much to the theory of Generative Grammar (Generative Phonology in particular) that was under development at MIT when they were being developed. This work is therefore a fine example of linguistically informed computational linguistic research.

From a computational point of view, DECOMP might be said to have some advantages over KIMMO because of the limited power of its spelling-change rules. Spelling changes can involve only the last letter of the residue of the analysis currently under consideration. Furthermore, there is no long-range sensitivity of the spelling-change rules, in that a particular decision to attempt a certain spelling change is made on strictly local grounds and cannot depend directly upon a spelling change made earlier in the analysis. DECOMP is therefore free from the criticisms of Barton et al., since there would be no way to encode NP-hard problems such as SAT in the DECOMP framework. Of course, this fact about DECOMP is not terribly interesting, since it falls out as a consequence of the fact that English spelling changes (unlike vowel harmony in Finnish) are indeed local in character—although English *phonological* rules (such as stress assignment) are definitely not local in the same way. DECOMP was specifically designed with such local rules in mind, and it could not therefore easily function as a model for other languages: to handle Finnish, for example, one would need to allow spelling changes with wider-reaching effects.

One other point which should be borne in mind—and this applies to many of the other systems discussed here—is that DECOMP is a morphological *analyzer*; since it was designed as part of a text-to-speech system, it cannot generate words.

3.6.2 Hankamer's *keçi*

The next finite-state morphological analyzer I shall discuss is the *keçi* system designed by Hankamer (1986) for Turkish.[43] According to Anderson (1988, p. 526), Hankamer's original motivation in designing this system was to check the typographical accuracy of a corpus of Turkish text that had been typed into a computer. This application of morphological analysis—

spelling checking—has already been discussed and the importance of having a means of analyzing morphologically complex words for such a system is even greater in Turkish than it is in English because of the relatively large number of productive morphological processes in Turkish.

Hankamer's system shares with URKIMMO (by which it was at least partly inspired), and also with DECOMP, the property of having a strictly finite-state morphotactics. What is particularly interesting about *keçi* is its treatment of phonological rules: *keçi* is perhaps the only truly working system that uses a generate-and-test procedure incorporating ordered phonological rules in the style of Generative Phonology. More on this momentarily; first I briefly outline the morphotactic model, which ought to look rather familiar by now.

***keçi*'s morphotactics** Turkish morphotactics are represented in Hankamer's system in a straightforward fashion by a finite-state machine. Now, as we have seen, Turkish is an exclusively suffixing language, so the first morpheme encountered in the word is guaranteed to be a root rather than an affix. Thus, the initial state of the machine allows transitions only to states corresponding to classes of root morphemes.[44] Subsequent states constrain the ordering of affixes. Naturally, each root is listed with its grammatical category, and each affix is listed with a specification of what category of stems it may attach to and what category of stem it produces. The plural suffix *-lar*, for example, is listed as $N2\backslash N3$, meaning that it takes an input of category $N2$ and produces one of $N3$; these category designations have no significance other than as a control for the order in which affixes may occur. The states of the FSM are labeled with these category labels so that the current state determines which affixes may attach at that point, and each affix determines the next state into which the FSM will go.[45] Finally, ε-transitions are allowed between certain states.

As an example, consider the word *çöp +lük +ler +imiz +de +ki +ler + den +mi +y +di* 'was it from those that were in our garbage cans?', from subsection 2.3.1. *keçi* will give the following analysis to this form, where the subscripts indicate the categorial entries of the affixes and where $\emptyset$ represents an ε-transition.

(55) $\text{çöp}_{N0} + \text{lük}_{N0} + \emptyset_{N0\backslash N1} + \emptyset_{N1\backslash N2} + \text{ler}_{N2\backslash N3} + \emptyset_{N3\backslash N4}$
$+ \text{imiz}_{N4\backslash N5} + \emptyset_{N5\backslash N7} + \text{de}_{N7\backslash N8}$
$+ \text{ki}_{N8\backslash NK} + \emptyset_{NK\backslash N2} + \text{ler}_{N2\backslash N3}$
$+ \emptyset_{N3\backslash N5} + \emptyset_{N5\backslash N7}$

$$+ \, \text{den}_{N7 \backslash N9} + \emptyset_{N9 \backslash Q1} + \text{mi}_{Q1 \backslash Q2} + y_{Q2 \backslash Q3} +$$
$$\emptyset_{Q3 \backslash V4} + \text{di}_{V4 \backslash V5} + \emptyset_{V5 \backslash V6} + \emptyset_{V6 \backslash V7} + \emptyset_{V7 \backslash WORD}$$

Phonological rules   We now turn to a description of Hankamer's generate-and-test approach to phonological rules. Imagine that we have identified a string of morphemes but still have more input to process, and we are now considering what to do with the remainder of the input string. Owing to the fairly constrained morphotactics of Turkish, the set of possible next morphemes will be quite limited. What is done, then, is to enumerate all the possible next morphemes, and then, for each morpheme, pass a copy of the lexical form of the proposed morpheme, along with a pointer to the current location in the string, to a matching function. This matching function then calls the relevant phonological rules to attempt to modify the lexical entry of the morpheme to match exactly what is found on the surface; in addition to the morpheme in question, the rules have access to the surface string, and so the phonological rules may be sensitive to properties of the surface string; they may also be sensitive to nonsurface phonological properties of the left, but not of the right since the nonsurface form of the string to the right of the current point in the input string is unknown at that point.[46] The phonological rules are applied in sequence, and *keçi* can therefore be said to have ordered phonological rules, like the rules of Generative Phonology. If the transmutation is successful—i.e., if there is a legitimate application of the rules that will yield a string identical to the first substring of the remainder of the input— a pointer is advanced past the end of that substring and the parse continues at the new location. This latter parse may fail, of course, and if that happens the system backtracks.

As an example of the application of a phonological rule consider the plural suffix *-lar*, which surfaces as *-ler* in (55). When *-lar* is posited as a possible next affix, the matching function is passed the rest of the string (*-lerimizdekilerdenmiydi*). Turkish has a rule of vowel harmony whose effect on /a/ after a front vowel in the preceding syllable is to change it into /e/. Since the preceding vowel was /ü/, which is front, this rule applies to the morpheme *-lar* and produces *-ler*, which matches with the first three characters of the surface string. These three characters are then stripped off and a pointer to the remainder of the surface string (*-imizdekilerdenmiydi*) is passed on to the next analysis phase.

This generate-and-test method is nice in that it allows a relatively straightforward implementation of Generative Phonological ordered rules. However (see also Anderson 1988, pp. 526–528), the reason Hankamer's system works well is that Turkish, as we have noted, has quite strict morphotactic constraints, meaning that the choice of morphemes at any given stage is limited. Furthermore, in Turkish phonological rules really do seem not to depend upon the right-hand morphological context. Thus there is no need for the system to make assumptions about what the morphological analysis of the string to the right may turn out to be in order to make decisions about which phonological rules to fire.

This lack of sensitivity to right-hand context is certainly not generally a characteristic of other languages. In English, for example, stress-shifting suffixes are a closed class, and one must therefore know whether or not one is dealing with a suffix that is marked as a stress-shifter. In analyzing a word such as *grammaticality* ([grə‚mæti'kælɪti]), one needs to know that the suffix on the word is *ity* in order to determine the expected stress pattern of the base. Yet that information cannot be known in a left-to-right analysis until the entire string has been processed. Therefore, while processing the stem *grammatical-*, one must make some guesses about the morphological content of what comes later.

So, although *keçi* incorporates some features, such as ordered phonological rules, that are rather interesting from the point of view of a Generative Phonologist, it is fair to say that the success of the system depends in large measure on the properties of the language for which the system was designed. In this sense, then, *keçi*, while certainly more powerful in what it can accomplish than was DECOMP, is more limited than KIMMO.[47]

A note on massively parallel morphology   It is possible to conceive of a system that uses a generate-and-test approach to phonological rules, but where the necessary search is not nearly as constrained as happens to be the case in Turkish. Such a system is proposed in somewhat sketchy form by Anderson (1988, pp. 534–540). Although Anderson's proposal probably takes us beyond finite-state morphology, it seems most fitting to describe it briefly here.[48]

Anderson's suggestion is to use a massively parallel machine, such as the Connection Machine, to run a brute-force algorithm wherein, for any surface word form, all roots of the language are initially proposed and most of them are subsequently weeded out by comparing morphological and phonological derivations from those roots with the input word form. In the Connection Machine implementation envisioned, each of the roots of the language would be assigned to its own processor of the 64,000 processors available on the machine. Each processor would then go to work deriving surface forms from its assigned root, with an analysis succeeding when a surface form that matches the input is generated. In Anderson's proposed system, there would also be mechanisms whereby obviously hopeless analyses are killed off early: perhaps a case would be the proposal that *beatings* is derived from the root *melon*, where one should not need to try all possible derivations before giving up the assumption. Since phonological rules are used to generate surface forms, and since furthermore it is intended that morphological affixation rules may apply interleaved with phonological rules, it is quite straightforward to model a Generative model of phonology and morphology in such a system, with full-blown cyclic phonology. This is something that seems problematic for other approaches to computational morphology (see subsection 3.7.2).

As far as I have been able to ascertain, Anderson's proposal has not yet been implemented and so it remains to be seen how well the proposal would work. To the extent that it can be shown that humans process linguistic structures in parallel (see Emmorey 1988 for some discussion of this point in the morphological domain), there may be something to be said for the proposal that one should consider parallel algorithms when designing morphological processing systems. On the other hand, as a practical matter, I suspect that most computational linguists would balk at the suggestion that one needs a Connection Machine to do morphological analysis. As with many considerations in computational linguistics, however, this is perhaps more a matter of taste than principle.

A note on Kay's morphological chart parsing model   There are two senses in which the work just discussed takes seriously the idea that one should model the ordered rules of generative phonology. The first sense is that the rules should be applied in an ordered fashion, and the second is that the rules should literally be used to *generate* surface forms from underlying forms. This generate-and-test model would not perhaps be the first thing that one would think of if one were considering the task of turning a generative phonological model into a computational phonological analyzer. One might instead consider running the phonological rule system backward, generating underlying forms from surface forms. I have already discussed one proposal of this form, namely that of Kay and Kaplan (1983). (More correctly, of course, Kay and Kaplan's system is bidirectional, since it can theoretically both generate and analyze word forms; however, it is correct to say that *qua* analyzer it models a generative phonological rule system run in reverse.) Here I discuss an earlier proposal by Kay (1977) with the same general approach.[49]

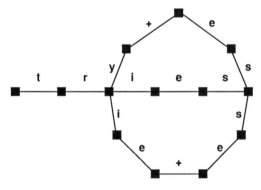

Figure 3.17
The upper diagram shows the input chart for *tries*. The lower diagram shows the
chart after the application of the rule that maps ⟨ies⟩ to ⟨y + es⟩. Also shown is the
output of another rule which allows for the possibility that they ⟨ies⟩ is
underlyingly ⟨ie + es⟩.

Kay proposed that morphological analysis be broken down into two
parts, the first part involving the application in reverse of phonological
rules (which Kay referred to as morphographemic rewriting rules) and
the second part involving dictionary lookup. The input string—the surface
form of the word—was represented as a trivial chart, as shown in the top
diagram in figure 3.17. Morphographemic rewrite rules were then successively checked for application by matching their conditioning specification
with the chart; if they applied, new edges were added to the chart to reflect
the output of the rule. Taking the hackneyed example of *tries* in English,
one might have a rule that rewrote the orthographic sequence ⟨ies⟩ as
⟨y + es⟩. Such a rule would reflect the fact that the surface form ⟨tries⟩
might have come from the underlying form ⟨try + es⟩. Another rule might
allow that surface ⟨ies⟩ could come from underlying ⟨ie + es⟩ The bottom
diagram in figure 3.17 shows the chart after edges corresponding to the
application of these two rules have been added.

Once all morphographemic rules have been generated, one has a chart that represents all and only the possible underlying strings for the given surface string. This chart then serves as input to morphological analysis, which involves using a tree-coded lexicon to search the chart for all possible sequences of morphemes; illegal sequences of morphemes are to be weeded out at this stage.

One property that makes Kay's system rather unusual is the extent to which the *conceptually* separate issues of phonological rule application and lexical access are really and truly separate (indeed logically ordered). While Kay does discuss the idea that one might want to "integrate the morphological rewriting rules [i.e., phonological rules—RWS] even more fully with the process of dictionary lookup" (p. 167), so as to allow rewriting rules to be linked to particular lexical entries, the bulk of the discussion centers around the model that I have sketched above. There are of course good computational reasons for disfavoring Kay's proposal. As we noted in the discussion of Kay and Kaplan 1983 above, one bad consequence of running a phonological rule system in reverse (i.e., without precompiling the system into a single automaton) is that one very easily gets an explosion of intermediate analyses. In Kay's model, this explosion is instantiated by the many proposed paths through the chart which must be retained simply because they could legally represent underlying forms for the given input. In any sufficiently complex system of rules, the vast majority of these paths have no chance of being the correct analysis simply because they could not correspond to a legal sequence of morphemes. Most morphological analyzers, as we have seen, get significant mileage out of the restrictions afforded by both the morphemes found in the lexicon and the grammar of their legal combination. Thus, a more intimate relationship between phonological rule application and lexical access in Kay's system could have the effect that at least some of these putative underlying representations could be weeded out early if it could be determined that no legal analyses could ultimately derive from these representations. I admit, however, that it is not obvious how one would generally be able to decide in Kay's system that a given intermediate analysis could not yield appropriate underlying forms. As Anderson (1988, p. 525) notes, Kay's proposal was never developed into a working system for a language with a sufficiently elaborate morphology and phonology, and this fact is surely significant.

To end this discussion on a more positive note, it is probably correct to say that Kay's proposal was the first computational model of morphology that was explicitly intended to be general in character. Nothing in Kay's model of phonology was particularly geared to the properties of any one language, though his model of dictionary lookup *was* evidently geared to a language with purely concatenative morphology. In this latter regard, however, Kay's proposal is no worse off than KIMMO.

3.6.3   Tzoukermann and Liberman's Spanish morphological analyzer

The Spanish morphological analyzer presented by Tzoukermann and Liberman (1990) (see also Feigenbaum et al. 1990 and the discussion in section 1.2.2 above for one application of a closely related system) is a *reductio* of one particular view that is common in the finite-state-morphology community. As we have seen, most work on finite-state morphology assumes that at least *some* alternations which Generative Phonologists would consider to involve phonological rules should be handled by listing the variant allomorphs in the system's lexicon. Tzoukermann and Liberman assume that *all* alternations due to phonological rules should be so listed. Rather than being run during the morphological analysis of a complex form, phonological rules are used in a compiler which takes as input a list of lexical items (derived ultimately from the typographer's tape of a Spanish dictionary) and generates as output an FST arc table, which Tzoukermann and Liberman term the *arc list* (the compiler is therefore termed the *arc-list compiler*).

As an example, consider the Spanish verb *jugar* 'play' and two of its stem alternates, *jueg-* and *jug-*. As we saw at the beginning of chapter 2 with the Spanish verb *poder*, there is a semi-productive rule that changes mid-vowels into diphthongs, so that /o/ becomes /ue/ and /e/ becomes /ie/. In the present indicative conjugations of such verbs, the underlying mid-vowel occurs in the first-person and second-person plural forms (*jugamos*, *jugáis*), whereas the diphthongal version occurs in the other forms (*juego*, *juegas*, *juega*, *juegan*). For the verb *jugar*, the arc-list compiler will run phonological rules to produce all the possible stem forms of the verb,[50] yielding entries of the form shown in (56) (Tzoukermann and Liberman 1990, p. 279).

(56) a.   1 7 *jug jugar*

   b.   1 8 *jueg jugar*

These arc list entries are to be interpreted in the following way: The first number in the entry refers to the input state number; since any verb stem can start a word in Spanish, both entries have the state number '1' corresponding to the initial state. The third entry is the stem alternate. The fourth entry is the lexeme of which the stem alternate is a surface form. The second entry is the state into which the FST moves after having read in the symbols in the third entry and outputting the lexeme in the fourth entry.[51] In analyzing the form *juego* 'play/1/SG/PRES/IND/ACT', the system would match the substring *jueg* to the third entry in (56b), would transduce it to the lexeme *jugar*, and would move the FST into state 8. The arc-list compiler creates the FST table in such a way as to guarantee that from state 8 one can reach only affixes that allow the diphthongized alternate, so an input such as **juegamos* is correctly ruled ill-formed.

If this were done carelessly, the resulting FST could in principle be very large, but Tzoukermann and Liberman reduce the size significantly by various straightforward methods. For example, if another verb *v* behaves exactly like *jugar* in that (a) it has the same number of stem alternates as *jugar* and (b) the verbal endings distribute in such a way that there is an isomorphism between the stem/ending pairings of *jugar* and *v*, then *v*'s arc list entries will have the very same set of output states as *jugar*'s (i.e., it will include states 7 and 8). The FST compiled by the arc-list compiler has about 225 states in all. The resulting analyzer can handle several tens of millions of inflected forms, including all and only the correct inflected forms of the roughly 55,000 verb, adjective, and noun lexemes given by the lexicon. (The system also handles a limited amount of derivational morphology.)

Tzoukermann and Liberman's system is interesting as a practical proposal because, as they note, the proposed model is extremely simple: the system's only run-time data structure is the FST described above, and it is easy to write an interpreter that can control access to this data structure. The system is, in practice, efficient to run (either as an analyzer or as a generator). Furthermore, although one might imagine that precompiling the effects of phonological rules would have the consequence that the resulting machine would be huge, this is evidently not the case; the FST is actually quite small, and it can at the same time handle a very large number of Spanish word forms. The reason for this can be seen when one considers that although many Spanish verbs have more than one stem form, the actual number of isomorphic classes is small—62 according to Tzoukermann and Liberman. So one does not need a very large machine to make sure that the right stems are combined with the right endings, even given that one has compiled out all of the stem alternates. This is interesting insofar as it lays to rest (at least for Spanish) any fears that not modeling phonological alternations on line necessarily has computationally nasty properties.

Very likely this approach would work for many languages. It is probably sufficiently often the case that one would not get the combinatorial explosion that one might expect to get from compiling out all the possible surface forms of all morphemes in the language. Of course, the drawback intrinsic to this method—as with any purely finite-state model—is that not all morphology is well modeled by finite-state machinery.

Still, from a linguistic (or psychological) point of view this is almost certainly the least interesting proposal we have discussed so far, because it simply removes from consideration the question of how to efficiently model the run-time application of phonological rules. While it is certainly true that not all the rules which Generative Phonologists have posited over the years can be argued to operate at run time,[52] it seems likely that at least some of them must be actively used (in this sense) by speakers of the language. As was noted above, even immature or impaired speakers of Finnish seem never to make errors in the application of vowel harmony, though they do make errors in the selection of suffixes which have morphological conditions on their occurrence. Koskenniemi (1983b, p. 151) argues that this supports a model where the mechanisms of affix selection are strictly separate from the application of phonological rules, a view that is basically consistent with the standard view taken in Generative Grammar. Tzoukermann and Liberman's model, in contrast, does not separate these two aspects, since the only constraint on affix selection—transitions in the FST—in principle confounds true morphological selection with phonologically conditioned alternations.

3.6.4 Word-based or paradigm-based systems

Word-based systems   As I mentioned above and as should be clear from the preceding discussion, by far the majority of work on computational morphology has assumed that words are to be derived by somehow combining roots and affixes. In contrast, a few strands of research, in particular those represented in represented by Byrd 1983, Byrd et al. 1986, Byrd and Tzoukermann 1988, and Church 1986, have followed Aronoff (1986) in assuming that words are to be derived from other words. I have already discussed Church's computational reasons for preferring such an approach in subsection 2.4.4. Here I shall briefly describe Byrd's work.[53]

Byrd's main interest in morphological analysis has been the development of tools for use with on-line dictionaries. Among other things, such tools should have the property that they know how to relate morphologically related dictionary entries, and they should also be able to relate novel words composed out of known morphemes to words in the dictionary. Since on-line dictionaries invariably give full word-form entries rather than roots, a word-based approach makes a great deal of sense.[54]

The work reported in Byrd 1983, Byrd et al. 1986, and Byrd and Tzoukermann 1988 is a rather direct implementation of Aronoff's word-based theory. The basic work in the system is done by a set of word-formation rules exemplified by (57), which implements the affixation of -ation.

(57) Name: + ion
      Change: ation*5e*
      Output Features: (verb)
      Input Features: (noun, + sg + abstract)

This rule is written from the point of view of word recognition; what it says is that if you find a word ending in the letters ⟨a-t-i-o-n⟩ you should take off five letters and look up either the residue or the result of concatenating the residue with ⟨e⟩. If the lookup succeeds, then the word found must be a verb, and the entire word (with -ation) will be marked as a singular, abstract noun.

In the work described in Byrd et al. 1986, the general approach of Byrd 1983 was extended. Using an approach similar in spirit to work on the DECOMP morph-lexicon, a base of 3000 "morphologically active" words was compiled using the word list of Kucera and Francis (1967); the term "morphologically active" is used to refer to a word that "can potentially serve as the base of a large number of affixed derivatives" (Byrd et al. 1986, p. 122).[55] A large word list of some 250,000 words was then analyzed using morphological rules as described above. From this analysis were derived tables giving information on which affixation rules were permitted for each given word. These tables consist of a list of words with associated bit vectors, each place in the vector corresponding to a particular rule. For example, *apprentice* would be listed as allowing the rule that suffixes -*hood* (*apprenticehood*) (by having a '1' in the location in its bit vector associated with that rule) but disallowing the rule that prefixes *over*- (*overapprentice). Similarly, *anchor* allows the rule that suffixes -*ed* (*anchored*) or -*like* (*anchorlike*) but disallows the rule that suffixes -*cy* (*anchorcy).

Tzoukermann's French verb generator   Vaguely similar to Byrd's work is Tzoukermann's (1986) system for generating French verbs. This system is notable in part for being one of the relatively few systems produced recently that deal solely with the generation of word forms. Tzoukermann's program takes as input verbs in their infinitival form and specifications for particular slots in the paradigm (i.e., person, number, tense, aspect, and mood specifications) and produces, for the verb in question, the appropriate forms. The system has only a minimal lexicon, which lists stem forms for **closed-class** verbs (e.g., -re infinitive verbs) and irregular verbs (e.g., avoir 'have', pouvoir 'be able'). Regular verbs, including most verbs ending in -er, are not listed in Tzoukermann's system, and one consequence is that the system can produce correct inflected forms for completely novel French verbs.[56]

The basic data structure of the generator is a set of tables—rather like the tables produced by the systems of Byrd et al. that specify which morphographemic rules may be applied with which classes of inflectional affixes. For example, Tzoukermann observes (p. 36) that verb stems ending in $\langle g \rangle$ (e.g., $\langle nag \rangle$, from nager 'swim') and those ending in $\langle c \rangle$ (e.g., $\langle trac \rangle$, from tracer 'draw') have those final consonants rewritten as in (58) when preceding the orthographic vowels $\langle a, o, u \rangle$.

(58) Rule 1: $\langle c \rangle \rightarrow \langle ç \rangle$
        Rule 2: $\langle g \rangle \rightarrow \langle ge \rangle$

In producing correct verb forms for -er verbs ending in $\langle g \rangle$ or $\langle c \rangle$ these rules are applied to produce stem alternants—e.g., $\langle nage \rangle$ and $\langle traç \rangle$—that must be used before endings beginning with the vowels specified above. But, rather than actually looking at the vowel of the ending (which is the approach a DECOMP-style model would have taken), Tzoukermann restricts the application of the rules in (58) by specifying classes of slots in the paradigm as either allowing or disallowing the rule's application. For example, for the two rules given above, the paradigm for the indicative mood, present tense for -er verbs includes the following specifications (adapted from Tzoukermann 1986, p. 40), where '1' means that the stated rule applies and '0' means that it does not:

(59) | Person | Rule 1 | Rule 2 |
|---|---|---|
| 1/SG | 0 | 0 |
| 2/SG | 0 | 0 |
| 3/SG | 0 | 0 |
| 1/PL | 1 | 1 |
| 2/PL | 0 | 0 |
| 3/PL | 0 | 0 |

The specified application of Rule 1, for instance, accounts for the following forms of tracer:

(60) 1/SG   *(je) tra**c** +e*
    2/SG   *(tu) tra**c** +es*
    3/SG   *(il/elle) tra**c** +e*
    1/PL   *(nous) tra**ç** +ons*
    1/PL   *(vous) tra**c** +ez*
    3/PL   *(ils/elles) tra**c** +ent*

Thus, in Tzoukermann's model, all morphographemic rules are morphologically conditioned in that they are associated with particular slots in the paradigm, and are never conditioned by phonological or orthographic content. This approach is somewhat in the spirit of the Word and Paradigm model; see in particular Matthews 1972, where various morphophonemic rules are linked to particular morphological operations. An even more explicit attempt to model certain aspects of the Word and Paradigm approach is that of Calder (1988), which I describe next.

Paradigmatic morphology   As we saw in chapter 2, paradigms have played a central role in the description of inflectional morphology in traditional grammar as well as in some theories of morphology. Most computational models of morphology have not explicitly used paradigms as a means of organizing morphological knowledge, and the paradigm thus is epiphenomenal. One exception to this is Calder 1988.[57]

In Calder's system, a paradigm is defined as a structure of the form

$$\langle \mathbf{Name}, \sigma : \varphi, [LR_1 \ldots LR_n], [S_1 \ldots S_n] \rangle,$$

where **Name** is the name of the paradigm, σ specifies a set of strings, and φ specifies a set of conditions (see below), and where, for $1 \langle i \langle n$, S_i specifies a string modification on σ under the application of lexical rule LR_i. For example, the general paradigm for English verbs could be given in part as follows (adapting somewhat from Calder 1988, p. 61):

(61) $\langle$**verb**, V:[verb, base, ...], [base 3sg non3sg ...], $[V\ V + s\ V ...]\rangle$

The paradigm named **verb** specifies that the variable V, which is constrained by the conditions [*verb, base,* ...] to range over strings corresponding to verbs, has lexical rules (specified separately) which give the morphological features for the base form, the third singular form, the non-third-singular form, and so on. Associated with each of these forms are specifications for each of the string transformations corresponding to each of the lexical rules: the base form has the same string form as the string specified by V, as does the non-third-singular form, whereas the third-singular form has the string form V concatenated with -*s*. Paradigms in this system are not to be interpreted procedurally (as rules in computational models of morphology generally are), but rather as a declarative statement of morphological relationships.[58]

One nice property of Calder's system is that it allows a straightforward treatment of lexical exceptions. Paradigms can subsume one another, and the system is set up in such a way that the most specific paradigm consistent with a given lexical form applies to that form, rather than the more general paradigm. For example, if one wants to model the fact that English nouns ending in $\langle o \rangle$ insert an $\langle e \rangle$ before the plural suffix, one can specify a paradigm for such nouns as in (62).

(62)

$\langle$**noun-o**, N:[noun, singular, $N = S + o$], [singular, plural], $[N \; N + \text{es}]\rangle$

This just says that a string N, which is the spelling of a noun, where N ends in $\langle o \rangle$ (this is what the equation $N = S + o$ means in the conditions), takes a plural form by concatenating $\langle \text{es} \rangle$ with the singular form. This handles a form like $\langle \text{potatoes} \rangle$, but what about a case like $\langle \text{pianos} \rangle$, where we don't want the $\langle e \rangle$ inserted? Recall from subsection 3.4.2 that Bear (1988) had proposed negative rule features, which simply block the application of $\langle e \rangle$ epenthesis in words like *piano*. In Calder's system one handles this case by providing a more specific paradigm; in this case, one of the conditions merely lists the lexical items that fail to undergo the epenthesis rule (see Calder 1988, p. 63):

(63) $\langle$**noun-o2**, N:[noun, singular, $N = [\,piano, piccolo \ldots\,]$],
        [singular, plural],$[N \; N + \text{s}]\rangle$

Since the paradigm in (63) is more specific than the paradigm in (62), a word like *piano* would match (63), and (62) would automatically be blocked from applying to this form.[59] Thus, in contrast with Bear's proposal, where lexical forms must be checked to see if a rule should have applied (and URKIMMO, where arbitrary diacritics are used to block rule applications), in Calder's system a word like *piano* would simply not be part of the paradigm where the $\langle e \rangle$-insertion rule takes place. This seems, conceptually, like the cleanest treatment of exceptionality.

3.6.5 Context-free systems: SIL's AMPLE

I turn finally to a description of one piece of work where the morphotactics is explicitly non-finite-state. Note again that the decision for what to include in this section is somewhat arbitrary. Clearly one could include some of the extensions to KIMMO in the above-described category, in particu-

lar the proposal in Bear 1986. However, one could also view those extensions as being a patch on a system which was originally finite-state in
design. In contrast, the system I describe here is non-finite-state from the
outset. I have already referred to one contribution of the Summer Institute
of Linguistics (SIL) to computational morphology: the implementation of
KIMMO reported in Antworth 1990. A somewhat earlier contribution of
SIL is a morphological exploration tool called AMPLE.[60]

According to Weber et al. (1988, p. 2), AMPLE is a descendant of a
morphologial parser for Quechua reported in Weber and Mann 1979. My
discussion of AMPLE is based on the extensive user's manual (Weber et al.
1988), another discussion, which I have not seen, is that of Simons (1989),
who discusses AMPLE from a linguistic point of view.

AMPLE models morphotactics with a version of categorial morphology
(see Hoeksema 1984): the lexical entry of the noun *courage* would give it a
categorial specification N, and the lexical entry for the prefix *en-*, which can
attach to nouns and make verbs, would be V/N. But unlike Hankamer's
system, where the categorial notation is a notational variant of KIMMO's
finite-state continuation lexicons, AMPLE has mechanisms that allow
long-distance dependencies between affixes and thus, in principle, have
greater-than-finite-state power.[61] For example, to model words like
en +courage +ment, where *en-* is V/N and *-ment* is $V \backslash N$ in AMPLE, one
lists such categorial specifications as part of the affixes' lexical entries. One
then writes a morphotactic rule (referred to as a *test* in Weber et al. 1988)
which allows that a suffix may attach to a root of the correct category (V in
the case of *-ment*), or may attach to a sequence of prefixes followed by a
root if the category which is the output of the prefix (V in the case of *en-*)
is of the appropriate type.[62] This will effectively give the analysis

$$[[en_{V/N} + courage_N]_V + ment_{V \backslash N}]_N$$

to *encouragement*.

In parsing a word, AMPLE proceeds from left to right doing a depth-
first search for a matching sequence of morphemes, trying shorter matches
first. As each morpheme is posited, morphotactic tests associated with the
class of that morpheme (be it prefix, infix, suffix, or root) are run to ascertain whether the posited morpheme is consistent with the analysis already
built. At the end of the word, a set of final tests are run; such tests might
check, for example, that the syntactic category of the morphological analysis is an appropriate category for a fully formed word of the language.

In addition to morphotactic tests, one may further constrain the distribution of morphemes by various lexical features. Affixes may be assigned

an order class, so that one can specify, for example, that a given affix of class n must occur after any affix of class $n - 1$. (This simple finite-state device is useful if one is describing a language with so-called **template morphology**—not to be confused with the templatic root-and-pattern morphology of Arabic; a typical example is verbal morphology in Athapaskan languages, where verbal prefixes seem to occur in a rigid order relative to one another, though see Kari 1989 for a recent in-depth assessment.)

Further constraints may be stated in AMPLE as regular expressions describing the constraining environment for the morpheme in question.[63] For example, one might place a constraint on the affixation of the past participle affix -en in German which stating that it can be affixed only if ge- is also affixed. This could be (approximately) stated with the following AMPLE morpheme environment constraint, which says that the morpheme must be preceded somewhere in the word by ge-:

(64) $+ /ge \dots -$

One can also constrain morphemes (or allomorphs) by stating phonological conditions on their occurrence. The allomorph em- of en- in English, for example, can be constrained in AMPLE to occur only before labials by first appropriately defining *Labial* and then writing the following constraint as part of the lexical entry of the allomorph em-:

(65) $/ - Labial$

(The other allomorph, en-, must be explicitly constrained to occur everywhere *but* before nasals.)

AMPLE has no direct model of phonological rules, and it is therefore necessary to list all the surface forms in which a morpheme might occur. However, as long as the distribution of a phonological variant of a morpheme can be stated in terms of surface phonological properties, it is possible to mimic the application of phonological rules by appropriately constraining the distribution of various allomorphs. Warlpiri progressive harmony could be modeled by listing both allomorphs of a suffix—-ŋku and -ŋki—and one would then constrain the /i/ alternate to occur when the last vowel in the stem is /i/, and the /u/ alternate to occur elsewhere (see subsection 2.6.3).

Finally, AMPLE has the conceptually cleanest model of infixing of any morphological analysis system of which I am aware. Infixes are constrained by directly stating phonological conditions for their occurrence. In a simple case like Bontoc (see subsecion 2.3.2), one would merely write a constraint forcing the infix to occur after the first consonant of the word. AMPLE checks for the presence of infixes at a given point in the analysis of a word, by first checking to see if any uninfixed morphemes occur at that point and then checking to see if there is an analysis xyz (where y is an infix and xz is a morpheme into which y may be inserted) that satisfies the conditions on y's occurrence. In AMPLE, the constraints on the Ulwa possessive infixes (see subsection 2.3.2) may be stated in part as in (66), where the symbol '$-$' refers to the location of the infix.[64]

(66) / # (C) V C $-$ C V
/ # (C) V (C) V C $-$ C V
/ # (C) V (C) V $-$ C V
/ # (C) V (C) (V) (C) $-$ #
/ # (C) V (C) V V (C) $-$ #

This is certainly a conceptually more appealing way to state the constraint on Ulwa infix placement than a large FST.

3.7 A PROSPECTUS: WHAT IS LEFT TO DO

Now that we have examined a variety of approaches to the computational treatment of morphology, it is time to look at some major areas which clearly need futher work. The list of topics here should not be taken to be definitive; rather, it is exemplary of the kinds of issues which are important and which (I feel) have not received a great deal of attention in computational morphology.

Before we turn to any of these issues, however, it would do well to summarize the general trends in the computational morphology literature. These seem to be the following:

• **The predominance of finite-state morphotactics.** While there have been a few exceptions (e.g., Bear 1986; Weber et al. 1988), most morphological analyzers assume that morpheme combinations are governed by a strictly finite-state grammar.

• **The predominance of item-and-arrangement-style morphology.** In the majority of systems, all morphemes are considered to be dictionary entries. Only in a few systems (e.g., Byrd 1983; Byrd et al. 1986; Calder 1988; Tzoukermann 1986) are affixes treated as rules or as properties of slots in paradigms, and thus viewed differently from stems.

• **The predominance of purely concatenative morphology.** Not only do finite-state models of morphotactics prevail, but the actual modes of combination expressible by those models are typically limited to the simple concatenation of morphemes; this effectively rules out a simple treatment of infixation or root-and-pattern morphology within those frameworks. Furthermore, morphemes are generally assumed to have some segmental content of their own, and mechanisms are not generally provided for handling reduplication. A few works (e.g., Kay 1987; Sproat and Brunson 1987; Weber et al. 1988) have looked at languages in which these assumptions are not valid.

All these issues pertain to morphology proper, and it can easily be seen that all the basic assumptions commonly found in various work in the literature are in particular found in URKIMMO. To be sure, the reason these assumptions are so prevalent is that they are approximately correct for many of the languages for which people have built morphological processing systems. If Koskenniemi had been interested in Arabic or Warlpiri rather than Finnish, his system might have taken on a rather different character from the start.

On the treatment of phonological (or orthographic) rules there is substantially less general agreement. Proposals have ranged from the fairly powerful general finite-state model of KIMMO and the potentially powerful generate-and-test model of Hankamer (1986), through the much more constrained string transformations allowed by DECOMP, to systems that eschew any on-line processing of phonological alternations, such as that of Tzoukermann and Liberman (1990). It is fair to say that Koskenniemi's proposal has been the most successful, if success is to be measured by the number of languages that have been described in the framework or the number of research projects that have adopted the general approach. If nothing else, KIMMO provides an implementation-independent language (either FST transition tables, or a real rule input language as discussed in Dalrymple et al. 1987) in which to write phonological or orthographic rules; this is something that Hankamer's system, for example, does not provide. Nonetheless, there are substantive problems with bringing the two-level assumption in line with assumptions commonly made in the linguistics literature, and where a generate-and-test approach may confer some advantages. I have already discussed the general issue of rule ordering (subsection 3.2.2), and noted that one can in principle model a system of ordered generative rules using a two-level model, albeit with much loss of elegance in some cases. Below I shall focus on a different question which is much harder to answer, namely the question of how to treat cyclicity in a computational framework.[65]

In addition to discussing these phonological problems, I will have a few further things to say about computational complexity as it relates to morphological analysis and generation. I will also discuss the relationship between morphology and syntax with a view to the lack of treatment of that topic within the computational morphology literature.

3.7.1 Issues of computational complexity

Let me start by addressing a problematic area where I feel the issues to be very unclear, namely the area of computational complexity and morphological or phonological analysis. As was noted above, Barton et al. (1987) have criticized the KIMMO approach to morphology (and, by implication at least, some others) on computational grounds. We have already examined Barton's suggestion for improving the computational complexity of KIMMO systems. However, we have also noted that (following Koskenniemi and Church 1988) there is a question as to how much of a practical concern Barton's criticism really is. Furthermore, even for the really hard computational problems, such as Barton's SAT generation problem, the exponential search required translates into exponential search time only on a serial machine. In a truly parallel machine such as the Connection Machine one could farm out each of the possible assignments of values to variables to a different processor, and the generation would proceed (in parallel) in time linear with the length of the input. The only limit on the number of processes that could be farmed out in this way is, of course, the number of processors on the machine. One answer to at least some questions of complexity would therefore seem to be to implement one's models in increasingly powerful hardware.

Indeed, as was noted in subsection 3.6.2, there have been proposals in the more psycholinguistically oriented corners of the literature (e.g., Anderson 1988; Dolan 1988) for the use of the Connection Machine for morphological analysis. The underlying theme in that discussion seems to be that a massively parallel architecture would allow one to throw considerations of computational complexity to the winds, and to pursue analyses (e.g., a general generate-and-test approach) that would be computationally prohibitive on a serial machine. The positive side of this approach is that there is reason to believe that humans use parallel processing in morphology (Emmorey 1988), and the Connection Machine may therefore afford a more psychologically realistic computational architecture than a standard serial machine. The down side is that many of the phenomena that would presumably be handled by such computationally expensive algorithms are morphological phenomena that have received fairly decent solutions using serial algorithms which, if not guaranteed to be efficient, are at least generally so.

The lack of clarity here is, I believe, a fair reflection of the state of the general understanding of these issues. With the exception of Barton's work and Koskenniemi and Church's response, there has been no systematic treatment of computational complexity as it relates to morphology. It is probably worth doing more: it is an open and interesting question as to what kinds of linguistic or computational constraints can be brought to bear on the design of algorithms for morphological analysis and generation so as to reduce their complexity. Barton's constraint-propagation method is a start on this, but it is only a start.

Finally, much more work needs to be done on modeling human morphological performance. This has been discussed to varying degrees in the literature—Koskenniemi 1983b, Anderson 1988, Dolan 1988, and Cornell 1988 are a few examples—but it has yet to be adequately treated. Of course, the problem is very hard: in order to model human behavior, one has to first understand what it is one is modeling; yet, although much is known about the human processing of morphological structure, it is also true that comparatively little is known. Psycholinguistically guided work on morphological analysis—whether using massively parallel machines or serial machines—will almost certainly end up having implications for arguments about computational complexity. The one thing that is certain about humans is that, when using a language with which they are familiar, they almost always analyze morphologically complex words very rapidly.[66] Yet to say that a program runs rapidly is not the same thing as saying that the algorithm it implements is provably efficient. It remains to be seen whether humans process words efficiently in the strictest sense of the word.

3.7.2 Cyclic and lexical phonology

Cyclic phonology   Cyclic rule application is one area of generative phonology that is most obviously interpreted computationally as part of a model of generation, and not analysis. It is rather easy to see how one might build a morphological generator that constructs words "from the inside out," interleaving the addition of morphemes with the application of phonological rules. If morphological *analysis* could generally be handled by a generate-and-test model, as Anderson suggests, then a morphological *analyzer* could presumably incorporate a model of the phonological cycle. However, in most currently available models, it is not easy to see how to model cyclic phonological rules (at least in an efficient fashion), since such rules would appear to require that we perform analysis by stripping off an affix, undoing phonological rules, and then repeating the process on the result. As in the system of Kay 1977, the intermediate results could get rather out of hand. And in a two-level system where one of the guiding principles is that phonological rules must directly relate lexical and surface forms, it is very hard indeed to see how to handle cyclic rules in any straightforward way; as an exercise, it is worth considering how one would build a two-level model of Mandarin Third Tone Sandhi, which was described in subsection 2.6.5.

To be sure, some kinds of cyclic interactions can be modeled readily enough. Consider the rules of Yer Deletion and Lower in Polish (Rubach 1984, pp. 184–190). Yers are a familiar topic in the Slavic phonology literature. A yer is a [−tense, +high] underlying vowel which, when followed by yer in the next syllable, becomes a [−high] vowel (/e/ in Polish); otherwise it deletes. An informal statement of the two rules, adapted from Rubach 1984 (p. 185), is given in (67) where /ĭ/, and /ī/ represent yers.

(67) a. Lower: $\{ĭ, ī\} \rightarrow e/ − C^* \{ĭ, ī\}$

 b. Yer Deletion: $\{ĭ, ī\} \rightarrow \emptyset$

Rubach argues that Lower is cyclic and that Yer Deletion is postcyclic, (i.e., applies at the end of the derivation of a word, after all of the cyclic rules have applied.)

Now, some of the examples Rubach discusses can be modeled in a two-level system. These are cases where the only yers occur in the root and suffixes, and hence the relevant cycles are built up from left to right.[67] Consider the word *pies +ecz +ek* /p'jes + eč + ek/ 'dog' (with two diminutive suffixes), for which Rubach gives the following derivation (p. 186, adapting somewhat), where the last cycle involves the addition of the nominative singular masculine ending ĭ:

(68) Cycle 2	pĭs + ĭ	
	pes + ĭk	Lower
	pjes + ĭk	Other rules
Cycle 3	pjes + ĭk + īk	
	pjes + ĭč + īk	Other rules
	pjes + eč + īk	Lower
Cycle 4	pjes + eč + īk + ĭ	
	pjes + eč + ek + ĭ	Lower
Postcyclic	pjes + eč + ek	Yer Deletion
	p'jes + eč + ek	Other rules

This can be modeled in a two-level system with two rules. The two-level version of Lower restricts the occurrence of the pairs ĭ:e and ī:e to

environments where another lexical yer follows (with possibly some intervening consonants) and furthermore forces the transduction to /e/ in that
environment:

(69) Lower (two-level version): Yer:e ⇔ − C* YER: =

With Lower stated in this way, Yer Deletion is handled by simply including the pairs ĭ:∅ and ĭ:∅ in the feasible pair set, and by allowing no further
surface transductions for the yers. A yer will therefore surface as zero if and
only if it is not followed by a lexical yer in the next syllable. This is the
desired result.

The problem arises when we consider the application of the two rules
in words that have both yer-containing prefixes and yer-containing suffixes, as in the case of *bez +den +n +y* 'bottomless' and *beze +cn +y* 'infa-
mous' (Rubach 1984, pp. 187–188). At issue is the negative prefix, which
shows up as *bez-* or *beze-*. Now, Rubach argues that Polish prefixes are
generally attached on a late cycle, after all suffixes have been attached; at
the point at which the negative prefix attaches, therefore, the underlying
forms *[[[dĭn] +ĭn] +i]* (-*denny*) and *[[cĭn] +i]* (-*cny*) have been transformed into *den +ĭn +i* and *cĭn +i*, respectively, via derivations similar to
that in (68).[68] According to Rubach, the underlying form of the prefix
bez(e)- is *bezĭ*. It attaches to the two stems above to form *[bezĭ+[den +
ĭn +i]* and *[bezĭ+[cĭn +i]]*, respectively. In the latter case the yer in the
prefix is followed by a yer in the following syllable, and the environment for
Lower is met. In *bez +den +n +y*, however, the underlying yer of the root
den has already been Lowered, thus removing the triggering environment
for Lower for the yer of the prefix. So the yer of the prefix cannot undergo
Lower, and later deletes. The surface forms of the two words are thus
[bez +den +n +i] and *[beze +cn +i]*. The latter form is not a problem
from the point of view of the two-level rule in (69), but the form *bez +den +
n +y* is; according to that rule, the second yer in *bez-* ought to surface as an
/e/ since it is followed in the next syllable (*den*) by a lexical yer, yet it deletes.
There is no clean way to modify the statement of Lower in (69) to handle
this case. One could of course add a diacritic such as '&' to the lexical entry
of prefixes. One could then add a second clause to the rule of Lower that
forces lexical yers to correspond to surface /e/ if followed by the diacritic
'&', any number of consonants, and a lexical yer corresponding to a surface
∅:

(70) Yer:e ⇐ − & C* YER:∅

Neither (70) nor (69) would apply to lexical yers followed by the context &
C* *yer:e*, so these would surface as ∅, as desired. But this analysis would

miss the point that is elegantly captured in the cyclic analysis: at the point where the prefix attaches, Lower cannot apply in *bez + den + n + y*, not because the general rule is blocked by some arbitrary symbol in the lexical entry of *bez(e)-*, but simply because the triggering environment has been removed by a previous application of the rule.

I do not see any straightforward solution to this kind of problem within the two-level framework. More generally, and assuming that one wants to eschew computationally expensive solutions, I do not see a neat general solution to dealing with cyclicity in any morphological analysis system.

A note on Lexical Phonology and Morphology   In view of the popularity in the phonological community of the constellation of assumptions of LPM, it is worth asking whether some of those assumptions may have computational import. I suspect that the answer, at least at present, is that there is relatively little computational import, though to my knowledge there has been essentially no discussion of this topic. I will merely offer a couple of suggestions along these lines.

The most obvious way in which LPM could be interpreted computationally is as a theory of word-form generation: recall that one of the ideas of LPM is that morphological operations are organized into ordered strata, with phonological rules marked to apply at particular strata. Unfortunately, as was noted in subsection 2.5.2, the constraints on morpheme combination afforded by LPM's stratum-ordering assumption are rather weak. It is therefore unlikely that LPM could be *usefully* interpreted as a computational model of word-form generation.

Probably the most interesting aspect of LPM from a computational point of view is the limitation of phonological rules to particular morphological strata. The interesting point here is that if we are doing morphological analysis, and if we posit the application of a rule which we know to be limited to a certain stratum, then the analyzer ought to be able to use that information to limit the search for affixes associated with the stratum in question. This idea has been used to some extent in the computational morphology literature—see, in particular, Sproat and Brunson 1987, and see also Coleman 1990. It seems to me, however, that this idea can be exploited further.

3.7.3   Morphology and syntax

We turn now to a question that has received little serious treatment: How might one incorporate a morphological analyzer (or generator) into a syntactic analysis (or generation) model? Computational models of morphology uniformly assume that a morphological analyzer should find all possible forms for a word and let some higher-level processor (such as a syntactic parser) decide which word form is most appropriate. Presumably, however, one would in general want to make use of syntactic context in guiding the analysis of a complex word form. If syntactic considerations tell us, for example, that a certain word must be a form of a verb (suppose that we are parsing Japanese and we come to the last word in the sentence, which is invariably a verb form), then there is probably no point in pursuing analyses that would end in the conclusion that the word is a noun. It is, of course, an open question to what extent one can depend on syntax to constrain the morphological analysis in this way: in practice, the percentage of cases where the syntax is sufficiently constraining to completely rule out the possibility that a word has a certain set of properties may well be quite low. But this question will surely come up as serious morphological analyzers are integrated into serious parsing systems.

A related issue which is clearly important in the morphological analysis of some languages is the handling of "syntactically relevant" morphology, such as noun incorporation or mirror-principle effects. Consider again the case of Huichol (subsection 2.5.1), where the order of the applicative and passive affixes on the verb mirrors the order in which (in Baker's [1988] model) the applicative and passive transformations apply in the syntactic derivation of the following sentence:

(71) *tiiri yi + nauka + ti nawazi me +* puutinanai + **ri** + YERI
     (children four + SUBJ knife 3/SG + buy + **APPL** + PASS
     'four children were bought a knife'

Clearly the order of the affixes on the verb gives useful information about the interpretation of the sentence, since it identifies the underlying function of the NP *tiiri yinaukati* 'four children': underlyingly this can only have been the indirect object (benefactive). One way to model this computationally would be to start with the common assumption that part of a verb's lexical entry is a frame giving information on what kinds of arguments it takes; for the sake of ease of explication, I will assume here a theory (like LFG) where such lexical entries are specified in terms of grammatical relations, but any representation that is essentially a notational variant of this would suffice. The lexical entry for *puutinanai* 'buy' might look as in (72), where the arguments are enclosed in angle brackets.

(72) *puutinanai*, V, ⟨SUBJ, OBJ, IOBJ⟩, 'buy'

Now, when the applicative affix -*ri* attaches to a verb such as *puutinanai*, we want the resulting form to have the frame ⟨SUBJ, OBJ, 2OBJ⟩ (where 2OBJ is 'second object'), with the further stipulations that whichever noun phrase is assigned to the derived OBJ slot should be related to the IOBJ slot in the original verb frame, and whichever noun phrase is assigned to the derived 2OBJ should be related to the original OBJ. This can be achieved by giving -*ri* its own frame, which is to be inherited by the mother node dominating the affix. Further equations stipulate the relation between the mother node's frame and the frame for the verb:

(73) -*ri*, LeftDaughter\MotherNode,
      MotherNode = V, LeftDaughter = V,
      MotherNode's Frame = ⟨SUBJ, OBJ, 2OBJ⟩,
      [MotherNode's OBJ] = [LeftDaughter's IOBJ],
      [MotherNode's 2OBJ] = [LeftDaughter's OBJ]

The passive affix -*yeri* would be treated similarly:

(74) -*yeri*, LeftDaughter\MotherNode,
      MotherNode = V, LeftDaughter = V,
      MotherNode's Frame = ⟨SUBJ, OBJ, (BY-OBJ)⟩
      [MotherNode's BY-OBJ] = [LeftDaughter's SUBJ],
      [MotherNode's SUBJ] = [LeftDaughter's OBJ]

Thus, in the complex verb form *(me +)puutinanai + ri + yeri* the subject (*tiiri yinaukati*) would be interpreted as being the same as the object of *puutinanai + ri* 'buy + APPL' (by (74)), which is in turn interpreted as the indirect object of *puutinanai* (by (73)).

The model for Huichol sketched above is fairly attractive computationally, since it is rather straightforward to implement such a scheme in a unification-based formalism (Shieber 1986). There is nothing particularly novel here; the analysis is quite similar to the original analyis of passive given within LFG (Bresnan 1982).[69] In the form in which I have given it, it is also rather crude. For one thing, I would expect that it would not be necessary to state quite so many details in particular lexical entries. For example, in many theories of grammatical relations, if some operation has the effect of changing an IOBJ into an OBJ, then it follows from general principles within the theory that the underlying OBJ should become a 2OBJ; one would therefore not need to state this fact explicitly, as I do in (73), but could have it follow from general mechanisms. Be that as it may, the above sketch is a plausible proposal for how to proceed in handling some of the kinds of morphology discussed in Baker 1988. Needless to say, no work has been done in this area, since there has to my knowledge not been any work on syntactic and morphological parsing for languages with the kind of mirror-principle effects exhibited in Huichol.

3.8   FURTHER READING

Apart from the present book (at the time of writing) there are no monograph-length treatments of computational morphology. There are, however, two review articles that discuss the topic. Anderson's 1988 is a brief overview of previous work on computational morphology (including Kay 1977, Hankamer 1986, and Koskenniemi 1983b) as well as a discussion of Anderson's own massively parallel generate-and-test proposal. Gazdar 1985 deals specifically with two-level finite-state morphology.

For a more in-depth introduction to two-level morphology, I particularly recommend Antworth 1990 (and see also my review of that book, Sproat 1991b). In addition to giving an excellent discussion of how two-level analyzers work and how to write two-level grammars, Antworth 1990 comes with software for a version of URKIMMO that can be run under a variety of systems (including IBM PC and compatibles running MS-DOS or PC-DOS, Macintosh, Unix System V, and 4.2 BSD UNIX). For more discussion of some of the formal properties of two-level morphology see Ritchie 1989 and Reape and Thompson 1988.

Standard references for finite-state automata and other issues in formal language theory are Hopcroft and Ullman 1979, Lewis and Papadimitriou 1981, and Harrison 1978. For the most complete discussion of the complexity of two-level morphology, and also for a discussion of complexity theory as it relates to other areas of computational linguistics, see Barton et al. 1987.

Chapter 4

Some Peripheral Issues

4.1 INTRODUCTION

In this chapter I discuss two areas which are somewhat peripheral to computational morphology. First, I review some models of the acquisition of morphology, paying particular attention to the connectionist work on this topic reported in by Rumelhart and McClelland (1986). Second, I discuss work on the analysis of compound nominals in English.

4.2 MORPHOLOGICAL ACQUISITION

Work on morphological acquisition is of two types. The first, represented by Golding and Thompson 1985 and Wothke 1986, is primarily concerned with the practical question of how to automatically calculate a set of word-formation rules for a language. Wothke's system, for example, learns morphological rules from a training corpus consisting of source-target pairs: for instance, if the rules to be learned are the pluralization rules of English nouns, then a set of pairs where the first member is the source (singular) and the second member is the target (plural) is presented to the system. The system then examines the source-target pairs and attempts to come up with a set of word-formation rules consistent with the data. If the data set contains the pairs *half/halves*, *calf/calves*, and *wolf/wolves*, Wothke's system will deduce a rule of the form shown in (1a). If the set also contains the pairs *boy/boys*, *girl/girls*, *mother/mothers*, and *father/fathers*, the system will deduce the rule given in (1b).

(1) a. $\langle f \rangle \rightarrow \langle ves \rangle / - \#$

    b. $\emptyset \rightarrow \langle s \rangle / - \#$

Of the two rules, (1a) is the more specific; it requires reference to the last letter of the input, whereas (1b) simply attaches an ⟨s⟩ to any stem. Wothke's system orders more specific rules before more general rules, so that rule (1a) will apply before rule (1b), and if (1a) applies it will block the application of (1b).[1] The system is presented as a pragmatic solution to the automation of certain types of morphological alternations; there is no pretense of trying to model how humans acquire morphology.

Two pieces of work that attempt to handle the acquisition of morphology, and at the same time to be psychologically realistic, are MacWhinney 1978 and Rumelhart and McClelland 1986. MacWhinney presents a very ambitious computational framework which is intended to model children's acquisition of morphology. The work is based heavily upon real acquisition data collected by MacWhinney and others. When MacWhinney 1978 was written the model was reportedly being implemented. As far as I know, however, the implementation was never completed, so MacWhinney's proposal cannot really be evaluated as a computational model of human morphological acquisition.

Rumelhart and McClelland's proposal, in contrast, was implemented and has been rather extensively evaluated, both by Rumelhart and McClelland themselves and by others—most notably Pinker and Prince (1988). Rumelhart and McClelland's work is interesting for a couple of reasons. First, as far as I know it is the only work in computational morphology that attempts to closely model the results of psycholinguistic studies of morphology; their psycholinguistic data were drawn from a study on the acquisition of the English past tense reported in Bybee and Slobin 1982. (As we saw in chapter 3, various work on computational morphological analysis has been claimed to be psycholinguistically realistic, but only Rumelhart and McClelland [1986] have really attempted to show that the behavior of their system fits the behavior of humans.) Second, Rumelhart and McClelland 1986 is one of the better-known, and arguably one of the more successful, applications of connectionist models to natural language. Since connectionism is currently flourishing as a field in its own right, it is worth reviewing the primary contribution of this field to computational morphology. In what follows I describe Rumelhart and McClelland's work, and I provide a critique of several of their claims to success. Included in this critique are some of the observations of Pinker and Prince, but there are some points included here which they do not discuss.[2] A great many issues which Pinker and Prince raise will not be discussed here; for these the reader is referred to their paper.)

4.2.1   Rumelhart and McClelland's connectionist morphology

Rumelhart and McClelland's connectionist network is capable, after a fashion, of learning the alternations inherent in English verbal morphology. When presented with data consisting of pairs of base forms and past-tense forms, its learning behavior is reminiscent of the behavior of children learning these alternations in English (Bybee and Slobin 1982). Also, their model is apparently able to extend what it has learned to novel verb forms, so that it is often able to come up with appropriate past-tense forms for verbs it has not seen. However, it also (somewhat less) often generates forms that seem wholly inappropriate.

According to Rumelhart and McClelland, there are two parts to their network, a diagram of which is given in figure 4.1. The first component consists of the encoding and decoding networks that take phonemic representations of words and convert them into a binary feature representation—the machine language of the network. The encoding and decoding algorithms are fairly complex. Rather than encode the phonemes of English verbs directly with vectors of features, as in standard phonology, Rumelhart and McClelland chose a representational scheme originally due to Wickelgren (1969), the basic units of which they call *Wickelphones*. Each phone is a triple consisting of the left context, the phone itself, and the right context; a Wickelphone model is thus a form of trigram model. Rumelhart and McClelland would represent /kat/ as $\{\#ka, kat, at\#\}$, where '$\#$' represents a word boundary. For the rather limited data in their set of English verbs, they are able to represent each word as an *unordered* set of Wickelphones, since this unambiguously defines a particular word—though, as Pinker and Prince (1988, pp. 96–98) point out, this will not work for linguistic data in general. Each Wickelphone is then translated into a set of binary-valued *Wickelfeatures*, which are rather loosely based upon standard phonological features. Finally, Rumelhart and McClelland added a certain amount of noise to the system by "blurring" the featural representation (pp. 238–239) "to promote faster generalization" over the data. As Pinker and Prince explain (p. 93), "[b]lurring the input representations makes the connection weights in the ... model less likely to be able to exploit the idiosyncrasies of the words in the training set and hence reduces the model's tendency towards conservatism."

Second, each node in the input layer is connected to every node in the output layer by a weighted connection (in figure 4.1 these connections are labeled as the Pattern Associator). The output value net_i of each output node i is computed by summing over the outputs of all the input nodes

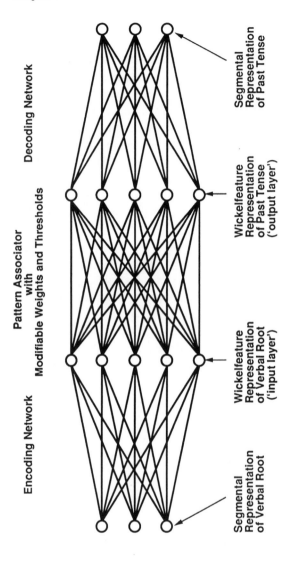

Figure 4.1
The two-layer connectionist network used in the simulations of English past-tense acquisition reported in Rumelhart and McClelland 1986. Adapted, with permission of The MIT Press, from Rumelhart and McClelland 1986, p. 222, figure 1.

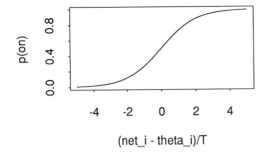

Figure 4.2
The form of the function for determining the probability of activation of an output node. Adapted, with permission of The MIT Press, from Rumelhart and McClelland 1986, p. 224, figure 2.

j multiplied by the adjustable weight from j to i, and applying to this sum a probability function of the form (Rumelhart and McClelland 1986, p. 224)

$$(2)\ \ p(a_i = 1) = \frac{1}{1 + e^{-(net_i - \theta_i)/T}}.$$

In this equation p is the probability of the output node's being turned on (i.e., having an output signal of 1 as opposed to 0), T is the (fixed) temperature of the system, and θ is the (adjustable) threshold of the unit. The probability function is plotted in figure 4.2. During training, the output of the network is compared with the desired output, and the weights and thresholds on the connections are adjusted using the perceptron convergence procedure (see Rumelhart and McClelland 1986, pp. 225–226, and elsewhere in the *Parallel Distributed Processing* volumes, for discussion).

In addition to these two components, Rumelhart and McClelland's model crucially depends upon a third design feature, namely the manner in which the data were presented. As noted, the morphological alternation which Rumelhart and McClelland were concerned with consisted of the mapping between present-tense and past-tense forms of English verbs. In addition to the regular verbs (which add -əd to words ending in the alveolar stops /t, d/, -t to words ending in voiceless consonants, and -d otherwise) there are a number of classes of irregular verbs. According to Rumelhart and McClelland, who derive their classification from that of Bybee and Slobin (1982), there are eight such classes of interest (class VI having two subclasses). These classes are outlined in (3) (adapted from Rumelhart and McClelland 1986, p. 247).

(3) **I.**   verbs that undergo no change: *hit, beat, cut*

    II.   verbs that undergo a change of final /d/ to /t/: *send/sent, build/built*

    III.   verbs that undergo an internal vowel change and also add /t/ or /d/: *fell/felt, lost/lost, say/said, tell/told*

    IV.   verbs that undergo an internal vowel change, delete a final consonant, and add a final /t/ or /d/: *bring/brought, catch/caught*

    V.   verbs that undergo an internal vowel change whose stems end in a dental: *bite/bit, find/found, ride/rode*

   VIa. verbs that have a vowel change /i/ to /æ/: *sing/sang, drink/drank.*

   VIb. verbs that have /i/ or /æ/ to /ʌ/: *string/stung, hang/hung.*

    VII. all other verbs that undergo an internal vowel change: *give/gave, break/broke*

   VIII. all verbs that undergo an internal vowel change and end in a diphthongal sequence: *blow/blew, fly/flew, go/went*[3]

Rumelhart and McClelland's data consisted of 506 English verbs, with both regular and irregular past tenses ranked in order of the frequency of their *-ing* form in the database of Kucera and Francis (1967). These verbs were split into three groups, the first consisting of the 10 most frequent (of which 8 are irregular), the second consisting of the 410 next most frequent, and the last consisting of the 86 least frequent verbs, including both regulars and irregulars. In training their network, Rumelhart and McClelland first presented the 10 most frequent verbs 10 times, and then went on to present these 10 along with the next 410 another 190 times. This method of presentation was designed by Rumelhart and McClelland to "capture approximately the experience with past tenses of a young child picking up English from everyday conversation" (pp. 240–241). The basic claim is "simply that the child learn first about the present and past tenses of the highest frequency verbs; later on, learning occurs for a much larger ensemble of verbs, including a much larger proportion of regular forms."[4] Finally, they tested the model on the last 86 verbs, to which the model had not been previously exposed, in order to evaluate how well it had learned the relevant generalizations.

According to Rumelhart and McClelland, the simulation exhibits humanlike behavior in two respects: the learning appears to proceed in a fashion reminiscent of children's acquisition of these alternations; and the final state of the machine deals appropriately with novel forms. These two points will be addressed in the next two sections.

The learning behavior of Rumelhart and McClelland's model   In learning the morphology of their language, children are exposed early on to high-frequency irregular forms and seem at first to learn those forms correctly before they learn to apply the regular productive rules. In the case of English verbal morphology, the child learns that *went* is the past tense of *go* and produces this form correctly before the regular rules for past-tense formation are learned. Once the regular rules are learned, the child initially *overregularizes*, producing such forms as *goed*. Gradually, the child re-learns the correct irregular forms, which it had seemingly forgotten. The learning curve for high-frequency words having irregular forms is thus "U-shaped": the child initially performs well on these forms, the performance then drops significantly, and finally the performance improves again. Figure 4.3 plots the learning curves for high-frequency regular and high-frequency irregular verbs for Rumelhart and McClelland's model; the horizontal axis represents the number of trials and the vertical axis the percentage correct by feature. The obvious dip in the learning curve for the irregular verbs would appear to suggest that Rumelhart and McClelland's model displays the same acquisition behavior as human learners. However, as Pinker and Prince note, there can be no doubt that this learning behavior does not stem from any intrinsic properties of Rumelhart and McClelland's model. Rather it is derivable from the manner in which the data were presented: after the model had converged upon the correct forms for the 8 most frequent irregular verbs, it was flooded with 410 more verbs,

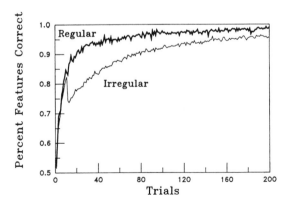

Figure 4.3
Percentage of correct features for regular and irregular high-frequency verbs as a function of trials. Reproduced, with permission of The MIT Press, from Rumelhart and McClelland 1986, p. 242, figure 4.

a substantial portion of which are regular. It is hardly surprising, then, that the model would "forget" what it had started to converge upon, since substantial amounts of data would favor adjusting the connection weights so as to produce regular endings.[5] But, although it is possible to get the U-shaped learning curve by presenting the data in two stages, this data presentation does not correspond in any reasonable way to the manner in which children are exposed to English verbal alternations (see Pinker and Prince 1988 for a discussion of this point). It is obviously not the case that children are first presented with the most common verbs and then, after they have achieved some predetermined level of competence on these, are presented with the next most frequent set.

A more subtle criticism that can be leveled against Rumelhart and McClelland's evaluation of their model's reproduction of the U-shaped curve is the following: As noted, the value along the vertical axis for the plot in figure 4.3 represents the percent correct by feature for the productions of the model over the first 200 trials. How this measure correlates with children's error rates is far from clear. At various times in their linguistic development, children produce greater or lesser numbers of regularized forms for irregular verbs. They do not, at different stages of their development, produce forms with various degrees of featural disparity with the correct response. For example, for *came* they do not initially produce *game* (which shares all but one feature with the intended form) and then, when they start to regularize, produce *gubbed* (which shares fewer features), and then relearn the production of more accurate renditions. On the other hand, as will become clearer when we consider some of the forms the system produced in its final state, the network is doing something rather like this, and it is partly for this reason that Rumelhart and McClelland use the extremely crude "features correct" measure. The use of this measure certainly gives a U-shaped learning curve, but not one that can sensibly be compared with real acquisition data.

A second way in which Rumelhart and McClelland's model is claimed to mimic human acquisition is in the differential regularization of the various classes of irregular verbs involving internal vowel changes (classes III–VIII). Bybee and Slobin observed that preschoolers' rates of regularization errors in spontaneous speech were not constant across the different classes of irregular verbs. For example, class VIII verbs (*blow*) were much more susceptible to regularization errors than class III verbs (*feel*). Now, one of the properties of the Wickelfeature encoding scheme which Rumelhart and McClelland used is that determining the actual response of the system to any given input is problematic; since the output of the system is a set of probabilities that particular Wickelfeatures are on, the only way that Rumelhart and McClelland could determine the actual response of the system was to compare the output response with the Wickelfeature representation of all possible strings which could be composed out of their set of Wickelphones. This set, while not infinite, is extremely large, and the problem is computationally expensive. What they actually did in the training sessions was to measure the strength of the model's response to the set of Wickelphones comprising each of a small set of what they deemed to be likely candidate outputs; so, if *ate* were deemed to be of interest, they would measure the system's response to the Wickelphones { #*et, et*# }. In comparing the model's behavior on Bybee and Slobin's different verb classes, Rumelhart and McClelland measured the system's response to the following forms: the *correct* form, the result of adding the regular past tense to the present tense form (*base +ed*), and the result of adding the regular past tense to the past-tense form (*past +ed*). Since the system could not be said to be regularizing in the same sense as Bybee and Slobin's preschoolers (that is, it was not at any time literally producing forms such as *blowed*, or *blewed*), Rumelhart and McClelland chose the following ratio as representing the tendency of the system to regularize on a particular verb:

$$(4) \quad \frac{(based + ed + past + ed)}{(base + ed + past + ed + correct)}.$$

As Rumelhart and McClelland observe, it would be difficult to be certain which stage of their model corresponded to preschool children. They therefore performed the regularization-response computation for the various classes of verbs over three different time periods taken over the period of maximal overregularization—namely the trials over which the upswing in the high-frequency irregular verbs occurs (figure 4.3). Their results are given here in table 4.1 (adapted from their table 14, p. 255), where the first two columns give Bybee and Slobin's data and the remaining columns give the rank ordering of the verbal classes by Rumelhart and McClelland's model (for the three time periods, plus an average for those time periods), derived by averaging the value of the ratio (4) computed for all the verbs in each class.

While they observe that there are discrepancies, Rumelhart and McClelland claim that "the simulation seems to capture the major features of the data very nicely" (p. 256). For the first five trials, as Pinker and Prince point out, Rumelhart and McClelland's claim seems to be somewhat true.[6] Indeed, some of the tendencies, such as for class VIII to be

Table 4.1

Rank order	Bybee and Slobin data		Trials 11–15		Trials 16–20		Trials 21–30		Average trials 11–30	
	Class	Percent	Class	Ratio	Class	Ratio	Class	Ratio	Class	Ratio
1	VIII	80	VIII	.86	VIII	.76	VIII	.61	VIII	.71
2	VI	55	VII	.80	VII	.74	VII	.61	VII	.69
3	V	34	VI	.76	V	.60	IV	.48	V	.56
4	VII	32	V	.72	IV	.59	V	.46	IV	.56
5	III	13	IV	.69	III	.57	III	.44	III	.53
6	IV	10	III	.67	VI	.52	VI	.40	VI	.52

most regularized and for class III to be among the least regularized, are at least consistent across trials and not hopelessly at odds with Bybee and Slobin's results.[7] Again, these results would be significant—suggesting that Rumelhart and McClelland's network has human-like behavior— *only if the behavior is due to properties of the network itself and is not an artifact of, e.g., the measurement chosen.*

However, there is good reason to believe that a large portion of Rumelhart and McClelland's results have nothing to do with the network, but have rather to do with the formula in (4) and the shape of the past-tense forms in the different classes. To see this, consider what the results of applying formula (4) would be if we were to simply assume that the network always produced a regularized form—a *base +ed* form, for example. Compare the output of the network with each of the three interesting possible responses, namely *correct*, *past +ed*, and *base +ed*. In any given case there will obviously be more or less of a disparity in feature specifications between the actual (*base +ed*) response and each of the alternatives; for example, the *base +ed* form will match perfectly with itself, but less well with *past +ed* or *correct*. If one then averages the values of (4) among verbs in each of the six classes of interest, the classes show rather different behavior, some classes showing "stronger regularization" than others. It is not difficult to see why this should be. Imagine that we take a verb of class VIII, such as *blow*, and consider how different a regularized form such as *blowed* is from the alternate forms *blew* and *blewed*. There is clearly quite a substantial difference between *blowed* and *blew*, since, among other things, the phoneme that ends the word is a consonant in the first case and a vowel in the second case. On the other hand, the featural disparity with *blewed* is much less. From formula (4) we would get a relatively large value for regularization, where 1.0 represents the perfect match for *blowed/blowed* and where the values for *past +ed* and *correct* are, respectively, less than 1.0 and *much* less than 1.0:

$$(5) \quad \frac{1.0 + past + ed(<1)}{1.0 + past + ed(<1) + correct(\ll 1)}.$$

On the other hand, for a class III verb such as *feel* we would be comparing *feeled* (*base +ed*) with *felt* (*correct*) and *felted* (*past +ed*); here, all forms end in consonants, with *felt* and *feeled* differing in only a few features but with *felted* (which, among other things, has two dental stops near the end of the word) and *feeled* differing more. This should result in a somewhat lower value for regularization than in the previous case:

(6) $\dfrac{1.0 + past + ed(\ll 1)}{1.0 + past + ed(\ll 1) + correct(<1)}$.

Egedi and Sproat (1988) performed these computations over the sets of verbs in the six different classes (III–VIII) measured by Rumelhart and McClelland.[8] These computations yield an ordering that correlates *exactly* with that achieved by Rumelhart and McClelland's model—cf. the average for trials 11–30 in table 4.1 above—with the notable exception of class VI, to which we will return momentarily:

(7) VI > VIII > VII > V > IV > III.

So Rumelhart and McClelland's formula (14) may be measuring nothing more than the intrinsic properties of English irregular verbs, since one can derive the ordering in (7) even assuming that the network *uniformly* regularizes; there is certainly no reason to believe that the formula measures properties of the network's behavior that correspond in any way to what Bybee and Slobin were measuring for the children's data.

Of course, an examination of the three trial time segments (11–15, 16–20, and 21–30 in table 4.1) will confirm that the network is not treating the different classes entirely uniformly, since the ranking of some of the classes changes between segments. Thus, there is *some* differential treatment of the verb classes, which suggests that the network might be exhibiting some interesting behavior. Unfortunately, it is by no means clear that this behavior corresponds in any way to the behavior of Bybee and Slobin's human subjects. The point can be made most dramatically by considering class VI. This class starts out (trials 11–15) ranked third. By the next segment it has plummeted to last position. In other words, by Rumelhart and McClelland's interpretation of their metric, class VI is quickly "learned" by the system, and quickly becomes the least regularized of the verb classes. There are two things to note about this. First, this quick "learning" of class VI apparently does not reflect human performance: in Bybee and Slobin's data, class VI was the second most commonly regularized group. Second, while the behavior may not be human-like, it *does* reflect a well-known property of connectionist models, namely that they very readily pick up on obvious generalizations (cf. Pinker and Prince 1988, p. 93). Surely one of the more obvious generalizations in English verbal morphology is that verbs which end in either /iN(C)/ or /æN(C)/—where /N/ is some nasal— often have past tenses where the stem vowel changes to /æ/ or /ʌ/.[9] This, of course, is precisely the set of verbs constituting class VI. What the data in table 4.1 suggest, then, is that the network is homing in on this fairly obvious generalization about English past tenses in a way that is rather characteristic of simple connectionist models. Indeed, in our three-layer network simulation, Egedi and I found precisely the same behavior with class VI as Rumelhart and McClelland. As in their simulation, class VI verbs ranked third during the earliest trials (11–15) and then plummeted to sixth place for the remaining trials (16–30); our network, too, was "learning" this apparent generalization. (The overall ranking of the other classes was also strikingly similar to Rumelhart and McClelland's results, but this can be derived under the assumption that the verbs are uniformly regularized, as argued above.) So, in summary, the behavior of Rumelhart and McClelland's network exhibited in table 4.1 probably has nothing to do with any human-like behavior on the part of their network, since the rank ordering of the classes can be obtained even if one assumes that the network uniformly regularizes. And the most significant piece of "interesting" behavior, the rank-order shift of class VI, seems to be more in keeping with the tendency of simple connectionist networks to "learn" obvious generalizations, than with children's observed treatment of this class of verbs.

The final state of the network According to Rumelhart and McClelland (1986, p. 265), their network, after being exposed 200 times to 420 verb alternations, has learned the "essential characteristics of the past tense of English." It seems to produce correct regular forms in the majority of cases, and it apparently "knows" some of the subgeneralizations for irregulars such as that manifested in class VI.

During the training, Rumelhart and McClelland had compared the output of the system for each input with a hand-selected set of candidates and measured the network's responses to these. However, in evaluating the final state of the machine by testing the machine's behavior on the 86 low-frequency verbs, they were substantially more liberal since they needed to discover what the network was actually producing as past-tense forms of the test verbs. They therefore measured how well each of the strings of phonemes of length less than 20 "which could be generated from the set of Wickelphones present in the entire corpus of verbs" (p. 271) could account for the activation of the output layer of the network. They also set a response threshold below which they would not consider a response to be valid. Despite this apparent freedom, the model seemed to have "acquired" some aspects of English past-tense formation. The list in (8) gives some of Rumelhart and McClelland's results (given in English orthographic rendition) for the novel verbs (from their tables 17 and 18, pp. 263–264).

(8) Input Word   Past Tense Response(s)

guard	*guard, guarded*
mate	*mated, maded*
squat	*squated, squat, squawked*
carp	*carped, carpted*
shape	*shaped, shipped*
sip	*sipped, sepped*
smoke	*smokted, smoke*
type	*typted*
hug	*hug*
mail	*mailed, membled*
tour	*toureder, toured*
bid	*bid*
bend	*bended*
weep	*weeped, wept*
catch	*catched*
cling	*clinged, clung*

Note that for many of the examples one of the responses is the correct form. Furthermore, for some of the irregular forms—e.g., *bid, weep, cling* —the correct past-tense form is generated, though a regularized form is also generated for *weep* and *cling*. Still, as Pinker and Prince (1988, pp. 124–125) point out, some of the past-tense forms produced are bizarre: *mail/membled, tour/toureder, sip/sepped*. With respect to the vowel changes which the network produces in such forms as *sepped, membled*, and *shipped* (for *shape*), Pinker and Prince note (p. 125): "Well before it has mastered the richly exemplified regular rule, the pattern-associator appears to have gained considerable confidence in certain incorrectly grasped, sparsely exemplified patterns of feature-change among the vowels. This implies that a major "induction problem"—latching onto the productive patterns and bypassing the spurious ones—is not being solved successfully." Still, it appears on the surface as if the model in many cases does manage to produce an appropriate regular(ized) form for the past tense. Furthermore, Rumelhart and McClelland (1986, p. 263) consider it to be quite an important point that in no case is the incorrect allomorph of the regular past-tense morpheme chosen when a regular(ized) form is produced: "... the model never chooses the incorrect variant of the regular past tense.... [V]erbs ending in a /t/ or /d/ take [-ɘd] in the past tense; verbs ending in unvoiced consonants take [-t], and verbs ending in vowels or voiced consonants take [-d]. On no occasion does the model assign a strength greater than .2 an incorrect variant of the past tense. Thus, the model has clearly learned the substructure of the regular correspondence and adds the correct variant to all different types of base forms. These results clearly demonstrate that the model acts in accordance with the regular pattern for English verbs and that it can apply this pattern with a high level of success to novel as well as familiar verbs." This might be an important observation if it were wholly due to the behavior of the network itself. It is clear, however, that this is not the case, and that the decoding algorithm is strongly influencing these results. As stated above, the only strings that are tested for coverage of the network's output layer are strings of length less than 20 *that could be formed out of the set of Wickelphones present in the data.* But this limits the choice quite substantially in most cases, since Rumelhart and McClelland's decoding algorithm is effectively allowing the network to produce only phonotactically well-formed outputs. For example, assume that a Wickelphone of the form ϕ-*dental*-$\#$, where ϕ is the final segment of the input stem, is consistent with the activation of the output layer of the network. Then, if ϕ is voiceless, *dental* will necessarily also be voiceless, since there are simply no final sequences of the form [-*voice*]$d\#$ in English. The decoding algorithm will therefore simply have no opportunity to posit such a sequence, since there are no candidate Wickelphones with the required properties: the network could not produce /karpd/ for *carp* even if it wanted to, since it is not allowed to "choose" the Wickelphone $pd\#$. Fortunately, since $pd\#$ differs from $pt\#$ only in the voicing of the second element, if $pd\#$ were highly consistent with the output layer's activation then $pt\#$ would also be quite consistent with it. So the right form is produced—with a fair amount of guidance from the decoding algorithm. The other choice for the past tense, -*əd*, is in principle available, since *pəd* is a phonotactically well-formed Wickelphone (though it is fair to ask if it actually occurs in the set of Wickelphones covering the 500 verbs of the data), so the decoder could allow */karpəd/ as an alternative. However, the system does not, as Rumelhart and McClelland seem to imply, have a three-way choice. A similar argument holds for the cases in which ϕ is a voiced obstruent, and for cases where ϕ is /t/ or /d/; in the latter case, neither /t/ nor /d/ could be affixed to either final segment, since the Wickelphones $tt\#$, $td\#$, $dt\#$, and $dd\#$ do not exist in English, so in these cases there is only one possible allomorph. In fact, once the network has "decided" to produce a past tense with one of the allomorphs -*d*, -*t*, and -*əd*, the *only* situation in which the decoding scheme allows a three-way choice is when ϕ is a voiced sonorant; in this case any of the allomorphs is in principle allowed by the phonotactics. Rumelhart and

McClelland give five examples (one assumes there are others) of novel verbs ending in consonant sonorants (no examples with vowel-final stems are given), for which the network correctly produces a form with the allomorph -*d*, never -*t* or -*əd*. In this case, one probably must presume that the network really *has* learned to produce the correct form, though in order to be certain of this for any given case one would have to be sure that all of the relevant Wickelphones were exemplified in the verb set.

Apparently, then, one of the important results of Rumelhart and McClelland's model turns out to be strongly influenced by the decoding algorithm, and is not due entirely to the behavior of the network itself. It is therefore quite unfair to say that the network has *learned* the regular verbal system of English, since the basic aspects of that system are in large measure given to it. Again, there are other criticisms that could be raised about the performance of Rumelhart and McClelland's model on the novel verbs; the interested reader should see Pinker and Prince's discussion of these.

So, in conclusion, there are a number of reasons to doubt that Rumelhart and McClelland's model is really doing what it is claimed to be doing. Much of its apparent humanlike learning behavior is due to the manner in which the data are presented to it or the manner in which they are analyzed, and an important component of its final behavior—namely its knowledge of the regular alternations in English—turns out to be strongly favored by the particular decoding algorithm used. Rumelhart and McClelland's work is the most significant work on connectionist morphology to date, and it remains to be seen whether connectionism will ultimately make clear contributions to the computational study of morphology in particular or of language in general.

4.3   COMPOUND NOMINALS AND RELATED CONSTRUCTIONS

I turn now to work on the structural and semantic analysis of compound nominals—more generally, premodified nominals—in English. To some it may seem strange to be discussing this topic as part of a treatment of computational morphology; would it not be more properly discussed in a book about (phrasal) parsing? There are in fact several justifications for discussing the topic here.

First, compound nominals have traditionally been treated as morphological rather than syntactic constructions. If tradition is to be any guide, then, it is just as important to discuss the computational analysis of compound nominals in this book as it is to discuss the computational treatment of Warlpiri reduplication. More generally, not only compound nominals, such as *spark plug*, but other types of premodified nominals, such as *electrical engineer*, must be treated here. As I argued in subsection 2.2.3, if one distinguishes compounds from other premodified (or complex) nominals by, e.g., stress behavior (*SPARK plug* versus *electrical ENGINEER*), one cannot decide that one *has* a compound until one has done some amount of analysis of the form in question. So any system that purports to handle compound nominals in unrestricted text must deal somehow with premodified nominals in general, even if the only decision that is made with a case like *electrical engineer* is to eliminate it from further consideration. In point of fact, all systems for treating compound nominals in English of which I am aware handle at least some cases that could be classified as phrases. So, combining the observation that compound nominals have traditionally been treated as morphological with the point that it is in practice hard to separate compounds from premodified nominals in general, we come to the conclusion that the analysis of premodified nominals is legitimately part of computational morphology.

Of course, one might point out that what makes premodified nominals in English different from more obviously morphological constructions is that many a premodified nominal consists of several orthographic words (see, again, subsection 2.2.3). If one were then to insist that computational morphology deals exclusively with constructions consisting of single orthographic words, thus relegating all multi-orthographic word constructions to the domain of syntactic analysis, then a good number of premodified nominals would fall outside computational morphology. Still, as we have seen, English compounds are often written as single words—*firefighter, handgun, mountaintop, fairground, firecracker*. And while it is true that one does not need to do a semantic analysis to analyze *mountaintop* as consisting of the morphemes *mountain* and *top*, if one were to do such an analysis it would legitimately be considered part of computational morphology. (Needless to say, while one would, on the basis of orthography, consider *firefighter* and *life insurance company employee* to be, respectively, morphological and syntactic constructions, in German the same distinction could not be made between *Feuerwehrmann* 'firefighter' and *Lebensversicherungsgesellschaftsangestellter* 'life insurance company employee'. So, even if *life insurance company employee* does not come under the rubric of computational morphology in English, its German counterpart surely must.)

Finally, if the structural and semantic analysis of nominal compounds in particular, and premodified nominals in general, is truly part of phrasal analysis rather than morphological analysis, then it is remarkable how little they are treated in the literature on (syntactic) parsing (see Sparck Jones 1985). The reason for this lack of attention is presumably that the assignment of structure to a noun compound like *computer communications network performance analysis primer* (see chapter 2 above) depends a great deal upon lexical or semantic facts, and (generally) very little on syntax. The work on syntactic parsing that does discuss these constructions generally presumes some sort of "oracle" that will tell the parser which way it should group the words (e.g., that *communications* forms a constituent with *network* rather than with *computer*), without saying anything specific about how the oracle should work; this is how the topic is treated in appendix A of Marcus 1980, for example.[10] So, since one does not generally find discussions of premodified nominals in a monograph on syntactic parsing, and since at least some of these constructions are arguably morphological, it seems justifiable to treat them here.

Broadly speaking, the extant work on the computational analysis of premodified nominals can be divided into two types, depending upon how rich a knowledge representation scheme is assumed. Analyses that assume a fairly rich scheme predominate, and include Gershman 1977, Brachman 1978, Finin 1980a, Finin 1980b, McDonald 1981, and (apparently) Wojcik et al. 1989. Analyses that assume a fairly impoverished scheme include Leonard 1984 and Sproat 1990 (see also Pun and Lum 1989 for some relevant work on Chinese). To illustrate the approaches, I will discuss Finin 1980a, Finin 1980b, and Sproat 1990. As we shall see, the richness of the knowledge-representation scheme used depends to some extent on the intended application and coverage of the system.

4.3.1   Finin's model of semantic interpretation

Finin's model of the semantic interpretation of compound nominals is designed to assign the most likely "discourse neutral" interpretation to a compound composed of two or more nominals. The system depends heavily upon a fairly rich model of knowledge representation. While the model is in principle capable of representing knowledge from any domain, Finin developed his system as one component of a natural language system, called JETS and based on an earlier system called PLANES, which allows the user to present the system with queries about the maintenance and flight records of naval aircraft, the answers to those queries being generated from a relational database. Such queries would routinely contain compound nominals such as *engine repairs, water pump, F4 water pump repairs,* and *engine housing acid damage.* A desideratum for such a system is that it be able to interpret such nominals and to retrieve the appropriate information from the database. In particular, it is important as Finin (1980a, p. 8) observes, that the system be relatively insensitive to the particular syntactic form of the nominal in the query. That is, to convey the notion *engine housing acid damage*, the user might use any of the following alternative noun phrases, among others:

(9) a. *acid damage to engine housings*

    b. *acid damage to the housings of engines*

    c. *damage by acid to engine housings*

    d. *damage resulting from the corrosion of the housings of engines by acid*

It is desirable to represent each of these alternative ways of conveying the same notion in a similar fashion in the internal semantic represention of the system. But in order to have *engine housing acid damage* interpreted in the same way as the wordier paraphrase in (10d), for example, it is necessary to store enough knowledge about acid, damage, engines, and housings: one must know that acid can damage things by causing corrosion, that engines are things which have housings, and that housings are physical objects (as opposed to abstract objects) and hence may be corroded. Since this, along with other information about each word, amounts to a great deal of information, a complete analysis system of this kind can currently be envisioned only in a limited domain, such as the one Finin chose.[11] Finin's system consists of three components: a *lexical interpreter*, a *concept modifier*, and a *modifier parser*. The lexical interpreter associates each of the input (orthographic) words to a concept or set of concepts. The concept modifier produces a set of possible interpretations for a head concept and a potential modifier, and an associated score for each of those interpretations. Finally, the modifier parser builds a structure for the compound consistent with the best-scoring local interpretations and produces an interpretation for the entire compound.

The concept modifier is driven by rules, which Finin divides into three general types. *Idiomatic rules* associate concepts to particular strings of words; for example, there is an idiomatic rule that associates the concept HANGAR-QUEEN to the string of words *hangar queen* (a Navy term for a plane with a poor maintenance record). *Productive rules* are intended to capture relationships which are "propert[ies] of the rule and not of the constituent concepts" (Finin 1980a, p. 108). One productive rule in Finin's system interprets *plane 30045* as 'plane with Bureau Serial Number 30045'. Arguably, there is nothing about the semantics of the word *plane* or the number *30045* that determines this interpretation; rather, it is determined by the mere existence of a pattern (and its concomitant interpretation in Navy usage) of the form PLANE + NUMBER. *Structural rules* are the most interesting rules in Finin's system; they provide interpretations for nominal compounds which are nonidiomatic and (unlike Finin's productive rules) depend upon the semantics of the individual words making up the compound. Some examples of the structural rules in Finin's system are given in (10), along with examples of the kinds of nominals they would handle.

(10) a. CONCEPT + ROLEVALUE: *maintenance crew,* 'a **crew** which **maintains** something'

b. CONCEPT + ROLENOMINAL: *water pump,* 'an instrument which **pumps water**'

c. SPECIFIC + GENERIC: *F4 plane,* where *F4* refers to a specific type of the generic concept PLANE.

In order to rank the applicability of a particular rule such as (10b) to a particular compound such as *water pump,* one must ascertain that there is a sufficiently good fit between the requirements of the rule and the representation of the concepts associated with the words involved. Knowledge is represented in Finin's system (as in other knowledge-representation systems) in terms of a tangled hierarchy where a specific concept such as PUMP may be a special instance of a more general concept (e.g. MECHANICAL-THING), and where specific concepts may inherit properties of more general concepts. In order for *pump* to be treated as a ROLE-NOMINAL, either the concept PUMP or else a more general concept of which PUMP is a specific instance must be interpretable as filling a particular role in some verbal concept. In this case, the interpretation is licensed by the fact that the concept PUMP is listed as (among other things) a possible filler of the INSTRUMENT role of the verbal concept TO-PUMP. One must then determine whether the concept WATER can fill one of the other roles of this verbal concept TO-PUMP. One role that WATER could fill would be the OBJECT role of TO-PUMP. Relative to other possible roles (such as AGENT, SOURCE, and LOCATION), the scoring heuristics give a high score to the interpretation that WATER fills the OBJECT role. Although Finin does not give the specific details by which his scoring algorithm gives a high numerical score to this particular example, it is clear from his discussion of how scoring is done in general that, among other things, the object of TO-PUMP (presumably) is typically a liquid (which would match with the general concept LIQUID, of which WATER is an instance). (The numerical scores assigned in Finin's system are heuristic and are not, for example, derived from the statistical analysis of a large database of compound nominals.)

In cases where a compound nominal consists of three or more words, the modifier parser is needed to compute the most likely grouping of the words. Finin's parsing algorithm is similar in spirit to that of Marcus (1980) in that it assumes a buffer of three constituents and it restricts interpretation rules to look only at the constituents in the buffer. It differs from Marcus' algorithm, however, in that a constituent may leave the left edge of the buffer without being attached to another constituent, and may later be pulled back unchanged into the buffer for further consideration when more structure has been built. As an illustration of the behavior of the modifier parser, consider the compound *January water pump shipment*. First, the lexical interpreter retrieves the concepts associated with the first three words, and these concepts are put into the buffer:

(11) **JANUARY WATER PUMP** *shipment*

The concept modifier will first attempt to analyze **JANUARY** as a modifier of WATER. Since JANUARY is not a very likely modifier for WATER, let us assume that any interpretation of this modification will receive a very bad score—i.e., one below some preset numerical threshold BAD. This will cause the interpretation to be rejected, and the buffer will shift one constituent to the right. The lexical interpreter will then replace *shipment* with its associated concept:

(12) *JANUARY* **WATER PUMP SHIPMENT**

The concept modifier will then attempt to interpret WATER as modifying PUMP, which works (as we have seen). The concept corresponding to the interpretation of WATER modifying PUMP, which I will notate here as [WATER PUMP], replaces PUMP in the buffer. This opens up the left position in the buffer, and JANUARY is brought back in:

(13) **JANUARY [WATER PUMP] SHIPMENT**

The parsing proceeds in a similar fashion: JANUARY is tested as a modifier of [WATER PUMP], which interpretation is rejected. [WATER PUMP] is tested as a modifier of SHIPMENT. This is acceptable, and finally JANUARY is tested as a modifier of [[WATER PUMP] SHIPMENT], which is acceptable, yielding the final interpretation [JANUARY [[WATER PUMP] SHIPMENT].

As can be seen from even this cursory description, Finin's system is quite complex, requiring an elaborate system for representing and interpreting concepts. The domain handled by his system is apparently rather small, and the task of scaling the system up to handle nominals in unrestricted text would be formidable indeed. (Actually, it is hard to know how well Finin's system works even on the domain to which he applied it, since he does not give any measures of coverage.) Still, the problem of providing a full semantic interpretation of compound nominals is a difficult one, and it seems unlikely that anything less intricate than Finin's system will suffice.

4.3.2   The assignment of stress to premodified nominals in English

Whereas Finin's goal was a detailed semantic interpretation of compound nominals, the goal pursued in Sproat and Liberman 1987 and in Sproat 1990 is the much more modest (but nonetheless complex) one of predicting appropriate stress for a premodified nominal. Being able to compute stress in such nominals is important for a natural-sounding English text-to-speech system. It is desirable, for example, to have a text-to-speech system say *COFFEE pot*, but *winter CHILL*. As I noted in subsection 2.2.3, there is some correlation between stress behavior and the kind of semantic relationship between the two elements of a premodified nominal, and it is therefore important to be able to do some amount of semantic analysis. However, it seems to be the case that one can do a fairly good job of predicting stress using some fairly simple heuristics, including a fairly simple-minded semantic grammar.

   I will review here the approach to this problem reported in Sproat 1990. The system—NP—attempts to assign reasonable structures to premodified nominals in unrestricted text by making use of syntactic, lexical, and semantic information (as well as some statistical information derived from large text corpora). NP then computes an appropriate stress pattern on that structure; in sufficiently long phrases, minor intonational phrase boundaries are inserted in appropriate places. It is assumed, following Chomsky and Halle (1968) and Liberman and Prince (1977) (see also subsection 2.2.3 above), that a nominal which is labeled as N^0—i.e., which is a word—will receive stress on the left member if and only if the right member is not itself complex. In all other cases, including cases where a nominal is syntactically labeled as a phrase (i.e., a nonzero projection of N such as $\bar{N}$), right-hand stress will be assigned. Thus, for simple binary cases, the correspondence between syntactic node labels and stress is as given in table 4.2. In all cases, the stress assignment predicted is for a "discourse neutral context."[12] The system will attempt an analysis of any premodified nominal, including noun phrases like *several very large ornamental*

Table 4.2

Type	Syntactic node label	Stress pattern	Example
Nominal compound	N^0	LEFT	*DOG house*
Nominal phrase	(e.g.) $\overline{N}$	RIGHT	*nice HOUSE*

ducks, (non-compound) complex nominals (in the sense of Levi 1978) such as *electrical engineer,* compounds such as *computer communications network performance analysis primer,* and proper names such as *former Attorney General Edwin Meese III* or *New York Avenue.*

NP takes as input text which has been labeled for part of speech and in which the left and right edges of noun phrases have been delimited; this labeling is accomplished using a stochastic part-of-speech assigner reported in Church 1988. For each noun phrase, NP uses a CKY (context-free) recognition algorithm (see Harrison 1978, section 12.4) to build a chart of possible constituents. The recognizer uses the following kinds of context-free rules:

• Phrase-structure rules—e.g., $NP \rightarrow DET + \overline{N}$. There are currently about 40 such rules.

• Context-free semantic/lexical schemata which predict the category label of the mother node. For example:

General schemata: a term for FURNITURE combines with a term for ROOM to form an $\overline{N}$ (i.e., right-hand stress—*kitchen TABLE*). (This is a specific instance of the TIME/LOCATION compounds exemplified in subsection 2.2.3, by *Monday MORNING* and *Washington APARTMENT.*) These correspond to Finin's productive and structural rules. (If several schemata apply to a given case, only one will be picked, but there is no mechanism to check that it is the most likely interpretation, unlike in Finin's system.)

Schemata with particular head nouns: street names ending in the word *Street* are N^0 (i.e., left-hand stress—*PARK Street*). Currently there are about 600 of these first two kinds of rules, about 95% of those being specific to food terms.

Lists of particular nominals with information about their phrasal status—e.g., *WHITE House* is an N^0 (taking left-hand stress). There are currently about 6500 entries of this kind. These are similar to Finin's idiomatic rules.

Having built the chart, NP picks one of the set of trees defined therein by doing a top-down walk and applying a number of heuristics at each node.[13] Once a (possibly partial) analysis has been provided for the nominal, NP passes the analysis to the phonology, where the position of the primary stress is determined, the rhythm rule (see, e.g., Liberman and Prince 1977) is applied, and (in long nominals) small intonational boundaries are inserted.

As an example, consider the sentence *I put it on the living room table.* The part of speech assigner assigns part-of-speech labels to the words in the sentence and brackets the nominal *the living room table.* NP then applies syntactic and semantic rules to the nominal. For example, NP has *living room* listed as being of the semantic type ROOM, and NP also knows that it is an N^0, so it places a node $[N^0, \text{ROOM}]$ in the chart, spanning *living room.* It also knows that *table* is a kind of FURNITURE, and that a ROOM term and a FURNITURE term can combine into an $\overline{N}$, so it places the node $[\overline{N}, \text{ROOM} + \text{FURNITURE}]$ in the chart, spanning the string *living room table.* Finally, the determiner *the* can combine with an $\overline{N}$ to make an NP. The final chart will contain (among other possibilities) the structure in (14a), which is the structure that happens to be picked by the heuristic top-down walk. Figure 4.4 gives an overview of part of the chart built over *the living room table.* Phonological rules (again, following Chomsky and Halle 1968 and Liberman and Prince 1977) are then applied to yield the correct stress pattern in (14b) (where *living* has secondary stress and *table* has primary stress).

(14) a. $[_{NP}$ *the* $[_{\overline{N}}[_{N^0}$ *living room*$]$ *table*$]]$.

   b. *the LIVING room TABLE.*

By far the most significant benefit afforded by NP is in the placement of primary stress on nominals; other effects, such as the correct placement of stress within the CN prior to the primary stress, are noticeable but are not as striking. The version of NP reported in Sproat 1990 was estimated to assign acceptable stress 96.4% of the time on randomly selected nominals. This is significantly better than what the Bell Labs synthesizer does by default, which is always assign stress on the rightmost member of a premodified nominal (this would treat *living room table* correctly, but would treat *dog house* incorrectly); that algorithm is right about 77% of the time. The simple alternative of assigning stress to the penultimate orthographic word in a long nominal if and only if the last two words of the nominal are nouns (which would treat *dog house* correctly but *living room table* incorrectly) does considerably better than this—93.8%—but still not as well as NP. This confirms that, while a fair amount can be achieved by just having part-of-speech information, this information alone (as is well known) is not

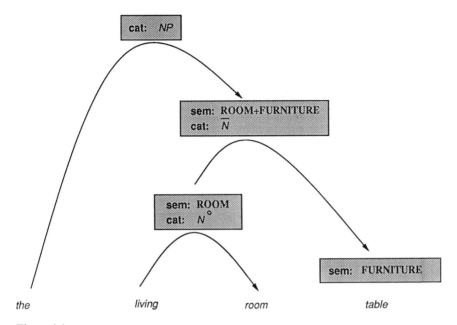

Figure 4.4
Part of the chart built for the noun phrase *the living room table.*

sufficient. A fairly simple nominal analyzer such as NP seems useful in doing a better job.

4.3.3   A summing up

As Brachman (1978, p. 144) cogently observes, a powerful knowledge-representation system is "a necessity, rather than a luxury" in the treatment of premodified nominals. But, since we are very far from being able to represent knowledge as a whole, we have always been forced to represent knowledge about a rather limited and well-circumscribed domain. For the treatment of premodified nominals in unrestricted input, we are thus in the unhappy predicament of requiring an extensive representation of knowledge about the world and being unable to provide such a representation. This, I would argue, is a good reason to try to see just how far one can go with the far shallower but more practicable analyses of the kind proposed in Sproat 1990. In this latter work I have, of course, been fortunate in being concerned not with providing a semantic analysis of anything close to the detail of, say, Brachman 1978, Finin 1980a, Finin 1980b, or even Leonard 1984, but rather with doing the minimal amount of syntactic, semantic, and lexical analysis necessary to achieve the goal of providing a reasonable assignment of stress to nominals. Any comparison between the two approaches must be understood with this important difference in mind. However, since the automatic assignment of stress to nominals is certainly a legitimate goal, it is heartening that at least this goal seems largely achievable without recourse to a complete knowledge-representation scheme.

Key to Abbreviations

The following abbreviations are used in the text to specify grammatical features:

1	first person
2	second person
3	third person
2INF	second infinitive (Finnish)
2OBJ	second object
ABL	ablative case
ACC	accusative case
ACT	active voice
AFF	affix
APPL	applicative
ASP	aspectual marker
AUG	augmentative
AUX	auxiliary
BY-OBJ	'by' object
CAUS	causative
COMP	comparative
CompAug	compounding augment
DU	dual number
EQU	equative
ERG	ergative case
EXP	experiential aspect
FEM	feminine gender
FUT	future tense
GEN	genitive case
IND	indicative mood

INST	instrumental case
INT	interrogative mood
IOBJ	indirect object
LOC	locative case
MASC	masculine gender
NEUT	neuter gender
NonPast	non-past tense (Warlpiri)
NOM	nominative case
OBJ	object
ObjAgr	object agreement
PART	partitive case
PASS	passive voice
PAST	past tense
PERF	perfect or perfective aspect
PL	plural number
POS	positive (adjectival form)
PRE	prefix
PRES	present tense
PROP	proprietive (Warlpiri)
REL	relative
SG	singular number
STRONG	strong (Germanic adjectives)
SUB	subjunctive mood
SUBJ	subject
SubjAgr	subject agreement
SUF	suffix
SUP	superlative
VOC	vocative case

Glossary

AFFIX   A **bound morpheme** that is not a root, and which attaches to a stem (or base). In the English word *overburdened*, *over-* and *-ed* are affixes.

AFFIX STRIPPING   The simplest technique for computational morphological analysis. One removes initial or final substrings of words corresponding to possible affixes, and tests the remaining substring against entries in the dictionary.

AGREEMENT   Two words α and β are said to agree with respect to some morphologically marked category μ if α's specification for μ is *not distinct from* β's. Agreement is any grammatical requirement that two or more words (or phrases) in a phrase agree as just described. In Spanish, for example, adjectives must agree in number and gender with the nouns they modify: *sop +as cremos +as* (soup + FEM/PL creamy + FEM/PL) 'creamy soups'; *gazpach +o cremos +o* (gazpacho + MASC/SG creamy + MASC/SG) 'creamy gazpacho'.

ALLOMORPH   One of a set of phonologically different surface forms for a morpheme. In English, *a* and *an* are allomorphs of the indefinite article.

APPLICATIVE   A grammatical-function-changing verbal affix that indicates that a verb's direct object is derived from an underlying benefactive (or other oblique) case.

ASPECT   A grammatical feature of verbs, indicating the state (inter alia) of the action described, which is morphologically marked in many languages. For example, a perfect marking on a verb indicates that the action described has been completed.

ASSIMILATION   A phonological or phonetic process whereby one phonological unit takes on a subset of the feature specifications of some other (often adjacent) phonological unit. In *impossible* (from *in +possible*), the final nasal of the prefix *in-* is said to assimilate in place of articulation to the initial /p/ of the stem *possible*.

AUGMENT   A semantically empty morpheme found between the stems of some compounds in some languages. An example from German is *-s-* in *Geschwindigkeit + s +begrenzung* (speed + CompAug + limit) 'speed limit'.

AUGMENTATIVE   A morphologically derived form (usually) of a noun, which typically denotes a large entity of the type designated by the base form: e.g., Italian *piazz +one* 'large square' from *piazza* 'square'. As opposed to **diminutive**.

AUTOSEGMENTAL PHONOLOGY   The theory of phonology wherein words or morphemes are phonologically represented as multiple parallel sequences of phonological units, where associations may be specified between units in different sequences. For example, the Mandarin word *lǎoshī* 'teacher', which has a low tone on the first syllable and a high tone on the second syllable, can be represented autosegmentally as a sequence of syllables *lao-shi*, and a sequence of tones *LH*, where the *L* is associated to the first syllable *lao* and the *H* is associated to the second syllable *shi*.

BASE   Equivalent to **stem**.

BINYAN (PLURAL BINYANIM)   In Semitic morphology, one of a set of derivational classes of verbs, formed with a nonconcatenative affix of a particular phonological shape. For example, the Arabic form *katab* 'write' is a binyan I stem form of the root *ktb*, formed with the affix *CVCVC*. Similarly, *kattab* 'cause to write' is a binyan II stem form.

BOUND MORPHEME   A morpheme that cannot stand alone as a separate word of a language (as opposed to a free morpheme). Typical bound morphemes are affixes, such as plural *-s* in English.

BRACKETING PARADOX   A situation in which a word has at least two contradictory bracketings of its constituent morphemes, depending upon the criterion one uses for analysis. For example, a word consisting of the morphemes $\alpha\beta\gamma$ might be bracketed as $[\alpha[\beta\gamma]]$ if one considers only phonological arguments for the structure, but as $[[\alpha\beta]\gamma]$ if one considers only morphosyntactic arguments for the structure.

BUNSETSU   An orthographic unit in Japanese, usually consisting of one or more Chinese characters (kanji) followed by one or more Japanese syllabary characters (kana).

CAUSATIVE   A form of a verb *V*, meaning roughly 'to cause *V*'. For example, the Chicheŵa verb form *a +na +u +gw +ets +a* (SubjAgr + PAST + ObjAgr + fall + CAUS + ASP) (Baker 1988, p. 11) means 'to cause to fall'.

CHART   A **directed acyclic graph**, built by any of various parsing algorithms (often called chart parsers), that represents the possible analyses of an input. A chart for the English sentence $_0I_1\,saw_2\,a_3\,cat_4$ might include the information that there are NPs spanning (0,1) and (2,4), that there is a VP spanning (1,4), and so forth.

CIRCUMFIX   An affix that attaches around its stem. The past participle affix(es) *ge-t* in German, as in *ge +täusch +t* 'deceived', may be thought of as a circumfix.

CLITIC   A (usually) syntactically independent word that behaves more or less like an affix as far as the phonology is concerned.

CLOSED CLASS   A class of words or morphemes that does not admit new members. For example, new prepositions are rarely formed, and so prepositions are said to be closed-class items.

COMPOUND STRESS   A stress pattern characterizing (English) complex nominals in which the rightmost member of the nominal does not bear primary stress in citation form. For example, *PARK Street* has compound stress.

CONCATENATIVE MORPHOLOGY   Morphology consisting purely of the concatenation of stems with prefixes, suffixes, or other stems.

CYCLE   In its use in Generative Phonology, a type of rule application whereby a phonological rule can apply once each time a morphological operation takes place. In a word $[[\alpha\beta]\gamma]$, a cyclic rule might apply first on $\alpha\beta$, then again on $\alpha\beta\gamma$ when γ is attached.

DERIVED NOMINAL   A noun which is derived from a verb, and which usually refers to an action, event, or result related to the verb. Examples from English are *destruction* from *destroy*, *emergence* from *emerge*, and *stagnation* from *stagnate*.

DETERMINISTIC FINITE-STATE MACHINE (AUTOMATON, TRANSDUCER)   A finite-state machine (automaton, transducer) whose transition relation δ is a function, so that, for any pair $\langle q_i, \sigma \rangle$, δ specifies a unique q_j.

DIMINUTIVE   A morphologically derived form of (usually) a noun, typically referring to a small entity of the type designated by the base form: e.g., Italian *piazz +ina* 'small square' from *piazza* 'square'. As opposed to **augmentative**.

DIRECTED ACYCLIC GRAPH (DAG)   A graph in which all edges are unidirectional—if one can pass from vertex v_i to vertex v_j along edge e, then one cannot pass from v_j to v_i along e; and there are no cycles—i.e., there is no vertex v such that there is a path $(e_1, e_2, \ldots, e_n)$ where v is the initial vertex of e_1 and the final vertex of e_n.

DISCRIMINATION NETWORK   Equivalent to **trie**.

ELSEWHERE CONDITION   A phonological condition stating that if two rules R_1 and R_2 apply to a form, and if (1) the environment in which R_1 applies is more specific than the environment in which R_2 applies (i.e., R_2 is the general or 'elsewhere' rule, and R_1 is the special rule) and (2) the result of applying R_1 is incompatible with the result of applying R_2, then R_1 applies and blocks the application of R_2.

ENCLITIC   A **clitic** that phonologically behaves like a suffix.

EQUATIVE   A form of comparison of adjectives, meaning 'as x as', where x is the adjective.

EXTERNAL ARGUMENT   In many theories of syntax, the argument of a verb which typically occurs outside the verb phrase—often the (underlying) subject.

EXTRAMETRICALITY, EXTRAPROSODICITY   In metrical phonology, the idea that the left or right edge of a morphological form may be "invisible" to metrical or other rules of the phonology. If the final syllable of a word is extrametrical, for example, a metrical tree built over that word will not include the final syllable, and the stress of the word will be computed as if the final syllable were not there.

FEATURE STRUCTURE   A feature matrix in which the features can have atomic values or can be other feature structures.

FINITE-STATE MACHINE (FSM), FINITE-STATE AUTOMATON (FSA), FINITE-STATE TRANSITION NETWORK   A quintuple $\langle q_1, Q, F, \Sigma, \delta \rangle$ in which Σ is an alphabet, Q is a set of states, q_1 is the unique initial state, F is a set of final states, and δ is a mapping from $Q \times \Sigma$ to Q. A finite-state machine can be thought of as reading a tape written with symbols from Σ and either accepting or rejecting the tape, depending upon whether the machine ends up in a final state after reading the last character of the tape. The set of languages accepted by all possible finite-state machines is exactly the set of **regular languages**.

FINITE-STATE TRANSDUCER (FST)   A **finite-state machine** whose alphabet consists of pairs of items, and which reads a pair of tapes instead of a single tape. A cascaded FST is a series of FSTs $M_1, M_2 \ldots M_n$ arranged such that the output tape of M_i is also the input tape of M_{i+1}.

FOOT   A unit in the metrical (or prosodic) hierarchy, consisting of one or more syllables, only one of which is stressed.

FREE MORPHEME   A morpheme that may stand alone as a separate word of a language. In English *cat* is a free morpheme, but in Latin *magn-* 'big' is not, since it must at least be marked with an inflectional suffix (e.g., *magn +us* 'big + NOM/ SG/MASC').

GEMINATION   The phonological or phonetic doubling of a segment.

GRAMMAR CONSTANT   In an equation expressing the complexity of a parsing system (or some other linguistic analysis system), a constant term determined only by the size of the grammar.

HARMONY   A phonological process that causes segments of a particular class to agree in the specifications for some phonological features across a certain domain (often, a phonological word). The best-known case is vowel harmony, in which vowels within a phonological domain must agree in specification for features such as [round] or [back].

HEAD OF A WORD   A morphological constituent, consisting of one or more morphemes, that determines the syntactic or semantic category of the word. In English this is often (but not always) the rightmost affix. For example, in *nominaliz +ation*, the suffix *-ation* would be said to be the head, since it determines that the whole word is a noun. In the case of a compound in English, the head would normally be the rightmost of the two combined stems.

HEAVY SYLLABLE   In most cases, a syllable whose **rime** is minimally of the form VV or VC.

IMPLICATIONAL UNIVERSALS   In works such as Greenberg 1966, a statistical statement of the form 'if a language has property X, then it is highly probable that it has property Y'.

INCORPORATION   A morpho-syntactic operation whereby a word that is underlyingly syntactically separate becomes morphologically a part of some other word in the sentence.

INFIX   An affix that attaches inside a stem, e.g. Bontoc *fikas* 'strong', *f-um +ikas* 'be strong', with infix *-um-*.

INTERNAL ARGUMENT   A verbal argument which, in a nonpassive sentence, typically occurs inside the verb phrase.

LATINATE AFFIX   In English morphology, affixes which are etymologically derived from Latin, such as *-able*, *-ity*, and *in-*. Contrast **native affix**.

LEMMATIZATION   The process of computing a normalized form—e.g., a dictionary entry—for a word of text. For example, *cats* would lemmatize to *cat*.

LETTER TREE   Equivalent to **trie**.

LEXEME   A "dictionary word." The set of lexemes of a language is given by the set of all word forms of the language after "normalization" for inflectional morphology. Both *overburdened* and *overburdens* are forms of the same lexeme, namely *overburden*. The words *overburden* and *burden* constitute different lexemes, though one is clearly derived from the other.

LEXICAL ACCESS   The retrieval of word forms from a dictionary in a processing model.

LEXICAL RULE   Any rule, phonological, morphosyntactic, or semantic, relating word forms.

LEXICAL TAPE   In two-level morphology, the transducer tape that contains the lexical or underlying form of the word being analyzed.

LIGHT SYLLABLE   In most cases, a syllable whose **rime** is maximally of the form *V*.

MATRIX CHART PARSING   A kind of chart parsing, described in Church 1986, where the chart specifying the possible spans for a particular constituent is represented by an upper triangular matrix consisting of zeros and ones, where ones occur in matrix entry i, j just in case there is a possible span for the constituent between i and j in the input. Concatenation is represented by matrix multiplication.

MINIMAL WORD   Following McCarthy and Prince 1990, a prosodic constituent corresponding to a single metrical foot (more accurately, a foot consisting of two morae).

MIRROR PRINCIPLE   The observation, due to Baker (1985), that the order of the morphemes that mark grammatical-relation-changing syntactic processes mirrors the order in which those syntactic processes apply.

MORPH   Occasionally used to refer to the parts of a word that "spell out" particular morphemes: *im-*, *pass*, and *-able* are morphs in *impassable*, spelling out the morphemes *in-*, *pass*, and *-able*.

MORPHEME   The minimal unit of morphological analysis. Morphemes are often (but not always) argued to be the minimal units of meaning. In *overburdened*, *over-*, *burden*, and *-ed* are all morphemes.

MORPHEME STRUCTURE CONSTRAINT   A constraint that specifies the possible phonological shapes of morphemes of a language. For example, morpheme structure constraints determine that **bnick* is not a **possible word** of English.

MORPHOGRAPHEMICS   A term referring to the orthographic spelling changes that take place when morphemes are combined to form written words. The $\langle y \rangle \rightarrow \langle i \rangle$ change in $\langle try \rangle$ and $\langle tries \rangle$ is an example of a morphographemic change.

MORPHOTACTICS   Broadly speaking, the "syntax of words," or the set of licit combinations of morphemes of a language.

MUTUAL INFORMATION   The measure of information between two events, a and b, defined as $log_2[p(ab)/p(a)p(b)]$, where $p(a)$ and $p(b)$ are the probabilities of those events and $p(ab)$ is the (joint) probability of the events' co-occurring.

NATIVE AFFIX   In English morphology, affixes that are etymologically derived from Anglo-Saxon, such as *-ing*, *-ness*, and *un-*. Contrast **latinate affix**.

NUCLEUS   The vowel (or other sonorant) at the "peak" of a syllable. In the syllable *string* /strɪŋ/, for example, /ɪ/ is the nucleus.

ONSET   Generally, the first part of the syllable leading up to, but not including, the nucleus: in the syllable *string* /strɪŋ/, for example, /str/ would be the onset.

OPEN CLASS   A class of words or morphemes that freely admits new members. Nouns typically form an open class, since one can fairly freely coin new nouns.

ORTHOGRAPHIC WORD   Usually, a sequence of alphanumeric characters surrounded by whitespace or punctuation.

OVERLAP   In recent phonological work (e.g. Bird and Klein 1991, Coleman 1990), two phonological "events" are said to overlap if there is an overlap in their temporal manifestations.

PARADIGM   Usually, a matrix of different inflected forms of the same lexeme. The following would be the paradigm for the present tense of the verb *be* in English:

am   are
are   are
is   are

PHONETIC IMPLEMENTATION   The mapping from phonological representations to phonetic (e.g. articulatory) representations.

PHONOLOGICAL WORD   Usually, a unit on the metrical hierarchy larger than a **foot** but smaller than a phonological phrase. In many languages, a phonological word is the minimal domain for stress or accent assignment, and is often the largest domain for such processes as vowel harmony.

PORTMANTEAU MORPHEME   A morpheme expressing a cluster of features in a language that are often expressed by separate morphemes in other languages. For example, the suffix *-o* in Spanish *puedo* 'I can' expresses the features first person, singular, present, and indicative, each of which might be expressed by separate morphemes in an agglutinative language such as Turkish.

POSSIBLE WORD   A form which satisfies a language's **morpheme structure constraints** but which is accidentally not a word of the language: e.g., *blick* in English.

PREFIX   An affix that attaches to the beginning of a stem.

PROCLITIC   A **clitic** that, phonologically, behaves like a prefix.

PRO-DROP LANGUAGE   A language in which pronominal subjects (more rarely, objects) are allowed to be deleted or non-overt, and in which the person/number interpretation of the subject is recoverable either by overt morphology on the verb or by discourse context. Italian and Spanish are canonical pro-drop languages.

REDUNDANCY RULE   A (usually lexical) rule that fills in a set of feature specifications which are redundant—i.e., determinable by default, and hence not specified in the underlying representation.

REDUPLICATION   A morphological operation involving the repetition of part or all of a stem. Partial reduplication involves the repetition of (usually) a part of a stem. For example, in the Australian language Yidinʸ, the form *gindal* + *gindalba* 'lizard' is formed by partial reduplication from the stem *gindalba*. Total reduplication, in contrast, involves the repetition of an entire morpheme: e.g., Indonesian *orang + orang* 'men', from *orang* 'man'.

REGULAR EXPRESSION   A specification for a **regular language**. Assuming an alphabet of symbols Σ, we can define a regular expression as follows:

1. $\varnothing$ (the Empty Set) is a regular expression.
2. ε (the Empty String) is a regular expression.
3. For any σ in Σ, σ is a regular expression.
4. For any regular expression ρ_i, $\rho_i *$—where $*$ is the Kleene star denoting Kleene closure—is also a regular expression.
5. For any two regular expressions ρ_i, ρ_j the following are regular expressions: $\rho_i \frown \rho_j$ (i.e., ρ_i concatenated with ρ_j) and $\rho_i | \rho_j$ (i.e., the disjunction of ρ_i and ρ_j).

REGULAR LANGUAGE   A language recognizable by a **finite-state machine** and specifiable by a regular expression.

RIME (RHYME)   Generally, the second part of the syllable, including the nucleus and following material. In the syllable *string* /strɪŋ/, for example, /ɪŋ/ is the rime.

ROOT   A morphologically unanalyzable form, which may or may not be a bound morpheme, from which stems and words may be derived via affixation. In *overburdened*, the root is *burden*.

ROOT-AND-PATTERN MORPHOLOGY   The kind of nonconcatenative morphology exhibited (e.g.) in Arabic verbs, where a (consonantal) root is autosegmentally associated with a skeletal pattern (specifying a morpheme).

SANDHI   A phonological rule that applies when two words (or, more generally, two morphemes) are placed adjacent to one another in a phrase.

SKELETON   In **autosegmental phonology**, the sequence of timing slots to which melodic material associates. In McCarthy's (1979) original analysis of Arabic nonconcatenative morphology, for example, the skeleton for the first binyan form of *ktb*, namely *katab*, would be $CVCVC$.

SPREADING   In **autosegmental phonology**, a spreading rule is a rule that causes a single melodic element to be associated to several skeletal (or other melodic) elements.

STEM   A (possibly polymorphemic) morphological unit to which an affix attaches. In *overburdened*, *overburden* is the stem to which *-ed* attaches, and *burden* is the stem to which *over-* attaches. In some authors' usage (see e.g. Bauer 1983, pp. 20–21), the term **base** is used as **stem** is used here, and **stem** refers only to the base for an inflectional affix; on this definition, *overburden* would be a stem, but *burden* would not be (since *over-* is not an inflectional affix.

STRATUM   In Lexical Phonology and Morphology, a stage in the "assembly" (i.e., generation) of a word form at which a well-defined class of phonological rules and morphological processes apply. There is a partial ordering over the strata in the assembly line. In English there is a stratum for **latinate morphology** ("stratum I"), where rules of stress also apply, and a later stratum for **native morphology** ("stratum II"), where some other phonological rules apply. The term level is also used in the literature to refer to a stratum.

SUBCATEGORIZATION   In the case of affixes, subcategorization is used to refer to a set of requirements (usually morphosyntactic, but sometimes phonological) on the stem to which the affix attaches. For example, *-ation* subcategorizes for verbs, meaning that the stem to which *-ation* (productively) attaches is usually a verb.

SUBTRACTIVE MORPHOLOGY   A morphological operation marked by the removal of material from the stem, rather than the addition of material to it.

SUFFIX   An affix that attaches to the end of a stem.

SURFACE TAPE   In two-level morphology, the transducer tape containing the surface form of the word being analyzed.

SYLLABLE   A basic unit of the metrical hierarchy, usually consisting of an **onset** and always having a **rime**, and combining into **feet**. (As has been often been noted, there are many definitions of syllable, none of them satisfactory.)

SYNCRETISM   A neutralization between the forms filling two or more distinct slots in a paradigm. In English, singular and plural forms of nouns are generally kept distinct, but in the cases of a few nouns—*sheep, deer*—there is a syncretism between the two forms.

SYNTACTIC WORD   A unit that is a word as far as the syntax is concerned: roughly speaking, it functions as a leaf in a phrase-structure tree. In English, we would say that *John's*, in *John's intelligent*, is one **phonological word** but two syntactic words, since the *John* part is a leaf dominated by the first NP of the sentence and the *(i)s* part is a leaf dominated by the VP of the sentence.

SYNTHETIC COMPOUND   A compound in which the head is a deverbal noun and the non-head is interpreted as one of the internal arguments of the head. A typical example from English is *dog-catcher*.

TEMPLATE MORPHOLOGY   Morphology in which particular morphemes that make up a polymorphemic word are rigidly ordered with respect to one another, and in which the ordering restrictions are hard to characterize by simple subcategorization statements. Such systems give the appearance of having morphemes assigned to slots in a template. The canonical example of a language with template morphology is Navajo, in which there are about 14 slots for affixes in a verb form.

TIER   In **autosegmental phonology**, the location of a melody which is parallel to the SKELETON, which occupies a single (half) PLANE, and which is associated to the skeleton (or, more generally, either to the skeleton or to an element on another tier). In McCarthy's analysis of Arabic morphology, for example, the root melody *ktb* would constitute the entry on the root tier in a form like *katab*, and *a* would constitute the entry on the vocalism tier. In many (older) versions of autosegmental phonology, **tier** is equivalent to **plane**.

TRIE   A linear-time method for storing a dictionary in a tree format. Each node of the tree is labeled with a letter, and for any traversal of the tree from the root to a leaf one will traverse nodes which spell out the letters of the entry stored at the leaf.

TRUNCATION   In Aronoff 1976, the removal of morphological material by a morphological rule that subsequently adds other morphological material. For example, in Aronoff's theory *nominee* is formed from *nominate* by the truncation of *-ate* followed by the addition of *-ee*.

UNDERSPECIFICATION   The idea that some features (e.g., phonological features) are not specified underlyingly, but are filled in later in the derivation by **redundancy rules**.

UNIFICATION   The unification of two **feature structures** F_1 and F_2 is the least-specified feature structure containing all the information in F_1 and F_2. If F_1 and F_2 have conflicting feature specifications for some feature(s), the unification of F_1 and F_2 fails.

WORD-BASED HYPOTHESIS   Aronoff's (1976) hypothesis that all instances of productive word formation involve derivations of words from other words.

WORD FORMATION   Traditionally equivalent to derivational morphology. Nowadays, often used to refer to any kind of morphology.

WORD-FORMATION RULE (WFR)   In certain theories of morphology (e.g., Aronoff's word-based theory, or the Extended Word and Paradigm theory of Anderson 1982), a rule that adds or deletes phonological material, or otherwise phonologically modifies a stem (or word), and which is usually triggered by some set of morphosyntactic features. Theories that use WFRs typically do not subscribe to the assumption that affixes are lexical entries; in such theories, roots would be lexical entries but affixes would be introduced by WFRs.

ZERO MORPHEME   A morpheme with null phonological content. A possible example of a zero morpheme would be found in the denominal verb *table*, which could be analyzed as the noun *table* affixed with a zero morpheme that **subcategorizes** for a noun and produces a verb. The existence of zero morphemes is controversial.

Notes

Chapter 1

1. One- and two-character words, taken together, account for about 99% of Chinese text.

2. We used a corpus of 2.5 million characters of newspaper text. The measure we used for association is related to **mutual information**. An approach similar to that of Sproat and Shih 1990, though more complex, is reported in Fan and Tsai 1988.

3. Ideally, then, the user could reconstruct the database only by querying every conceivable key. Since the set of particular keys of the database is not necessarily known to the user and furthermore may be a very large set, someone who is interested in protecting a database is not likely to be terribly concerned that this brute-force approach is in principle possible.

One might ask why anyone would actually want to encrypt something like a dictionary. As Feigenbaum et al. point out, the construction of dictionaries is a laborious and expensive procedure, and those who produce electronic dictionaries are therefore often concerned about piracy by a competitor. Yet the contents of a dictionary are not patentable—one cannot patent the fact that *eat* is a verb in English or that *ate* is its past tense—and copyright laws may not protect a publisher against someone making minor modifications to the form of the database while leaving the content intact. Thus, the only way one can publish an on-line dictionary and still protect its contents is by encrypting it.

4. Thanks to Alexandra Gertner for help with these Hebrew orthographic forms.

5. Attar et al. refer to these words as compounds, but their use of this term is not standard in discussions of morphology.

Chapter 2

1. Some general texts on morphology are listed at the end of the chapter for anyone who wants to read in more depth on some of the issues presented here.

2. There is little doubt that a great deal of confusion about Chinese morphology, and about Chinese linguistics in general, can be traced to the properties of the Chinese writing system. See DeFrancis 1984 for a lengthy discussion of this

point, and see chapter 1 above for some discussion of problems with Chinese orthography.

3. The traditional four-way classification of languages was based purely on the characteristics of each language's inflectional morphology—or lack thereof. So, one would not have classified English as agglutinative on the basis of examples like *antidisestablishmentarianism*, despite the apparent similarity to the example in (6).

4. At least one model of generative morphology, the Extended Word and Paradigm Theory (Anderson 1982; Thomas-Flinders 1981) (and see also Matthews 1972 and Matthews 1974 for discussion of the earler Word and Paradigm model), is constructed around this very distinction between inflectional and derivational morphology in that the two kinds of morphology are handled in different modules of the grammar. Derivational morphology applies "before" syntax in that derived words are inserted into syntax before the application of syntactic rules. Inflectional morphology takes place after the application of syntactic rules and may thus be sensitive to syntax.

5. There is a problem with the notion of productivity as it pertains to affixes. For an affix to be literally fully productive, it would have to be the case that it could attach freely to any word in the language. But there are probably no such affixes in any language; there are always some restrictions, and this point clearly applies equally to inflectional morphemes and derivational ones. The question then arises: What kinds of restrictions one must have in order to judge an affix to be nonproductive? Clearly, if one must simply list all the words that the affix in question attaches to (as may be the case with *-th* in (11) above) then it is probably fair to deem the affix nonproductive. On the other hand, it is not sufficient that the list of words to which the affix can attach merely be small in order for the affix involved to be judged nonproductive; it might be the case that the affix has severe semantic restrictions on its distribution and that these semantic restrictions can be met by only a very few words. See Aronoff 1976, chapter 3, for some discussion of these issues.

6. The last category is often classified separately under the term voice; see, for example, Bybee 1985, p. 20.

7. One other thing to notice about (21) is that many of the forms are used in more than one place in the paradigm; so *magn + is* serves as the ablative and dative plural in all of the genders. This replication of form, termed **syncretism**, is common in inflectional paradigms.

8. Derived nominals have a rather important status in the history of Generative Linguistics, since their properties in English (treated in Chomsky 1970) led both to the development of one of the more widely accepted theories of phrase structure—$\overline{\text{X}}$ theory—and to the renewed interest in morphology within Generative Grammar. See Sproat 1991a for discussion of these points.

9. It has been suggested that *-ability* can be thought of as a kind of compound suffix; see Aronoff and Sridhar 1983.

10. At least as far as noun compounds are concerned. Adjectival compounds such as *red hot* do not behave in the same way as nominal compounds from the point of

view of stress, though this is typically taken to be predictable from theories of stress (Chomsky and Halle 1968; Liberman and Prince 1977; Hayes 1980).

11. In contrast to the rather complicated picture of the distinction between compounds and phrases I have presented here, much recent work on morphology—in particular, work within the Lexical Phonology and Morphology (LPM) paradigm, e.g. Kiparsky 1982, Mohanan 1982, Halle and Mohanan 1985, and Mohanan 1986 —seems to portray the distinction as clear-cut.

12. Systematic exceptions to this claim are so-called **synthetic compounds** (Marchand 1969; Roeper and Siegel 1978; Selkirk 1982; Lieber 1983; Sproat 1985; Levin and Rappaport 1988), such as *dog catcher*, where the head is deverbal, e.g. an agentive nominal or a derived nominal. In such cases, the semantics are much more restricted, and it is typically the case that the left member is interpreted as being an argument of the verb contained within the right member. So a *dog catcher* is someone who catches dogs, with *dog* functioning as the object of *catch*.

13. Further complications arise from the fact that derivational affixes can often attach to compounds in English. Whereas compounds may consist of several orthographic words, affixes must be written attached (possibly with the use of a hyphen) to some following or preceding orthographic word This leads to constructions such as *ex-Reagan official*, which is interpreted as a 'former Reagan-official' (not an 'official of ex-Reagan') despite what the orthography would suggest.

14. The term **morph** is sometimes used to refer to the form(s) in which a morpheme is "spelled out."

15. Though see subsection 2.5.2 for a discussion of cases where even purely concatenative morphology runs afoul of a finite-state model.

16. The existence of purely suffixing languages—and the concomitant absence of purely prefixing languages—may attest to this processing advantage, since humans (arguably) process words from left to right. Thus, an advantage is conferred if the stem is at the left edge of the word (see Cutler et al 1985).

17. The technical term for such invisibility of initial and final elements is **extrametricality**, a notion that has received a great deal of attention in the phonological literature over the last decade or so.

18. Thanks to Bill Poser and Ken Hale for pointing out this example. The transcription used here differs slightly from the transcription used in CODIUL 1989 in that long vowels are represented here by writing the vowel twice ($\langle$uu$\rangle$), whereas a circumflex ($\langle$û$\rangle$) is used in the cited reference.

19. The affix *-ka-*, in addition to serving as the third-person possessive marker, is also used when the noun is preceded by a demonstrative: *suulu* 'dog'; *yaka suu +**ka**-lu* 'that dog'. Many nouns also allow the option of attaching the *-ka-* as a suffix even when the word is longer than the foot: *tingsuba* 'devil'; *ting +**ka**-suba* or *tingsuba + **ka**. See CODIUL 1989, pp. vi–vii, for discussion. There appear to be a few irregularities in the system of infixation, which slightly complicate the picture presented here.

20. English "expletive" infixation (McCarthy 1982) also serves as an example:

*Alabama   Ala***fuckin***bama*
*fantastic   fan***fuckin***tastic*

McCarthy argues (roughly) that the infix must be placed between prosodic feet.

21. Another option is for the association to be "driven" by the template. A great deal of the literature on reduplication has investigated the various ways in which association between the segmental melody and the reduplicative prefix proceeds; a discussion of this complex topic is not appropriate here.

22. Some cases of reduplication are more intricate in that the reduplicative template sometimes comes with its own segmental material. For example, in the Philippine language Cebuano (McCarthy and Prince 1990) one reduplicative morpheme (in a certain prosodically defined class of words) has the form *Culu*, where the *C* is copied from the stem to which the morpheme is prefixed. So, from *balibad* 'refuse offering' we get **bulu** + *balibad*, and from *paŋutana* 'ask question' we get **pulu** + *paŋutana*.

23. To avoid any possible misunderstanding, I note that partial reduplication is found in many languages outside Australia. Australian languages just happen to be a rich source of types of reduplicative morphology.

24. This is what the pseudo-categorial notation $A\backslash N$ represents.

25. See Aronoff 1976 and Wurzel 1989 for definitions of the notion 'morpheme' that allow for such cases.

26. In terms of ID/LP grammar, the *dominance* relations can be thought of as being specified for the morphological structure proper, whereas the *linear precedence* information is specified on the phonological structure.

27. The use of '*' here to mean phonological attachment is similar to its use in McCarthy and Prince 1990, described above in subsection 2.3.4. To my knowledge, this similarity is entirely fortuitous.

28. As I have argued (Sproat 1985, 1988), not all conceivable mappings are licit.

29. The idiomatic sense of *goer* in some dialects is irrelevant to its use in *church-goer*.

30. A good discussion of the topics raised in this section is to be found in Bauer 1983, chapter 4.

31. Readers familiar with recent trends in syntax will have noted that the kind of description just given of the applicative and passive "rules" is not in keeping with current parlance within government/binding theory. Be that as it may, the mode of description given here will serve for present purposes.

32. Indeed, Chomsky and Halle (1968, p. 49) argued that English orthography was a near-optimal representation of English precisely because it abstracted away from the application of phonological rules such as vowel shift and trisyllabic laxing, and thus purportedly gave a purer representation of the underlying structure of words. It has generally been concluded that Chomsky and Halle overstated the case; see Sampson 1985, pp. 200–201, for a recent discussion.

33. A further justification for concentrating on phonology in the present discussion is that linguists have primarily concerned themselves with describing the phono-

logical properties of a language, and with how phonology interacts with morphology, and have considered orthography only secondarily if at all. Orthography has usually been viewed—with some justification—as being in the ideal case (Finnish) a notational variant of a phonemic transcription for the language, and in the worst case (English) a reliquary for curious fossils of previous stages of the language. A result of this view is that it is possible to coherently discuss generalizations about how different kinds of phonological rules interact with morphology, as well as to discuss properties that seem to be true of phonology across languages, whereas a coherent discussion of similar generalizations about orthography (assuming such exist) seems much harder to come by.

34. See section 3.5 for a discussion of the complexity of certain computational morphological models.

35. An additional rule, called regressive harmony, applies from right to left, causing the vowels in certain stems to harmonize with suffixes. This rule will be discussed in subsection 3.4.4. Note that in my discussion of Warlpiri progressive harmony I am ignoring the fact that the labial consonants /p,w/ also affect the behavior of vowel harmony.

36. For '[labial]' one can read '[round]', at least as far as the present discussion is concerned. Nash uses the feature [labial], as do others who have worked on Warlpiri vowel harmony, and I am merely adopting this usage.

37. There has been a fair amount of work on **redundancy** in phonology (see Stanley 1967 and Archangeli 1984, inter alia). I will depart from some of the assumptions of that literature in the analysis of Warlpiri presented here.

Some of the notions employed in this area are, of course, familiar from information theory. The vowel /a/ requires only one bit ([−high]), whereas /i/ and /u/ generally require two bits. But since vowel harmony is predictable in its outcome, one needs only one bit (encoding the feature [high]) to distinguish vowels in suffixes, since the [labial] bit's value is predictable; see below.

38. The situation is more complicated than (103) suggests, since a stem whose vowels are all harmony-neutral requires [−back] harmony on the suffixal vowels, e.g. *kive* +ä (rock + **PART**) 'of a rock.'

39. More generally, one finds cyclic rule application even in phrasal phonology, where one can analyze larger phrasal units as being constructed out of smaller phrasal units. Mandarin 3TS is cyclic when it applies in phrases; see Shih 1986.

40. This section was aided significantly by the review in Emmorey 1988, and the interested reader is referred to that paper for discussion of issues not touched upon here.

41. Data from aphasia also often provide evidence that morphological knowledge is used in the understanding of language, since comprehension is often impaired in part because of the inability to process various kinds of inflectional morphology.

Further evidence for the role of morphological structure in language production is provided by data from speech errors among unimpaired speakers. Various work has been done on morphological speech errors on and speech errors more generally; see Fromkin 1973 and Stemberger 1982. Stemberger's conclusion is that words are not simply listed as unanalyzed wholes but rather are listed with some indication of their morphological structure. The rules that access that structure when people speak can be broken occasionally, resulting in morphological speech errors. This, then, can be taken as evidence that speakers make use of morphological structures when they *produce* language.

42. The most commonly used piece of methodology in psycholinguistic studies of word recognition—and something quite common in psycholinguistics in general—is the lexical decision task. The subject is presented with either words or nonwords of the language under investigation, and is asked to respond as quickly and as accurately as possible to the question "Is this a word?" Depending upon the particular task, the experimenter may be interested primarily in the affirmative responses, in the negative responses, or in both.

43. Though, as Bradley (1980) and others argue in later work (see note 47), the frequency effect becomes much more complicated when one is considering the retrieval of morphologically complex words.

44. Also, no evidence exists on how various kinds of nonconcatenative morphology (such as infixing or root-and-pattern morphology) are handled by speakers of the relevant languages.

45. As well as orthographically similar forms. It is assumed that activation is not a simple binary decision, but rather that various forms are activated to greater or lesser degrees.

46. Thanks to Andrej Ljolje for help with this paradigm.

47. According to the satellite-entries model, nouns are accessed in time inversely correlated with the frequency of the lexeme, where information about frequency is stored with the nucleus of the cluster (the nominative singular form). This predicts some access time associated with the cluster as a whole. Then, for any form other than the nucleus of the cluster, an additional computation is needed to get to that form, thus deriving the result we have seen.

There appears to be some disagreement in the literature on one point which is relevant to this model: Is the access time for a morphologically complex word sensitive to the frequency of the word in question, or is it merely sensitive to the frequency of the stem or the cluster of related forms as a whole? For example, Bradley (1980) argues that access to words derived with native affixes in English, such as *-ness*, is sensitive to the frequency of the stems (and their derivatives) and not to the frequency of the surface form. So, *briskness* and *sharpness* are identical in frequency, but *brisk* and its derivatives are far less frequent than *sharp* and its derivatives. In fact, *sharpness* was found to be accessed much more rapidly than *briskness*. In contrast, word pairs such as *heaviness* and *happiness*, which are identical in frequency for their stems (*heavy*, *happy*) but differ in frequency for their derived forms, did not show significantly different reaction times. This suggests that it is the frequency of the stem, not the frequency of the derivative, that matters. On the other hand, as Emmorey (1988, p. 114) notes, other researchers have concluded that both the stem's and the derived forms' frequencies are relevant. So, for derived forms of equal frequency, the frequency of the stem can be shown to have an effect, confirming half of Bradley's results. However, if the stem forms do not differ in frequency, then it has often been found that the frequency of the derived form is relevant.

In any event, returning to the satellite-entries model, it is very clear from Lukatela et al.'s results that, while it is certainly true that nominative case forms are more frequent than the other case forms, one cannot explain the difference in access times to the nominative form and the other forms on the basis of frequency. The genitive form is actually only slightly less frequent than the nominative form, whereas the instrumental form is almost one-tenth as frequent. Yet, as we have noted, there is a significant difference in reaction time between the nominative form and the genitive form, and no significant difference between the genitive form and the instrumental form.

48. See DeFrancis 1984 for an excellent discussion of many of the facts, as well as the myths, surrounding Chinese characters.

49. At the Association for Computational Linguistics Meeting in Vancouver (June 1989), Mark Liberman argued for a figure numbering in the many tens of thousands.

Chapter 3

1. I postpone until the next chapter discussion of various work where either the linguistic data or the mechanisms are *radically* different from the normal meat and drink of the computational morphologist.

2. KIMMO is Koskenniemi's first name. The appellation KIMMO is due to Karttunen (1983, p. 163). KIMMO thus shares with AWK (Aho et al. 1988) the property of being a computational system named after its author. Such naming practices are surely more honored in the breach than in the observance.

3. Because a model of this kind depends only upon a local context of 1 (morpheme)—since to determine the allowability of a morpheme in position n one looks only at the morphemes in positions $n - 1$ and n—such models are often called *first-order* models. In fact, the only difference between a simple model of morphotactics of the kind described above and the Markov models commonly used in speech recognition is that the latter have probabilities associated with each of the transitions, whereas it is implicitly assumed in models such as the one diagramed in figure 3.1 that the transitions are equiprobable.

4. Knuth is responsible for the name **trie**, which is the second syllable of *retrieval*.

5. I assume familiarity here (as in the previous chapter) with **regular expressions** and **regular languages**, as well as with their relationship with FSMs. Some good sources for those not familiar with these notions are Hopcroft and Ullman 1979, Lewis and Papadimitriou 1981, Harrison 1978, and Partee et al. 1990.

6. Other cases, such as *downdrift* (Johnson 1972, pp. 108–111), would now be considered to be outside the domain of phonology proper. Downdrift (often called *downstep* or *catathesis*) is a process whereby the pitch value of a high tone is lowered (relative to preceding high tones) by a directly preceding low tone. Such phenomena were traditionally described in generative phonology by means of rules with integral-valued features; one might describe downdrift by a rule that resets the value of a high tone to some higher integer (corresponding to a *lower* tone) than the

previous high tone's value whenever that high tone is preceded by a low tone. Since the entire set of integers is in principle available as feature values, we are no longer dealing with a finite alphabet and we therefore can no longer model this rule with an FST. But recent work on the relationship between phonology and phonetics has argued that such rules do not belong in the phonological component anyway; rather, they belong as part of phonetic implementation, where the phenomena are handled by continuous rather than discrete models; see Pierrehumbert and Beckman 1988 for a recent example of work which demonstrates this point nicely.

Note in this connection that Gibbon (1987) has presented an FST-based analysis of tonal interactions of this type in a couple of African languages. However, his model of downdrift is purely symbolic in that it essentially takes a lexical high tone (labeled 'H') and outputs a "downstepped" high tone (labeled '!H') whenever the lexical high tone occurs in the right context (usually after a lexical low tone). Thus no actual pitch values (or even abstract scaling values) are output, and one must still presume a model of phonetic implementation that interprets the outputs of Gibbon's machines.

7. Occasionally one sees '@' used for this purpose, as in Antworth 1990.

8. There is a glitch here: the sets specified by the pairs must either be nonintersecting or be in a subset relation. If the two pairs in question specify intersecting sets that are not in a subset relation, then there is no way to know how to classify a pair that falls in the intersection. For example, in the rule in (8), the correspondence pair $r :=$ is subsumed both under $[+son] :=$ and under $R :=$. This is why, for example, there is one column for each of $r :=$ and $ş :=$ in the table in (9), since we need to allow that $r :=$ but not $ş :=$ will be treatable both as a sonorant and as a retroflex continuant. If we know only that $R :=$ is treated by the rule in one way and $[+son] :=$ in another, we have no way of knowing in a given case whether to treat $r :=$ qua retroflex continuant or qua sonorant.

9. This is not true if unbounded deletion is allowed (Fernando Pereira, personal communication).

10. Still, one wonders if the increased power of computers in the approximately ten years since Kay and Kaplan first proposed their idea would not render tractable some of the cases that one might want to handle.

11. As Barton et al. (1987, pp. 153–155) point out (attributing the observation to R. Kaplan), the interpretation of intersection is complicated somewhat when rules allow insertions or deletions. Normally, the intersection of two regular languages L_1 and L_2 accepted by machines M_1 and M_2 is a third regular language L_3 which is accepted by the (machine) intersection of M_1 and M_2. In the case of FSTs with insertions, things are more complicated: two FSTs can be constructed (Barton et al. 1987, pp. 154–155), one of which accepts pairs of strings of the form $\langle a^n, b^n c^* \rangle$ and the other of which accepts pairs of strings of the form $\langle a^n, b^* c^n \rangle$. The intersection of the two *languages* of these machines is $\langle a^n, b^n c^n \rangle$, for which there is no accepting FST. The intersection of the two *machines* is a machine that accepts only a pair of null strings. It is this latter machine intersection (which Barton et al. call *internal intersection*) that is performed in systems such as those of Gajek et al. (1983) and Dalrymple et al. (1987), rather than the language intersection (which Barton et al. call *external intersection*).

To give a sense of how large an intersected machine for a practical application is likely to be, Koskenniemi (1983b, p. 119) claims that if the machines running the 55-odd rules in his description of Finnish (see subsection 3.3.2) were intersected, the resulting machine would have fewer than 4000 states. This is quite a manageable number, though one would have to be careful to do the intersection in stages and minimize the intermediate results, since otherwise the nonminimized intermediate intersection machine could be horrendously large.

12. It remains true, however, that *cyclic* rule orderings are not statable in either Kay and Kaplan's model or Koskenniemi's model; see subsection 3.7.2 for further discussion.

13. Of course, there is still the difference that Generative Phonological rules do not generally relate lexical and surface forms directly, whereas two-level rules always do.

14. From informal testimony which I have heard from colleagues over the years, Koskenniemi's description is indeed quite complete in that it can handle a very large percentage of the words which one is likely to find in Finnish text (or which a Finnish linguist can concoct).

15. As was pointed out to me by Stephen Anderson, Koskenniemi's decision to put only very productive rules in the phonology and handle less productive alternations in the lexicon is similar in spirit to the approach taken in Natural Generative Phonology (Stampe 1973; Hooper 1976—and see again Anderson 1988, p. 530). The latter theory also argued against the extremely abstract underlying phonological representations posited by Standard Generative Phonology, preferring instead to list many alternations in morphemes in the lexicon. For his part, Koskenniemi (1983b, p. 152) relates his ideas to concrete morphology.

16. There is also a form -*Vn*, but that need not concern us.

17. See Stemberger 1982, where a particularly strong stance is taken against Generative Phonology on precisely these kinds of grounds.

18. Thanks to Janet Pierrehumbert for bringing these issues to my attention.

19. Note that for any FSM with ε-transitions one can construct an equivalent FSM without ε-transitions.

20. See Bear 1988 for further details. Note that Bear is assuming a somewhat different interpretation of two-level rules than Koskenniemi, and it is straightforward in his system to ascertain that the relevant part of a rule has been applied.

21. The particular theory of word syntax adopted in Ritchie et al. 1987 is that of Selkirk (1982).

22. Antworth (1990, pp. 158–159) also discusses how to handle cases where both infixation and reduplication occur in a word. This interaction does not require an increase in the number of states in the reduplication machines, but it does require that they include arcs which admit of the possibility of an intrusive infix. In effect, infixation must be duplicated by the reduplication machine.

23. This is actually not a real word of Arabic, since the root *ktb* 'write' doesn't occur in this Binyan (IX). It is, however, structurally well formed according to the analysis of McCarthy 1979.

24. Berwick claims a proof that recognition with a multi-tape model is computationally undecidable in the general case; the proof supposedly consists of a reduction to Post's correspondence problem (Hopcroft and Ullman 1979, pp. 193–201). Unfortunately, I have not seen a citation for the proof. One should nonetheless be aware of the possible computational dangers of multi-tape systems, since it is tempting to consider using them to implement directly the multi-dimensional representations which have become popular in phonology in recent years and which we briefly examined in the preceding chapter. Dolan (1988) makes a suggestion along these lines.

25. This may seem like a loss of elegance, but note that the association of vowel segments to vowel slots in McCarthy's description is more complicated in general than in the simple example that I gave in the previous chapter. The association rules are slightly different among some of the binyanim, and Beesley's solution is therefore not a bad compromise.

26. Of course, Beesley's system also handles the strictly concatenative person-number agreement affixes. These are handled in the conventional way. See the discussion in subsection 3.4.3.

27. The input could actually consist of an entire sentence with no word breaks. Since primary stress is predictably on the first syllable of the word in Warlpiri, recovery of word boundaries is easy.

28. The rules were implemented directly as rejection sets, but this need not concern us here.

29. More recently, Coleman (1990) has taken a similar approach in modeling domains of English morphology. In his system a [+latinate] word is defined as the **overlap** of [+latinate] morphology and [+latinate] stress. The interpretation of overlap in this instance is that a string analyzable as a [+latinate] word must be analyzable both as an instance of [+latinate] stress assignment and as an instance of [+latinate] morphology; in other words, the string is a member of the intersection of the set of [+latinate] stressed items and the set of [+latinate] morphological items.

30. See, however, Aone and Wittenburg 1990 for a system incorporating zero morphemes in a categorial-grammar-based model of computational morphology.

31. A more recent piece of work dealing with German umlaut within a two-level model is Trost 1990.

32. For a more complete overview of complexity issues, and their relevance to natural language, see Barton et al. 1987—in particular, chapter 1.

33. It hardly needs to be pointed out that there is a confusion of issues here. FSTs in Koskenniemi's and Karttunen's original descriptions are by and large used to implement phonological alternations, the real *morphology* being handled by the finite-state dictionary model. It is not at all clear that Finnish *phonological* rules—the issue that Karttunen is really raising—*are* more complex than English phonological rules, and if anything one suspects that the reverse may be true.

34. Of course, that need not be the case. An interesting thought is that one could apply surface phonotactic constraints to bear on limiting the possible surface forms

of words in a language. These constraints would function like the dictionary to constrain some of the hypothesized transductions. I have never seen any development of this idea, however.

35. As was noted above, prefixes are outside the domain of root-suffix vowel harmony, and *pirri-* is therefore not affected by regressive harmony.

36. I ignore here complications arising from deletion or insertion rules; see Barton et al. 1987, pp. 179–181.

37. Koskenniemi and Church do not report the total number of tokens used.

38. Koskenniemi and Church claim (p. 338) that nondeterminism is a property of *generation* only in a regressive harmony language. However, this is true only if one can assume that the input to the *analyzer* is a well-formed word. If it is not (e.g., **pirri + kiji + ŋu*), then the system will backtrack. Of course, in most real applications (as in analyzing the words in Finnish newspapers, or Warlpiri texts) the input words *will* be well formed, and one's only task is to figure out what they are. However, one of the functions of a morphological analyzer is to recognize that an input form is ill formed, so one cannot generally eliminate the nondeterminism as Koskenniemi and Church claim.

39. Barton's constraint-propagation technique has been applied, apparently to good ends, in the work reported in Trost 1990.

40. Long-distance consonant harmony processes, though attested, are much rarer than vowel harmony processes, and I will therefore not consider them here.

41. In addition to the DECOMP module discussed here, there are some morphological-analysis routines in the letter-to-sound module; see Allen et al. 1987, chapter 6.

42. According to Church (1986), although DECOMP could certainly handle words which involved stress-shifting affixes such as *-ity*, there was no mechanism in MITalk to handle the stress shift and its effect on pronunciation. This is not a problem in the word *scarcity*, since *scarce* has only one syllable, but in a polysyllabic case like *festivity* there was no way for MITalk to handle the pronunciation change in the root *festive*, conditioned by the affixation of *-ity*. Such cases, therefore, had to have their pronunciations listed.

43. *keçi*, according to Hankamer, is the unofficial mascot of the linguistics department at the University of California at Santa Cruz. Also, Hankamer has stated categorically that *keçi* should not be capitalized, so I haven't.

44. The grammar actually allows more than one root morpheme to occur at the beginning of the word, this being the case in compounds.

45. The categorical designations in *keçi* are, of course, formally equivalent to the continuation lexicons in KIMMO.

46. Hankamer notes that the rules could in principle also be sensitive to the actual morphemes on the left side, but that the version reported did not have this feature.

47. Another drawback of Hankamer's particular implementation of his model compared with the various versions of the KIMMO model is that phonological rules in *keçi* are coded in C rather than in an implementation-independent meta-

language, and there is thus no way to easily adapt the system to another language (even if the model were well suited to that language).

Wallace (1988b) reports on a system for parsing Quechua morphology that follows Hankamer's parser in basic design: in particular, the generate-and-test methodology for modeling phonological rules is retained. Like Turkish, Quechua is an exclusively suffixing language in which morphologically complex words can consist of numerous suffixes attached to the stem. Wallace's system is more powerful than Hankamer's purely finite-state design in that morphosyntactic features for morphemes are combined as the parse proceeds. This allows one to model co-occurrence restrictions between nonadjacent affixes, something which is necessary in Quechua. Wallace's extension to Hankamer's model is thus analogous to Bear's (1986) extension to the URKIMMO model, as discussed in subsection 3.4.3.

48. Dolan's (1988) system is also parallel in design, as were other systems reported in the Wallace 1988a volume, following Anderson's influence, though there are differences in the algorithms proposed. Note also that Anderson's proposal, as advertised, is intended primarily to handle inflectional morphology, though this restriction does not seem to relate to any general formal differences between inflectional and derivational morphology.

49. Out of dissatisfaction with some of the linguistic shortcomings of Koskenniemi 1983b, I did a summer project in which I implemented a toy system (reported in Sproat 1984) remarkably similar in design to Kay's, if somewhat less sophisticated. I had no knowledge of Kay's earlier work at the time, and this would appear to uphold my claim that the most obvious way to implement ordered generative rules is to run them in reverse.

50. For truly irregular verbs, such as *tener* 'have', which has stems such as *tuv-*, the arc-list compiler does not produce such stem alternates by rule, but obtains them from the dictionary.

51. Although Tzoukermann and Liberman's system can, like KIMMO, function as both an analyzer and a generator, the primary focus in the practical application of the system is on analysis.

52. See Bybee 1985, pp. 66–67, for some evidence that the alternations in Spanish verb stems are *not* handled at run time by Spanish speakers in the way that might be predicted by the standard Generative account.

53. Church's main contribution in this area was to provide some useful statistics on lexical relatedness. Church provides a statistical measure for the 'derived from' relation, which he notates '$>$':

$$Probability(suf_1 > suf_2) = \frac{Number\ Of\ Stems\ Allowing\ Both\ Suf_1\ And\ Suf_2}{Number\ Of\ Stems\ Allowing\ Suf_1}.$$

For example, the probability measure for words ending in *-ency* (*presidency*) being derived from words in *-ent* (*president*) is 73%.

54. In this respect, Byrd's line of research is similar to the work on Finnish reported by Jäppinen and Ylilammi (1986), who are particularly interested that the form of lexical entries should be "natural" to casual users (p. 271)—i.e., they should look more or less like entries found in a Finnish dictionary.

Jäppinen and Ylilammi's system differs from Koskenniemi's approach to Finnish in a number of respects. Perhaps the most striking difference is that whereas Koskenniemi tends to treat root allomorphs as separate lexical entries (unless the alternate form can be derived by fairly general two-level rules), Jäppinen and Ylilammi develop a set of 280 stem-alternation rules, which, for many kinds of alternations, compute the allomorph of a root appropriate to the particular morphological context. The other main difference is that their system processes Finnish words from right to left (like DECOMP or Byrd's system for English); since roots come at the beginning of Finnish words, this allows Jäppinen and Ylilammi to analyze well-formed morphologically complex words based on unknown roots, because the affixes are stripped off before the root is reached. Furthermore, because of the stem-alternation rules, the system can offer for the unknown root a set of plausible lexicon entries of the kind that would be found in an ordinary Finnish dictionary. In the KIMMO approach, appropriate handling of unknown roots is rather less straightforward; see Antworth 1990, pp. 237–238, for some discussion of how to approach this problem in that framework. In general, *open lexicon* systems such as Jäppinen and Ylilammi's are unusual; most morphological analyzers assume that all the morphemes of the word being parsed are in the system's lexicon.

55. The 3000 bases include homographs, meaning that *record* is listed only once although it can be either a noun or a verb; the number of actual words is larger (apparently 4350).

56. The *-er* class happens to be completely productive in French in that newly created verbs overwhelmingly tend to be put in the *-er* class.

57. One might add to this Jäppinen and Ylilammi 1986, and perhaps a few others.

58. String operations are handled by *string unification*, which allows several non-contradictory partial descriptions of a string to be unified into a single (partial) description of that string; see Calder 1988 for further details. String unification is more powerful than finite-state mechanisms, and allows for the straightforward modeling of such phenomena as reduplication as well as providing a natural way for encoding other kinds of nonconcatenative morphology.

59. As Calder notes, this effectively implements the **Elsewhere Condition** of Kiparsky (1973).

60. In yet another SIL contribution, Grimes (1983) reports on tools for the analysis of morphotactics in morphologically elaborate languages.

SIL is perhaps most famous for its extensive contributions to descriptive linguistics (and not a few areas of theoretical linguistics) in the form of grammars of previously undescribed languages. Much of what we know about languages from various parts of the world (especially South and Central America) comes from SIL work; in the case of quite a few languages, SIL grammars would appear to be the only available description. Since SIL has a large team of affiliated field linguists, it has a very practical concern with providing tools to help those linguists in their job of describing unknown languages. This was the motivating force behind the development of the morphological-analysis tools PC-KIMMO and AMPLE. With respect to the former, Antworth (1990, p. xii) notes that "in 1985, after learning about Koskenniemi's two-level processor, Gary Simons envisioned a project that would implement a version of it on personal computers, thus making it available to field linguists." Many of the languages described by the field workers in question have relatively elaborate morphology, and it is therefore important to have good tools to aid in the study of the structure of the word. (SIL has traditionally been interested in the Word in a different sense: many of its affiliates have also engaged in providing different linguistic communities with new translations of Scripture. This explains the discussion of file-name conventions for biblical names dictionaries and biblical texts found on pp. 46 and 63 of Weber et al. 1988.)

61. Since AMPLE does require one to specify (or else specifies by default) the upper limit on the number of prefixes, infixes, and suffixes, any particular AMPLE grammar has a weakly equivalent finite-state model.

62. One *must* provide such a rule, since AMPLE does not automatically do the right thing. AMPLE is fairly general in the sense that one can implement a variety of morphological theories in the model; therefore, very few morphotactic principles are encoded in the system. AMPLE provides a small programming language in which tests of this kind can be stated.

It is apparently easiest in AMPLE to encode constructions where, say, all prefixes are morphologically inside (lower in the parse tree than) suffixes, as is the case in *encouragement*. Cases such as *unencourageable*, which has the interleaved structure [*un* + [[*en* + *courage*] + *able*]], are trickier to describe.

63. More specifically, they are drawn from a proper subset of regular expressions. See Weber et al. 1988, pp. 237–238, for a formal description of these constraints.

64. Actually this covers the singular and first-person inclusive infixes: the plural infix -*na* will need further constraints.

65. I have also said some things about the treatment of prosodic structure in computational models, especially proposals such as those of Sproat and Brunson (1987). I do not view this issue as closed; but I do not have much to add to what I have already said, so I will not address it in this section.

66. Even here one must be careful, since there is at least anecdotal evidence suggesting that some morphologically complex words must be in appropriate sentences in order to be understood. Mark Baker once told me that when he was doing some fieldwork on Winnebago (a Siouan language spoken in Wisconsin and Nebraska) his informant was unable to give interpretations for some morphologically well-formed words when those words were removed from sentences in which they were appropriate. This brings up the question of how much knowledge of phrasal syntax should interact in models of morphological analysis and generation, a topic which I discuss below.

67. Presumably one could imagine cases where yers are found only in roots and prefixes, where the two-level analysis that I am about to propose would also work. I don't believe that Polish has very many relevant cases, however. I note also, for readers familiar with Rubach's work, that the two-level analysis below does not correctly handle all cases of suffixation: the nominalizing suffix -*stw* +*o* (Rubach 1984, p. 189) is not handled, for example.

68. The /i/ in the final suffix (orthographic ⟨y⟩) is not a yer: it does not delete and it does not trigger Lower.

69. In this context, it is of some interest that Baker's original work on what was later to be called the mirror principle was written in the LFG framework (Baker 1983). Baker argued in that paper that LFG was the only grammatical formalism that directly predicted the observed morpheme orders.

Chapter 4

1. In other words, Wothke's system encodes Kiparsky's Elsewhere Condition.

2. My discussion of this topic is based heavily on an unpublished paper I wrote a few years ago with Dania Egedi (Egedi and Sproat 1988). In that paper, in addition to critiquing Rumelhart and McClelland's work, we showed how a three-layer connectionist network—i.e., a different architecture from Rumelhart and McClelland's two-layer model—showed rather similar behavior to their system when the data were presented in a similar way. We also showed that our model was capable to a point of learning alternations which are never found as morphological alternations in natural language (e.g., string reversal); this, we argued, raised the question of how useful connectionist models are in *explaining* why certain alternations never occur in natural language morphology, and hence how useful (simple-minded) connectionist models could be in providing a *theory* of why language has the characteristics it has.

3. Some of these groupings seem bizarre, to say the least. In particular, one can hardly take seriously the proposal that *go/went* belongs in the same class as *fly/flew*.

4. See Pinker and Prince 1983, pp. 136–145, for a critique of this design.

5. In the three-layer network replication of Rumelhart and McClelland 1986 reported in Egedi and Sproat 1988, we obtained a U-shaped learning curve when data were presented as in the Rumelhart and McClelland study. However, when we trained the network without separating the high-frequency verbs—i.e., presenting the entire set from the first trial onward—the learning curve was not U-shaped.

6. Pinker and Prince computed the "rank-order correlation between degree of overregularization by children and model across classes as .77 in that first interval [trials 11–15]" (p. 152).

7. Still, as Pinker and Prince point out, it is significant that the behavior of Rumelhart and McClelland's model is very similar to that of Bybee and Slobin's subjects only for a short time slice, whereas Bybee and Slobin's data span $3\frac{1}{2}$ years of development.

8. In performing these computations, we did not use the Wickelfeature representation. Rather, we used a segmental feature set taken from Halle and Clements 1983, p. 33, which we also used in our own network simulations; a simple features-correct measure was used to compute the matches. Since Wickelfeatures are largely phonetically sensible, and therefore correspond fairly well to (trigrams of) ordinary phonological features, one would not expect the overall results to be different if the computation had been done with Wickelfeatures.

9. Even though there are two choices of output vowel, the system would not get many features wrong if it simply generalized one of the output vowels.

10. Marcus' reason for discussing these constructions at all is to argue that they are not problematic for his model of deterministic parsing. As Finin (1980a, pp. 46–47) argues, there are empirical problems with Marcus' argument in that a good fraction of compounds cannot be handled by his algorithm.

11. Finin does not report on how many words have representations in his system, so it is not clear just how limited the system is.

12. See Hirschberg 1990 for methods that model the effects of discourse on stress in premodified nominals and other constructions.

13. Additionally, in the case of a ternary nominal like *Wall Street Journal* a statistical (mutual-information-like) measure was used to decide which way to group the triple (i.e., *[[Wall Street] Journal]* or *[Wall [Street Journal]]*). The method is similar to that used for Chinese in Sproat and Shih 1990 and discussed briefly in subsection 1.2.1 above. Unfortunately, the method has not been nearly as successful for English as it was for Chinese, in part because of the sparseness of the training data: for any given bigram of words in a nominal, the chances are high that that bigram will not occur in the corpus from which the bigram statistics were derived.

References

Abe, M., Ooshima, Y., Yuura, K., and Takeichi, N. 1986. A Kana-Kanji translation system for non-segmented input sentences based on syntactic and semantic analysis. In *COLING-86* (Association for Computational Linguistics).

Ahmad, K., and Rogers, M. 1979. GERAD: An adjective morphology teaching program. *Journal of Computer-Based Instruction* 6: 55–59.

Aho, A., Kernighan, B., and Weinberger, P. 1988. *The AWK Programming Language*. Addison-Wesley.

Alam, Y. 1983. A two-level morphological analysis of Japanese. *Texas Linguistic Forum* 22: 229–252.

Allen, J., Hunnicutt, M. S., and Klatt, D. 1987. *From Text to Speech: The MITalk System*. Cambridge University Press.

Allen, M. 1978. Morphological Investigations. Ph.D. thesis, University of Connecticut, Storrs

Anderson, S. 1982. Where's morphology? *Linguistic Inquiry* 13: 571–612.

Anderson, S. 1988. Morphology as a parsing problem. *Linguistics* 26: 521–544.

Andron, D. 1962. Analyse morphologique du substantif russe. Technical report, Centre d'Etudes pour la Traduction Automatique, Université de Grenoble 1.

Antworth, E. 1990. *PC-KIMMO: A Two-Level Processor for Morphological Analysis*. Occasional Publications in Academic Computing 16, Summer Institute of Linguistics, Dallas.

Aone, C., and Wittenburg, K. 1990. Zero morphemes in unification-based combinatory categorial grammar. In *ACL Proceedings, 28th Annual Meeting* (Association for Computational Linguistics).

Archangeli, D. 1984. Underspecification in Yawelmani Phonology and Morphology. Ph.D. thesis, Massachusetts Institute of Technology.

Arens, Y., Granacki, J., and Parker, A. 1987. Phrasal analysis of multi-noun sequences. In *ACL Proceedings, 25th Annual Meeting* (Association for Computational Linguistics).

Aronoff, M. 1976. *Word Formation in Generative Grammar*. MIT Press.

Aronoff, M., and Sridhar, S. N. 1983. Morphological levels in English and Kannada; or, atarizing Reagan. In *Papers from Parasession on the Interplay of Phonology, Morphology and Syntax* (Chicago Linguistic Society).

Attar, R., Choueka, Y., Dershowitz, M., and Fraenkel, A. 1978. KEDMA: Linguistic tools for retrieval systems. *Journal of the Association for Computing Machinery*, 25: 52–66.

Bailly, G., and Benoit, C., editors. 1990. *Proceedings of the ESCA Workshop on Speech Synthesis*, Autrans, France.

Baker, M. 1983. "Assume GF" and the order of morphemes. In Massam, D., and Haïk, I., editors, MIT Working Papers in Linguistics, Volume 5 (Department of Linguistics and Philosophy, MIT).

Baker, M. 1985. The Mirror Principle and morphosyntactic explanation. *Linguistic Inquiry* 16: 373–416.

Baker M. 1988. *Incorporation: A Theory of Grammatical Function Changing.* University of Chicago Press.

Baker, M., and Hale, K. 1990. Relativized minimality and pronoun incorporation. *Linguistic Inquiry* 21: 289–297.

Barton, G. E. 1986. Computational complexity in two-level morphology. In *ACL Proceedings, 24th Annual Meeting* (Association for Computational Linguistics).

Barton, G. E., Berwick, R., and Ristad, E. 1987. *Computational Complexity and Natural Language.* MIT Press.

Bauer, L. 1983. *English Word-Formation.* Cambridge University Press. lucid (123)

Bear, J. 1986. A morphological recognizer with syntactic and phonological rules. In *COLING-86* (Association for Computational Linguistics).

Bear, J. 1988. Morphology with two-level rules and negative rule features. In COLING-88 (Association for Computational Linguistics).

Becker, J. 1984. Multilingual word processing. *Scientific American*, July: 96–107.

Beesley, K. 1989a. Computer analysis of Arabic morphology: A two-level approach with detours. In *Proceedings of the Third Annual Symposium on Arabic Linguistics* (University of Utah).

Beesley, K. 1989b. Computer analysis of Aymara morphology: A two-level, finite-state approach. In *Proceedings of the Fifteenth Annual Deseret Language and Linguistics Symposium* (Brigham Young University).

Berendsen, E. 1986. *The Phonology of Cliticization.* Foris.

Berko, J. 1958. The child's learning of English morphology. *Word* 14: 150–177.

Bernard-Georges, A., Laurent, G., and Levenbach, D. 1962. Analyse morphologique du verbe allemand. Technical report, Centre d'Etudes pour la Traduction Automatique, Université de Grenoble 1.

Blåberg, O 1985. A two-level description of Swedish. In Karlsson, F., editor, *Computational Morphosyntax: Report on Research 1981–1984* (University of Helsinki).

Black, A., Ritchie, G., Pulman, S., and Russell, G. 1987. Formalisms for morphographemic description. In *ACL Proceedings, 3rd European Meeting* (Association for Computational Linguistics).

Bloomfield, L. 1933. *Language*. Holt, Rinehart and Winston.

Boussard, A. and Berthaud, M. 1965. Présentation de la synthèse morphologique du français. Technical report, Centre d'Etudes pour la Traduction Automatique, Université de Grenoble 1.

Brachman, R. 1978. A Structured Paradigm for Representing Knowledge. Technical report 3605, Bolt, Beranek and Newman, Inc., Cambridge, Mass.

Bradley, D. 1978. Computational Distinctions of Vocabulary Type. Ph.D. thesis, Massachusetts Institute of Technology.

Bradley, D. 1980. Lexical representation of derivational relation. In Aronoff, M., and Kean, M.-L., editors, *Juncture* (Anna Libri).

Brand, I., Klimonow, G., and Nündel, S. 1969. Lexiko-morphologische Analyse. In Nündel, S., Klimonow, G., Starke, I., and Brand, I., editors, *Automatische Sprachübersetzung: Russisch-deutsch* (Akademie-Verlag).

Bresnan, J. 1982. *The Mental Representation of Grammatical Relations*. MIT Press.

Bresnan, J., and Mchombo, S. 1987. Topic, pronoun and agreement in Chicheŵa. *Language* 63: 740–782.

Brodda, B., and Karlsson, F. 1981. An Experiment with Automatic Morphological Analysis of Finnish. Technical report, Department of General Linguistics, University of Helsinki.

Broselow, E., and McCarthy, J. 1984. A theory of internal reduplication. *Linguistic Review* 3: 25–88.

Brunson, B. 1986. A Processing Model for Warlpiri Syntax and Implications for Linguistic Theory. Master's thesis, University of Toronto.

Büttel, I., Niedermair, G., Thurmair, G., and Wessel, A. 1986. MARS: Morphologische Analyse für Retrievalsysteme: Projektbericht. In Schwarz, C., and Thurmair, G., editors, *Informationslinguistische Texterschliessung* (Georg Olms Verlag).

Butterworth, B. 1983. Lexical representation. In Butterworth, B., editor, *Language Production*, Volume 2 (Academic Press).

Bybee, J., 1985. *Morphology*. John Benjamins, Amsterdam.

Bybee, J., and Slobin, D. 1982. Rules and schemas in the development and use of the English past tense. *Language* 58: 265–289.

Byrd, R. 1983. Word formation in natural language processing systems. In *IJCAI-83* (International Joint Conference on Artificial Intelligence).

Byrd, R., Klavans, J., Aronoff, M., and Anshen, F. 1986. Computer methods for morphological analysis. In *ACL Proceedings, 24th Annual Meeting* (Association for Computational Linguistics).

Byrd, R., and Tzoukermann, E. 1988. Adapting an English morphological analyzer for French. In *ACL Proceedings, 26th Annual Meeting* (Association for Computational Linguistics).

Cahill, L. 1990. Syllable-based morphology. In *COLING-90*, Volume 3 (Association for Computational Linguistics).

Calder, J. 1988. Paradigmatic morphology. In *ACL Proceedings, 4th European Meeting* (Association for Computational Linguistics).

Caramazza, A., Laudanna, A., and Romani, C. 1988. Lexical access and inflectional morphology. *Cognition* 28: 297–332.

Caramazza, A., Miceli, G., Silveri, M., and Laudanna, A. 1985. Reading mechanisms and the organization of the lexicon: Evidence from acquired dyslexia. *Cognitive Neuropsychology* 2: 81–114.

Carson, J. 1988. Unification and transduction in computational phonology. In *COLING-88*.

Carstairs, A. 1984. Constraints on Allomorphy in Inflexion. Ph.D. thesis, University of London. Distributed by Indiana University Linguistics Club.

Chapin, P., and Norton, L. 1970. A Procedure for Morphological Analysis. Technical report MTP-101, MITRE Corporation, Bedford, Mass.

Chomsky, N. 1970. Remarks on nominalization. In Jacobs, R., and Rosenbaum, P., editors, *Readings in English Transformational Grammar* (Ginn).

Chomsky, N. 1981. *Lectures on Government and Binding*. Foris.

Chomsky, N., and Halle, M. 1968. *The Sound Pattern of English*. Harper and Row.

Church, K. 1980. *On Memory Limitations in Natural Language Processing*. Master's thesis, Massachusetts Institute of Technology.

Church, K. 1986. Morphological decomposition and stress assignment for speech synthesis. In *ACL Proceedings, 24th Annual Meeting* (Association for Computational Linguistics).

Church, K. 1988. A stochastic parts program and noun phrase parser for unrestricted text. In *Proceedings of the Second Conference on Applied Natural Language Processing* (Association for Computational Linguistics).

CODIUL. 1989. Diccionario elemental del Ulwa (sumu meridional). Technical report, CODIUL/UYUTMUBAL, Karawala Región Autónoma Atlántico Sur, Nicaragua; Centro de Investigaciones y Documentación de la Costa Atlantica, Managua and Bluefields, Nicaragua; Center for Cognitive Science, Massachusetts Institute of Technology.

Cohn, A. 1989. Stress in Indonesian and bracketing paradoxes. *Natural Language and Linguistic Theory*, 7: 167–216.

Coker, C. 1985. A dictionary-intensive letter-to-sound program. *Journal of the Acoustical Society of America, Supplement 1*, 78: S7.

Coker, C., Church, K., and Liberman, M. 1990. Morphology and rhyming: Two powerful alternatives to letter-to-sound rules for speech synthesis. In Bailly, G., and Benoit, C., editors, *Proceedings of the ESCA Workshop on Speech Synthesis*.

Cole, J. 1987. Planar Phonology and Morphology. Ph.D. thesis, Massachusetts Institute of Technology.

Coleman, J. 1990. Unification phonology: Another look at "synthesis-by-rule." In *COLING-90*.

Coleman, J., and Local, J. 1990. The 'no crossing constraint' in autosegmental phonology. *Linguistics and Philosophy* 14: 295–338.

Corbin, D. 1987. *Morphologie Dérivationnelle et Structuration du Lexique*. Max Niemeyer Verlag.

Cornell, T. 1988. IceParse: A model of inflectional parsing and word recognition for Icelandic ablauting verbs. In Wallace, K., editor, *Morphology as a Computational Problem* (Department of Linguistics, University of California, Los Angeles).

Culy, C. 1985. The complexity of the vocabulary of Bambara. *Linguistics and Philosophy* 8: 345–351.

Cutler, A., Hawkins, J., and Gilligan, G. 1985. The suffixing preference: A processing explanation. *Linguistics* 23: 723–758.

Dalrymple, M., Kaplan, R., Karttunen, L., Koskenniemi, K., Shaio, S., and Wescoat, M. 1987. Tools for Morphological Analysis. Technical report CSLI-87-108, Center for the Study of Language and Information, Stanford University.

Davis, S. 1988 On the nature of internal reduplication. In Hammond, M., and Noonan, M., editors, *Theoretical Morphology* (Academic Press).

DeFrancis, J. 1984. *The Chinese Language*. University of Hawaii Press.

DiSciullo, A. M., and Williams, E. 1987. *On the Definition of Word*. MIT Press.

Dolan, W. 1988. A syllable-based parallel processing model for parsing Indonesian morphology. In Wallace, K., editor, *Morphology as a Computational Problem* (Department of Linguistics, University of California, Los Angeles).

Dolby, J., Earl, L., and Resnikoff, H. 1965. The Application of English-Word Morphology to Automatic Indexing and Extracting. Technical report M-21-65-1, Lockheed Missiles and Space Company, Palo Alto, Calif.

Downing, P. 1977. On the creation and use of English compound nouns. *Language* 53: 810–842.

Drewek, R., and Erni, M. 1982. LDVLIB(LEM): A system for interactive lemmatizing and its application. In *COLING-82* (Association for Computational Linguistics).

Egedi, D., and Sproat, R. 1988. Connectionist Networks and Natural Language Morphology. Presented at the University of Maryland Conference on Grammar and Language Processing.

Ejerhed, E., and Bromley, H. 1986. A self-extending lexicon: Description of word learning program. In *Papers from the Fifth Scandinavian Conference on Computational Linguistics* (University of Helsinki).

Elgot, C., and Mezei, J. 1965. On relations defined by generalized finite automata. *IBM Journal of Research* 9: 47–68.

Emmorey, K. 1988. Do people parse? In Wallace, K., editor, *Morphology as a Computational Problem* (Department of Linguistics, University of California, Los Angeles).

Ettinger, S. 1974. *Diminutiv- und Augmentativbildung: Regeln und Restriktionen*, volume 54. Tübinger Beiträge zur Linguistik.

Fabb, N. 1988. English suffixation is constrained only by selectional restrictions. *Natural Language and Linguistic Theory* 6: 527–539.

Fan, C.-K., and Tsai, W.-H. 1988. Automatic word identification in Chinese sentences by the relaxation technique. *Computer Processing of Chinese and Oriental Languages* 4: 33–56.

Feigenbaum, J., Liberman, M., and Wright, R. 1990. Cryptographic protection of databases and software. In Feigenbaum, J., and Merritt, M., editors, *Proceedings of the DIMACS Workshop on Distributed Computing and Cryptography* (AMS and ACM).

Finin, T. 1980a. The Semantic Interpretation of Compound Nominals. Ph.D. thesis, University of Illinois, Urbana-Champaign.

Finin, T. 1980b. The semantic interpretation of nominal compounds. In *AAAI-80* (American Association for Artificial Intelligence).

Fleck, M. 1982. Design Options for a Morphological Analysis System. Unpublished essay, Massachusetts Institute of Technology.

Forster, K. 1976. Accessing the mental lexicon. In Wales, R., and Walker, E., editors, *New Approaches to Language Mechanisms* (North-Holland).

Fromkin, V. 1973. *Speech Errors as Linguistic Evidence*. Mouton.

Fromkin, V., and Rodman, R. 1983. *An Introduction to Language*. Holt, Rinehart and Winston.

Fudge, E. 1984. *English Word-Stress*. Allen and Unwin.

Fujimura, O., and Kagaya, R. 1969. Structural patterns of Chinese characters. In Proceedings of the International Conference on Computational Linguistics, Sånga-Såby, Sweden.

Gajek, O., Beck, H., Elder, D., and Whittemore, G. 1983. LISP implementation. *Texas Linguistic Forum* 22, 187–202.

Gazdar, G. 1985. Review article: Finite state morphology. *Linguistics* 23: 597–607.

Gazdar, G., Franz, A., Osborne, K., and Evans, R. 1987. *Natural Language Processing in the 1980s*. University of Chicago Press.

Gazdar, G., Klein, E., Pullum, G., and Sag, I. 1985. *Generalized Phrase Structure Grammar*. Harvard University Press.

Gershman, A. 1977. Conceptual analysis of noun groups in English. *In IJCAI-77* (International Joint Conference on Artificial Intelligence).

Gibbon, D. 1987. Finite-state processing of tone systems. In *ACL Proceedings, 3rd European Meeting* (Association for Computational Linguistics).

Golding, A., and Thompson, H. 1985. A morphology component for language programs. *Linguistics* 23: 263–284.

Goldsmith J. 1976. Autosegmental Phonology. Ph.D. thesis, Massachusetts Institute of Technology.

Goldsmith. J. (1989). *Autosegmental and Lexical Phonology: An Introduction.* Basil Blackwell. 123

Görz, G., and Paulus, D. 1988. A finite state approach to German verb morphology. In *COLING-88* (Association for Computational Linguistics).

Graham, S., Harrison, M., and Ruzzo, W. 1980. An improved context-free recognizer. *ACM Transactions on Programming Languages and Systems* 2: 415–462.

Greenberg, J. 1966. Some universals of grammar with particular reference to the order of meaningful elements. In Greenberg, J., editor, *Universals of Language* (MIT Press).

Grimes, J. 1983. *Affix Positions and Cooccurrences: The Paradigm Program.* Publication 69, Summer Institute of Linguistics, Arlington, Texas.

Gross, M. 1986. Lexicon-grammar: The representation of compound words. In *COLING-86* (Association for Computational Linguistics).

Hajič, J. 1988a. Formal morphology. In *COLING-88*.

Hajič, J. 1988b. Morphotactics by attribute grammar. Presented at Fourth European Meeting of ACL.

Halle, M., and Clements, G. N. 1983. *Problem Book in Phonology.* MIT Press.

Halle, M., and Mohanan, K. P. 1985. Segmental phonology of Modern English. *Linguistic Inquiry* 16 :57–116.

Hankamer J. 1986. Finite state morphology and left to right phonology. In *Proceedings of the West Coast Conference on Formal Linguistics*, Volume 5 (Stanford Linguistic Association).

Harris, J. 1983. *Syllable Structure and Stress in Spanish.* MIT Press.

Harrison, M. 1978. *Introduction to Formal Language Theory.* Addison-Wesley.

Hayes, B. 1980. A Metrical Theory of Stress Rules. Ph.D. thesis, Massachusetts Institute of Technology. Distributed by Indiana University Linguistics Club (1982).

Hirschberg, J. 1990. Using discourse context to guide pitch accent decisions in synthetic speech. In *ESCA Workshop on Speech Synthesis* (ESCA).

Hockett, C. 1954. Two models of grammatical description. *Word* 10: 210–231.

Hoeksema, J. 1984. Categorial Morphology. Ph.D. thesis, Groningen University. Distributed by Garland Press.

Hoeppner, W. 1982. A multilayered approach to the handling of word formation. In *COLING-82* (Association for Computational Linguistics).

Hogg, R., and McCully, C. 1987. *Metrical Phonology: A Coursebook.* Cambridge University Press. 123

Holman, E. 1988. FINNMORF: A computerized reference tool for students of Finnish morphology. *Computers and the Humanities* 22:165–172.

Hooper, J. B. 1976. *An Introduction to Natural Generative Phonology.* Academic Press.

Hopcroft, J., and Ullman, J. 1979. *Introduction to Automata Theory, Languages and Computation.* Addison-Wesley.

Inkelas, S. 1989. Prosodic Constituency in the Lexicon. Ph.D. thesis, Stanford University.

Isabelle, P. 1984. Another look at nominal compounds. In *COLING-84* (Association for Computational Linguistics).

Jakobson, R., Fant, G., and Halle, M. 1952. *Preliminaries to Speech Analysis*. MIT Press.

Jäppinen, H., Lehtola, A., Nelimarkka, E., and Ylilammi, M. 1983. Knowledge engineering approach to morphological analysis. In *ACL Proceedings, 1st European Meeting* (Association for Computational Linguistics).

Jäppinen, H., Niemisto, J., and Ylilammi, M. 1985. FINTEXT: Text retrieval for agglutinative languages. In *RIAO-85: Actes du Premier Congrès International sur la Recherche d'Informations Assistée par Ordinateur* (Institut d'Informatique et de Mathematiques Appliquées de Grenoble).

Jäppinen, H., and Ylilammi, M. 1986. Associative model of morphological analysis: An empirical inquiry. *Computational Linguistics* 12: 257–272.

Jarvella, R., Job, R., Sandström, G., and Schreuder, R. 1987. Morphological constraints on word recognition. In Allport, D., Mackay, D., Prinz, W., and Scheerer, E., editors, *Language Perception and Production* (Academic Press).

Jespersen, O. 1942. *A Modern English Grammar on Historical Principles, Part VI, Morphology*. Allen and Unwin.

Johnson, C. 1972. *Formal Aspects of Phonological Description*. Mouton.

Johnson, M. 1984. A discovery algorithm for certain phonological rules. In *COLING-84* (Association for Computational Linguistics).

Kaisse, E. 1985. *Connected Speech: The Interaction of Syntax and Phonology*. Academic Press.

Källgren, G. 1981. FINVX: A system for the backwards application of Finnish consonant gradation. Papers from the Institute of Linguistics publication 42, University of Stockholm.

Källgren, G. 1983. Computerized analysis and synthesis of Finnish nominals. In *Paper from the Seventh Scandinavian Conference of Linguistics*, Volume 2 (University of Helsinki).

Kari, J. 1989. Affix positions and zones in the Athapaskan verb complex: Ahtna and Navajo. *International Journal of American Linguistics* 55: 424–454.

Karlsson, F. 1985. Morphological tagging of Finnish. In *Computational Morphosyntax: Report on Research 1981–1984* (University of Helsinki).

Karlsson, F. 1986. A paradigm-based morphological analyzer. In *Papers from the Fifth Scandinavian Conference of Computational Linguistics* (University of Helsinki).

Karttunen, L. 1983. KIMMO: A general morphological processor. *Texas Linguistic Forum* 22: 165–186.

Karttunen, L., and Wittenburg, K. 1983. A two-level morphological analysis of English. *Texas Linguistic Forum* 22: 217–228.

Kataja, L., and Koskenniemi, K. 1988. Finite-state description of Semitic morphology: A case study of ancient Akkadian. In *COLING-88* (Association for Computational Linguistics).

Katz, L., Boyce, S., Goldstein, L., and Lukatela, G. 1987. Grammatical information effects in auditory word recognition. *Cognition* 25: 235–263.

Kay, M. 1977. Morphological and syntactic analysis. In Zampolli, A., editor, *Linguistics Structures Processing* (North Holland).

Kay, M. 1984. The dictionary server. In *COLING-84* (Association for Computational Linguistics).

Kay, M. 1985. When meta-rules are not meta-rules. In Sparck Jones, K., and Wilks, Y., editors, *Automatic Natural Language Parsing* (Ellis Horwood).

Kay, M. 1986. Machine translation will not work. In *ACL Proceedings, 24th Annual Meeting* (Association for Computational Linguistics).

Kay, M. 1987. Nonconcatenative finite-state morphology. In *ACL Proceedings, 3rd European Meeting* (Association for Computational Linguistics).

Kay, M., and Kaplan, R. 1983. Word Recognition. Manuscript, Xerox Palo Alto Research Center.

Kenstowicz, M., and Kisseberth, C. 1979. *Generative Phonology: Description and Theory*. Academic Press.

Keyser, S. J., and Kiparsky, P. 1984. Syllable structure in Finnish phonology. In Aronoff, M., and Oehrle, R., editors, *Language Sound Structure* (MIT Press).

Khan, R. 1983. A two-level morphological analysis of Rumanian. *Texas Linguistic Forum* 22: 253–270.

Khan, R., Liu, J., Ito, T., and Shuldberg, K. 1983. KIMMO user's manual. *Texas Linguistic Forum* 22: 203–215.

Kiparsky, P. 1973. "Elsewhere" in phonology. In Anderson, S., and Kiparsky, P., editors, *A Festschrift for Morris Halle* (Holt, Rinehart and Winston).

Kiparsky, P. 1982. Lexical morphology and phonology. In Yang, I.-S., editor, *Linguistics in the Morning Calm* (Hanshin).

Kiparsky, P. 1987. The Phonology of Reduplication. Manuscript, Stanford University.

Klatt, D. 1987. Review of text-to-speech conversion for English. *Journal of the Acoustical Society of America* 82: 737–793.

Klavans, J. 1985. The independence of syntax and phonology in cliticization. *Language* 61: 95–120.

Klavans, J., and Chodorow, M. 1988. Using a morphological analyzer to teach theoretical morphology. Technical report RC 13794, IBM Thomas J. Watson Research Center.

Klein, W., and Rath, R. 1981. Automatische Lemmatisierung deutscher Flexionsformen. In Herzog, R., editor, *Computer in der Übersetzungswissenschaft: Sprachpraktische und terminologische Studien* (Verlag Peter Lang).

Knuth, D. 1973. *The Art of Computer Progamming*, volume 3. Addison-Wesley.

Koktova, E. 1985. Towards a new type of morphemic analysis. In *ACL Proceedings, 2nd European Meeting* (Association for Computational Linguistics).

Koskenniemi, K. 1983a. Two-level model for morphological analysis. In *IJCAI-83* (International Joint Conference on Artificial Intelligence).

Koskenniemi, K. 1983b. Two-Level Morphology: A General Computational Model for Word-Form Recognition and Production. Ph.D. thesis, University of Helsinki.

Koskenniemi, K. 1984a. An application of the two-level model to Finnish. In *Computational Morphosyntax: Report on Research 1981–1984* (University of Helsinki).

Koskenniemi, K. 1984b. FINSTEMS: A module for information retrieval. In *Computational Morphosyntax: Report on Research 1981–1984* (University of Helsinki).

Koskenniemi, K. 1984c. A general computational model for word-form recognition and production. In *COLING-84* (Association for Computational Linguistics).

Koskenniemi, K. 1984d. A general computational model for word-form recognition and production. In *Computational Morphosyntax: Report on Research 1981–1984* (University of Helsinki).

Koskenniemi, K. 1985. A system for generating Finnish inflected word-forms. In *Computational Morphosyntax: Report on Research 1981–1984* (University of Helsinki).

Koskenniemi, K. 1986. Compilation of automata from morphological two-level rules. In *Papers from the Fifth Scandinavian Conference of Computational Linguistics* (University of Helsinki).

Koskenniemi, K., and Church, K. 1988. Complexity, two-level morphology and Finnish. In *COLING-88* (Association for Computational Linguistics).

Kotsanis, Y., and Maistros, Y. 1985. "Lexi Fanis": A lexical analyzer of modern Greek. In *ACL Proceedings, 2nd European Meeting* (Association for Computational Linguistics).

Kucera, H., and Francis, W. 1967. *Computational Analysis of Present-Day American English*. Brown University Press.

Ladd, D. R. 1984. English compound stress. In Gibbon, D., and Richter, H., editors, *Intonation, Accent and Rhythm* (W. de Gruyter).

Ladefoged, P. 1982. *A Course in Phonetics*, second edition. Harcourt Brace Jovanovich.

Lapointe, S. 1980. A Theory of Grammatical Agreement. Ph.D. thesis, University of Massachusetts, Amherst.

Lau, P., and Perschke, S. 1987. Morphology in the EUROTRA base level concept. In *ACL Proceedings, 3rd European Meeting* (Association for Computational Linguistics).

Leben, W. 1973. Suprasegmental Phonology. Ph.D. thesis, Massachusetts Institute of Technology. Distributed by Indiana University Linguistics Club.

Lee, K.-F. 1989. *Automatic Speech Recognition: The Development of the SPHINX System*. Kluwer.

Leonard, R. 1984. *The Interpretation of English Noun Sequences on the Computer.* North-Holland.

Levi, J. 1978. *The Syntax and Semantics of Complex Nominals.* Academic Press.

Levin, B., and Rappaport, M. 1988. Non-event -*er* nominals: a probe into argument structure. *Linguistics* 26: 1067–1083.

Levin, J. 1985. A Metrical Theory of Syllabicity. Ph.D. thesis, Massachusetts Institute of Technology.

Lewis, H., and Papadimitriou, C. 1981. *Elements of the Theory of Computation.* Prentice-Hall.

Li, C., and Thompson, S. 1981. *Mandarin Chinese: A Functional Reference Grammar.* University of California Press.

Liberman, M., and Prince, A. 1977. On stress and linguistic rhythm. *Linguistic Inquiry* 8: 249–336.

Liberman, M., and Sproat, R. 1991. The stress and structure of modified noun phrases in English. In Sag, I., editor, *Lexical Matters* (University of Chicago Press).

Lieber, R. 1980. On the Organization of the Lexicon. Ph.D. thesis, Massachusetts Institute of Technology. 76

Lieber, R. 1983. Argument linking and compounds in English. *Linguistic Inquiry* 14: 251–286.

Lieber, R. 1987. *An Integrated Theory of Autosegmental Processes.* SUNY Press.

Lin, L.-J. 1985. A Syntactic Analysis System for Chinese Sentences. Master's thesis, National Taiwan University, Taipei.

Lindstedt, J. 1984. A two-level description of Old Church Slavonic morphology. *Scando-Slavica* 30: 165–189.

Lukatela, G., Gligorijeŕć, B., Kostić, A., and Turvey, M. 1980. Representation of inflected nouns in the internal lexicon. *Memory and Cognition* 8: 415–423.

Lun, S. 1983. A two-level morphological analysis of French. *Texas Linguistic Forum* 22: 271–278.

MacWhinney, B. 1978. *The Acquisition of Morphophonology.* Monographs of the Society for Research in Child Development. University of Chicaco Press.

Marantz, A. 1982. Re reduplication. *Linguistic Inquiry* 13: 435–482.

Marantz, A. 1984. *On the Nature of Grammatical Relations.* MIT Press.

Marantz, A. 1988. Clitics, morphological merger, and the mapping to phonological structure. In Hammond, M., and Noonan, M., editors, *Theoretical Morphology* (Academic Press).

Marantz, A., and McIntyre, L. 1986. Reduplication Revisited. Manuscript, University of North Carolina.

Marchand, H. 1969. *The Categories and Types of Present-Day English Word-Formation.* C. H. Beck. best (123)

Marcus, M. 1980. *A Theory of Syntactic Recognition for Natural Language.* MIT Press.

Marsh, E. 1984. A computational analysis of complex noun phrases in navy messages. In *COLING-84* (Association for Computational Linguistics).

Marslen-Wilson, W. 1980. Speech understanding as a psychological process. In Simon, J., editor, *Spoken Language Generation and Understanding* (Reidel).

Martin, J. 1988. Subtractive morphology as dissociation. In *Proceedings of the Seventh West Coast Conference on Formal Linguistics* (Stanford Linguistic Association).

Martin, P. 1990. Automatic assignment of lexical stress in Italian. In *Proceedings of the ESCA Workshop on Speech Synthesis.*

Matthews, P. 1966. A procedure for morphological encoding. *Mechanical Translation* 9: 15–21.

Matthews, P. 1972. *Inflectional Morphology: A Theoretical Study Based on Aspects of Latin Verb Conjugations.* Cambridge University Press.

Matthews, P. 1974. *Morphology.* Cambridge University Press.

McCarthy, J. 1979. Formal Problems in Semitic Morphology and Phonology. Ph.D. thesis, Massachusetts Institute of Technology. Distributed by Indiana University Linguistics Club (1982).

McCarthy, J. 1982. Prosodic structure and expletive infixation. *Language* 58: 574–590.

McCarthy, J., and Prince, A. 1990. Foot and word in prosodic morphology: The Arabic broken plural. *Natural Language and Linguistic Theory* 8: 209–284.

McCloskey, J., and Hale, K. 1984. On the syntax of person-number inflection in Modern Irish. *Natural Language and Linguistic Theory* 1: 487–533.

McDonald, D. 1981. Compound: A program that understands noun compounds. In *IJCAI-81* (International Joint Conference on Artificial Intelligence).

McIlroy, M. D. 1982. Development of a spelling list. *IEEE Transactions on Communications* 30: 91–99.

Meya-Lloport, M. 1987. Morphological analysis of Spanish for retrieval. *Literary and Linguistic Computing* 2: 166–170.

Mithun, M. 1984. The evolution of noun-incorporation. *Language* 60: 847–895.

Mohanan, K. P. 1982. Lexical Phonology. Ph.D. thesis, Massachusetts Institute of Technology. Distributed by Indiana University Linguistics Club.

Mohanan, K. P. 1986. *The Theory of Lexical Phonology.* Reidel.

Nash, D. 1980. Topics in Warlpiri Grammar. Ph.D. thesis, Massachusetts Institute of Technology.

Nida, E. 1949. *Morphology: The Descriptive Analysis of Words.* University of Michigan Press.

Partee, B., ter Meulen, A., and Wall, R. 1990. *Mathematical Methods in Linguistics.* Kluwer.

Pesetsky, D. 1979. Russian Morphology and Lexical Theory. Manuscript, MIT.

Pesetsky, D. 1985. Morphology and logical form. *Linguistic Inquiry* 16: 193–246.

Pierrehumbert, J., and Beckman, M. 1988. *Japanese Tone Structure*. MIT Press.

Pinker, S., and Prince, A. 1988. On language and connectionism: Analysis of a parallel distributed processing model of language acquisition. In Pinker, S., and Mehler, J., editors, *Connections and Symbols* (MIT Press).

Postal, P. 1962. Some Syntactic Rules of Mohawk. Ph.D. thesis, Yale University. Distributed by Garland Press (1979).

Pounder, A. and Kommenda, M. 1986. Morphological analysis for a German text-to-speech system. In *COLING-86* (Association for Computational Linguistics).

Pulman, S., Russell, G., Ritchie, G., and Black, A. 1988. Computational morphology for English. *Linguistics* 26: 545–560.

Pun, K. H., and Lum, B. 1989. Resolving ambiguities of complex noun phrases in a Chinese sentence by case grammar. *Computer Processing of Chinese and Oriental Languages* 4: 185–202.

Quang, P. D. 1970. The applicability of transformations to idioms. In *Papers from Seventh Regional Meeting* (Chicago Linguistic Society).

Ralli, A., and Galiotou, E. 1987. A morphological processor for Modern Greek. In *ACL Proceedings, 3rd European Meeting* (Association for Computational Linguistics).

Rankin, I. 1986. SMORF–an implementation of Hellberg's morphology system. In *Papers from the Fifth Scandinavian Conference of Computational Linguistics*, (University of Helsinki).

Rappaport, M. 1983. On the nature of derived nominals. In Levin, L. E., editor, *Papers in Lexical-Functional Grammar* (Indiana University Linguistics Club).

Reape, M., and Thompson, H. 1988. Parallel intersection and serial composition of finite state transducers. In *COLING-88* (Association for Computational Linguistics).

Ritchie, G. 1989. On the generative power of two-level morphological rules. In *ACL Proceedings, 4th European Meeting* (Association for Computational Linguistics).

Ritchie, G., Pulman, S., Black, A., and Russel, G. 1987. A computational framework for lexical description. *Computational Linguistics* 13: 290–307.

Roe, D., Pereira, F., Sproat, R., Riley, M., Moreno, P., and Macarrón, A. 1991. Toward a spoken language translator for restricted-domain context-free languages. In *EUROSPEECH 91: 2nd European Conference on Speech Communication and Technology*.

Roeper, T. and Siegel, M. 1978. A lexical transformation for verbal compounds. *Linguistic Inquiry* 9: 199–260.

Rubach, J. 1984. *Cyclic and Lexical Phonology*. Foris.

Rumelhart, D., and McClelland, J. 1986. On learning the past tense of English verbs. In McClelland, J., Rumelhart, D., and the PDP Research Group, *Parallel Distributed Processing: Explorations in the Microstructure of Cognition*, Volume 2 (MIT Press).

Russel, G., Pulman, S., Ritchie, G., and Black, A. 1986. A dictionary and morphological analyser for English. In *COLING-86* (Association for Computational Linguistics).

Russi, T. 1990. A framework for morphological and syntactic analysis and its application in a text-to-speech system for German. In *Proceedings of the ESCA Workshop on Speech Synthesis*.

Sadock, J. 1980. Noun incorporation in Greenlandic. *Language* 56: 300–319.

Safir, K. 1987. The syntactic projection of lexical thematic structure. *Natural Language and Linguistic Theory* 5: 561–602.

Sagey, E. 1988. On the ill-formedness of crossing association lines. *Linguistic Inquiry* 19: 109–118.

Sagvall-Hein, A.-L. 1978. Finnish morphological analysis in the reversible grammar system. In *COLING-78* (Association for Computational Linguistics).

Sampson, G. 1985. *Writing Systems*. Stanford University Press.

Scalise, S. 1986. *Generative Morphology*, second edition. Foris.

Schane, S. 1973. *Generative Phonology*. Prentice-Hall.

Schane, S., and Bendixen, B. 1978. *Workbook in Generative Phonology*. Prentice-Hall.

Schnabel, B., and Roth, H. 1990. Automatic linguistic processing in a German text-to-speech system. In *Proceedings of the ESCA Workshop on Speech Synthesis*.

Schützenberger, M. 1961. A remark on finite transducers. *Information and Control* 4: 185–196.

Schveiger, P., and Mathe, J. 1965. Analyse d'information de la déclinaison du substantif en hongrois (du point de vue de la traduction automatique). *Cahiers de Linguistique Théorique et Appliquée* 2: 263–265.

Segui, J., and Zubizarreta, M. 1985. Mental representation of morphologically complex words and lexical access. *Linguistics* 23: 759–774.

Selkirk, E. 1982. *The Syntax of Words*. MIT Press.

Shieber, S. 1986. *An Introduction to Unification-Based Approaches to Grammar*. University of Chicago Press.

Shih, C.-L. 1986. The Prosodic Domain of Tone Sandhi in Chinese. Ph.D. thesis, University of California

Siegel, D. 1974. Topics in English Morphology. Ph.D. thesis, Massachusetts Institute of Technology.

Simons, G. 1989. A tool for exploring morphology. *Notes on Linguistics* 44: 51–59.

Sparck Jones, K. 1985. So what about parsing compound nouns? In Sparck Jones, K., and Wilks, Y., editors, *Automatic Natural Language Parsing* (Ellis Horwood).

Spencer, A. 1988. Bracketing paradoxes and the English lexicon. *Language* 64: 663–682.

Sproat, R. 1984. Parsing Morphology. Technical memorandum, AT&T Bell Laboratories.

Sproat, R. 1985. On Deriving the Lexicon. Ph.D. thesis, Massachusetts Institute of Technology.

Sproat, R. 1988. Bracketing paradoxes, cliticization and other topics: The mapping between syntactic and phonological structure. In Everaert, M., Evers, A., Huybregts, R., and Trommelen, M., editors, *Morphology and Modularity* (Foris).

Sproat, R. 1990. Stress assignment in complex nominals for english text-to-speech. In *Proceedings of the ESCA Workshop on Speech Synthesis*.

Sproat R. 1991a. The lexicon in generative grammar. In Bright, W., editor, *Oxford International Encyclopedia of Linguistics* (Oxford University Press).

Sproat, R. 1991b. Review of *PC-KIMMO*. *Computational Linguistics* 17: 229–231.

Sproat, R., and Brunson, B. 1987. Constituent-based morphological parsing: A new approach to the problem of word-recognition. In *ACL Proceedings, 25th Annual Meeting* (Association for Computational Linguistics).

Sproat, R., and Liberman, M. 1987. Toward treating English nominals correctly. In *ACL Proceedings, 25th Annual Meeting* (Association for Computational Linguistics).

Sproat, R., and Shih, C. 1990. A statistical method for finding word boundaries in Chinese text. *Computer Processing of Chinese and Oriental Languages* 4: 336–351.

Stampe, D. 1973. A Dissertation on Natural Phonology. Ph.D. thesis, University of Chicago.

Stanley, R. 1967. Redundancy rules in phonology. *Language* 43: 393–436.

Stemberger, J. 1982. The Lexicon in a Model of Language Production. Ph.D. thesis, University of California, San Diego. Distributed by Garland Press.

Strauss, S. 1982. *Lexicalist Phonology of English and German*. Foris.

Taft, M., and Forster, K. 1975. Lexical storage and retrieval of prefixed words. *Journal of Verbal Learning and Verbal Behavior* 14: 635–647.

Thomas-Flinders, T. 1981. Inflectional morphology: Introduction to the extended word and paradigm theory. UCLA Occasional Papers 4.

Thomason, R. 1985. Some issues concerning the interpretation of derived and gerundive nominals. *Linguistics and Philosophy* 8: 73–80.

Thurmair, G. 1984. Linguistic problems in multilingual morphological decomposition. In *COLING-84* (Association for Computational Linguistics).

Torre, L. 1962. Analyse morphologique de l'adjectif russe. Technical report, Centre d'Etudes pour la Traduction Automatique, Université de Grenoble 1.

Traill, A. 1970. Transformational grammar and the case of an Ndebele speaking aphasic. *Journal of the South African Logopedic Society* 17: 48–66.

Trost, H. 1990. The application of two-level morphology to nonconcatenative German morphology. In *COLING-90* (Association for Computational Linguistics).

Tufis, D. 1988. It would be much easier if WENT were GOED. In *ACL Proceedings, 4th European Meeting* (Association for Computational Linguistics).

Tzoukermann, E. 1986. Morphologie et Génération des Verbes Français. Ph.D. thesis, Institut National des Langues Orientales, Sorbonne Nouvelle, Paris III.

Tzoukermann, E., and Liberman, M. 1990. A finite-state morphological processor for Spanish. In *COLING-90*, Volume 3,

Vauquois, B. 1965. Présentation d'un programme d'analyse morphologique russe. Technical report, Centre d'Etudes pour la Traduction Automatique, Université de Grenoble 1.

Vergne, J., and Pagès, P. 1986. Synergy of syntax and morphology in automatic parsing of French language with a minimum of data. In *COLING-86* (Association for Computational Linguistics).

Wackernagel, J. 1892. Über ein Gesetz der indogermanischen Wortstellung. *Indogermanische Forschungen* 1: 333–436.

Wald, B. 1987. Swahili and the Bantu languages. In Comrie, B., editor, *The World's Major Languages* (Oxford University Press).

Wallace, K. 1988a. Morphology as a Computational Problem. Technical report, University of California, Los Angeles.

Wallace, K. 1988b. Parsing Quechua morphology for syntactic analysis. In Wallace, K., editor, *Morphology as a Computational Problem* (Department of Linguistics, UCLA).

Wang, J. 1983. Toward a Generative Grammar of Chinese Character Structure and Stroke Order. Ph.D. thesis, University of Wisconsin, Madison.

Weber, D., Black, H. A., and McConnel, S. 1988. *AMPLE: A Tool for Exploring Morphology*. Occasional Publications in Academic Computing, 12. Summer Institute of Linguistics, Dallas.

Weber, D., and Mann, W. 1979. Prospects for computer assisted dialect adaptation. *Notes on Linguistics* Special Publication 1.

Wehrli, E. 1985. Design and implementation of a lexical data base. In *Association for Computational Linguistics, 2nd European Meeting* (Association for Computational Linguistics).

Wickelgren, W. A. 1969. Context-sensitive coding, associative memory, and serial order in (speech) behavior. *Psychological Review* 76: 1–15.

Williams, E. 1981. On the notions 'lexically related' and 'head of a word'. *Linguistic Inquiry* 12: 245–274.

Winograd, T. 1983. *Language as a Cognitive Process*. Addison-Wesley.

Winston, P. 1984. *Artificial Intelligence*. Addison-Wesley.

Wojcik, R., Hoard, J., and Duncan-Lacoste, L. 1989. Lexical and phrasal issues in NP disambiguation. Presented at LSA Annual Meeting, Washington, D.C.

Wolfart, H. C., and Pardo, F. 1979. Computer-aided philology and algorithmic linguistics: A case study. *International Journal of American Linguistics* 45: 107–122.

Wolff, S. 1984. The use of morphosemantic regularities in the medical vocabulary for automatic lexical coding. *Methods of Information in Medicine* 23: 195–203.

Woodbury, A. C. 1987. Meaningful phonological processes. *Language* 63: 685–740.

Wothke, K. 1986. Machine learning of morphological rules by generalization and analogy. In *COLING-86* (Association for Computational Linguistics).

Woyna, A. 1962. Morphological Analysis of Polish Verbs in Terms of Machine Translation. Technical report, Machine Translation Research Project, Georgetown University.

Wurzel, W. U. 1989. *Inflectional Morphology and Naturalness.* Kluwer.

Yang, Y. 1985. Studies on an Analysis System for Chinese Sentences. Ph.D. thesis, Kyoto University.

Zimmer, K. 1964. *Affixal Negation in English and Other Languages.* Supplement to *Word* 20. International Linguistics Association.

Zinglé, H. 1990. Morphological segmentation and stress calculus in German with an expert system. In *Proceedings of the ESCA Workshop on Speech Synthesis.*

Zwicky, A. 1977. On Clitics. Technical report, distributed by Indiana University Linguistics Club.

Index

Abe, M., 10–11
Ablaut, 61
Abstract pair, 146
Affixation. *See* Infixation, Prefixation,
   Suffixation
Affix stripping, xiii
Agentive nominal, 33
Agglutinative language, 19–21, 44
Agrammatism, 111
Agreement, 28
Ahmad, K., 14
Akkadian, 163
Allen, J., 185–188
Allen, M., 87
Allomorph, 92
Allomorphy of English latinate verbs ending
   in *-mit*, 66
Alphabet, 104
ALPNET, 153
Altaic. *See* Turkish
AMPLE, 202–205
   categorial morphology in, 203
   morphotactics in, 203
Anderson, S., 76, 108, 142, 189, 191–192, 195,
   207–208, 214
Andron, D., 3
Antworth, E., 146, 159–161, 203, 214
Aphasia, 110–111
Applicative, 26, 212–214
Arabic
   broken plural in, 53–56
   computational analysis of binyanim in, 162
   computational analysis of broken plurals
      in, 160
   discontinuous morphology in, 158
   non-concatentative morphology of, 65–66,
      69

prosodic templates in, 58
quantity sensitive stress in, 103
root-and-pattern morphology in, 51–56
Argument structure, inheritance of, 34
Aronoff, M., 35, 75–77, 198
Aspect, 27
Associated Press, xii
Athapaskan, 204
Attar, R., 13–14
Augmentative, 79–80
Augmented addressed morphology, 115–
   116
Augments in compounds, 42
Autosegmental association line, 58
Autosegmental phonology, 52–55
   vs. to segmental phonology, 101
Autosegmental spreading, 98

Baker, M., 26, 29, 42–43, 84–85, 87, 123,
   212–213
Bambara, reduplication in, 61
Bantu. *See* Chicheŵa, Ndebele, Swahili
Barton, G. E., 96, 144, 160, 171–176, 179,
   181–183, 207–208, 214
Bauer, L., 37, 79, 123
Bear, J., 156–158, 169, 202–203, 205
Becker, J., 11
Beesley, K., 153, 158, 163–164
Bendixen, B., 96, 123
Berendsen, E., 72
Berko, J., 110
Bernard-Georges, A., 3
Berthaud, M., 3
Binyan, 51–52
Bloomfield, L., 19, 38
Bontoc, 159
   infixation in, 45–46, 204

Boolean satisfiability, 173–180, 189, 207
  as linguistically unnatural, 175–176,
    179–183
Bound form, 19
Boussard, A., 3
Brachman, R., 232, 240
Bracketing paradox, 69–72
Bradley, D., 113, 117
Brand, I., 3
Bresnan, J., 26, 28–29, 85, 213
Broca's aphasia, 111
Broselow, E., 58
Brown corpus, 185, 220
Brunson, B., 75, 83, 104, 108, 162, 164–169,
    206, 211
Bunsetsu, 11
Büttel, I., 13
Butterworth, B., 114
Bybee, J., 22, 25, 90, 123, 216–217, 219, 223,
    225
Byrd, R., 78, 198–200, 205

Cahill, L., 170
Calder, J., 201, 205
Caramazza, A., 115, 117
Carstairs, A., 22
Case marking, 23–24
Causative, 26–27
Central Alaskan Yupik, 114
  as polysynthetic language, 21
Chart, 11. See also Matrix chart parsing
Chicheŵa
  agreement in, 28
  applicative and causative in, 26–27
Chinese, 3–5. See also Mandarin
  characters, 121–122
  compounds, 232
  as lacking orthographic words, 3–5, 73
Chodorow, M., 14
Chomsky, N., 26, 38, 43, 55, 94, 96, 105, 134,
    153, 169, 238
Church, K., xii, 77–78, 90, 164, 174–175,
    179–181, 184, 188, 198, 207–208, 237
Circumfixation, 50, 158
Clitic, 72–73
Cliticization, 72–73
  in computational setting, 74–75
  in Hebrew, 13
Cohn, A., 70, 72
Cohort model, 112–113
Coker, C., 8
Cole, J., 98

Coleman, J., 58, 211
Complex nominal. See Compound
Composite rule, 145–146
Compound, 8, 37–43, 230–240
  correlation of stress with semantics in, 40
  semantic interpretation of, 232–236
  semantics of, 39–40
  stress, 37–39, 236–240
Computational complexity, 171–184, 207–
    208
Concatenative morphology, 44–45, 205–206
Concord, 28
Concrete pair. See Feasible pair
Connection machine, 192–193, 207
Connectionism, 216–230
Constraint propagation, 175–179, 208
Context restriction rule, 145
Continuation lexicon, 129–131
Continuation pattern, 129–131
Cornell, T., 170, 208
Correspondence pair, 135
Culy, C., 60
Cutler, A., 45
Cycle, 105–108, 208–211

Dalrymple, M., 141, 145, 154–155, 206
Davis, S., 60
DECOMP, 74, 124, 184–189
  Generative grammar and, 189
DeFrancis, J., 3
Deletion, 95–97
  as source of complexity, 96
Derivational morphology, 33–36
  vs. inflectional morphology, 21–25
Derived nominal, 33–34
DiSciullo, A. M., 82
Diacritic, 148–149
Dictionary, on-line, 4, 5–7. See also Lexicon
Directed acyclic graph, 157
Discrimination network. See Trie
Document retrieval, 13–14
Dolan, W., 50, 169, 207–208
Dolby, J., 13
Downing, P., 40
Drewek, R., 7
Dutch, compound augments in, 42

Egedi, D., 226–227
Elgot, C., 132
Elsewhere case, 135
Emmorey, K., 115, 193, 207
Encliticization, 72

Encryption, 5–6
English, xi–xii, 7, 87, 114, 153
  acquisition of past tense in, 216–230
  augments to KIMMO for, 156–159
  classes of irregular verbs in, 219–220
  clitics in, 73
  complexity in two-level lexicon for, 172
  compounding in, 37–41
  concatenative morphology in, 45
  dative shift in, 85
  differential regularizations of irregular
    verbs in, 222–227
  finite-state characterization of
    morphotactics in, 126–127
  irregular plurals compared with Arabic
    broken plurals, 56
  latinate affixes in, 80, 87
  lexical restrictions on affixes in, 80
  morpheme structure constraints in, 102
  native affixes in, 87
  orthography, 93–95
  percolation in compounds in, 81
  percolation in affixes in, 81
  phonological restrictions on affixes in, 79
  pluralization in nouns, 215–216
  semantic restrictions on affixes in, 79
  stress in, 94–95, 103, 169, 192
  syntactic restrictions on affixes in, 79
  text-to-speech in, 185
  trie lexicon for, 128–131
  trisyllabic laxing in, 94
  vowel shift in, 94
  word-formation rules for affixation in,
    75–76
  zero morphology in, 64
Erni, M., 7
Eskimo. See Central Alaskan Yupik
Ettinger, S., 79
Etymology, in lexical phonology and
  morphology, 87
Exclusion rule, 145
Extended word and paradigm theory, 76,
  254n4
External argument, 33

Fabb, N., 88
Feasible pair, 135
Feature. See Phonological feature
Feeding, 105
Feigenbaum, J., 5–6, 196
Finin, T., 232–236, 240

Finite-state automaton. See Finite-state
  machine
Finite-state machine, 126–127
  complementation of, 155–156
  concatenation of, 155
  intersection of, 141
  minimization of, 139
Finite-state morphotactics, predominance of
  in computational morphological systems,
  205
Finite-state transducer, 6, 132–143
  alignment of, 140
  cascaded, 137–139
  composition of, 139
  computational complexity of systems of,
    141
  non-determinizable, 144–145
Finnish, 100, 105
  as basis for design of KIMMO, 45
  Consonant gradation in, 149–150
  English spelling changes vs. vowel
    harmony in, 189
  gemination in, 149–150
  illative form in, 150
  as morphologically more complex than
    English, 171
  as morphologically simple, 152–153
  nominal cases in, 31
  orthography, 93
  prosodically conditioned morphology in,
    169
  two-level description of, 147–153
  vowel harmony in, xii, 97, 100–101, 180
Finno-Ugric. See Hungarian, Finnish
Foot, 46–47, 102–103
Forster, K., 112–113, 115–116, 119
Francis, W., 185, 199, 220
French
  clitics in, 73
  closed-class verbs in, 200
  generator for verb forms in, 199–201
Frequency effect, 113–114, 118
FSM. See Finite-state machine
FST. See Finite-state transducer
Fromkin, V., 45
Fudge, E., 40
Full text retrieval. See Document retrieval

Gajek, O., 141
Gazdar, G., 134, 152, 159, 214

GB. *See* Government-binding theory
Generalized phrase-structure grammar
  (GPSG), 159
Generate-and-test procedure, 190, 192–193
Generation, morphological, 143
Generation system, 3
Generative phonology, 95–100
  vs. two-level phonology, 148–151
Georgian, agreement in, 28
German, 8
  circumfixation in, 50, 158, 204
  clitics in, 73
  compounds in, 41–42, 231
Germanic. *See* Dutch, English, German,
  Icelandic
Gershman, A., 232
Golding, A., 215
Goldsmith, J., 58, 123
Government-binding theory, 26
  noun incorporation in, 43
Grammar constant, 141
Grammatical-function-changing
  morphology, 26, 32, 84–87
Greenberg, J., 29–30, 45, 90

Hale, K., 29
Halle, M., 38, 55, 94, 96, 105, 134, 153, 238
Hankamer, J., 20, 45, 189–190, 206, 214
Harmony. *See* Vowel harmony
Harris, J., 102
Harrison, M., 126, 214, 237
Hash table, 112
Hayes, B., 47, 103
Head of a word, 37, 82
Hebrew, 13–14
Hockett, C., 75–76
Hoeksema, J., 42, 113, 203
Hogg, R., 123
Holman, E., 14
Hopcroft, J., 126, 139, 141, 155, 214
Huichol, grammatical-function-changing
  morphology in, 85–87, 212–214
Hungarian, vowel harmony in, 100

IA. *See* Item and arrangement
Icelandic, 170
  ablaut in, 61–62
Implicational universal, 30, 90
Incorporation, 21, 29, 42–43, 212
Indo-European
  agreement in, 28
  gender in, 31

nominal case in, 120
Indonesian, 169
  circumfixation in, 50
  reduplication in, 57
Infixation, 45–50
  in KIMMO, 159–160
Inflectional language, 19
Inflectional morphology, 21–33
  vs. derivational morphology, 21–25
Inkelas, S., 67
Insertion, 97
Irish
  as pro-drop language, 29
  plural formation in, 61
Iroquian, noun incorporation in, 42–43
Isolating language, 19
Italian, 8, 115–116
  semantic restrictions on affixes in, 79–80
Item and arrangement, 75–78
  in computational morphological systems,
  205
Item and process, 75

Jakobson, R., 96
Japanese, 153
  inputting of, 10–13
Jäppinen, H., 13, 92
Jarvella, R., 112
Javanese, 167
  habitual-repetitive reduplication in, 57
Jespersen, O., 35
JETS, 232–236
Johnson, C., 96, 134
KIMMO, 74, 92, 112, 124–125
  augments to, 153–170
  complexity in, 144–145
  and concatenative morphology, 45
  continuation patterns in, 119
  Finnish analyzer in, 93
  as having basically segmental
    representation, 104
  problems with long-distance dependencies
    in, 92
  "psychological reality" of, 151–152
  real theory of morphology in, 131
Kaisse, E., 72
Kana-kanji conversion, 10
Kaplan, R., 135–137, 139, 193, 195
Kari, J., 204
Karttunen, L., 110, 125, 136, 157, 171
Kataja, L., 163
Katz, L., 113, 117

Kay, M., 135–136, 139, 162–163, 193–196, 206, 209, 214, xiii
keçi, 189–192
vs. KIMMO and DECOMP, 192
and concatenative morphology, 45
morphotactics of, 190
phonological rules in, 191–192
Kenstowicz, M., 123
Keyser, S. J., 105, 148–150
Kiparsky, P., 57, 87, 105, 135, 148–150
Kisseberth, C., 123
Klatt, D., 7, 185, 188
Klavans, J., 14, 72
Klein, W., 7
Knuth, D., 112, 128
Koasati, subtractive morphology in, 64, 170
Koskenniemi, K., 13, 92–93, 100, 110, 125, 129, 135–136, 139–141, 145–146, 149–152, 154–155, 159, 163, 171, 174–175, 179–181, 184, 198, 207–208, 214
Kucera, H., 185, 199, 220

LFG. See Lexical functional grammar
LPM. See Lexical phonology and morphology
Ladd, D. R., 38
Ladefoged, P., 104
Language processing by humans, 109–122
Latin
lexemes in, 37
as inflectional language, 20
nominal declension in, 30–31
participles in, 23
passive in, 26
quantity-sensitive stress in, 103
segmental deletion in, 96–97
tense and aspect in, 27
Leben, W., 63
Lee, K.-F., 8
Lemmatization, 7
Leonard, R., 232, 240
Letter tree. See Trie
Levi, J., 37, 39–40, 237
Levin, B., 33–34
Levin, J., 53–54, 58
Lewis, H., 126, 214
Lexeme, 22, 37
as one notion of "word", 73
Lexical access, 111–114, 166–167
using tries, 128–131
Lexical functional grammar, 26, 85

Lexical phonology and morphology, 87–89, 255n11
computational models and, 211
Lexicographic word, 73
Lexicon
notion of in generative morphology, 76
mental, 111–114
as source of complexity in two-level descriptions, 171–172
Li, C., 27–28
Liberman, M., 38, 92, 184, 196–197, 206, 236, 238
Lieber, R., 61, 76, 81–82, 157
Lin, L.-J., 4
Local, J., 58
Long-distance dependencies, in morphology, 90–92
Lukatela, G., 117, 119–120, 131
Lum, B., 232
Lure of the Finite State, 171

MITalk, 7, 124, 185
MacWhinney, B., 216
Mandarin
A-not-A verbs in, 4
aspect in, 27
cyclic rules in, 106–108
as isolating language, 19–20
Third Tone Sandhi in, 209
third tone sandhi in, 106–108
Mangarayi, infixing reduplication in, 60, 65–66
Mann, W., 203
Mapping principle, 67–69, 70–71
Marantz, A., 58, 60, 67, 70, 72, 81, 123, 151
Marchand, H., 33, 38, 123
Marcus parser, 235
Marcus, M., 232, 235
Marslen-Wilson, W., 112
Martin, J., 64
Martin, P., 8
Massively parallel morphology, 192–193
Mathe, J., 3
Matrix chart parsing, 164
Matthews, P., 3, 22, 69, 75–76, 123, 201
McCarthy, J., 46, 51, 53–58, 162
McCawley, J., 122
McClelland, J., 215–217, 219–223, 225, 226–230
McCloskey, J., 29
McCully, C., 123

McDonald, D., 232
McIlroy, D., 9–10
McIntyre, L., 60
Mchombo, S., 28–29
Melody, 52
Meya-Lloport, M., 13
Mezei, J., 132
Minimal word, 53–54
Mirror principle, 84–87
  computational models and, 212–214
Mithun, M., 42–43
Modifier, 37
Mohanan, K. P., 87–88, 105, 123
Morph, 185
Morpheme, 17
  more formal definition of, 65–66
  prefixes, suffixes, and roots as only
    examples of, 51
Morpheme structure constraint, 102–103
Morphographemics, 185, 187
Morphological acquisition, 215–230
Morphological analysis, 15
Morphological chart parsing, 193–195
Morphological generation, 15
Morphological parsing. See Morphological
  analysis
Morphological recognition. See
  Morphological analysis
Morphology, teaching aids for, 14
Morphotactics, 83–92
  computational models of, 82–83
  finite-state, 125–127, 205
  in DECOMP, 185–186
  syntactic constraints on, 83–87
Mutual information, 253n2

NP-hardness
  of KIMMO systems, 171
  of KIMMO-generation, 173–174
  of KIMMO-recognition, 181–182
Nasal assimilation, 96
Nash, D., 57, 57–58, 72, 79, 97, 161, 166
Ndebele, 110–111
Negative rule feature, 156
Ngbaka, tonal morphology in, 63, 101
Nida, E., 25, 63, 123
Non-concatenative morphology
  in KIMMO, 159–161
  in computational morphology, 159–170
Noun incorporation. See Incorporation
Nucleus, 102
Number marking, 23

Old Church Slavonic, 153
Onondaga, noun-incorporation in, 42–43
Onset, 46
Order of morphemes, 17
Orthographic word, 231
  as one notion of "word", 73
Orthography, vs. phonology, 93–95
Overregularization, 221–222

PATR, 153
PLANES, 232
PSPACE-hardness, of KIMMO-
  recognition, 171
Papadimitriou, C., 126, 214
Paradigm, 22, 201–202
  defective, 24
Paradigmatic morphology, 201–202
Parsing system, xi, 2–4
Part of speech assignment, 237
Passive, 26
Perceptron convergence procedure, 219
Percolation, 81
Pesetsky, D., 69–70, 70, 87, 105
Philippine languages, infixation in, 45–46
Phonetic implementation, vs. phonology,
  259–260n6
Phonological feature, 95
Phonological rule, 17
  iterative, 134–136
  in lexical phonology and morphology, 88
  in computational morphological systems,
    136–143, 206
Phonological word, 46
  vs. syntactic words, 69–73
Phonology, 92–108
  finite-state, 132–143
Pinker, S., 216–217, 221–223, 226, 228, 230
Polish, cycle in, 209–211
Polysynthetic language, 19
Portmanteau morpheme, 20, 28
Possible word, 102–103
Postal, P., 42
Prefixation, as less favored than suffixation,
  45
Prince, A., 46, 53–57, 162, 216–217,
  221–223, 226, 228, 230, 236, 238
Pro-drop language, 28
Procliticization, 72
Productivity, 24–25
Prosodic representation, 102–104
Psycholinguistics, 109–122
  and computational complexity, 208

Pun, K. H., 232

Quang, P. D., 122
Quechua, 203

Rappaport, M., 33–34
Rath, R., 7
Reape, M., 214
Reduction, 173
Redundant feature specification, 97–98
Reduplication, 56–61
  computational complexity of, 60–61
  in KIMMO, 160–161
  Mandarin, 28
  partial, 57–60
  total, 57, 61
Regular expression, and vowel harmony,
  100–101
Rejection set, 155
Resource Management Task, 8
RESPONSA, 13
Restrictions on affixes, 78–83
  Phonological, 78–79
  Syntactic, 79
Rhythm rule, 238
Righthand head rule, 82, 159
Rime, 64, 102–103
Ritchie, G., 158–159, 214
Rodman, R., 45
Roe, D., 8
Rogers, M., 14
Root, 37
  in Arabic root-and-pattern morphology,
    51–52
Root-and-pattern morphology, 50–56
Roth, H., 8
Rubach, J., 209, 209
Rule ordering, 104–108
  in keçi, 190–192
Rumanian, 153
Rumelhart, D., 215–230
Russel, G., 158
Russi, T., 8
Russian
  as non-pro-drop language, 29
  percolation in diminutive in, 81

Sadock, J., 42
Safir, K., 34
Sagey, E., 58
Sampson, G., 104
Sanskrit, 134–136

SAT. *See* Boolean satisfiability
Satellite entries model, 117–120
  vs. continuation patterns, 131
Scalise, S., 123
Schane, S., 96, 123, 123
Schnabel, B., 8
Schützenberger, M., 132, 139
Schveiger, P., 3
Second object, 27, 213
Segmental representation, 95–96
Segui, J., 117
Selector feature, 149–150
  and prosodically conditioned morphology,
    169
Selkirk, E., 69, 157
Semantic restrictions on affixes, 79–80
Semitic, gender in, 31
Serbo-Croatian, 117–120
Shieber, S., 82, 157, 213
Shih, C.-L., 4, 106
Siegel, D., 87
Simons, G., 203
Skeleton, 52–53
Slobin, D., 216–217, 219, 223, 225
Spanish, 5
  agreement in, 28
  computational analysis of morphology in,
    196–198
  as inflectional language, 20
  morpheme structure constraints in,
    102–103
  as pro-drop language, 28–29
  verb conjugation in, 16–17
Sparck Jones, K., 232
Speech-recognition system, xi, 8–9
Spelling checker, 9–10
Spelling, checking of, 190
SPHINX, 8
Sproat, R., 4, 34–35, 38, 67, 70, 72, 75, 83,
  104, 108, 162, 164–169, 206, 211, 214,
  226–227, 232, 236, 238, 240
State-transition table, 133–134
Stem, 17
Stratum (in lexical phonology and
  morphology), 87–89
Strauss, S., 70
Stress
  in Arabic, 103
  in English, 94–95, 103, 169, 192
  in English compounds 37–40, 236–240
  in Latin, 103
  in Ulwa, 46–7

Stress (cont.)
  in Warlpiri, 166
Subtractive morphology, 64–65, 170
  vs. truncation, 77
Suffixation, 17, 44
Summer Institute of Linguistics (SIL), 203
Sumu. *See* Ulwa
Suprasegmental morphology, 63
Surface coercion rule, 145
  compilation of, 154–156
Swahili
  class agreement in, 32
  noun-classes in, 31
Syllabary, 104
Syllable, 46–7, 102–104
Syllable weight, 103
Syncretism, 254n7
Syntactic word, vs. phonological word,
  69–73
Synthetic compound, 255n12

Tableau, 176–179
Taft, M., 115–116, 119
Tagalog
  as counterexample to righthand head rule,
    82
  infixation in, 159–160
  reduplication in, 161
Tape, 132–143
Template, in Arabic root-and-pattern
  morphology, 51–55
Template morphology, 204
Tense, 27
Text-to-speech, 7–8, 184–185, 236
Thomas-Flinders, T., 76
Thomason, R., 34
Thompson, H., 214, 215
Thompson, S., 27–28
Thurmair, G., 13
Tier, 52
Torre, L., 3
Traill, A., 110–111
Trie, 112–113, 128–131
Trost, H., 158
Truncation, 77
Turkish, 114
  as agglutinative language, 20–21
  as basis for design of keçi, 45
  computational morphology of, 189–192
  concatenative morphology in, 44
  as ideal item-and-arrangement language,
    78

vowel harmony in, 100, 191
TWOL, 154–156
Two-level morphology, 125
  vs. generative phonology, 105
  computational complexity of, 171–184
  as misnomer, 92–93
Two-level phonology, 139–143
  shallowness of, 141–143
Two-level rule
  formalism of, 145
  rule compiler for, 154–156
Tzoukermann, E., 92, 184, 196–200,
  205–206

U-shaped learning curve, 221–222
Ullman, J., 126, 139, 141, 155, 214
Ulwa
  infixation in, 79, 160, 205
  infixes in, 46–49
  stress in, 46–47, 103
Underspecification, 98
Unification, 82, 157–159, 213
Uto-Aztecan. *See* Huichol

Vauquois, B., 3
Vietnamese, as counterexample to righthand
  head rule, 82
Voice, 254n6
Vowel harmony, 97–101
  autosegmental analysis of, 98
  phonological and physical constraints on,
    184
  as similar to Boolean satisfiability, 175–
    176, 179–180
WFR. *See* Word-formation rule
Wackernagel, J., 72
Wald, B., 31
Waltz, D., 176
Warlpiri
  cliticization in, 72
  phonological restrictions on affixes in, 79,
    82–83
  progressive vowel harmony in, 72, 97–101,
    204
  reduplication and other prosodic
    morphology in, 58–59, 161, 164–169
  regressive vowel harmony in, 166–168, 175,
    182
  stress in, 166
Weber, D., 203, 205–206
Wehrli, E., xiv
Welsh, adjectival comparison in, 32

Wickelfeature, 217
Wickelgren, W. A., 217
Wickelphone, 217
Williams, E., 70, 82, 159
Winston, P., 176
Wojcik, R., 232
Wolff, S., 6
Woodbury, A., 21
Word. *See* Lexeme, Orthographic word,
    Phonological word, Syntactic word
Word and paradigm theory, 76, 201, 254n4
Word formation, 21–22
Word processing, 9–13
Word structure, 66–75
Word-based hypothesis, 76–78
  in computational systems, 198–202
Word-formation rule, 75–78
  automatic acquisition of, 215
Word-head convention, 159
Wothke, K., 215–216
Woyna, A., 3
Wug test, 110
Wurzel, W., 22, 51

Yang, Y., 4
Yidinʸ, reduplication in, 57–58
Ylilammi, M., 92

Zero morpheme, 63–64, 170
Zimmer, K., 79
Zinglé, H., 8
Zubizarreta, M., 117
Zwicky, A., 72